# Therapeutic Trances

## The Cooperation Principle in Ericksonian Hypnotherapy

# *Therapeutic Trances*

## *The Cooperation Principle in Ericksonian Hypnotherapy*

*By*

## Stephen G. Gilligan, Ph.D.

BRUNNER/MAZEL, *Publishers* • New York

**Library of Congress Cataloging-in-Publication Data**

Gilligan, Stephen G., 1954–
  Therapeutic trances.

  Bibliography: p. 349
  1. Hypnotism – Therapeutic use.   2. Patient
compliance.   3. Psychotherapist and patient.
4. Erickson, Milton H.   I. Title.   [DNLM: 1. Hypnosis.
WM 415 G481t]
RC495.G48   1986        616.89′162        86-20706
ISBN 0-87630-442-0

Copyright © 1987 by Stephen G. Gilligan

*Published by*
BRUNNER/MAZEL, INC.
19 Union Square
New York, New York 10003

MANUFACTURED IN THE UNITED STATES OF AMERICA

10  9  8  7  6  5  4

To Milton H. Erickson, M.D.,
with my deepest respect and love.

# Acknowledgments

Many people have participated in the birth of this book, and special thanks go to the following:

—to those colleagues who read and provided feedback on the manuscript, especially Chris Beletsis, Lisa Chiara, Steve Dwoorman, Hank Freedman, John Klinkert, Barbara Larocca, Marc Lehrer, Carol Locke, Neil Perrine, Eileen Shields, and Jeff Zeig;

—to Julianna St. John, who helped considerably with her secretarial skills;

—to Ann Alhadeff of Brunner/Mazel, who contributed invaluable editorial assistance;

—to Paul Carter, who was my teaching partner for most of the years in which the manuscript was being written and who therefore contributed meaningfully to the ideas presented below;

—to my students and clients, without whose partnership I would have learned nothing;

—to Denise Ross, my wife and soul mate, whose love and presence inspired me at a time when the manuscript was in danger of never being completed;

—and to Milton Erickson, whose unorthodox and multifaceted ways transformed all my images and ideas of therapy, not to mention life itself.

To all of these individuals and then some, I would like to say, "Thank you."

# *Foreword*

I had the good fortune to serve with Stephen Gilligan on the faculty of the 1986 Second Annual San Diego Conference on Hypnotic and Strategic Interventions sponsored by The Milton H. Erickson Institute of San Diego. During one of his presentations, Gilligan told this joke: "How many Ericksonians does it take to change a light bulb? Why, eight: one to change the bulb and seven to tell metaphors about how Erickson would have done it better."

Fortunately, this is not a book about how Milton H. Erickson did it better. In fact, it is not even about Erickson. Although the central topic is Ericksonian hypnotic induction, this is actually a manual about psychotherapeutic change – a book that teaches you as a therapist to improve your ability as a communicator.

Certainly all psychotherapists can benefit from improving their communication skills. One of the exciting aspects of this trade is that we have no tangible tools – only our artistry at communication. Our only tool is ourselves.

In order to communicate therapeutically, one needs to grow increasingly aware of the effect of one's message and the effect one's message *can* have. And so this book *is* about Erickson in a way, because there is no one who was a better model of communication than Erickson. He spent his career improving his awareness of and power at interpersonal effect.

Many sought out Erickson and were intrigued by his original and enduring contributions, including Jay Haley, Ernest Rossi, Richard Bandler and John Grinder, Stephen and Carol Lankton, Michele Ritterman, and Bill O'Hanlon. Subsequently, these experts developed models to help practitioners manifest in their own clinical work some of the spectacular effects that Erickson achieved. Even the great anthropologists, Margaret Mead and Gregory Bateson, contacted Erickson to study his methods.

In *Therapeutic Trances*, Gilligan brings to bear his training as an experimental psychologist and synthesizes the approaches of his mentors,

Erickson, Bandler and Grinder, and Bateson. From these three well-springs he creates his own model – fresh and new. But his approach bears the imprint of the lessons he learned well: generative creativity, boldness, and intellectual incisiveness – how to effectively join hypnosis, linguistics, and philosophy.

Gilligan is not a mere synthesizer. He is a pioneer and developer. His contributions to psychotherapy are original and enduring, just as the contributions of this book are original and enduring.

In order to place *Therapeutic Trances* in historical perspective, we need to understand some things about the phenomenon that was Milton Erickson. Erickson was a psychiatrist who has been dubbed both the father of modern hypnosis and its offspring, brief strategic psychotherapy. He was a master therapist who used hypnosis because it was a model par excellence of influence communication. Erickson was known for his use of indirect, hypnotically based methods, and he used this technique because it was the most effective way to get patients to realize their power to change – and to elicit their cooperation.

One of the main problems in therapy is to increase patient compliance. Patients often come to therapy because they have lost the ability to cooperate within themselves and among important people. They are lost in recursive patterns of limited choice and have lost track of intrinsic abilities to change.

Hypnotic induction definitely promotes cooperation, and this is true even with direct suggestions. For example, if a patient is told, "Cigarette smoke will taste bad," it is more likely the response will be positive if the suggestion follows an effective hypnotic induction. In fact, during his middle years, Erickson noted that the main purpose of induction was to elicit patient cooperation.

Gilligan helps us to understand how to effectively tailor nonconventional Ericksonian therapeutic communication, especially in inducing trance states. Induction is a procedure by which the therapist helps the patient to pattern a new flexible perspective; the patient learns how to elicit trance phenomena such as perceptual alterations, automatic (nonvolitional) behavior, altered memory function, and so forth.

When one examines the effects that can be achieved by hypnosis, one can see a striking similarity between symptoms and trance phenomena. For example, a phobic patient could scare himself by vividly (and even nonvolitionally) imagining "horror movies" about the future. However, in hypnosis, the same patient could imagine a pleasant scene with equal vividness.

Erickson used a phrase to describe the underlying principle: "If you can have phantom pain, you can have phantom pleasure." Following in Erickson's footsteps, I have pointed out that the mechanism by which a problem is maintained is a mechanism of solution. Actually, the mechanism is always benign. The end result (presenting complaints) might be problematic, but just because the end point is a problem doesn't mean the therapist should throw out the baby with the bath water. The well-developed symptom strategies in the patient can be conceived as benign or even positive. Because these strategies are well developed, it is better to use them rather than to try to tear them down and resurrect new ones.

Like no previous writer, Gilligan elaborates and develops the similarities among mechanisms to maintain problems, generate trance phenomena, and generate solutions. It is an important concept and by itself it would make studying this book invaluable. However, there are other important contributions. Notable examples are the explication of the "both/and" reasoning of the hypnotized patient, associational and dissociational strategies, and the confusion technique. In fact, Gilligan's chapter on confusion is the most important advance on this technique since Erickson's original article more than two decades ago. It is astonishing that more has not been written about therapeutic confusion, because Erickson considered it one of the most important techniques he contributed to hypnosis. Gilligan's chapter mines a rich therapeutic vein and will be cited for years to come.

Another exceptional quality of this book is that it is the closest one can come to experiencing Gilligan without attending one of his internationally renowned workshops. In his workshops, Gilligan stresses the growth and development of the therapist.

This book is similar. It is the first hypnosis book that focuses as much on the therapist as it does on the patient, problem, technique, or theory. Actual methods are presented for the therapist to maintain an effective externally directed trance and to deal with "unacceptable experiences," for example, the problems the therapist brings to the situation.

*Therapeutic Trances* is a manifesto of the fundamentals of Ericksonian hypnotherapy — fundamental principles and fundamental techniques. It is a treasure trove of practical ideas, giving therapists specific questions to ask and general therapeutic ideas to pursue. Scholarly and well-written concepts are developed in a logical and orderly fashion. We are privy to actual transcripts so that techniques are demonstrated rather than explained. At a time when Ericksonian methods have brought interest back to hypnosis, this book will stimulate its growth and development.

So, how many Ericksonians does it take to change a light bulb? The answer is one. But it sure helps to have Gilligan show us how we can do it better.

It is a pleasure to learn from Gilligan and I look forward with anticipation to the sequel to this book.

Jeffrey K. Zeig, Ph.D., Director
The Milton H. Erickson Foundation
Phoenix, Arizona
August 1986

# Contents

# Introduction

This is a book about the therapeutic use of trance states. It is written primarily for therapists, although other health professionals may find applications as well. Based on the seminal work of Milton H. Erickson, M.D., it is intended to provide a sense of how therapists may cooperate with clients to translate problems into solutions.

A major premise of the book is that hypnosis is an excellent model for describing how experience is generated. Hypnosis is conceptualized as an experientially absorbing interactional sequence that produces an altered state of consciousness wherein self-expressions begin to happen automatically (i.e., without conscious mediation). As we will see, this naturalistic approach enables both the induction of "out-of-control" symptoms and the induction of therapeutic trance states to be described with a common language; thus, an orientation to a problem is an orientation to a naturalistic "hypnotic induction" already in effect (cf. Ritterman, 1983). Using the same language to describe problems and solutions allows the hypnotic induction and other therapeutic communications to be fashioned directly from the "problem induction" employed by the client. In this way, the Ericksonian practitioner utilizes the very patterns by which the client is maintaining limiting realities to expand the range of possibilities.

Another major premise underlying this view is that the value of an experience depends primarily on its context. For example, a young woman entered therapy with the complaint that for several months she had, upon closing her eyes and trying to relax, been confronted by an intense "pair of eyes." These eyes were disembodied (i.e., disconnected from a face or body), staring steadfastly at her until she opened her eyes and reoriented externally. The experience was becoming increasingly troubling to the woman, so she sought therapeutic assistance in dealing with it.

Interestingly enough, a similar phenomenological experience was reported several months later in a therapist training group in Germany. During a group trance process, it was generally suggested that participants could develop an enjoyable dissociation state ("the Middle of Nowhere"), wherein their unconscious minds might share with them a meaningful symbol for further self-development. When the trance was concluded and experiential reports were solicited, a woman raised her hand to disclose an experience of great value to her. She described developing a pleasurable immersion in a "voidlike" state during the trance, then gradually becoming aware of a pair of eyes slowly moving towards her from a distance. She sensed that this unusual experience was somehow deeply meaningful, as if "something or somebody was returning back" to her. Deeply moved and touched, she felt no need to consciously analyze the experience.

Thus, the same trancelike phenomenon of "disconnected eyes" was experienced by two different people. For one it was a problem, for the other a solution. The "difference making the difference" (cf. Bateson, 1979), it will be argued, can be summarized in a word: Context. As we will see, context ("that which goes with the text or story") can be described in multiple languages: (1) bio-logic (the experiential presence and rhythms of participants), (2) socio-logic (the community in which an expression is offered), (3) ideo-logic (the intentions or ideas to which a person or community is committed), and (4) psycho-logic (the structures by which a person represents and makes sense out of an experience).

Depending on the values of these various contexts, a phenomenological experience can take on radically different meanings. For example, the "disconnected eyes" phenomenon was experienced as a problem within a context involving arrhythmic biological patterns (e.g., suspended breathing and tense muscle tone), no community support, no sense of asking the eyes to appear, and a sense of needing to relate to the eyes by avoiding them. In vivid contrast, the same phenomenon was experienced as a solution within a context distinguished by balanced biological rhythms, community support and acknowledgment, a sense of inviting an unusual symbol to emerge, and relationship patterns emphasizing acceptance and appreciation of whatever occurred.

All this suggests that the task of the therapist is to recontextualize problematic processes so they can function as "value-able" solutions in the developmental growth of the person. With the woman troubled by the eyes, for example, I first secured her attention in a soft yet absorbing fashion. After receiving a detailed description of her experience (such as when, where, how, with whom the eyes showed up), I asked her to keep her eyes open and look at mine as hypnotic communications were offered. These communications elaborated how absorption in my eyes could remain constant, even as my face might change in a variety of surprising yet secure ways. By thus disengaging (my) eyes from face, the disembodied eyes technique she developed naturalistically was experientially recreated within the therapeutic relationship. Further hypnotic suggestions described the many possible ways that her unconscious could begin to explore and relate to the eyes as a means of secure self-discovery and self-development, knowing that she could use my voice as a guide and security anchor throughout the explorations. In this way, the problem was experientially reconstructed as an opportunity to master a meaningful hypnotic process developed by her unconscious.

This paradoxical approach of translating problems into solutions via the hypnotherapeutic relationship is elaborated over the following eight chapters. The first chapter develops a general framework for understanding the Ericksonian approach to hypnotherapy. It contrasts the more traditional views of the authoritarian approach (emphasizing the hypnotist's "power") and the standardized approach (emphasizing the subject's "susceptibility") to the interactional view of the Ericksonian approach (emphasizing the cooperative relationship between hypnotist and su˙ject). The chapter then identifies other key ideas underlying Ericksonian hypnotherapy: (1) each person is unique; (2) hypnosis is an experiential process of communicating ideas; (3) each person has generative resources; (4) trance potentiates resources; (5) trance is naturalistic and biologically essential; (6) Ericksonian approaches orient to solutions more than to problems; (7) a person's uniqueness may be appreciated at many levels; and (8) the unconscious can operate generatively.

Chapter 2 explores the experience of trance. Theories and metaphors used to describe trance are first overviewed, followed by a naturalistic view of trance as a cross-contextual and biologically essential process serving multiple functions. Phenomenological characteristics of the trance experience (e.g., effortless expression, time/space variability, trance logic) are then identified. This chapter elaborates how symptom phenomena and hypnotic phenomena are the same phenomena expressed in different contexts, such that the therapeutic context can be used to translate liabilities into assets.

Chapter 3 overviews the general approach of the Ericksonian hypnotherapist, developing three key ideas in the process. First, integrity is an essential context for therapeutic effectiveness. Second, the hypnotherapist may develop an "interpersonal trance" with the client as a means for stimulating unconscious creativity and achieving therapeutic outcomes. Third, the principle of cooperation (that is, accepting and utilizing the client's reality) is the primary basis for all techniques.

Throughout the chapter, the need for flexibility and sensitivity to on-going processes is underlined.

Chapter 4 details how this adaptation to another person's reality may be achieved on multiple levels. Methods of joining and directing a person's behavior via verbal and nonverbal channels are identified, followed by a discussion of how to observe and utilize micro-behavioral ("minimal") cues. Application of cooperation principles to macro-behaviors (e.g., symptoms, lifestyles, skills, and assets) is then explored. Throughout, the notion of hypnotic communication as unfolding within a experiential feedback loop is emphasized.

Chapter 5 focuses on the more specific area of the initial phase of hypnotherapy. This phase includes the complementary processes of (1) gathering information about how a client generates and maintains a reality and (2) introducing the experiential and naturalistic process of therapeutic trance. Thus, the hypnotherapist seeks to identify invariant values in the client's world (e.g., social relationships, intentions, fixed behavioral patterns, beliefs), then uses these values to develop experiential processes within the therapeutic field.

Chapter 6 details ways to elicit hypnotic responses. Specific accessing techniques include asking questions, interspersing suggestions, presupposing hypnotic responses, speaking generally, telling stories, using associational cues, developing new associational bondings, pacing and leading dominant cognitive modalities, and framing and ratifying hypnotic responses. All of these techniques use naturalistic communications within a sensitive interpersonal feedback loop to immerse a person in experiential realities conducive to both trance development and therapeutic change.

Chapter 7 discusses how the client's responses may interfere with the straightforward development of therapeutic trance, and how the therapist may utilize such responses as the basis for hypnotic confusion techniques. These "deframing" techniques, pioneered by Milton Erickson, involve aligning with client patterns and then either interrupting or overloading the patterns to initiate hypnotic receptivity. The importance of contextual factors (relationship, nonverbal communication, etc.) are emphasized throughout the discussion.

The final chapter seeks to demonstrate how the principles and techniques explored in the various chapters come together in various areas of practical application. A detailed transcript of an induction is first examined, followed by discussions of applications with children, psychotics, emergency situations, and groups. Finally, a series of questions for identifying where a hypnotherapist may be stuck in relating to clients is offered.

Throughout the book there is an emphasis on unconscious generativity, both in the therapist and the client. It is argued that creative solutions to vexing problems can emerge when therapist and client trust their unconscious processes to cooperate in a joint endeavor. Because some mistakenly assume that this view advocates the mindless and narcissistic free association of the therapist, it should be made clear from the outset that nothing could be further from the heart of the matter. The approach outlined in the following pages requires the therapist's complete commitment to the client, involving a full experiential presence as well as the ability to join and differentiate patterns at many levels. Dedication and rigor are needed as the therapist discovers how to be "a part of and apart from" the client's reality in this process of "controlled spontaneity." As we will see, therapists must be in tune with and draw on both their own and their clients' unconscious capacities if this process is to succeed.

As a final note, it should be emphasized that the book is neither exhaustive nor definitive. It is one possible approach to Ericksonian therapy; different perspectives have been outlined by others (see Zeig, 1985a, 1985b). Furthermore, this volume is the first in a planned series; additional volumes will elaborate hypnotherapy structures and psychotherapy models helpful in applying Ericksonian principles and processes in "vari-able" fashions. Having stated these caveats, I invite you to explore the book at your own rate and style. Whether you find the various techniques relevant or not, my major hope is that you sincerely consider the principle of cooperation as the basis for transformational change, not only in therapy but also in other areas of human interaction.

# Therapeutic Trances

## The Cooperation Principle in Ericksonian Hypnotherapy

# CHAPTER 1

# *The Ericksonian Approach to Hypnosis*

Hypnosis suggests many things: power, magical cures, mystery, loss of control, and so forth. Unfortunately, many of these pervasive notions are misleading. This chapter distinguishes the Ericksonian approach from some of these popular misunderstandings. The first section overviews different conceptualizations of the hypnotic relationship: the authoritarian approach emphasizing the hypnotist; the standardized approach emphasizing the subject; and the cooperation approach emphasizing the relationship between hypnotist and subject. The second section outlines eight further ideas underlying the Ericksonian approach: (1) Each person is unique; (2) hypnosis is a process of communicating ideas; (3) each person has generative resources; (4) trance potentiates resources; (5) trance is naturalistic; (6) transformational change is course-corrective rather than error-corrective; (7) a person's uniqueness can be appreciated on many levels; and (8) the unconscious can operate autonomously and generatively.

## THE HYPNOTIC RELATIONSHIP

Traditionally, hypnosis is seen as a social interaction between two people enacting roles of hypnotist and subject. This interaction is intended to produce in the subject a special "trance" state. In this state, the subject's behavior and experience are presumably different from that characterizing his or her regular waking state.

Although most hypnotic practitioners would concur with this general description, they disagree sharply about the specific nature of the hypnotic relationship. To clarify some of these differences, three approaches

3

can be distinguished: the authoritarian approach, the standardized approach, and the cooperation approach.

## The Authoritarian Approach

The extreme version of this approach involves some "powerful" individual (the hypnotist) with "special" mental abilities (e.g., the "hypnotic eye," a "strong will") who *causes* another individual (the subject) to enter a relatively passive state wherein he or she is "susceptible" to the hypnotist's "suggestions." These suggestions can "force" subjects to perform various behaviors (from barking like a dog to stopping a smoking habit) that they ordinarily would not be willing or able to do. Notions of "mind over matter," "loss of control," "implanting suggestions," and "susceptibility" abound within this viewpoint, themselves in part "implanted" by books, movies, and folklore. These conceptions are often held openly by lay persons, but many therapists who use hypnosis also believe them implicitly.

The authoritarian approach is especially exploited in the stage hypnosis situation. Here subjects are usually individuals who attend a night club act with a group of friends. They typically volunteer to climb up on the stage where the hypnotist first administers a brief (5–10 minutes) flurry of inductional communications, then issues authoritative commands directing the subjects to enact unusual and often amusing behaviors, such as losing a shoe, acting like an animal, or beginning a striptease act. Upon returning to their tables following the hypnosis, subjects are showered with the good-natured adulations of jubilant and intrigued friends. In this sense, stage hypnosis serves the same function as a bottle of alcohol: normally inhibited persons can act in a "wild and crazy" fashion, then attribute responsibility for such behavior to someone (the hypnotist) or something (the trance state) other than themselves.

This direct and authoritarian approach is also used by many clinical hypnotists, albeit in a less spectacular fashion. Although clinicians operate in a different situational context and have different intents (e.g., to help people change), they often implicitly conceive of the hypnotic process as one in which they assume control over (i.e., hypnotize) clients' mental processes, then order them to change undesirable behavioral patterns (e.g., smoking, overeating).

Although adherents to the authoritarian approach are often well-intentioned, they promote misleading ideas about hypnosis. For example, the unconscious is generally construed to be something that is *not* the individual; it is considered as some "blank state" or "fertile ground" in which suggestions may be "written in" or "planted." These suggestions allegedly exert a powerful control over subjects' behavior, sometimes forcing them to act in ways inconsistent with their conscious volition or normal behavioral habits. Perhaps the most unfortunate implication is that the hypnotist holds power over the subject. As we will see in later chapters, this highly erroneous belief regarding loss of control strongly discourages many individuals from fully participating in the hypnotic process.

The authoritarian conceptions derive partly from the writings of historical figures such as Mesmer, Bernheim, Charcot, and Freud. Although these men claimed different theoretical positions (see Ellenberger, 1970, for detailed comparisons), they all emphasized hypnosis in terms of an asymmetrical relationship in which the hypnotist (usually a charismatic male) held sway over a generally passive subject (usually a woman). For example, consider Ellenberger's (1970) description of Charcot, one of the most eminent scientists of the late 19th century:

> In the eyes of the public, Charcot was the man who had explored the abysses of the human mind, hence his nickname, "Napoleon of Neuroses." He had come to be identified with the discovery of hysteria, hypnotism, dual personality, catalepsy, and somnambulism. Strange things were said about his hold on the Salpetriere's hysterical young women and about happenings there. Jules Clareties relates that during a patient's ball at the Salpetriere, a gong was inadvertently sounded, whereupon many hysterical women instantaneously fell into catalepsy and kept the plastic poses in which they found themselves when the gong was sounded. (p. 95)

By focusing on the power of the hypnotist, the authoritarian approach does not take into account the uniqueness of each subject in terms of his or her learnings, beliefs, capabilities, and so forth, nor does it recognize the client's ability to choose how (or whether) to participate in the hypnotic events. Thus, as we will see, this approach has limited value for developing lasting therapeutic changes.

The limiting conceptions of the authoritarian approach have lingered so long partly because Freud's categorical rejection of hypnosis around the turn of the century all but eliminated serious scientific examination of the topic for many years. As Cheek and LeCron (1968) have commented:

> In the 1890's when Freud first began to practice, he worked with a general practitioner named Breuer, one of the best medical hypnotists of that time. Freud knew little about hypnosis, was a poor

operator, and had the mistaken idea that a deep trance was necessary for good results. Only about one in ten of his patients would enter a deep trance and Freud found this frustrating. Breuer was having far better results. There was much rivalry between them and Freud could not tolerate the situation. He therefore sought other methods, gave up hypnosis, and developed free association and dream interpretation.

Although Freud's contributions to our knowledge of the mind and of psychotherapy are great, his abandoning hypnosis was harmful, for he blocked hypnotherapy for nearly fifty years. Today many psychiatrists and most analysts have minimal interest in hypnosis. They know nothing about it and believe it worthless because Freud first used it and then gave it up. Many of them firmly believe that hypnotherapy is only a matter of suggesting away symptoms, as Bernheim used it. Hence it is often claimed that hypnotherapy has only temporary results, although Bernheim and other physicians of that day certainly proved this idea false. (p. 18)

Fortunately, this model of hypnosis in terms of authoritarian and direct suggestions is slowly being rejected. This is largely due to what might be called *the standardized approach*.

*The Standardized Approach*

This approach is especially dominant among experimental psychologists. Instead of focusing on the power of the hypnotist, this view emphasizes the *subject* as the major unit of study, generally assuming hypnotic responsiveness to be some durable trait within the subject. As such, the hypnotist can employ a standardized set of communications that remain unchanged across different subjects. In other words, the subject is either hypnotizable or he or she is not; the hypnotist's behavior really does not matter too much.

The most influential advocates of the standardized approach have been academicians seeking to legitimize hypnosis by subjecting it to the rigorous tests of experimental psychology (e.g., Hilgard, 1965; Hull, 1933). Their efforts are certainly to be commended, as they rescued hypnosis from its "Mesmer metaphor" role (i.e., the authoritarian conceptions), thereby reestablishing its respectability in the scientific community. However, in strictly adhering to the tacit assumption in experimental psychology that the fundamental unit of study is the individual, the approach minimized the relative importance of contextual variables (e.g., the hypnotist-subject relationship). Since the phenomenon of interest was the subject's behavior, efforts were taken to experimentally control all other factors. For example, much work was devoted to developing standardized induction procedures that could be played on records or tapes, thereby completely eliminating the need for an operator (who might bias the experimental tests). Of course, this in itself is not objectionable; in fact, if by such a procedure the majority of subjects could experience a trance state, it would be quite laudable.

However, it soon became apparent that only a portion of subjects are hypnotically responsive to standardized inductions. Specifically, about 15% are highly susceptible, 65% are moderately susceptible, and 20% are not susceptible at all (see Hilgard, 1965). These individual differences, coupled with the finding that a given subject's responsiveness to the standardized test remains generally stable over time (see, e.g., Hilgard, 1965), led many experimentalists (Hilgard, 1965; Shor, Orne, & O'Connell, 1966) to consider hypnotizability a stable trait. Some people have it; some do not. As Hilgard (1965) remarked:

> Whenever a human ability is subjected to measurement the question arises as to how stable that ability is, how enduring it is through time. The historical studies of the constancy of the IQ are addressed to this problem, and we face the same kind of problem concerning the stability of the ability to enter hypnosis. . . . The evidence . . . shows that *under standard conditions* [italics added] hypnotic susceptibility is a quite dependable trait. . . . (p. 69)

In this sense, the standardized approach attributes both success and failure in the hypnotic encounter to the *subject*. The hypnotist is not that important.

There are some major problems with this approach. First, it assumes that a standardized induction, which essentially instructs a person to relax and imagine various things, is a valid way of assessing an individual's general hypnotic ability. This is like assessing dancing skill in terms of one's ability to do the fox-trot. The point is that some people can disco but not waltz; others can square dance but not boogie, and so forth. Some subjects can readily mold their experience to relaxation instructions; others, particularly those with a good deal of internal dialogue, will only be responsive to other inductional communications. As we will explore in detail, there are many ways of going into trance; the therapist's task is to find that induction most appropriate for a given client.

A second problem with the standardized approach is that it defines hypnotic ability in terms of *behavioral* responses to test suggestions.

Thus, individuals who cannot, say, experience their hands as tremendously heavy are probably not great trance subjects. While using external behaviors to assess an internal state is understandable, especially in the experimental domain, it shades a major point: trance is primarily an *experience*, like love or anger, which will be different for different individuals. One would not conclude that a person is not angry because he or she did not hit somebody, or that a person could not be in love because she or he did not kiss the experimenter. Similarly, some hypnotized subjects are unwilling or unable to comply with all of the behavioral demands of an experimental test; others will come out of trance in order to do so (see Erickson, 1967). To say that these individuals therefore lack the ability to experience trance is, in the present view, an unwarranted conclusion.

A third problem is that the standardized approach does not seriously account for the finding that susceptibility scores can be significantly influenced by a variety of factors, including alternate induction strategies (Kubie & Margolin, 1944), drugs (Sjoberg & Hollister, 1965), attitudes (Kroger, 1963), expectancies (Barber, 1969, 1972; Wolberg, 1948), environmental setting (Kramer, 1969; Tart, 1964), special training (Blum, 1961; Sachs, 1971), and modeling (Zimbardo, Rapaport, & Baron, 1969). Theorists believing hypnotic ability to be a stable trait explained these repeated demonstrations of enhanced hypnotic responsiveness (see Diamond, 1974, for comprehensive review) as due to attitudinal improvement (Hilgard, 1965); that is, subjects' willingness to participate increased over time. But rather than discarding their theories in the face of such evidence, theorists advanced notions such as *plateau hypnotizability* (Shor, Orne, & O'Connell, 1966), which assumes that each individual has an upper limit to his or her hypnotic ability. A person can perform below that limit (which will often happen, especially in the first few sessions), but cannot exceed it.

These constraints within the standardized approach discourage hypnotists from being flexible with and adaptive to subjects (cf. Dorcas, 1963). They also convince some individuals that they will never be able to experience trance. For example, in discussing hypnosis with both friends and clients, I have had a number of people disappointedly confess that they are not "good" hypnotic subjects. Most of these people developed such a belief after being informed by an experimenter or clinician that their inability to comply with a standardized induction *meant* they could never experience trance. My own experience, as well as that of colleagues, strongly suggests that this is not true: Most of these "resistant" or "insusceptible" individuals can experience trance with specialized training.

*This is not to say that all individuals are equally hypnotizable.* Some subjects can respond promptly and profoundly to direct hypnotic suggestions; others will forever be experientially unresponsive to such techniques. Experience reveals that there can be little disagreement about this point. The point of contention is whether individuals hypnotically unresponsive to direct suggestions given under standardized conditions may be responsive to more flexible hypnotic techniques offered within interpersonally intense contexts (e.g., therapy). The standardized approach answers negatively on this point, while the present view asserts that each individual possesses the capacity to become experientially immersed in a hypnotic relationship. Individuals do vary tremendously across many parameters, such as time to develop trance, behaviors exhibited in trance, and interpersonal needs while in trance. Thus, it is the task of the therapist to identify and create those conditions favorable for hypnotic developments. In short, how to do this is a central concern of this book.

Before concluding our brief discussion of the standardized approach, it should in all fairness be noted that it is useful in some respects. Standardized instructions are often necessary in the experimental context, where the need for strict controls is paramount. Also, standardized tests may identify subjects who can experience trance without any trouble whatsoever (i.e., subjects scoring high on the test). They may also indicate which trance phenomena (e.g., hypnotic dreams, age regression) a client can easily develop. This is valuable information for researchers using hypnosis, as it permits them to select subjects suitable for their purposes. It can also help the clinician assess how much attention must be given to individualized inductions for a given client; in addition, it suggests hypnotherapeutic strategies (e.g., hypnotic dreams) appropriate for a particular client (see, e.g., Spiegel & Spiegel, 1978). The point here is that standardized tests can provide insight about what a person can do with ease, but they do not reveal what an individual is intrinsically incapable of doing. In other words, a high score on a susceptibility test generally means that the subject will be responsive to just about any hypnotic instructions; a low score suggests that a different strategy by the hypnotist or more training is needed.

## The Cooperation Approach

Many contemporary hypnotherapists believe hypnotic responsiveness to reflect an interaction among the client's motivations and interests, the therapist's flexibility and sensitivity, and the degree of rapport obtaining between therapist and client.

The major developer of this clinical approach to hypnosis was Milton H. Erickson, M.D. In devoting almost 60 years of psychiatric investigation to innovative and therapeutic uses of hypnosis, Erickson developed an approach to psychotherapy that was truly unique. Erickson's approach was first and foremost one of *cooperation*:

> . . . hypnosis should primarily be the outcome of a situation in which interpersonal and intrapersonal relationships are developed constructively to serve the purpose of both the hypnotist and subject. This cannot be done by following rigid procedures and fixed methods nor by striving to reach a single specific goal. The complexity of human behavior and its underlying motivations makes necessary a cognizance of the multitude of factors existing in any situation arising between two personalities engaged in a joint activity. (1952; in Rossi, 1980a, pp. 166–167)

Thus, the cooperative approach emphasizes an interpenetrating triad of units involved in the hypnotic interchange. As Figure 1.1 illustrates, the hypnotist, the subject, and the hypnotist/subject relationship are each recognized as autonomous systems cooperating in a "common-unity." This approach emphasizes that trance always occurs in a relationship *context* in which neither hypnotist nor subject can be considered independently of each other.

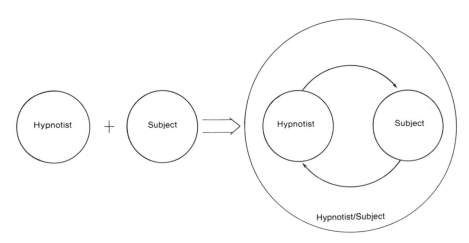

Figure 1.1. The cooperative hypnotic relationship

Within this cooperative context, hypnotist and subject assume different roles:

> Whatever the part played by the hypnotist may be, the role of the subject involves the greater amount of active functioning – functioning which derives from the capabilities, learning, and experiential history of the total personality. The hypnotist can only guide, direct, supervise, and provide the opportunity for the subject to do the productive work. To accomplish this, he must understand the situation and its needs, protect the subject fully, and be able to recognize the work accomplished. He must accept and utilize the behavior that develops, and be able to create opportunities and situations favorable for adequate functioning of the subject. (Erickson, 1952; in Rossi, 1980a, p. 167)

Thus, the Ericksonian practitioner cooperates according to a principle of *utilization*, wherein the client's patterns of self-expression are recognized as constituting the basis for therapeutic trance development. This requires adaptive rather than standardized instructions, as the hypnotist follows and then guides the ongoing behavior of the subject. In this fashion, the path into trance is always a unique one, based on the unique expressions of both hypnotist and client. In other words, trance unfolds from an experiential, interpersonal encounter in which therapist aligns with client, thereby enabling both parties to become increasingly receptive to each other. Methods for accomplishing this process are outlined in depth in subsequent chapters. For now, the important point is that the Ericksonian approach is based on cooperation, utilization, and flexibility.

*Summary of Differences*

We have thus far seen how the hypnotic relationship is conceptualized in different ways: the authoritarian approach assumes the hypnotist's power to be of major importance; the standardized approach focuses upon the subject's susceptibility; and the cooperation approach emphasizes the interaction between hypnotist and subject. These and other differences have engendered seemingly endless arguments, especially between experimentalists and clinicians. For example, the experimentalists tend to accuse clinicians of refusing to acknowledge "scientific fact," a claim that many clinicians refute by arguing that the laboratory findings lack ecological validity. Although many investigators are not entrenched in this mutual antagonism (see, e.g., Perry,

Gelfand, & Marcovitch, 1979), the existing polarization is unfortunate, as it denies each side the other's contributions.

Why do these differences exist? As Table 1.1 illustrates, they may in part be attributed to the various situational contexts and interests of each approach.

Subscribers to the authoritarian approach are usually in situations where they must show themselves to be charismatic and powerful. The laboratory researcher is trained in and devoted to dispassionate observation of the phenomenon in question. The contemporary clinician does whatever he or she can to help clients and must constantly question the nature of the therapeutic relationship. Accordingly, the entertainer or charismatic showman, the experimentalist, and the clinician will necessarily employ different observational frameworks, intentions, and communicational strategies.

TABLE 1.1
Aspects of the Hypnotic Relationship

| | General Type of Approach | | |
| --- | --- | --- | --- |
| | *Authoritarian* | *Standardized* | *Cooperation* |
| *Situational Context* | Nightclub; clinic | Experimental laboratory | Clinical practice |
| *Intent* | Impress, mislead, and entertain the audience | Study specific phenomena | Create opportunities for transformational change |
| *Focal Point* | Hypnotist | Subject | Cooperative relationship |
| *Types of Communication by Hypnotist* | Direct and overbearing commands | Standardized and changing suggestions (usually permissive) | Extremely flexible, adaptive to client pattern |
| *General Task of Subject* | Perform bizzare and unusual behaviors | Follow experimental instructions | Develop intimate intra-personal experience within safe interper-sonal context |
| *Length of Induction* | Short | Short | Varies, but usually longer (30–60 minutes) |
| *Interpretation of "Nonhypnotic" Response* | Subject is "resistant" | Subject is "insusceptible" to hypnosis | Therapist needs to adjust to the client's particular patterns |
| *Major Data of Interest* | Subject's behavior | Subject's behavior | Client's internal experience and subse-quent behavioral changes |

They will also interpret their data differently. For example, consider the common situation of the subject failing to go into trance. The authoritarian operator tends to see this as "resistance"; the experimentalist concludes that the subject is "insusceptible" to hypnosis; the cooperative therapist recognizes the need to utilize a more appropriate communicational strategy. By understanding how such fundamental differences arise from the different situational contexts, one can begin to see the potential complementarity of the approaches.

Of course, there will probably remain some irreducible differences, perhaps the most important being the question of whether all individuals are hypnotizable. Many clinicians answer in the affirmative, most experimentalists in the negative. However, even this seemingly irreconcilable disagreement may be due to semantic or procedural differences. As Perry, Gelfand, and Marcovitch (1979) point out, trance is often defined by clinicians in terms of the subject's subjective involvement, whereas experimentalists assess it in terms of the number of behavioral items passed; in addition, experimental procedures stipulate an unchanging set of items, whereas clinical practice demands that the hypnotist use those techniques that will be most effective for a given client. Thus, the opponents may be talking about two different phenomena and arguing from different sets of data (cf. Erickson, 1967; Perry & Laurence, 1980; Perry & Walsh, 1978; Weitzenhoffer, 1980). By establishing a common basis for discussion, the positions may somehow be integrated.

## FURTHER IDEAS UNDERLYING
## THE ERICKSONIAN APPROACH

We have thus far seen that the Ericksonian approach emphasizes an interpersonal relationship characterized by a principle of cooperation. This section identifies further assumptions central to the approach. Each distinction is only briefly discussed here, then elaborated in subsequent chapters.

*1. Each person is unique.* One of the qualities that impressed me most about Milton Erickson was his willingness and ability to *actualize* his cornerstone belief that each person is unique. This central belief arose, it seems, partly from Erickson's own uniqueness. Among other distinctions, he was color-blind, tone deaf, twice paralyzed with polio, and dyslexic. He learned to appreciate these and other distinctions as special attributes which would allow him to learn and enjoy life. This same orientation was then applied to helping his patients utilize their own circumstances as the basis for self-development.

Applying this belief to hypnotic work, Erickson (1952) commented:

> A primary problem in all hypnotic work is the induction of satisfactory trance states. . . . The securing of comparable degrees of hypnosis in different subjects and similar trance states in the same subject at different times frequently constitutes a major problem.
>
> The reason for these difficulties derives from the fact that hypnosis depends upon inter- and intrapersonal relationships. Such relationships are inconstant and alter in accord with personality reactions to each hypnotic development. Additionally, each individual personality is unique and its pattern of spontaneous and responsive behavior necessarily will vary in relation to time, situation, purposes served, and the personalities involved.
>
> Statistically, certain averages may be obtained for hypnotic behavior but such averages do not represent the performance of any one subject. Hence, they cannot be used to appraise either individual performances or specific hypnotic phenomena. (in Rossi, 1980a, p. 139)

Erickson repeatedly stressed that therapeutic communications should be based neither on theoretical generalizations nor on statistical probabilities, but on actual patterns distinguishing the client's present self-expressions (e.g., beliefs, behavior, motivations, symptoms). This is a truly radical proposition in that it requires therapists to begin each therapy in a state of experiential ignorance. It assumes that clients' expressions are individualized models of "reality" and that therapy is based on accepting and utilizing these models. To do so, therapists must develop a receptive state of *experiential deframing* in which they set aside their models and become "students" to learn a new "reality" (i.e., that of the client).

*2. Hypnosis is an experiential process of communicating ideas.* An idea is a distinction, a "difference that makes a difference" (Bateson, 1979), a correlation, a bit of information. An idea is a form of closure, an act of generating boundaries, a way of differentiating a figure in a field (cf. Brown, 1979). In emphasizing hypnosis as idea communication, Hartland (1971) commented:

> The induction of hypnotic states and phenomena is above all a matter of the communication of ideas and the eliciting of trains

of thought and associations within the subject which ultimately lead to behavioral responses. Even when the hypnotist does something to the subject, or tells him what to do and how to do it, the trance that is produced is still the result of ideas, associations, mental processes, and understandings that are already in existence in the subject's mind, and are consequently merely aroused within the subject himself. Far too many therapists in the hypnotic field regard their own activities, their intentions and desires, as the effective forces and uncritically believe that it is their own utterances to the subject that elicit or initiate specific responses. They fail to realize that what they say or do serves only as a means of stimulating or arousing within their subjects past learnings and understandings, some of which have been consciously and some unconsciously acquired. . . . Every effort should be made to direct the subject's attention to processes within himself, to his own body sensations, his memories, emotions, thoughts, feelings, ideas, past learnings and past experiences. A good hypnotic technique organized in this way can be remarkably effective even under seemingly adverse circumstances. (p. 375)

Thus, effective hypnotic suggestions or ideas activate ideas or distinctions already contained in a person's field of self-identification.

To appreciate this view, it is important to realize that ideas can be contained in many forms or modalities: A distinction may be expressed as a sensation, an image, a perception, a belief, a motor expression, or a cognition. *Thus, a person is always absorbed in various ideas: The task of the Ericksonian therapist is to identify and utilize those absorbing ideas as the basis for hypnotic development.* For example, a client sought relief from "anxiety." Investigation revealed that this symptom complex contained, among other ideas, the simple distinction of sensation in the chest. A portion of hypnotic communications thus elaborated on this simple idea:[1]

Now, Bob, you've got the ability to develop absorption in a wide variety of different things . . . we all do . . . and you have the ability to experience sensation in a variety of different ways and in a variety of different areas . . . now I'm not going to mention *variation in sensation* in your hands or feet *right* yet, because you apparently have selected your chest as the place to *focus attention*

---

[1]Italics are used in all examples and transcripts in the book to indicate words and phrases delivered in a different (usually softer and more intense) nonverbal style. The value of these "embedded suggestions" is explored in Chapter 5.

*experientially* . . . and you have indicated you feel so much sensation in your chest . . . and yet I'd like to challenge you with the
assertion that you haven't paid enough attention to all the *different
sensations* you can begin to develop in your chest . . . so as you
breathe in and out . . . in and out . . . and as you look at me here . . .
that's right . . . and as you listen to my voice and *feel the sensation* in your chest . . . I'm wondering how and where you feel the
sensation start and where and how you feel it diffuse . . . whether
it stops above your navel or below your neck . . . how it might
change as you *become deeply absorbed* in your own ability to *let
your unconscious develop appropriate sensations* in your chest as
the need arises and to respond *in a secure and comfortable way*. . . .

Thus, an idea (sensation in the chest) distinguishing a person as an
individual was utilized to absorb attention and develop trance. Many
futher examples of this sort will be offered.

In orienting to hypnosis as idea communication, the goal is experiential participation rather than conceptual understanding. As we will see,
the nonverbal presentation of ideas constitutes a good portion of the
hypnotic technique. The therapist works to absorb a client experientially and then redirect attention hypnotically to accomplish therapeutic
goals.

*3. Each person has generative resources.* The Ericksonian practitioner assumes that individuals have far more abilities and resources
than they are consciously aware of. In fact, a person has resources
sufficient to generate a happy and satisfying life. Unfortunately, many
of these resources are dissociated from the client's ongoing experience.
For example, everyone has the ability to be gentle with another person,
and yet many people deny themselves this way of being. And even if
such resources are available, they are often constrained in unnecessarily
limiting ways. Thus, one client assumed he could only be gentle with
his little boy; another believed that if she were gentle with someone, she
would need to enter into some sort of long-term commitment with that
person. Both reality models disallowed spontaneous and appropriate
expressions of gentleness.

Based on these observations, the Ericksonian therapist usually does
not attempt to *add* anything to the client. Instead, he or she assists
clients in learning to utilize the skills and resources they already have.
It is assumed that these resources will be actualized via the client's
experiential explorations, not the therapist's (or client's) conceptual
understandings. As we will see, this is true in both hypnotic induction,

where trance is developed from the client's naturalistic experiences, and therapy in general, where transformational strategies are designed to elicit and/or reorganize the client's relevant resources.

*4. Trance potentiates resources.* A major therapeutic benefit of trance is that it can deframe a person from rigid sets and thereby enable restructuring and reorganization of self-systems. The assumption here is that conscious, goal-oriented activity typically involves taking on some mental set or frame that narrows or focuses attention to frame-relevant stimuli. Demonstrations of this biased processing abound in the experimental literature. For example, Gordon Bower and I conducted a series of studies (Bower, Gilligan, & Monteiro, 1981; Gilligan, 1982b; Gilligan & Bower, 1984) in which hypnotized subjects were trained to develop certain emotional moods (happiness, sadness, anger) and then tested on various cognitive tasks of memory, perception, story interpretation, prediction, subjective estimates, and so forth. The general finding across numerous experiments was that mood biased cognition in the direction of the affect; for example, happy subjects remembered happy memories, while sad subjects recalled sad ones. This finding that frames (e.g., affective, cognitive, postural) sharply constrain information processing has been demonstrated repeatedly (e.g., Higgins, Herman, & Zanna, 1981).

These sorts of biases are relevant clinically in that persons with problems can be observed to be fixated in some invariant processing structures. That is, their conscious processes become self-contained in endless looping, thereby dissociating from unconscious resources. As Chapter 5 will explore, this dissociation will be demonstrated by repetitive behavior in multiple channels – e.g., posture, verbal output, behavioral acts, images, accessed memories, ways of thinking. Such fixation will disallow flexible adaptation to changing needs, changing situations, changing relationships; instead, it will ensure the same undesirable outcome again and again. Trance potentiates the resources needed for transformational change by offering a deframed (i.e., *unbiased*) state of self-receptiveness wherein new ways of being may unfold. This idea is explored in depth in subsequent chapters.

*5. Trance is naturalistic.* Trance experiences are not divorced from a person's normal patterns of functioning. As will be extensively discussed in the next chapter, they are not in any way bizarre or artificial. They resemble processes commonly experienced by each of us, such as reading an absorbing novel, being in love, or daydreaming. What is often different in trance is that the experiential involvement is *intensified* and extended for a longer duration for specific purposes. As Erickson noted (in Rossi, Ryan, & Sharp, 1983):

> What are the behaviors you can perform under hypnosis? There really is no behavior you can carry out in the hypnotized state that you cannot carry out in the ordinary, everyday waking state. The advantage with hypnosis is that you can control, direct, and prolong that behavior that just pops up in ordinary, everyday life. Perhaps the best example is amnesia. If I were to ask any one of you to forget some item, you would have very great difficulty doing so in your ordinary, waking state. But how many times have you been introduced to a person, been told the person's name, repeated the name, shook hands with the full resolution of remembering that name you have been told; and yet the moment you drop the hand you forget the name? Instant forgetting is as easy in the ordinary waking state, despite your wishes, as it is in the hypnotic state. And so you make use of hypnosis to ask people to function as they do in ordinary, everyday life but to do so at a given time, and for a given length of time. You ask them to use experiential learnings and capacities in ways of which they were formerly unaware. . . . Most of us don't really know what we are capable of doing. (p. 183)

That trance states operate in accord with a person's normal processes means they are best developed through naturalistic communications. For example, rather than attempting to induce an age regression through some standardized and artificial-sounding communications as the experimental hypnotist does, the Ericksonian practitioner might ask the subject to revivify and describe an imaginary playmate or a pet, neighborhood, nursery rhyme, from childhood.

That trance is naturalistic makes it an ideal context wherein a person can establish deep systemic changes by accessing, acknowledging, and then transforming basic experiential relationships. In other words, the entranced individual can experientially connect with underlying aspects of the problem state within a deeper context of self-valuing and then utilize various resources to generate transformational changes. As the following chapters will make clear, this can be done in a myriad of ways.

Finally, that trance is naturalistic means that it can be self-valuing or self-devaluing. That is, the processes of hypnotic trance are present not only in everyday trance states but also in symptomatic (problem) states. For example, consider the central hypnotic principle of *ideodynamicism*, whereby an action is felt to "just happen" automatically, without conscious mediation or effort. In hypnotic trance, this might be manifested as, say, hand levitation; in the everyday trance of a jogger's "second wind," it might be reported as "my whole body was just moving in this effortless way"; in a symptomatic trance, a person may complain that processes like overeating "just happen" automatically, despite best efforts to control (suppress, annihilate, overpower) them consciously. In each case, ideodynamic expressions signal the onset of trance states.

Thus, trance can give rise to problems or solutions, depending on the value of the context. As we will see, this understanding allows the Ericksonian practitioner to utilize therapeutic trance states to transform and value the symptomatic expressions recurring for clients in self-devaluing trance states.

*6. Ericksonian approaches orient to course-alignment rather than error-correction.* Erickson focused on achieving the goals and needs of the present self, not understanding the past. His approach was a profoundly positive one: The past signifies multiple learnings, most of them forgotten and some framed in self-devaluing ways, yet all are "value-able" resources:[2] the present offers endless possibilities for new learnings and self-appreciation; the future holds many potential ways to further self-development. Thus, the client's present understandings and learnings – whether they are presented as assets or deficits, "good" or "bad" – are appreciated as the basis for further developmental learnings. The Ericksonian practitioner orients clients to their goals and interests and provides opportunities for them to achieve these.

This orientation emphasizes self-development as a natural biological course of personal evolution and problems or errors as deviations from that plan. Problems are seen as an essential yet secondary aspect of development, with solutions (growth) a primary aspect. This view is explicated beautifully by Pearce (1981) in the following passage:

> . . . a biological plan of magnificent proportions . . . is built into our genes. The plan is flexible, to accommodate an infinite number of variables. . . .

---

[2]Again, therapeutic trance allows a deframed context wherein a person can explore events without being identified with, and thus bound by, an evaluative frame marking an experience as "good" or "bad." This variability in relation to experience allows reevaluation of relationships in accord with the present needs of the self. And, as Erickson noted (personal communication, 1977), " . . . it's just as important to know what you don't like as what you do like."

Development is learning to walk this straight-line system built
into us. As is natural to any skill, our walking is crude at first. We
wobble about, stumble and fall. The wobbles and falls are inciden-
tal so long as we keep our eye on that straight line of development — so long as we stay aligned. Everything unfolds in its good
time when we do that and wobbles and wide excursions amount
to nothing. (p. 92)[3]

This metaphor of learning to walk is especially relevant to Milton
Erickson's self-development. For example, Erickson recollected a key
developmental challenge in his life, that of learning to walk as an adolescent after being crippled by polio:

I learned to stand up by watching baby sister learn to stand up:
use two hands for a base, uncross your legs, use the knees for a
wide base, and then put more pressure on one arm and hand to get
up. Sway back and forth to get balance. Practice knee bends and
keep balance. Move head after the body balances. Move hand and
shoulder after the body balances. Put one foot in front of the other
with balance. Fall. Try again. (In Rossi, Ryan, & Sharp, 1983, pp.
13–14)

This beautiful description can be applied to virtually any developmental
learning process.

Consistent with this description the Ericksonian therapist focuses
on appreciation and utilization of the present processes and explores
how they will naturally unfold to further developmental growth. Thus,
the therapeutic goal is to expand rather than restrict a person's range
of self-expressions. As Figure 1.2 illustrates, this is a major difference
between Ericksonian therapy and more traditional approaches: The
former works toward solutions by identifying boundaries and expanding
them, while the latter attempts to correct "problems" by restricting the
range of self-expressions (e.g., getting the person to stop expressing the
symptom). Processes for accomplishing this orientation are explored
throughout the book.

*7. A person's uniqueness can be appreciated on many levels.* For hypnotherapeutic purposes, I find it especially useful to distinguish four
levels: the Deep Self, the unconscious mind, the conscious mind, and

---

[3]From *The Bond of Power* by Joseph Chilton Pearce. Copyright © 1981 by Joseph
Chilton Pearce. Reprinted by permission of the publisher, E. P. Dutton, a division of New
American Library.

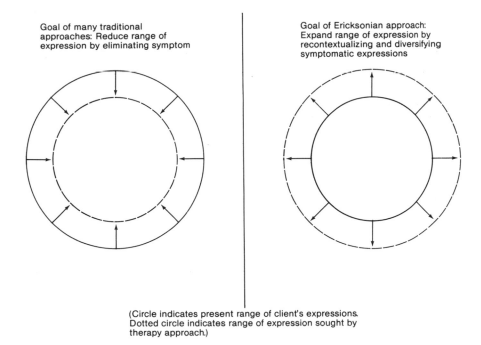

Goal of many traditional approaches: Reduce range of expression by eliminating symptom

Goal of Ericksonian approach: Expand range of expression by recontextualizing and diversifying symptomatic expressions

(Circle indicates present range of client's expressions. Dotted circle indicates range of expression sought by therapy approach.)

Figure 1.2. The traditional approach and the Ericksonian approach to problem-solving

the contents of consciousness. As Figure 1.3 shows, each level can be considered as a concentric circle.

*First*, an essence of Self can be recognized as the nonconceptual, ineffable Deep Self. Erickson (1962b, in Rossi, 1980b) referred to this essence as "that vital sense of the 'beingness' of the self (that) is often overlooked" (p. 345); T. S. Eliot (1963) pointed to it as "a condition of complete simplicity costing not less than anything" (pp. 222–223). This essence cannot be captured by an image, description, or other form; it is the rhythm and identity that characterizes a being as unique. I propose this essence as the source of life energy and generativity. It cannot be divided, being a natural integral ("whole"); yet it can be denied or devalued.[4] I see one of the tasks of generative hypnotherapy as reconnecting clients with their Deep Self via hypnotic explorations.

---

[4]Precisely because Self cannot be divided, it is unavailable to phenomenological experience since such experience requires splitting Self into subject (perceiver) and object (perceived); nevertheless, Self can be intuited in special transpersonal states such as love and generative trance.

It should be repeatedly recalled that Deep Self is an entirely fictional term used to point

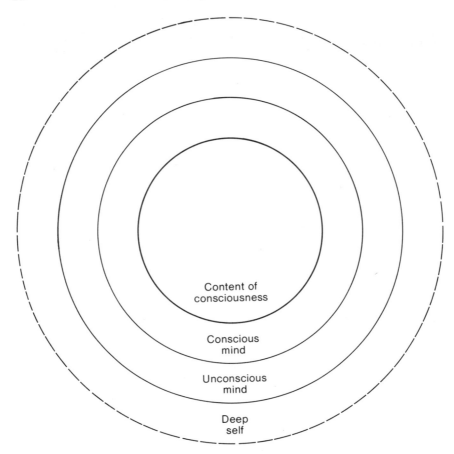

Content of
consciousness

Conscious
mind

Unconscious
mind

Deep
self

Figure 1.3. Levels of self

to an ineffable Self. Other metaphors can and should be used, along with the understanding
that "whatever you say it is, it isn't."

We might imagine the Deep Self as a four-dimensional hypersphere enfolded in the
topological form of a torus. The torus, also called "mobius sphere" or "doughnut sphere,"
has been proposed by Einstein and Eddington as a model of the universe (see Davis &
Hersh, 1981; Young, 1972; Zukav, 1979). Among its fascinating properties is that every
point in the sphere is a center point, being described by the same Fourier transformation
mathematics used to generate holograms (cf. Davis & Hersh, 1981). Thus, the whole is
contained in each of the points, as in holograms. In this view, each person is a unique
"representation" of the common-unity Self.

*Second*, the differentiations of self over time give rise to a system of organizational identity conventionally called the *unconscious mind*. Mind is a tool, a computational device, an amazingly complex information system, the task of which is to preserve the integrity (wholeness) of self while expanding its autonomy ("domain of self-regulation"). Following Bateson's (1972, 1979) orientation, mind is seen as a cybernetic system consisting of closed (i.e., circular) information loops or networks of pathways through which differences (i.e., distinctions or ideas) or transformations of differences are transmitted. Thus, mind is a map of the territory, expressing and representing the correlations of self-in-context; it is the pattern and patterning of relationships, a matrix or constellation by which we differentiate and navigate the "space" all around us.

In this view, mind is not contained within the body. As Bateson (1972) proposed:

> . . . the delimitation of individual mind must always depend upon what phenomena we wish to understand or explain. Obviously there are lots of message pathways outside the skin, and these and the messages which they carry must be included as part of the mental system whenever they are relevant. (p. 458)

> Individual mind is immanent but not only in the body. It is immanent also in pathways and messages outside of body; and there is a larger Mind of which individual mind is a subsystem. Larger mind is perhaps what we mean by God . . . immanent in the totally interconnected social system and planetary ecology. (p. 461)

Thus, mind refers not only to intrapersonal "patterns that connect" (Bateson, 1979) but to interpersonal loops as well. For example, the client may be absorbed in the "group mind" of the family or a cult; relatedly, we will see in Chapter 3 how an "interpersonal trance" between therapist and client may be developed.

*Third*, the *conscious mind* can be seen as the figure to the ground or field of the unconscious. While the unconscious mind tends to act holistically, the conscious mind is lineal in orientation. Its major functions include structuring information into action frames or programs ("mental sets") and sequencing and computing conceptual relationships. The conscious mind is viewed here as a manager or regulator; it is primarily conservative, not generative, in nature. It is the domain of roles, sensory-motor cybernetic loops, goal-achieving plans, scripts, strategies, structures, and rationality ("ratio-making" or self-dividing). As we will discuss further, it arises from and is maintained by muscular tension patterns.

The conscious mind selects out and re-presents transforms of the unconscious mind; in doing so, it divides the unconscious (awareness) field into focal (inner) and peripheral (outer) regions. If this same conscious patterning (division) persists (i.e., if the same frame is constantly active), dissociation between conscious and unconscious processes can occur. As we will see, this gives rise to symptomatic expressions, which are understood here as symbolic attempts to reunite the two orders of mind.

*Fourth*, we may distinguish the content elements filtering through mind. These include individual perceptions, motor expressions, images, cognitions, and sensations. These distinctions are the information units by which experience is represented, manipulated, and communicated.

In summary, a person can be appreciated as being a unique essence (Self), as operating within a unique psychobiological organizational system (unconscious mind or context of Self), as using unique strategies in attempting to achieve goals (conscious mind or structure of Self), and as being absorbed at a given time in distinctive mental content (content of Self). This multilevel model suggests multilevel therapeutic goals. At the primary level, unconditional valuing of Deep Self is essential to generative expression. At the level of organizational identity, the hypnotherapist works to 1) synchronize and align with the biological rhythms underlying self-expressions and 2) align with and recontextualize the intentions (i.e., commitments or injunctions) underlying behavioral strategies. At the level of goal structures, the hypnotherapist joins, balances, reframes, and modifies the client's strategies of self-expression (i.e., sensory/motor loops). And at the level of content, the therapist works to diversify the specific content of a person's experience. Each of these levels of intervention are explored further in the book.

*8. Unconscious processes can operate generatively and autonomously.* As Table 1.2 shows, a distinction between conscious and unconscious minds has been proposed by various thinkers over the years.[5] The present approach assumes that the two systems are complementary in nature, although it places the conscious mind as responsive to the more inclusive unconscious system (see Figure 1.4). Thus, while the conscious mind can be clever and efficient, the unconscious mind is needed for

---

[5]To these complementarities, others can be added: whole/part, unifying/separating, continuous/discontinuous, etc.

TABLE 1.2
Conscious/Unconscious Complementarities
(adapted from Bogen, 1969)

| | Complementarities | |
| --- | --- | --- |
| *Suggested by* | *Unconscious* | *Conscious* |
| C. S. Smith | Gross | Atomistic |
| Price | Synthetic or concrete | Analytic or reductionist |
| Wilder | Geometric | Numerical |
| Head | Perceptual or nonverbal | Symbolic or systematic |
| Goldstein | Concrete | Abstract |
| Reusch | Analogic or eidetic | Digital or discursive |
| Bateson and Jackson | Analogic | Digital |
| J. Z. Young | Maplike | Abstract |
| Pribram | Analogic | Digital |
| W. James | Existential | Differential |
| Spearman | Education of correlates | Education of relations |
| Hobbes | Free or unordered | Directed |
| Freud | Primary process | Secondary process |
| Pavlov | First signaling | Second signaling |
| Sechenov (Luria) | Simultaneous | Successive |
| Levi-Strauss | Mythic | Positive |
| Bruner | Metaphoric | Rational |
| Akhilananda | Manas | Buddhi |
| Radhakrishnan | Integral | Rational |

wisdom and generativity. The fundamental limits of conscious processes were described by Bateson (1972) as follows:

*The cybernetic nature of self and the world tends to be imperceptible to consciousness, insofar as the contents of the "screen" of consciousness are determined by considerations of purpose.* The argument of purpose tends to take the form "*D* is desirable; *B* leads to *C*; *C* leads to *D*; so *D* can be achieved by way of *B* and *C*." But, if the total mind and the outer worlds do not, in general, have this lineal structure, then by forcing this structure upon them, we become blind to the cybernetic circularities of the self and the external world. Our conscious sampling of data will not disclose whole circuits but only arcs of circuits, cut off from their matrix by our selective attention. Specially, the attempt to achieve a change in a given variable, located either in self or environment, is likely to be undertaken without comprehension of the homeo-

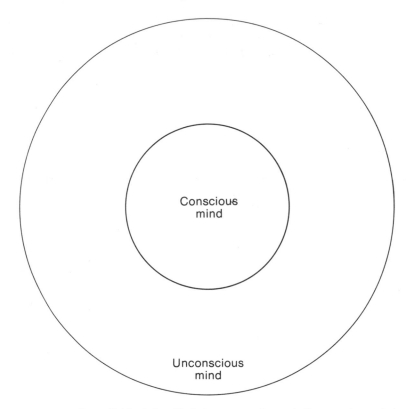

Figure 1.4. Figure/field relationship between conscious mind/unconscious mind

> static network surrounding that variable. . . . It may be essential
> for *wisdom* that the narrow purposive view be somehow corrected.
> (p. 444) (original italics)

Thus, problems can be seen to arise when a person identifies with self-containing processes of the conscious mind and dissociates from a deeper source of integrity.

Perhaps the most radical claim in all of this is that unconscious processes are intelligent, organized, and creative resources. Furthermore, the unconscious can operate autonomously from conscious processes (this is generally called *dissociative processing*), and is capable of deep transformational changes. Thus, rather than viewing the hypnotic context as one in which suggestions are "planted" into some passive receptacle, the Ericksonian practitioner conceptualizes trance as process in which the client's conscious processes are set aside, thereby enabling unconscious processes to generate meaningful transformational experiences. In this view, *conscious insight is not necessary for such changes to occur*. It is in this sense that Erickson (personal communication, 1978) would frequently emphasize,

> Your conscious mind is very intelligent, but your unconscious is a lot smarter.

Thus, the unconscious is seen as an integral and central aspect of Self, not as something to avoid or try to control. The major task of the Ericksonian hypnotherapist is to assist clients in realizing this in a practical way.

In emphasizing the potential generativity of unconscious processes, the therapist needs to appreciate that the ultimate value of such processes depends upon the context in which they are expressed. In other words, that the unconscious *can* be generative does not mean it always is so. As we will see, the therapist thus strives to facilitate those conditions enabling unconscious generativity, such as (1) establishing a coherent intention (or commitment to change), (2) ensuring a rhythmic and balanced biological context, and (3) developing ways to cooperate effectively with social structures.

Furthermore, a working complementarity between unconscious processes and conscious processes is increasingly sought as the person begins to integrate changes into the desired social contexts. It is assumed that for most creative accomplishments, both systems are ultimately needed. As an illustrative example, consider the famous case of Fredrich Kekule, the German chemist who solved the structural riddle of the benzene molecule. Kekule labored for a long time attempting to consciously solve the problem at hand. Finally, in a daydream, his unconscious processes generated an analogical structure involving six snakes connected in the structural form of a hexagon. Upon arousing, he consciously recognized this metaphor as representing the elusive structure of the benzene ring. Thus, his conscious mind identified and posed the problem; his unconscious generated a metaphorical solution; and his conscious mind was subsequently able to interpret its significance. Without the participation of the similarity relations of the unconscious, which bonded two form-related but content-unrelated structures (i.e., "the pattern of X is *similar* to the pattern of Y"), it is doubtful whether the answer would have been discovered. The conscious mind would probably have confined its inquiry to those categories immediately related to the problem's content, such as concepts within the domain of chemistry. The unconscious, however, was able to disregard the content and instead seek similarity relations of a structural and analogical (i.e., metaphorical) type. Just as important, the abstracting properties of the conscious mind were then needed to represent and communicate the solution in a standardized format (i.e., chemistry), thereby making it technologically applicable.

Although interaction between unconscious and conscious systems may be necessary for creative achievement, it unfortunately seems to be the exception rather than the rule for many people. Individuals may be totally dominated by unconscious processes; in the extreme case, this is called psychosis. Or more commonly, a person may strongly distrust the intuitive processes of the unconscious and thus try to rigidly control life through rational ("divisive") means. This dissociation may be due to implicit cultural mores or to specific personal experiences; for example, an individual may dissociate from unconscious resources by attempting to disown or "forget" an incomplete or traumatic experience related to him or her. The task of the therapist is to find ways whereby the person learns to appreciate the value of both conscious and unconscious processes.

An important variable in pursuing this task is the *quality* of the relationship between conscious and unconscious minds. Specifically, the relationship boundary (the circumference in Figure 1.4) may be *translucent* (i.e., flexible, permeable, open, and soft) or *opaque* (closed, rigid, impermeable, and hard), depending on factors such as muscle tension, psychological security, and whether an experience is accepted (i.e., valued) or dissociated (i.e., devalued). When the boundaries are translucent, conscious and unconscious minds complement each other; when the boundaries are opaque, the systems oppose (i.e., compete) with each other (e.g., man "against" environment, self vs. other). Thus, a major goal in the present approach is to soften the boundaries so that complementary interactions can occur. As we will see, hypnotic communications are major tools for accomplishing this goal.

In all of this, a person should not be confused as "being" either the unconscious or conscious mind. To reiterate, mind is a computational tool by which the Self knows and expresses Self in the world of experience. *The potential of a tool to create is equivalent to its potential capacity to destroy or oppress: Its effects depend on how it is used by the Self.* Dynamite can be used for peaceful or violent purposes; a leader can destroy or incredibly enhance a culture (e.g., Hitler vs. Christ). In the same sense, the psychological processes that create pain for an individual can be used to generate satisfaction and creative solutions. This explains in part why the unconscious can be benevolent (the humanistic view) or oppressive (the Freudian view): It depends upon the individual's relation to it and his or her willingness to accept all parts of the self as valid.

A primary factor in all of this is the extent to which the individual equates his or her self-identity with that tool. In other words, a person identifying himself as *being* (rather than *expressing*) a particular process will be *used by* (and thus cannot use) that process. For example, suppose an individual has a strong rule that states that he *must* be intelligent (and thus cannot be unintelligent). He will thus be highly motivated to exhibit behaviors that support such a claim, while simultaneously avoiding at all costs behaviors that could challenge the validity of such a proposition. As such, he will hesitate to experiment with behaviors that have uncertain outcomes associated with them, and consequently will become entrenched in familiar (habitual) patterns of thinking and behaving that simulate intelligence. This would of course inevitably disallow the expression of intelligence, as such a process requires independence, spontaneity, and creativity. Of course, the individual might act "intellectually," though at best this would be a painful simulation.

This general metaphor of mental processes as tools with equivalent destructive and constructive capacity is highly relevant to hypnotherapeutic practice. Specifically, the Ericksonian hypnotherapist's communicational strategies are designed to establish the desired state by "getting into gear with" the subject's ongoing processes and then shifting them toward the identified goal. Chapter 7 outlines, for example, how the person whose incessant internal dialogue constitutes a difficulty for traditional trance inductions can be offered a set of inductional communications that effectively utilize the internal verbalizations as the basis for trance development. This utilization principle of "whatever a person is doing is exactly that which will allow him or her to change" will be continually demonstrated and emphasized.

## SUMMARY

This chapter sought to establish a general framework for understanding the utilization approach to clinical hypnosis. This was initially done by emphasizing how many hypnotic practitioners conceptualize the hypnotic relationship in terms of either the hypnotist's power (the authoritarian approach) or the subject's susceptibility (the standardized approach). These more traditional orientations were contrasted with the cooperation (or utilization) approach developed by Milton Erickson, which emphasizes the *relationship* between hypnotist and subject as being of primary importance. Further assumptions of the cooperation approach include the following: (1) each person is unique; (2) hypnosis is an experiential process of communicating ideas; (3) each person has generative resources; (4) trance potentiates resources; (5) trance is naturalistic; (6) Ericksonian approaches orient to course-alignment more than error-correction; (7) a person's uniqueness can be appreciated on many levels (Deep Self, unconscious mind, conscious mind, and contents of consciousness); and (8) unconscious processes can operate generatively and autonomously. Each of these assumptions is developed in greater detail in the ensuing chapters.

# CHAPTER 2

# *The Experience of Trance*

*Trance* is a word that conjures up many associations. This chapter explores some of these associations, the major intention being to develop a general sense of trance as a pervasive and naturalistic phenomenon. The first section outlines major theories of trance, starting with 19th century speculations and then proceeding onward to present-day proposals. The view is taken that the various proposals can be seen, for the most part, as complementary to each other. The second section expands the discussion to distinguish the *experience* of trance from the specific *ritual* of hypnosis, emphasizing trance as a cross-contextual and pervasive phenomenon with profound therapeutic potential. The third section overviews some of the phenomenological aspects of the experience of trance, noting how such aspects apply to both symptom phenomena and trance phenomena. The final section briefly discusses how the therapeutic use of trance can be organized into the four steps of (1) creating a context (*preparation for trance*), (2) making the transition (*development of trance*), (3) promoting transformations (*utilizing the trance*), and (4) consolidating learnings (*concluding and extending the trance*).

### THEORIES OF TRANCE:
### WHAT THE THEORISTS CLAIM

*Early Speculations*

During the past several centuries there have been many scholarly speculations regarding the phenomenon of hypnotic trance. The majority of these ideas were developed in the 19th century; most contemporary theories are modified versions of these earlier ones. The following are sketches of the most important early metaphors used to describe the experience of trance; more detailed accounts can be found in Ellenberger (1970), Rosen (1959), and Tinterow (1970).

*1. Trance as energy channeling.* Franz Mesmer (1734–1815) is most often credited with fathering the modern theory and practice of hypnosis. Mesmer believed that human health is influenced by the action of planetary and lunar forces on an invisible magnetic bodily fluid. He suggested that disease results from a disequilibrium in (i.e., an unequal distribution of) this magnetic fluid. Therefore, channeling magnetic forces into the sick person should restore equilibrium through a convulsive healing "crisis." It is interesting to contrast the convulsive behaviors of "Mesmeric trances" to the relaxed behaviors generally associated with contemporary hypnotic trances, as it shows how the phenomena ("appearances") of trance can vary according to the beliefs and values implicit in the social context.

Mesmer's hypnotic rituals were initially performed with actual magnets; later "discovery" revealed that animal magnetism could be transferred to other therapeutic objects. These included trees, the mesmerizer's hands, and a device known as a *baquet*, described by a visitor to Mesmer's home:

> I was in his home the other day and was witness to his method of operating. In the middle of the room is placed a vessel of about a foot and a half high which is called here a *baquet*. It is so large that twenty people can easily sit around it; near the edge of the lid which covers it, there are holes pierced corresponding to the number of persons who are to surround it; into these holes are introduced iron rods, bent at right angles outwards, and of different heights, so as to answer to the part of the body to which they are to be applied.
>
> Besides these rods, there is a rod which communicates between the *baquet* and one of the patients, and from him is carried to another, and so on the whole round. The most sensible effects are produced on the approach of Mesmer, who is said to convey the fluid by certain motions of his hands or eyes, without touching the person. I have talked with several who have witnessed these effects, who have convulsions occasioned and removed by a movement of the hand. . . . (cited in Ellenberger, 1970, p. 64)

Mesmer insisted that the spectacular healings that often seemed to result from such rituals were due solely to the physical energy of animal magnetism. He rejected any suggestions that there was a psychological component. (This failure to seriously consider psychological explanations is not surprising when we remember that psychology as a scientific discipline developed well after Mesmer's time.) Since only Mesmer and a few other charismatic men seemed to possess this ability to channel magnetism, Mesmer rapidly developed a lucrative practice in France and Austria. However, the questionable nature of his theories and practice soon brought him under intense scientific scrutiny. Several major scientific commissions concluded that there was no truth to his physical theories. Interestingly, none of the commissions seems to have considered the possibility that the undeniably dramatic effects of mesmerism indicated the therapeutic potential of imagination, suggestion, or the charismatic interpersonal relationship.

*2. Trance as sleep.* A number of 19th century investigators likened trance to sleep. One of the first was Jose Faria (1755–1819), a Portuguese priest who lived in Paris. Originally a practitioner of animal magnetism, Faria advanced a theory of *somnambulism* which held that the hypnotized subject entered a state of "lucid sleep." This state occurred when the subject voluntarily concentrated his or her thoughts and withdrew from sensory experience, thereby restricting the conscious will and inner freedom. Faria claimed that somnambulists were capable of extraordinary acts, such as diagnosing their own illnesses and dissociating from surgical pain. He was one of the first to claim that the development of trance was due to characteristics of the subject, not the magnetizer. He believed that the best subjects were those who possessed a "liquidity of the blood" and a certain "psychic impressionability" (suggestibility), went to sleep easily, and perspired freely.

James Braid (1795–1860), a Scottish surgeon, was another early proponent of modified sleep theory. In his early work, Braid would ask the subject to gaze steadily at a spot slightly above eye level. After several minutes the subject's eyes would usually tire and then close. Braid thought this indicated the onset of a sleeplike neurophysiological state that caused fatigue and consequent paralysis of the nervous centers controlling the eyes and eyelids. He originally called this condition "neurohypnotism," then shortened it to "hypnotism" (from the Greek *hypnos*, or sleep). Braid later altered his initial conclusion about the sleeplike nature of trance, proposing it instead to be a state of mental concentration, which he termed "monoideism" (having one dominant mental idea).

A third advocate of the sleep theory of trance was Ivan Pavlov (1849–1936), who explained the trance state as an "incomplete sleep state" resulting from hypnotic suggestions. These suggestions purportedly created excitation in some parts of the brain cortex and inhibition in others, allowing the hypnotized subject to attend exclusively to the hypnotic communications and dissociate from the external world.

As in Braid's early theories, the trance state was assumed to be a peculiar neurophysiological condition.

The metaphor of "trance as sleep" has been shown to be inaccurate on at least several counts. First, no physiological similarity exists between sleep and hypnotic trance (Barber, 1969; Sarbin, 1956); the latter more closely resembles a relaxed waking state. Second, the hypnotized subject rarely loses full awareness and response capabilities. Although appearing lethargic at times, the subject's internal world is far from being passive or inactive.

*3. Trance as pathology.* Jean Martin Charcot (1825–1893) was perhaps the most distinguished neurologist in Europe when he decided to investigate hypnosis in 1878. His experiments used a minimum of subjects, all female patients with diagnoses of hysteria from the Salpêtrière hospital in Paris. After an investigation similar to ones he used for neurological diseases, Charcot concluded that the trance state was a pathological state similar to hysteria.[1] Further, he theorized three levels of trance – catalepsy, lethargy, and somnambulism. Many people, influenced by Charcot's reputation in neurology, accepted his claims regarding hypnosis. These people, collectively known as the Salpêtrière school, upheld the validity of Charcot's theories against, and fought bitterly with, supporters of the Nancy school theory of suggestibility.

*4. Trance as suggestibility.* Auguste Liébeault (1823–1904), originator of the Nancy school, was a French country doctor who likened trance to sleep, with the major exception that trance resulted from direct suggestion. This theory attempted to explain why a trance subject remained in rapport with the hypnotist. Liébeault's method of hypnosis was to look deeply into the subject's eyes and suggest that the subject become increasingly sleepy, whereupon he would issue direct suggestions for symptom removal. His work would have gone unnoticed but for Hippolyte Bernheim (1840–1919), a famous Nancy university professor who became Liébeault's pupil and public admirer. Bernheim assumed leadership of what came to be known as the Nancy school. In contrast to Mesmer's physical and Charcot's neurological theories, Bern-

---

[1]Charcot apparently conducted none of the investigations directly, relegating the work to assistants (see Ellenberger, 1970). Although his conclusion that trance is a pathological state is misleading by ignoring the potential healing aspects of trance, it is useful in emphasizing severely dissociated states as trance-like in nature. As we will see, the present approach assumes that trance can be generative or degenerative, depending on contextual factors.

heim (1895) advanced a psychological explanation of trance as a state of enforced suggestibility resulting from suggestion. (As we will see, this obviously circular argument led some contemporary investigators to completely reject terms such as "trance" and "hypnosis.") Bernheim (1895) believed that, to some extent, everyone possessed suggestibility, which he defined as "the aptitude to transform an idea into an act" (p. 137). An excellent clinician, he successfully utilized hypnosis for a variety of medical purposes, and his scathing attacks on Charcot's theory helped to discredit it. Bernheim gradually stopped using hypnosis, however, contending that the observed effects could be obtained by suggestion in a waking state. He and his followers named this new procedure "psychotherapeutics."

5. *Trance as dissociation.* Dissociation may be generally defined as a mental process in which systems of ideas are split off from the normal personality and operate independently (cf. Hilgard, 1977). Pierre Janet (1849–1947), one of the first proponents of this theory, described the hypnotic trance as a state in which the subject's subconscious mind executed cognitive functions away from conscious awareness. Janet (1910) introduced the term *subconscious* to avoid using the term *unconscious*, which he believed to have erroneous connotations. His notion of the subconscious, emphasizing the ability to carry out intelligent, creative, and autonomous activity, is very close to the notion of the unconscious as Erickson used it. Janet also believed that, in addition to the dissociational aspects of trance, there existed a "role-playing" component in which the subject would perform to please the hypnotist.

In Janet's experience, hypnotic dissociation often involved regression to an earlier period in the subject's life. While in trance, the subject could remember incidents that occurred in previous dissociated (trance) states, as well as events that transpired during the normal waking state; upon awakening, the dissociated subject would have amnesia concerning the trance state. This general theory derived from Janet's intense investigations into many areas, including hypnosis, automatic writing, and psychopathology (multiple personality and hysteria).

Janet (1910) distinguished two types of dissociation: *total automatism*, in which the subject shifted entirely into a different personality; and *partial automatism*, in which a part of the personality split off and operated unbeknownst to the normal personality. Janet's ideas influenced many theorists, including William James (1890) and Morton Prince (1975) in the United States. Prince (1975) described personality alterations that could be hypnotically developed and emphasized the possibilities for using the trance state for therapeutic work with multiple personalities.

## Contemporary Proposals

This brief overview indicates how hypnosis aroused considerable interest and controversy among 19th century scientists. This interest declined during the first half of the 20th century. This was due partly to the strong upsurge of behaviorism, partly to Freud's rejection of hypnosis, and partly to the overtones of mystery that still shrouded the nature of hypnosis. This slide toward oblivion reversed itself after World War II, when hypnosis was demonstrated to be effective in treating victims of war neuroses, dental patients, and obstetrical cases (Hilgard, 1965). In the 1950s, the British and American medical societies both formally recognized hypnosis as a valid treatment modality. Since then, an increasing number of researchers and clinicians have been attracted to the subject.

Most contemporary theorists reject physical and neurological explanations (the sleep and pathology metaphors) in favor of psychological approaches emphasizing suggestion, imagination, motivation, dissociation, and role playing. The following are among the most prominent of the contemporary proposals.

*1. Trance as regression.* Many psychodynamicists have interpreted the hypnotic experience in terms of Freudian and neo-Freudian concepts of psychic regression and transference. Kris (1952) advanced the concept of *partial regression in the service of the ego.* Gill and Brenman (1959) similarly characterized the hypnotic trance as regression to a primitive state in which rationality yields to impulse and the subject develops a transference relationship with the hypnotist. Fromm (1972; Fromm, Oberlander, & Gruenwald, 1970) reviewed these and other psychodynamic theories of trance and offered a refined version stressing the "passive ego" and "adaptive regression" of the hypnotized subject.

In one of the first attempts at a comprehensive theory, Shor (1959, 1962) proposed three dimensions of the trance experience: (a) *depth of role-taking involvement*, in which the subject initially strives to think and act like a hypnotic subject but then (upon entering trance) begins to do so nonvolitionally and unconsciously; (b) *depth of trance*, which develops as the subject's general "reality orientation" diminishes, and allows the subject to become immersed in an arbitrary and purely subjective world; and (c) *depth of archaic involvement*, which involves the regressive-transference properties presented above.

2. *Trance as acquired learning.* Clark Hull, the eminent American psychologist, believed that all hypnotic processes could be explained by the laws of formal learning theory – associative repetition, conditioning, habit formation, habituation, and so forth. In his classic 1933 work, *Hypnosis and Suggestibility*, Hull proposed that hypnotic phenomena were acquired responses similar to other habits. His conclusion was that the subject's trance experiences resulted from the hypnotist's suggestions and were due to "the strictly physical basis of the association between stimuli and responses, ideas becoming purely physical symbolic acts." (I must admit being puzzled as to how a "symbolic act" can be "purely physical.") Other theorists, including Weitzenhoffer (1953, 1957), have employed learning concepts such as habit extinction and drive reduction in discussing the hypnotic process. This theoretical approach has some merit in emphasizing trance as a naturalistic experience that can become easier and more complete with practice. Yet even Weitzenhoffer (1957, pp. 56–58) points out the extremely limited nature of this view. Aside from the currently acknowledged deficiencies of classical learning theories (see Bandura, 1977), there is no allowance for the phenomenological aspects of trance, the uniqueness of individual subjects, or the interpersonal relationship.

3. *Trance as dissociation.* Ernest Hilgard, whose theorizing on trance has undergone various shifts over the years (for comparisons, see Sheehan and Perry, 1976), recently revived and modified Janet's dissociation concepts. Hilgard's (1977) neodissociation theory borrows concepts from contemporary cognitive psychology in describing the hypnotic experience as a temporary detachment by the subject from the usual conscious planning and monitoring functions. By operating independent from reality testing, the subject becomes less critical and thus able to develop dissociative experiences such as amnesia, hypnotic deafness, pain control, and automatic writing.

4. *Trance as motivated involvement.* For many years, T. X. Barber (1969, 1972) has ardently criticized the metaphor of "trance" as "an altered state of consciousness," claiming that such vague hypothetical constructs are strongly misleading. Not only do they distract the operator (hypnotist) from operationally defining the important variables of the "hypnotic" interaction, but they also convince many subjects that they cannot develop "amazing and mysterious hypnotic phenomena," such as pain control, hallucinations, and age regression. As an alternative, Barber (1969) advanced a cognitive-behavioral viewpoint that assumes "trance" experiences to result from "positive attitudes, motivations

and expectation toward the test situation which lead to a willingness
to think and imagine with the themes that are suggested" (p. 5). In
this view, any willing individual can be trained to develop "hypnotic"
phenomena. Barber believes formal (traditional) inductions to be unnecessary, while considering contextual variables such as the operator's
behavior and the interpersonal relationship to be of paramount importance.

   Many people think Barber's position is in direct and complete opposition to Erickson's approach. Leaving aside obvious differences in terminology, there are similarities between the two positions, particularly the
emphasis on all individuals being capable of "hypnotic" experiences,
alternatives to formal trance inductions, trance as naturalistic, and the
importance of motivational and interpersonal variables. On the other
hand, Barber's straightforward equation of trance with imagination
appears flawed, as many subjects experience trance as qualitatively different from any other experience.

   *5. Trance as role enactment.* This view emphasizes the social psychological aspects of the hypnotic situation. White (1941) described
trance as a goal-directed state in which the subject is highly motivated
to behave "like a hypnotized person" (as defined by the operator and
understood by the subject). Sarbin (1950, 1956; Sarbin & Coe, 1972), the
most eloquent proponent of this theory, depicted the hypnotic subject
as an individual enacting a "role." Like Barber, Sarbin expressed disdain
for vague and circular mentalistic terms such as "trance," "state," and
"the unconscious," arguing for a more descriptive language to identify
the variables and conditions responsible for "trance experiences." Sarbin
contended that it was more helpful to view hypnotic behavior as *"as if"*
conduct. His repeated portrayal of "trance" as an abstract metaphor
wrongly assumed to be concrete (and thus a misleading one), taken with
his strong emphasis on social psychological variables, led many to assume erroneously that his position denied *any* validity to the "trance
experience."

   In actuality, Sarbin invoked the role enactment metaphor to describe
*all* social behavior, and emphasized that the level of *organismic involvement* in a role may vary considerably, from "casual role enactment" and
"ritual acting" to the extremes of "ecstasy" and (death-inducing) "object
of sorcery and witchcraft" (Sarbin & Coe, 1972). Sarbin placed classical
hypnotic behavior midway along this "involvement" continuum by
claiming that a skilled and motivated individual could become deeply
immersed in the hypnotic role to the extent of experiencing dramatic
qualitative shifts in subjective reality.

## An Eclectic View

In surveying these contemporary theories of trance, it can be seen that each position seems to emphasize or highlight important characteristics of the hypnotic experience, while ignoring or downplaying others. This is not to diminish these views; rather, it is to call attention to the multidimensional nature of hypnotic experience. There exist many important situational and interpersonal variables affecting the general development of a trance state; additionally, the unique qualities of each subject act against characterizing trance as being essentially the same experience for everyone.

Erickson was extremely aware of this complexity; over the years he maintained a fairly constant atheoretical position. On the frequent occasions in his later years when he was asked to define specifically the nature of trance or of unconscious processes, he would typically demur, explaining that "whatever I say it is . . . will distract me from recognizing and utilizing the many possibilities that are" (Erickson, personal communication, 1977). (After his disclaimer, however, he would often relate elaborate metaphorical stories on the topic.)

In general, simplistic and categorical statements about trance experience can offer comfort to the theoretician, but may bias and unnecessarily limit the practitioner. As Erickson (1952) noted:

> It must be recognized that a description, no matter how accurate or complete, will not substitute for actual experience, nor can it be made applicable for all subject (sic). Any description of a deep trance must necessarily vary in minor details from one subject to another. There can be no absolute listing of hypnotic phenomena as belonging to any one level of hypnosis. Some subjects will develop phenomena in the light trance usually associated with the deep trance, and others in a deep trance will show some of the behavior commonly regarded as characteristic of the light trance state. Some subjects who in light trances show behavior usually typical of the deep trance may show a loss of that same behavior when deep hypnosis actually develops. For example, subjects who easily develop amnesia in the light trance may just as easily fail to develop amnesia in the deep trance. The reason for such apparent anomalies lies in the entirely different psychological orientation of the deeply hypnotized person as contrasted to his orientation in lighter states of hypnosis. (In Rossi, 1980a, pp. 144–145)

Thus, the Ericksonian practitioner remains wary of any categorical claims about hypnotic trance. This does not rule out the practitioner's developing an opinion about the nature of trance. Erickson tended to favor dissociational models of trance, as evidenced in the following quotations:

> Deep hypnosis is that level of hypnosis that permits the subject to function adequately and directly at an unconscious level of awareness without interference from the conscious mind. (1952; in Rossi, 1980a, p. 146)

> Therapeutic trance is a period during which the limitations of one's usual frame of reference and beliefs are temporarily altered so one can be receptive to the patterns and associations and modes of mental functioning that are conducive to problem-solving. (Erickson & Rossi, 1979, p. 3)

The quality that is most needed by the Ericksonian is an elastic, open-minded position. Table 2.1 indicates some valuable points made or implied by each of the previously presented contemporary theories. In this way, the hypnotic practitioner can view these theories as complementary, not mutually exclusive. Later chapters will further explore these points and demonstrate their interlocking nature.

### TRANCE AS NATURALISTIC AND CROSS-CONTEXTUAL

In the Ericksonian approach, the *naturalistic* use of trance processes plays a central role. To appreciate this orientation, the general *experience* of trance should be distinguished from the specific *ritual* of hypnosis. The latter is but one means to elicit the former. By recognizing how trance occurs in other ways and in other situations, the ability to utilize trance processes is markedly enhanced. To facilitate such a recognition, the following distinctions may be of value.

*1. Trance experiences are distinguished by the principle of ideodynamicism and both/and logic.* To develop a feel for the nature of trance, several principal features might be noted. First, experience in trance "just happens," without the regulation, control, or other active participation by self-conscious processes. As is discussed further in the next section, this characteristic of effortlessness is described by the principle of ideodynamicism, which states that ideas can be expressed in dynamics (sensations, images, cognitions, motor acts, perceptions, emotions) without any conscious mediation.

Second, trance involves a paradoxical, both/and logic. That is, a

TABLE 2.1
Some Valuable Points Made by Contemporary Theories of Trance

| Theory | Some Valuable Points |
|---|---|
| 1. Psychodynamic | a. In hypnotherapy, a strong relationship develops between the hypnotist and subject.<br>b. The trance subject shifts to a less analytic and more primary style of processing (e.g., less critical and defensive, more image-oriented). |
| 2. Learning | a. Trance is a naturalistic skill to be learned.<br>b. Trance ability can improve with practice.<br>c. Other learnings may interfere with trance development; they need to be addressed and depotentiated. |
| 3. Neo-Dissociation | a. The deeply hypnotized subject is often dissociated from normal monitoring and control processes.<br>b. This general dissociation permits the development of specific dissociational phenomena such as age regression, hypnotic dreams, automatic writing, hallucinations, and pain control.<br>c. Dissociative experiences can occur without formal hypnosis (e.g., night dreams, state-dependent recall). |
| 4. Motivated Involvement | a. Trance is a naturalistic experience phenomenologically similar to other psychological experiences.<br>b. As such, any willing subject can be trained to develop ''trance'' phenomena.<br>c. Formal inductions and rituals are not needed to develop ''trance'' experiences.<br>d. It is most important to establish rapport and to effectively inform and motivate the subject. |
| 5. Role Playing | a. Hypnosis and trance are really just metaphors and should not be reified.<br>b. Because trance is a response occurring within a social psychological context, situational variables (e.g., the hypnotist's communications, the relationship) must always be taken into account. |

person identifies with both sides of a complementary distinction of "this" and "that," "inside" and "outside," "subject" and "object." Thus, in trance I can feel both "here" and "there," connected with you and disconnected from you, "a part of" and "apart from" an experience, both a child and an adult. This both/and logic gives rise to a nonconceptual and nonverbal experiential state of unity. It is a more primary, inclusive way of relating than the separating, "either/or" logic characterizing analytical, conscious processes. In other words, trance processes tend to unify relations ("this" *and* "that"), while conscious processes tend to differentiate relations ("this" *vs.* "that").

Other features of trance to be explored in the next section include experiential absorption, continuity, time distortion, time/space variability, and perceptual alterations. Taken together, they suggest trance as a state of deep experiential absorption where a person can operate independently from the constraints of regulatory, error-oriented conscious processes.

*2. Trance is experienced in many situations.* Given even this brief description of trance, we can recognize its occurrence in many situations. It frequently develops in cultural transition rituals; for example, my experience in recently getting married was decidedly trancelike in nature. It can be heard in the descriptions of athletes and other artists, who describe processes of letting go and getting in the "flow." It can be felt by those who become deeply absorbed in the sound of music or the rhythm of dance. It can be seen in the person so immersed in reading a book, or the child so glued to the television show, that they heed not our calls. It can be observed in the daydreaming student, the deeply depressed client, the reminiscing old person. In short, trance occurs in many contexts.

*3. Trance is developed in many ways.* Among the means by which trance can be induced are *rhythmic and repetitive movement* (dancing, running, rocking, breathing exercises, etc.); *chanting* (meditation, prayer, group rituals, chants at rallies or sports events, the repetitive self-talk of depression, etc.); *attentional absorption* (on a mantra, the hypnotist's voice, an image, an idea, the television, etc.); and *balancing of muscle tonus* (via relaxation processes, massage, drugs such as alcohol or valium, rhythmic movement, etc.). These interrelated methods all tend to decrease the discontinuous, arrhythmic movements of deliberate conscious orientation, thus giving rise to a more unified mode of experience. The strong skin-bounded differentiation between self and other is dissipated by muscle tone shifts, thereby enabling the person to synchronize with complementary biological rhythms and align with unitary psychological processes.

*4. Trance is biologically necessary.* Anthropologists have noted that trance rituals can be found in virtually every culture (see Richeport, 1982). Historians have noted that such rituals have been around for centuries. This prevalence of trance across cultures and through time suggests that it is a biologically essential phenomenon for human beings.

One of the implications of this view is that trance will occur, like it or not. That is, we need opportunities to let go of trying, to immerse in a deeper communal context, to surrender to our Deep Self. We need to periodically depotentiate the error-correcting regulation of conscious goal achieving and experience anew an unbiased sense of wholeness. (As I tell many clients, if you don't let yourself in the front door, no amount of dead bolts will secure the back.) In fact, I see many symptoms developing when avenues to self-valuing trance states are blocked or otherwise denied by a person or community.

*5. Trance serves multiple functions.* If trance is biologically essential, it must be so for specific evolutionary purposes. In the present view, trance plays an integral role in the balancing of bio-logical and psychological systems. More specifically, trance aids in the achievement of several complementary motivations intrinsic to humans: *preserving* and *expanding* the integrity ("wholeness") of an autonomous ("self-regulating") self-identity. This self-identity is always in terms of multiple systems: individual, dyadic, familial, social, etc.

Identity preservation (i.e., not changing) via trance can occur in many ways. A person or group may develop trance to renew a sense of security — for example, through daily meditation, autohypnotic trance, group chanting. Severe threat to survival may trigger a protective trance involving complete withdrawal from conscious orientation (shock, catalepsy, depression, imaginal projection). Trance may also provide expression of consciously prohibited roles; for example, Bateson (1958) described how the Iatmul tribe in New Guinea perform *naven*, a trance ritual wherein men dress like women and vice versa and then act out certain roles normally associated with the complementary gender. Trance can be used to affirm a deeper experiential connection; for example, American Indian tribes use rain dance rituals to enter a communal state with the natural environment. In short, trance is an opportunity to return to a basic essence of one's identity.

Trance can also expand a person's or community's circle of identity. It appears in meaningful rituals of developmental transition (marriage, passage into adulthood, etc.). It can allow a person to disidentify with and move beyond certain attachments (e.g., to pain, a behavior pattern, a perceptual style). It gives rise to solution-seeking metaphorical expressions, such as symptoms, artistic expression, and story-telling. And it may facilitate psychological integrations (i.e., the unification of disconnected parts), a major concern of psychotherapy.

   *6. Trance can be self-valuing or self-devaluing.*  As with any experience, the value of a trance depends on the context in which it occurs. Self-valuing trances tend to be gentle, rhythmic, and continuous (fluid); self-devaluing trances tend to be violent, arrhythmic, and rigid. Over time, the content of self-valuing trances tends to change, since integrations occur and new gestalts thus form. The content of self-devaluing trances tends to repeat itself, since no integration (only more violence) occurs. In self-valuing trances, no attempt is made to actively control experience; in self-devaluing trances, efforts are made to control, deny, or otherwise negate experience in self and/or other (self). For example, persons expressing psychological symptoms may be seen as manifesting trance phenomena that they are attempting to control ("get rid of it") and deny ("this is not me"). Similarly, persons engaged in systematic violence (e.g., war) attempt to wipe out the other (self); when doing so, a trancelike state often develops.[2]
   That a trance is not necessarily useful shifts a therapist's focus from *how much* of a trance is developed to its *therapeutic quality*. Thus, the Ericksonian practitioner is more interested in the *breadth* than the *depth* of trance, that is, in how much of the client's resources are accessible within a given trance. It is assumed that a client knows how to develop trance in one way or another; of interest is how the therapeutic context can be utilized to enhance the self-valuing processes (and hence pragmatic value) occurring in such trances.

   *7. Trance phenomena are the basic processes by which psychological experience is generated.*  When an individual or community becomes immersed in hypnotic trance, certain phenomena ("appearances") are likely to emerge. These include regression into the past, progression into the future, heightened remembering (hypermnesia) or selective forgetting (amnesia), perceptual distortions, and perceptual dissociations (positive

---

   [2]The rigid trancelike states engendered in expressions of war can be observed in the multiple inductions surrounding it: the repetitive and stiff marches, the drum beats, the symbols (e.g., flags). As a child, I often wondered when watching war movies why, for example, the British would devote a significant number of soldiers to drum playing in battle marches. In retrospect, these men were clearly needed to induce the appropriate trance in those around them.

and negative hallucinations).[3] Although at first glance such phenomena may appear unusual, they are entirely naturalistic. In fact, trance phenomena can be seen as the basic psychological processes by which experience is generated and maintained. What *is* different is that phenomenological experience is intensified and amplified in trance states, thereby making it appear spectacular or otherwise unusual. Thus, we experience hallucinations when we fully dissociate from the imagery we have projected; we heighten our ability to forget something (amnesia) when we emphasize an ability to become immersed in something unrelated. By allowing a more intimate and intense involvement with the ways we regularly construct our world of experience, while also providing a sense of detachment from it (i.e., you have the sense in trance of not needing to control or hold on to experience), therapeutic trance enables fundamental shifts in our relationship to patterns of self-expression. In short, this process allows deep, transformative changes to be made.

*8. Trance phenomena and clinical symptoms are the same phenomena expressed in different contexts.* One of the first tasks Milton Erickson assigned me when I began to study with him was to study psychotics. After securing a part-time position enabling me to do so, I periodically visited Erickson and discussed various cases with him. In describing his extensive interactions with psychotics, he seemed to stress three points over and over again. First, the phenomenological experience of psychotics is remarkably similar to that of deep trance subjects: Both are characterized by regressions, dissociations, amnesias, perceptual and sensory alterations, symbolic expressions, and so forth. Second, the *quality* of experience could not differ more: Psychotics generally experience a very painful and limiting world, while deep trance subjects are enjoying themselves thoroughly. In other words, the phenomenological *form* of the experiences is the same, while the *context* differs radically. Third, the psychological processes of both groups are amplified expressions of normal unconscious processes.

These ideas suggest the therapeutic context of trance to be ideal for

---

[3]These phenomena are not common to all trances. They tend to be minimized, for example, in the meditational trances of Eastern cultures, where traditional values favor detachment from the phenomenological domain as a means of self-development. Hypnotic trance phenomena may thus be artifacts arising from Western values and biases. This suggests that the specific expressions occurring in a trance indicate primary values of the individual in whom and the community in which trance occurs.

transforming devaluing symptom expressions. Symptom expressions can be seen as valid hypnotic phenomena occurring in invalidating psychological contexts. The therapist thus seeks to generate interpersonal and intrapersonal relationship contexts where the same processes are validated, defined as legitimate autonomous expressions of the unconscious (i.e., trance phenomena), and utilized as the basis for problem solutions and self-integrations.


## THE PHENOMENOLOGICAL EXPERIENCE OF TRANCE

We have thus far explored general ideas regarding the nature of trance. This section discusses more specifically some of the particular phenomenological characteristics prominent in the experience of trance.

*1. Experiential absorption of attention.*  In trance, subjects can develop attentional absorption to the extent of becoming fully immersed in one particular experiential context for a sustained period. Contrast this to the waking state, in which attentional processes stay scattered and unfocused by continual reorientation to changing external stimuli. While in trance, hypnotized subjects will often not be aware of irrelevant stimuli (noises, other voices); even if aware of them, they will usually not be distracted or bothered nor feel a need to attend to them. This is especially true in deep trance.

The subject's attentional focus may be internally or externally oriented. Most traditional hypnotic rituals require the hypnotist to first fixate the subject's attention on an external object (a crystal ball, the hypnotist's eyes, a tack on the wall, a metronome, etc.). The hypnotist then gradually shifts the subject's attention to internally directed absorption. Sometimes, however, it is more appropriate for the subject to remain externally oriented while in trance. This would be the case if the hypnotist wished to induce trance in subjects who object to closing their eyes or in order to enhance subjects' performance in public (speeches, social interactions, athletic competition). Another situation calling for external direction is the therapist's going into trance while working with the client; the method and benefits of this will be outlined in Chapter 3.

This characteristic of sustained experiential absorption applies to "symptom" trances as well as hypnotic trances. A person beset by a recurrent problem can be observed to develop a singular fixation to that problematic process. Like the hypnotically entranced person, the problem-plagued individual does not have to try to remain absorbed; the experiential process sustains itself without deliberate conscious effort. In contrast to the hypnotic subject, however, the symptomatic individual reiteratively attempts to disrupt the experiential absorption through various regulatory strategies. This dissociates conscious processes from unconscious processes, the latter remaining absorbed in the problem field. In other words, the unconscious mind remains fixated on an incomplete experiential relationship, while the conscious mind attempts to move away from (i.e., negate or deny) it; this creates an opposition between conscious and unconscious processes. As we will see, Ericksonian induction strategies strive to join with both types of processes in moving to integrate them.

2. *Effortless expression.* The hypnotized subject usually feels little need to *try* to do anything or the compulsion to "plan ahead." Experience "just seems to happen" and "flows quite effortlessly." This manifestation of the trance state is not necessarily due to the subject relegating directive control to the hypnotist; it is just as common in autohypnotic experience and is reflective of a shift from conscious to unconscious processing.

This characteristic reflects the principle of *ideodynamicism* ("ideas" into "dynamics"), which postulates that ideas can be transformed into dynamic expression (e.g., images, behaviors, sensations, cognitions, etc.) *independently of*, and sometimes unbeknownst to, volitional conscious process.[4] As Bernheim (1895) pointed out, *ideodynamic processes seem to be more intense and occur more often in trance.* For example, the subjects receiving a suggestion that their hand will begin to automatically lift will often develop the *ideomotoric* experience of that hand *involuntarily* drifting up; in listening to a hypnotist's communication, they might develop *ideosensory* visualizations of feelings. The repeated expression of ideodynamic processes by hypnotic subjects led Erickson and Rossi (1979) to describe hypnotic suggestions as ideas that utilize a person's mental processes in ways that are outside his or her usual range of ego control.

In other words, the client's unconscious processes are encouraged to express themselves autonomously in the hypnotherapeutic context.

---

[4]William James (1890) is often credited with proposing the ideomotor principle, but Hilgard (1977) notes that James developed this concept from Alexander Bain's "Law of Diffusion" and Fere's concept of "dynamogenesis." Bain (1859) assumed that every sensory or emotional feeling had motoric consequences. Féré (1887) stated that any sensory stimulation increased muscle action. These were general theories about behavioral processes, not just those in the hypnotic context.

Such encouragement was often provided indirectly by Erickson. For example, he would often elicit trance response by telling anecdotes about *other* people experiencing trance phenomena, such as hand levitation or relaxation. While attentively listening to Erickson, the subject would begin to experience *similar* images. As this occurred, the subject would ideomotorically communicate a general sense of what was occurring through *minimal cues* – subtle changes in physical features such as facial coloration, breathing patterns, and pupil dilation. Erickson would closely observe these minimal cues and use them to guide his subsequent communication during the induction. This interpersonal "feedback loop" of communication would often result in the subject dropping into trance without a direct suggestion to do so. In these and other ways, ideodynamic processes can be utilized therapeutically.

It should also be noted how ideodynamic processes characterize self-devaluing (symptomatic) trances. A major feature of any problem context is that its symptom components are automatically expressed. Self-defeating feelings just seem to develop; troublesome images keep coming back; repetitive internal dialogue cannot be shut off. The Ericksonian practitioner accepts such automatic expressions as legitimate ideodynamic expressions from the person's unconscious mind and seeks to provide opportunities for them to be expressed in self-valuing, balancing, and diverse ways. With a client complaining of anxious feelings in the chest, for example, the following hypnotic communications were offered after appropriate rapport had been developed:

> That's right, Mary. And I really want to emphasize to you an idea that may at first seem a little unusual, yet an idea that I think you can begin to appreciate more and more as you begin to develop an experiential understanding of it even as I talk to you now. And what idea am I referring to? Simply this: You've got an ability to let your unconscious express itself autonomously in so many different ways . . . we all do. . . . For example, you've been expressing an ability to have *sensations develop autonomously . . . that's right, Mary . . . sensations* in your chest . . . you know that you've given them *different* names and had *different* thoughts about them. . . . And I simply want to affirm that your unconscious mind can develop those feelings *and then some* . . . because why have your chest hog all the action? I don't know if your arm will at first join in immediately, or whether it will be your legs that begin to *feel warm* or cool or tingly or numb . . . all I know is that you can express that autonomous *unconscious* ability to *experience sensations* developing in so many secure ways. . . .

In this conversational hypnotic approach, the symptom is defined as one instance of a general unconscious ability. Suggestions to diversify the ability via related (self-valuing) ideodynamic responses are offered to recontextualize the symptom as an (unconscious) gift to be valued. In this way, the automaticity shared by hypnotic and symptom phenomena is used to transform the latter into a therapeutic development.

*3. Experiential, nonconceptual involvement.* Entranced individuals usually are quite immersed in experiential, rather than conceptual, domains. They are more able to directly experience "things as they are" and generally show little need to logically understand or conceptually analyze experience. Thought processes typically become less critical, less evaluative, less verbal, and less abstract; concurrently, they grow more descriptive and image-based, more sensory, and more concrete. This experiential mode of processing gives rise to an ability to connect in a deeper way with resources and current realities. This ability is especially valuable to therapy clients. By "getting to know oneself at a different level of experience" (Erickson, personal communication, 1977) via setting aside habitual, dysfunctional conscious processes, a person is free to explore experiences from multiple perspectives.

This unbinding of experiential processes from conceptual frames distinguishes therapeutic trances from symptomatic trances. In the latter, a person typically is experientially immersed in a process, while at the same time attached to a rigid conceptual set that molds and biases the values of experiential stimuli. This results in recurrent (and thus predictable) experiential outcomes. The goal of hypnotic inductions is to dissipate fixation to these rigid frames, thereby enabling experiential processes to unfold according to a deeper intelligence within the person.

*4. Willingness to experiment.* The person in a hypnotic trance will usually be quite willing to experiment with new perspectives. Although this characteristic is often described as *suggestibility*, such a term sometimes implies the erroneous assumption that the subject is a passive automaton whose experience results from another person's (the hypnotist's) commands. This was not Erickson's (1948) belief, as he states emphatically:

Too often, the unwarranted and unsound assumption is made that ... whatever develops from hypnosis must necessarily and completely be as a result and primary expression of suggestion. Contrary to such misconceptions, the hypnotized person remains the same person. . . . His altered behavior derives from the life experience of the patient and not from the therapist. At the most, the therapist can influence only the manner of self-expression. The induction and maintenance of a trance serve to provide a special psychological state in which the patient can reassociate and reorganize his inner psychological complexities and utilize his own capacities in a manner concordant with his own experiential life. It serves to permit him to learn more about himself and to express himself more adequately. (In Rossi, 1980d, p. 38)

Hypnotic subjects are not gullible and will generally not follow instructions incongruent with their personal values.[5] Attempts to force entranced individuals to do something they do not want to do will almost always bring them *out of trance*; usually, such attempts create distrust and anger toward the therapist, thereby severely impairing the relationship.

The hypnotized person retains full choice about the experience; the security and state of well-being felt in a therapeutic trance will generally enhance one's sense of choice. Like a harried businessman on vacation, the trance subject — temporarily free from domination by the worried and fixed point of view of normal conscious processes — is more willing and able to experiment with creative and spontaneous behavior.

*5. Flexibility in time/space relations.* Phenomenological experience generally occurs within a time/space context. In trance you can relate to time and space in many ways. You can completely *dissociate* from the present and shift to alternative time/space realities. For example, you might subjectively *age regress* to the past or *age progress* into the future; you can *time distort*, experiencing a minute like an hour (*time expansion*) or an hour like a minute (*time condensation*); you can *positively hallucinate* something which is not really there or *negatively hallucinate* something that is actually there.

---

[5]Rosenhan (1967) offers an excellent review of the experimental literature on hypnosis and suggestibility, concluding that hypnotic subjects show no more suggestibility than individuals in waking states. At the same time, all of us are influenced by each other in any relationship. The point to be made is that a person in a therapeutic trance is less fixated to a position (i.e., a frame or set), though still grounded in personal values. To the extent that these values are threatened or otherwise disrespected, refixation to a frame will occur. Thus, the therapist must work to respect at all times a person's individual values and needs. To the extent this is accomplished, clients will allow themselves to become immersed in a receptive trance.

Underlying these and other trance phenomena is the ability to relate to time and space as *variables* to be manipulated rather than *constants* to be limited by. In other words, the hypnotized person becomes unbound from fixation to a single time/space coordinate (the "present"), thereby making available an infinite number of other potential realities. The tremendous therapeutic value of this flexibility (e.g., in reorganizing the past, changing one's present point of view, altering beliefs about the future) is explored in great detail in later chapters.

A beautiful example of this time/space variability can be found in *The Wizard of Oz*. In an opening scene, Dorothy's conscious mind is "depotentiated" by a thump on the head. The next thing she knows, she's whirling (in "the middle of nowhere") in her house. Circulating all around her are various objects from her mundane world: kitchen sinks, bicycles, baskets, and so forth. These floating objects are "deframed" from the contexts in which they usually occur. Similarly, the various elemental units usually bound in rigid configurations in a person's waking-state experience unbind in trance, thereby enabling reassociation of the elemental learnings into new, more appropriate configurations (frames).

*6. Alteration of sensory experience.* Trance subjects frequently experience alterations in their sensory experience, such as perceptual distortions, heightening, selectivity, and hallucinations. These changes can develop in any of the sensory modalities. For example, kinesthetic alterations are quite common. Subjects might feel quite relaxed and drowsy (the body becoming heavy and warm), or may feel motorically immobilized (*catalepsy*) with a sense of lightness or disconnection from the body. Perceptual distortion of body parts sometimes develops: The head might feel disproportionately large, the hand may seem to be operating independently from the rest of the body (as in arm levitation), and so on. Various shifts in the vestibular system, such as a pleasant sense of whirling or spinning about, are occasionally experienced.

Visual alterations are also common. Subjects whose eyes remain open may develop a *tunnel vision* in which their peripheral fields become dark or foggy. Tunnel vision is especially apt to occur if the subject is fixated on a single stimulus (e.g., the hypnotist's eyes) without moving or blinking. The color perception of the open-eyed subject may become aesthetically heightened, or shift into black and white, or perhaps change into a sequence of different colors. If looking at the hypnotist, the subject may see his or her face distort into that of another person (familiar or unfamiliar). The deeply hypnotized person may also experience positive or negative visual hallucinations.

The trance subject with eyes closed will often be immersed in vivid visual imagery. This may involve revivified memories, geometric patterns and designs, or interesting symbolic imagery (as in the hypnotic dream).

Alterations in the auditory system may also occur. The subject will often selectively attend to the hypnotist's voice to the extent of not hearing other external noises. At the same time, the hypnotist's voice might begin to sound quite different to the subject: It may seem to move closer or further away, the tone may sound different, or it may fade away altogether. (The subject generally remains in rapport with the hypnotist, as evidenced by responses to hypnotic directives.) Finally, the subject frequently develops a heightened sensitivity to the hypnotist's paralinguistic communications, such as tonal emphasis, intonation pattern (especially in relation to his or her own nonverbal "rhythms," such as breathing), and auditory localization in space (see, e.g., Erickson, 1973). Thus, subjects may have difficulty developing or maintaining a trance if the hypnotist speaks in a harsh or choppy manner, or at a rate which is much quicker or slower than the subject's own internal processing.

These various sensory alterations are usually experienced as quite pleasant and intriguing. They serve to disorient subjects from their normal realities, thereby contributing to the development of trance. They are particularly effective as "convincer" experiences for subjects who worry and wonder whether they are in trance, enabling them to drop their concerns and shift deeper into trance.

These sensory alterations also characterize symptomatic trances. They are easily observable in severely dissociated individuals (e.g., psychotics), but occur in other problems as well. For example, a client who experienced intense jealousy whenever any other woman was around her husband would, in doing so, develop tunnel vision (with her peripheral fields completely blacked out) followed by highly selective visual orientation. Another client, a businessman who feared public speaking, would, right before a presentation, develop an out-of-body experience in which he would be looking down at himself. Such unusual perceptual alterations are often accompanied by muscular rigidity (usually from fear) and arrhythmic behavioral reactions (usually attempts to short-circuit the response), thereby creating a dissociated problem state.

But in more self-valuing hypnotic environments (where motor responses can remain relaxed and rhythmic), these sorts of symptom phenomena can be appreciated as spontaneous and autonomous expressions of unconscious processes utilizable as solutions. For example, the jealous client was taught to hypnotically utilize tunnel vision in a variety of self-valuing ways, including focusing on her husband in a fashion that elicited a variety of secure and pleasurable feelings. The dissociating businessman learned to hypnotically view himself from across the room as a means to successfully be "a part of" and "apart from" himself. Thus, perceptual alterations are problems or solutions, depending on their context value and expression variability.

*7. Fluctuation in involvement.* The traditional "depth of trance" metaphors — e.g., light, medium, and deep — emphasize trance as more of a continuum of involvement than an all-or-none phenomenon. This "depth of hypnotic involvement" will often fluctuate during a trance, especially with novice subjects. The subject may, for instance, develop a deep trance, shift up to a light or medium one, and then arouse from trance altogether before again dropping into a deep state. This fluctuation in the level of trance may be described as *the floating phenomenon.*

The *level of trance* refers to the relative degree of conscious vs. unconscious processing. To clarify this, three general levels might be identified: *conscious, mixed*, and *dissociated*. Subjects in a *conscious state* (usually called a *waking state*) are essentially dominated by rational and reality-oriented conscious process; they are not in a trance at all. Subjects in a *mixed state* (usually called *light trance*) experience an interaction of conscious and unconscious processes. For example, they may still be aware of external stimuli, but do not feel compelled to actively orient to them; internal dialogue may be present, but in a less directive and dominant fashion. In this relaxed state, subjects generally do not feel attached or fixated to a single point of view. Subjects in a *dissociated state* (usually called *deep trance*) are immersed fully in unconscious processing and will usually experience many of the trance characteristics described in this section.

The hypnotherapist is wise to attend to the floating phenomenon because *different levels of trance require different utilizations.* For example, inductional communications are intended to shift the subject from a conscious to a mixed or dissociated state. Many hypnotherapeutic utilization procedures are introduced only when the induction has been adequately accomplished (as assessed by methods mentioned later). Even then, the hypnotherapist should remain sensitive to possible lightening of the trance, since such an occurrence might limit the efficacy of the procedure, especially if it is one requiring a dissociated state. (This is not to advance the fallacious assumption that "the deeper the trance, the more likely the therapeutic change"; as we will see, many hypnotherapeutic procedures require only a mixed state, as long as the person's conscious processes do not actively interfere with hypnotic explorations.)

The subject's level of trance can also be used in deciding upon the most appropriate style of communication. For example, it is often best to use indirect communications (e.g., metaphorical stories) with the subject in a conscious or mixed state, so as to bypass any possible interference from conscious processes. With dissociated-state subjects, however, the need for indirect communication is greatly reduced, since conscious processes are not prominently active.

*8. Motoric/verbal inhibition.* Hypnotically entranced individuals often do not feel like moving or talking in any elaborate fashion. To reiterate, this lack of movement partly reflects a value implicit in most hypnotic rituals. Other trance rituals favor dancing (e.g., around the fire, in circles), chanting, singing, or other expressive rhythms to induce trance. The point to be made is that trance can be developed and maintained via inhibition of movement or *rhythmic* (circular and repetitive) movement, i.e., an absence of the irregular and arrhythmic orienting responses (and muscle tension) that give rise to a conscious mind. The relative immobility of the hypnotic subject may have developed as a needed complement to the incessant movement (goal-oriented action) occurring in the waking-state style favored by Western culture; it may also reflect the dissociation from the physical self (man dominating nature, including his body) that generally occurs in our culture.

Thus, entranced individuals usually can move or talk if they so desire, but they often experience such externally oriented behaviors as irrelevant and distracting to internally directed experience. To understand this, imagine you are deeply absorbed in an interaction with somebody and an experimenter kept interrogating you about your experience; naturally, such questions would interrupt the flow of your experience. Also, verbalizing is usually strongly associated with conscious processing and thus tends to shift the subject into that mode of experience.

The potential disruptiveness of such activities suggests several things. First, the hypnotherapist should keep requests to talk or move to a minimum. In fact, I rarely ask internally absorbed subjects to explain, conceptualize, or talk in detail about their hypnotic experience. This restriction need not be a handicap, since information about the subject's ongoing experience can be readily discerned from minimal cues, ideomotoric responses, posttrance discussion, or automatic talking. But, as we will see, the task of the Ericksonian hypnotherapist is to introduce general processes which the client can autonomously use to establish the desired changes. In other words, the therapist does not try to impose solutions; rather, he or she guides clients into a context (therapeutic trance) in which they can generate their own solutions. As such, the particular details of the client's experience often need not be known; but extremely close attention needs to be paid to ongoing general responses (e.g., emotional state, depth of trance), so that hypnotic communications can be flexibly adapted. As we will see, these general responses can be observed from the client's nonverbal behavior.

A second point about this trance-indicative motoric/verbal inhibition is that an increase in these outputs often signals a lightening of the trance. For example, the subject who begins to shift about in the chair is usually coming to a lighter stage of trance. This may simply be due to the floating phenomenon just described, or it may indicate a specific difficulty. Regardless, it should be promptly utilized. For example, the therapist might shift to inductional communications that describe the process of "being able to shift up and down in trance, knowing that you can come to a lighter state for a while, rest a bit, wonder about things, and then begin to wander back down into trance."

Finally, the rhythmically repetitive or inhibited behavior characterizing hypnotic trances is also present in symptom trances, albeit in self-devaluing ways. Rhythmically repetitive symptoms include compulsive acts such as hand washing, the rocking of the hyperactive child, the self-defeating internalized chants of the depressed person ("I can't do it, nothing works"), the slow and methodical eating pattern of some compulsive overeaters, and so forth. (One such client of mine had an incredible ability to eat for close to an hour in a trancelike rhythm of continual shoveling of food from hand to mouth while watching television.) Motoric inhibition symptoms include, for example, the person fearing public speaking frozen in panic, the person withdrawn into a depression, or the person frozen in shock or fear. If maintained, either pattern (rhythmic or immobile) will tend to develop into a trance. To reiterate, recontextualization and expression diversification of such processes can result in transformational events.

*9. Trance logic.* Entranced individuals tend to relate to their experience with a different logic than that used in waking states. To reiterate, unconscious (primary process) thinking is generally more associational, metaphorical, and concrete (image-oriented) than the rational, linear (sequential), and causal logic favored by the conscious mind. In particular, trance logic (see Orne, 1959) allows "both/and" relations to obtain. For example, entranced subjects find nothing bizarre or discomforting about experiencing themselves in two different places at the same time, or in exploring fantasy worlds whose rules or structures violate real-world constraints. Such trance logic is much less restrictive than rational ("ratio-making" or dividing) logics, thereby making it better suited for tasks in which a wider range of possibilities is sought (e.g., in therapy). The "both/and" (distinct from "either/or") relations of trance logic enable seemingly contradictory relationships to be simultaneously valued, thereby allowing "win/win" relationships to obtain. Since conflicts always contain (apparent) contradictions, trance logic is especially useful for integration ("making whole") in clinical processes.

It is interesting to note that both/and logics are the stuff of which both therapeutic double binds (e.g., Zen koans) and nontherapeutic double-binds (e.g., Bateson's schizophrenogenic systems) are made (see Rossi & Jichaku, 1984). Thus, the Zen master says to the student: "If you say this is a stick, I will hit you. If you say this is not a stick, I will hit you. What is this I'm holding?" In a structurally equivalent way, the schizophrenogenic parent says, "If you say or do X, you're bad. If you don't say or do X, you're bad. Be a good boy (or girl) and respond." The difference can be seen in the context: The Zen master (presumably) creates an underlying self-valuing context that allows the student to see beyond the world of opposites and discover the "middle third" or "middle way" described by Buddhists.

In a similar vein, most clinical problems can be seen as double binds or "hypnotic koans." The client presents a loop containing both sides of a seemingly contradictory relationship: "I want to change/I don't want to change," "I want to be by myself/I want to be with others," "I want to leave/I want to stay."[6] From the point of view of the conscious mind, either one or the other must be chosen; that is, the conscious mind identifies with one side against the other. This creates a problem, since both are equally prominent, despite repeated attempts to bias toward one side. Trance dissipates the either/or frame biases and allows the unity underlying positions to be felt, thereby enabling the unfolding of creative integrations.

*10. Metaphorical processing.* This is a central and unifying concept of the Ericksonian approach and thus will be explored in great detail. A symbol is generally defined here as *something that stands for that*

---

[6]In this view, symptoms (or identified patients) can be seen as metaphorical (unconscious) attempts to integrate complementarities. That is, symptoms are condensations of complements bound by negation (i.e., dissociation) operators. This idea is the focus of a work in preparation.

*which it is not*; symbolic (or metaphorical) processing refers to trance subjects' strong tendency to comprehend and represent communications in *self-referential* fashion. For example, they might begin to develop trance while hearing a story about *somebody else* who became deeply absorbed; or access and explore their own problem(s) while listening to a description of a problem that is content-unrelated (e.g., different characters and setting) but structurally similar to their own; or solve a problem by generating hypnotic dreams that symbolically develop and then transform the problem state; or change pessimistic self-fulfilling prophecies by age progressing several months into the future and then "reviewing" how they made many unexpected changes; or even develop a desired skill by *trance identification* with (i.e., assuming the personality of) some person who embodies that skill. Each of these processes constitutes a chapter in the forthcoming volume, *Hypnotic Transformations: Experiential Reframing in Ericksonian Hypnotherapy*, which I have written as a sequel to the present volume.

The unusual nature of some of these procedures should not distract from the fact that metaphorical processing is a common and naturalistic process. For example, everybody has witnessed or observed countless conversations in which listeners responded by relating a similar experience of their own (see, e.g., Bower & Gilligan, 1979). Thus, for instance, a description of my "first love" will tend to elicit your experiences involving the same, especially if they are similar. As we will see, many other phenomena further suggest the pervasiveness of this naturalistic process (e.g., the popularity of a movie like *Rocky*). We will also explore in detail how the extent to which such processing occurs depends on variables such as the speaker's delivery style (e.g., absorbing vs. interpersonal), the situational context (e.g., hypnosis vs. business), and the listener's experiential state (e.g., trance vs. waking). Of importance here is that trance facilitates symbolic processing.

Metaphors also play a prominent role in problem processes. To reiterate, recurrent symptoms can be seen as symbolic condensations of double-bound complementarities, that is, the co-existence of seemingly opposite motivations or injunctions. In other words, they are unconscious attempts to integrate conflicts, much like a problem child's symptoms often reflect parental conflict. When such symbolic expressions (symptoms) are evident, metaphorical communication is an excellent way to match the client's style.

*11. Time distortion.* As mentioned earlier, the experience of time is often quite different for the hypnotized person. In fact, many individuals speak of trance as having a "timeless" quality to it. If asked to

estimate how long the trance experience lasted, subjects may look somewhat surprised and confused, as if the concept really had no relevance
during the trance experience. I understand this by distinguishing two
types of time: *bio-logical time*, which is rhythmic, circular, pulsating,
and primary; and *psycho-logical time*, which is cultural, lineal, successive, and secondary. Psycho-logical time seems to be a construct of
analytical thinking, useful for organizing goal-oriented actions and sequential events with certain social markers. Reduction of analytical
orientation in trance dissipates these markers and, along with them, the
lineal sense of time.

Given the decreased value of psycho-logical time in trance, subjects
may provide estimates remarkably different (usually shorter) from the
actual elapsed clock time. For example, an hour of clock time might be
estimated as 10 minutes.[7] As Cooper and Erickson (1959) and Masters
and Houston (1972) have discussed, this time distortion ability has
many therapeutic applications, especially in the area of accelerated
learning processes.

*12. Amnesia.* Hypnotic subjects will sometimes arouse from trance
and remember few (*partial amnesia*) or none (*full amnesia*) of the transpired trance events. Interestingly, it was once believed that full amnesia always occurred in the trance subject. This belief originated with
the Marquis de Puysegur, who in 1784 "mesmerized" a young shepherd
who afterwards had no memory for his trance experience. Today, however, we know that amnesia is neither a necessary nor sufficient condition of trance (Cooper, 1972; Orne, 1966). Although subjects will occasionally exhibit spontaneous amnesia, most of this temporary forgetting
results from techniques applied by the hypnotherapist, or from state-
dependent learning processes (see Gilligan and Bower, 1984).

The Ericksonian hypnotherapist frequently uses amnesia to "protect"
unconscious change processes from conscious interference. Specifically,
clinical progress may be significantly hampered if clients become consciously aware of hypnotic learnings or instructions before they are able
to comfortably integrate them (into conscious representations). Such
premature conscious awareness is particularly inadvisable with, for
example, clients who may be tremendously distressed and overwhelmed
by consciously remembering a repressed childhood trauma; or clients

---

[7]It should be pointed out that differences between estimated and actual elapsed time
do not necessarily indicate time distortion; they may instead be evidence of hypnotic
amnesia. That is, since the subject remembers little about the trance, he or she assumes
that not much happened and therefore estimates that little time elapsed.

who may consciously doubt or incessantly question the validity of trance learnings or posthypnotic instructions, thereby interfering with their completion or consolidation; or with clients who might try to consciously "help" in implementing new behaviors, thereby reintroducing the very conscious processes that created difficulties in the first place. In such cases, amnesia and other dissociative methods allow a person to become consciously aware of unconscious processes at a rate and in a style most beneficial to the entire self.

In this regard, it is extremely important to recognize that the intent in suggesting amnesia is *not* to have clients permanently forget some memory or part of themselves. Rather, it is to permit the uninhibited development of new learnings. Any attempt to permanently ablate a memory will result in the most deleterious of outcomes.

The futility of using (naturalistic) amnesia techniques to obliterate memories can be observed in many clinical problems. In such cases, individuals attempting to stop thinking about certain events or experiences usually end up dominated by the targeted processes. Thus, the Ericksonian hypnotherapist works to engage the client in selectively thinking about *other* processes, thereby protecting the unconscious learnings. Naturalistic techniques for accomplishing this are discussed by Zeig (1985c).

## HOW THE HYPNOTHERAPIST CAN ORGANIZE TRANCE EVENTS

As previously noted, situational contexts influence how trance is experienced and conceptualized. In the clinical context, where the primary goal is therapeutic change, I have found it most useful to organize trance events into four major phases: (1) *preparation*; (2) *induction*; (3) *utilization of trance*; and (4) *consolidation of trance learnings*. In actual practice, these phases often overlap and interact with each other. They can be used to describe a single hypnotic session, or more generally to organize a multi-session hypnotherapeutic endeavor. To clarify, each phase will be briefly commented on.

### 1. Creating a Context: Preparing for Trance

This initial phase, which is the major topic of Chapter 5, has two goals. The first is to *receive* communication from the client. The therapist needs to develop a general sense of the client's world model, and thus gathers information about major beliefs, occupation, education level, interests, skills, family life, and so forth. In addition, the therapist identifies the changes desired by the client, as well as any strategies or objections that might interfere with development of such changes. The therapist also needs to find out the client's general understandings and previous experiences regarding hypnosis.

A second major goal is to communicate *to* the client about the nature of the hypnotic process. Perhaps most important, *rapport* and *trust* need to be established before any inductions are offered. The therapist also needs to create an expectancy that something meaningful can and will happen, and to establish agreements about the client's commitment to the change process. Finally, the therapist begins to indirectly access trance responses during this phase.

## 2. Making the Transition: Induction of Trance

A hypnotic induction is an experientially absorbing interactional sequence that culminates in an altered state of consciousness wherein self-expressions develop without analytical or effortful mediation. There are an endless number of ways in which this can be done. The Ericksonian practitioner does not rely on artificial or standardized communications. Instead, he or she assumes that effective inductions are those that utilize a given client's unique needs and patterns, and therefore strives to continually adapt communications to the client's ongoing experience. Guiding the therapist in this endeavor are three general principles of induction:

1. Secure and focus the subject's attention;
2. Pace and depotentiate the conscious mind;
3. Access and utilize the unconscious mind.

The many ways to apply these principles are the primary focus of Chapters 6, 7, and 8.

## 3. Establishing the Desired Changes: The Utilization of Trance

Once trance develops, the question becomes: "What do we do now?" This third phase seeks to fruitfully answer this query by utilizing trance for therapeutic changes. That is, the therapist follows experiential *deframing* (i.e., trance induction) with multiple possibilities for experiential *reframing*. Many hypnotherapeutic procedures are available for such purposes, especially those involving dissociational methods, hypnotic dreams, metaphorical stories, age regression, age progression, and personality alterations.[8] Each of these procedures generally involves (a) accessing and then transforming unacceptable experiences (limits) and/or (b) accessing and then making regularly available the powerful but previously dissociated resources (assets) of the client. Instead of trying to add anything new or take something away, these strategies usually guide the client to realize and reorganize already present resources.

### 4. Consolidating Trance Learning: Concluding and Extending the Trance

This final phase has two major steps:

1. Concluding the trance;
2. Generalizing the trance learnings.

The first step involves taking the client out of trance. This transition usually consists of general self-appreciation suggestions, posthypnotic suggestions, general or specific amnesia instructions, and trance-terminating communications. This usually takes 10–15 minutes.

The trance learnings can then be extended into other contexts of the client's life. This second step often includes 10–15 minutes of posttrance discussion regarding the client's trance explorations. But perhaps more important, the hypnotherapist also usually introduces additional procedures, such as homework assignments (e.g., diaries, behavioral tasks, practicing new choices), self-hypnosis instruction, and "nonhypnotic" strategies (e.g., behavior therapy, family therapy, body work, job development). The therapist might also work with clients on applying the hypnotic learnings in a practical way. For example, role playing may be employed to develop specific behavioral strategies and to identify possible obstacles to implementing them. As we will see, hypnosis alone is often not sufficient to establish lasting therapeutic changes; the effective hypnotherapist thus complements hypnotic work with various other approaches.

### SUMMARY

This chapter discussed the experience of trance. The first section reviewed the major metaphors used to explain the trance experience. Early speculations described trance in terms of energy channeling,

---

[8]These procedures are the primary focus of the forthcoming *Hypnotic Transformations*.

sleep, pathology, suggestibility, and dissociation; modern accounts emphasize regression, acquired learning, dissociation, motivated involvement, and role enactment. Each approach may identify an important aspect of the experience of trance, though none seems complete in itself; thus, clinicians need to assume an open-minded, eclectic approach.

The second section characterized trance as naturalistic and cross-contextual. It was argued that trance (1) is distinguished by the principle of ideodynamicism and by both/and logic, (2) is experienced in many situations, (3) is developed in many ways, (4) is biologically necessary, (5) serves multiple functions, and (6) can be self-valuing or self-devaluing. It was further suggested that trance phenomena are the basic processes by which psychological experience is generated, and that trance phenomena and clinical symptoms are the same phenomena expressed in different contexts.

The third section explored 12 phenomenological characteristics common in the experience of trance: (1) experiential absorption of attention, (2) effortless expression, (3) experiential, nonconceptual involvement, (4) willingness to experiment, (5) flexibility in time/space relations, (6) alteration of sensory experience, (7) fluctuation in involvement, (8) motoric/verbal inhibition, (9) trance logic, (10) metaphorical processing, (11) time distortion, and (12) amnesia. Generally speaking, these phenomena suggest trance as an ideal state for experiential learning, one in which a person can develop deep attentional absorption in ways that allow unconscious processes to operate creatively.

The final section briefly overviewed how therapists can organize their experience about trance events into four phases: preparation, induction, utilization, and consolidation of learnings. This organization applies to a single session as well as to an entire therapy.

# CHAPTER 3

# The General Approach of the Ericksonian Hypnotherapist

Consider for a moment the master jazz musician, the champion basketball player, the innovative thinker, the adroit communicator. What commonalities do such luminaries share? For one, they are totally committed to their art form. They have to be: artistic excellence demands it. Only from rigorous and devoted training can the artist develop the refined behavioral skills and gracefulness needed for a truly creative act.

Master practitioners surrender to their art form and move in the "flow" of creative expression. The musician begins to experience his or her instrument as an extension of self, and in doing so generates novel and creative melodies; the ballplayer develops an affinity with teammates, and begins to anticipate and merge with their actions in an intangible yet undeniable fashion.

This state of "controlled spontaneity" also characterizes effective hypnotic communicators. On the one hand, they never know what they are going to do next; on the other, they adhere to a set of general guidelines that enable systematic effectiveness along with complex flexibility. This chapter describes some of these guidelines. The first section discusses the need for integrity; the second outlines some effective communicational processes for the hypnotherapist; the third introduces general principles governing the Ericksonian practitioner's strategies.

## THE INTEGRITY OF THE HYPNOTHERAPIST

### The Value of Integrity

Integrity is the most important aspect of the hypnotherapist's approach. In formal terms, a system's integrity is the degree of self-consistency and interdependent support of its various parts. In the hypnotherapeutic system, it is the degree to which the therapist's intentions and expressions are aligned with the needs of the client. More specifically, the hypnotherapist with integrity is willing and able to:

- fully support the client's quest for transformational change;
- set aside individual biases and needs and fully accept (while not necessarily agreeing with) the client's experience;
- refrain from imposing solutions and personal beliefs on the client.

The seemingly abstract nature of these points should not distract from their practical relevance. *A context of integrity is essential for therapeutic success.* Lacking integrity, even technically proficient therapists will find that clients may develop hypnotic phenomena but not therapeutic changes; or may be duly impressed with the therapist's abilities but not their own; or may assume the therapist's beliefs and lifestyle rather than developing their own. In short, the client's quality of experience will not be significantly enhanced.

Conversely, the hypnotherapist operating with integrity can secure rapport with the client. In trusting the therapist, the client begins to trust his or her self more. This enhances the willingness to examine shortcomings and actualizes the potential to develop new ways of being. Clients become more willing (both in trance and waking states) to cooperate with hypnotic directives, no matter how strange and irrelevant they may seem. As we will see, such cooperation is rather important to the Ericksonian practitioner, who employs many unorthodox strategies.

It is difficult, if not impossible, to convey in words the practical necessity of integrity. This is due partly to its seemingly abstract nature: Integrity cannot be quantitatively defined as this or that set of behaviors. But this makes it no less real: *Integrity is the context from which all self-valuing expressions are generated.* It distinguishes the true leader from the despot, the creative artist from the technician, the wise from the merely clever. In interpersonal terms, integrity is the ability to become entirely aligned and absorbed in cooperating with another individual or living system. Although the exact behaviors will of course vary, the intent does not.

I believe strongly that Erickson's startling effectiveness was in great part due to his integrity. Prior to training with him, I fervently studied his many clinical writings. While deeply impressed and intrigued, I often wondered how he could get his patients to cooperate with his highly unorthodox strategies. The explanations set forth by him and others (e.g., Haley, 1973) emphasized seemingly vague generalities about "accepting and utilizing the patient's reality." For example, Erickson (1952) cautioned:

> A subject needs to be protected at all times as a personality possessed of rights, privileges, and privacies and recognized as being placed in a seemingly vulnerable position in the hypnotic situation.
>
> Regardless of how well informed and intelligent a subject may be, there always exists, whether recognized or not, a general questioning uncertainty about what will happen or what may or may not be said or done. Even subjects who have unburdened themselves freely and without inhibition to the author, a psychiatrist, have manifested this need to protect the self and to put the best foot forward no matter how freely the wrong foot had been exposed.
>
> This protection should properly be given the subject in both waking and trance states. It is best given in an indirect way in the waking state and more directly in the trance state.
>
> . . . Depriving the subject of this constitutes a failure to protect him as a sentient being. Such failure may imperil the validity of hypnotic work since the subject may feel that his efforts are not appreciated, and this may result in lesser degrees of cooperation. (In Rossi, 1980a, pp. 149–151)

Only after meeting and observing Erickson did the importance of these ideas become apparent to me. Erickson manifested an unmitigated intention to fully respect and support patients and students. While clearly directive, he was also clearly not out to manipulate or control people for his own personal gains.[1] Accordingly, those with whom he communicated would most often "let go" and fully cooperate in the hypnotic endeavor.

## The Issue of Manipulation

From a context of integrity Erickson would often issue specific behavioral directives. The prominence of such directiveness demands that Ericksonian practitioners critically examine the issue of *manipulation*. The term is generally and nonevaluatively defined here as *the process of influencing behavior*. This process is pervasive: whether we are aware of it or not, our behavior always affects others. In this real sense, *all*

---

[1] I knew Erickson in his later years. He may have impressed some people differently earlier in his career.

*behavior is manipulation.* As Haley (1963) pointed out, this is especially true in the therapeutic context, where the explicit goal is to change behavior. Thus, I think it imperative that the therapist frequently ask, What is my intention in communicating with this client? How am I affecting this individual's behavior? (As Chapter 5 will explore, this question can be straightforwardly answered by identifying recurrent expressions in an interaction.) By honestly exploring such questions, the therapist can enhance his or her ability to influence others with integrity.

*This is not a trivial matter to be sidestepped or disregarded.* In training many mental health professionals, I have noticed that failing to come to grips with these issues creates many problems. Some trainees experience great difficulty in acknowledging that they can and do powerfully affect another person's behavior. They consequently demur from developing awareness of how to intentionally use hypnotic techniques, especially those involving disorientation (see Chapter 8). Others are overpowered by an insecure need to prove themselves and consequently wield techniques in a domineering and insensitive fashion. Both types of students are controlled by their ability to manipulate: the former by attempting to dissociate from it, the latter by using it irresponsibly. In both cases, the ability to enhance experience through therapeutic cooperation is stifled.

Once therapists become aware of the intent and effect of their behavior, they can express themselves in powerful ways. But one need only remember a Hitler or a Jim Jones to realize that developing this ability does not guarantee happy endings.[2] To reiterate, the outcome of a relationship ultimately depends upon (and thus reflects) the intent of the "cooperators": the same technique (or any distinction, for that matter) can be used for mutual support or oppression. Of course, the latter choice cannot always be implemented. Most hypnotic subjects, for example, will quickly distrust and hence become uncooperative with a "nonsupportive" hypnotist. (As noted in the previous chapter, an individual can "resist" suggestions just as strongly [if not more] while in trance.) Choosing to *cooperate* with clients is much easier than attempting to oppose, control, or dominate them, since there really can be no "resistance" when one is totally aligned with another individual. Besides, it is a far more personally satisfying and professionally effective posi-

---

[2]For an excellent article on the similarity of Ericksonian techniques to those used in cults, see Zeitlin (1985). As Chapter 2 emphasized, trance can be Self-valuing or Self-devaluing, depending on the context of the participation.

tion. In this sense, integrity is equivalently a pragmatic and an ethical issue. Simply stated, the more integrity you develop, the more fun and success you are likely to experience.

*Developing and Maintaining Integrity*

The question thus becomes, How can the hypnotherapist achieve and then maintain integrity? For starters, three possibilities might be mentioned:

*1. Identify and handle unacceptable personal experiences.* Personal attachments (limits, fears, problems, etc.) bias perceptions and reactions to similar limits in others. For example, a colleague had a strong personal rule about being assertive with others. He complained that his outstanding therapeutic record was being blemished by several "resistant" clients. In investigating the issue with him, I realized that these recalcitrant clients held similar constraints about being assertive. Only after expanding his own limits in this area did the therapist let go of *his* "resistance" to accepting and utilizing the clients' realities. Consequently, his therapy with them became much more effective. The assumption here is that "unacceptable experiences" strongly constrain one's behavior. That is, the person who develops the belief, "If I experience 'X' (the unacceptable experience), then something terrible will happen," will avoid behaviors *in self and others* that may lead to "X." Thus, the therapist repelled and disgusted by, say, binge eating will be hard pressed to assist an individual mired in such a process.

Regarding this key idea of valuing experiences, I am not suggesting that all behaviors are acceptable in all contexts. Certainly, violent acts are intolerable in most situations, and persons committing such acts must bear social responsibility and its consequences (e.g., social containment). At the same time, therapists are not part of the criminal justice system: In the criminal domain, behavior is to be evaluated and regulated according to social norms; in the clinical domain, experience is to be valued so its behavioral expressions can be amplified to include more satisfying choices. To accomplish their task of expanding rather than constraining ways of being, therapists are faced with the "hypnotic koan" of realizing that self-devaluing expressions are the basis of self-valuing expressions; the difference is the context from which such expressions unfold. The utilization principle, which encourages alignment with expressions to transform their context and thus allow for their "reformation," is fundamental in this regard.

Implicit in this is the notion that experience is distinguishable from (behavioral) expression of experience. Behaviors are acts designed to achieve basic experiential outcomes (e.g., security, love, satisfaction). Most dysfunctional behaviors arise when the person is unclear about the desired experience, often because of a learned association of that experience with a particular set of behaviors or behavioral outcomes. For example, a person might learn that his anger leads to unbearable rejection by others, and thus desperately tries to not be angry.

Furthermore, Self is distinguishable from experiential intention. Expressions are variables; Self is (an ineffable yet generative) constant. Hence, while persons are fully responsible for ("able to respond to") their experience, they are not reducible to it.

Finally, there is a difference between acknowledging the reality of an experience and supporting its continuation. I acknowledge that hate is a possible experience but choose not to become immersed in the self-devaluing act of violence. I think that acknowledging the reality of an experience is necessary if one is to become unfettered from any irrational or compulsory attachment to (*"must* have it"), or dissociation from (*"must not* have it"), that experience. Only then does one truly have the choice to develop or reject the experience. The work of Christ, Ghandi, M. L. King, and others attests to this. Such assumptions also seemed to underlie Erickson's work.

Hence, therapists should strive to identify and handle their own "unacceptable experiences." Such limits may become apparent during therapy sessions or in other social situations. They may identified through various cues—for example, pejorative labeling, emotional arousal, and universal quantifiers (see Gilligan, 1985). Or they may be uncovered during intense personal explorations, which, incidentally, I strongly recommend that any hypnotherapist regularly engage in. Regardless of the context of discovery, one powerful method for expanding such limits is self-hypnosis.

Because Ericksonian hypnotherapy is such an intense interpersonal process, it is inevitable that the therapist will periodically access "unacceptable experiences" during hypnotic "cooperation." This may be evidenced by emotional discomfort developing in response to the client's behavior or experience. For instance, one therapist became aware of her own sexual frustrations while listening to a client describe his; another therapist found himself reacting with overwhelming fear when a client blamed him for her troubles. Accessing "unacceptable experiences" may be evidenced in less obvious ways, such as when a therapeutic impasse is reached, or when therapists themselves accuse a client of being "sick" or "resistant," or otherwise "uncooperative." Whatever the case, it is rather important that therapists continue by utilizing their accessed personal limits. One way to do this is to (1) acknowledge the active "unacceptable experience(s)," (2) utilize processes (described in the next section) to set them aside for the remainder of the session, then (3) explore and transform them through (postsession) private work (e.g., self-hypnosis). A complementary strategy is to utilize the unacceptable experience as the basis for hypnotic expression. For example, the therapist may begin to tell a story describing his or her own experience in which the question is continually raised rhetorically as to how the story character could let go and accept the experience in a way that satisfied the needs of the entire self. Since much of the technique's effect will depend on nonverbal delivery, the therapist should be nonverbally "letting go" while talking about such a process. To do this naturally, the therapist needs to establish a relatively "centered" state – breathing rhythmically, posturally balanced, muscularly relaxed, and so on. If this state is not achievable, the technique should not be used.

*2. Be nonevaluative.* In particular, the therapist should refrain from believing in diagnostic categories. These generalizations frequently blind the therapist from realizing the unique situation of each individual. In addition, they imply that the client is "sick" and that their experience is invalid. Unfortunately, this makes both therapist and client quite unwilling to accept the latter's experience, thereby prohibiting transformational changes.

A clear example of this is with so-called "psychotics," who are so often solemnly informed that their experience is "unreal" or "bad" and that therapeutic progress can occur only when they "get rid of" their hallucinations, delusions, and so on. This essentially reinforces a major process responsible for the "psychotic" experience in the first place – that of trying to destroy (i.e., dissociate from) some major part of experience of one's self – thereby ensuring the continuation of the dysfunctional state. By shedding a compulsion to evaluate experience in terms of "wrong vs. right" or "good vs. bad," the therapist becomes able to acknowledge and utilize the particular experiences that the client is having difficulty with. Transformation then becomes possible.

My strong beliefs on this matter developed in no small part from training experiences with Erickson. One series of interactions was especially valuable. After spending years diligently studying his approach, I felt I had a fairly good grasp of his sophisticated techniques. Yet something was clearly missing. My work was not as effective as I felt it could be, but I was unclear about how I was limiting myself. Finally, on the last day of a week-long visit with Erickson, I respectfully requested some guidance in the matter. Instead of launching into one of his lengthy and indirect answers, he stated in a simple but intensely meaningful fashion: "You've got a tendency to overcompartmentalize your experience . . . and it gets in the way of your unconscious." He then immediately ended the session.

As I walked out with a colleague, I confessed my disappointment about not being given any useful feedback, but sympathetically suggested that maybe it was because Erickson was getting old, and besides, he never did seem to have a good conscious understanding of what he did. In other words, I "compartmentalized" his response! Several months later, at the end of a similar training session, I again advanced the question, to which he replied a bit more sternly: "You've got a tendency to overcompartmentalize your experience . . . and it gets in the way of your unconscious!" My disappointment was even more marked this time, for Erickson was "clearly" getting a bit senile: he didn't remember what he told me before.

Four months later, my despair deepened when a third phrasing of the question was met with the same response. Why was Milton being so uninformative? Why couldn't he remember what he had said before? Did he give such unhelpful advice on such matters to all of his students? If so, what happened to his emphasis on unique solutions for each person? I gave the question one more try several months later, to which he replied: "You've got a tendency to overcompartmentalize your experience . . . and it gets in the way of your unconscious!" Flash! I was suddenly overwhelmed with the blinding (or rather unblinding) insight: *I had a tendency to overcompartmentalize my experience . . . and it did get in the way of my unconscious*!! When I finally looked at Erickson, his eyes were twinkling. "That's right," he softly said.

This realization led to others. It became all too clear that most of my time as a hypnotist was spent in internal dialogue, trying to classify the client's behavior and then come up with some sophisticated response. The more I indulged in these conceptual evaluations, the less I attended to what clients were actually experiencing and doing. In addition, I was forced to "objectify" clients into this or that "compartment," thereby limiting the degree of possible rapport. As I relinquished the need for such conceptualizations, my appreciation for the uniqueness of each individual grew. Most important, my communications became more fitting and my work more effective.

Of course, I sometimes find myself mired again in this evaluative mode. On those not infrequent occasions, I think back to Erickson's simple but persistent suggestion, which cues me to shift into more spontaneous processes (described in the next several sections).

*3. Let clients generate their own experience.* It is often thought that the therapist is responsible for the client's trance experience. This puts a lot of pressure on the therapist, often compelling him or her to unwittingly violate the client's integrity. For example, it creates in some hypnotherapists an air of superiority towards their clients, thereby encouraging a domineering and condescending approach. Other hypnotherapists, especially novices, feel overwhelmed and unsure about knowing what's right for the client, and retreat to using standardized techniques, or strategies that work for them (but not necessarily for the client). Regardless of intention, the hypnotherapist who attempts to assume responsibility for the client's hypnotic experiences will experience much disappointment and frustration. The therapist will tend to convey messages that the client is incompetent and should thus passively submit to paternalistic hypnotic programming. Clients will resist this message either directly (e.g., by outrightly refusing to participate) or indirectly (e.g., by "trying" to hypnotically respond but experiencing difficulty in doing so). As such, it is critical to realize that *the hypnotherapist does not cause the client's experience.* As Erickson (1948) emphasized:

> Hypnotic psychotherapy is a learning process for the patient, a procedure of reeducation. Effective results . . . derive only from the patient's activities. The therapist merely stimulates the patient into activity, often not knowing what the activity might be, and then he guides the patient and exercises clinical judgement in determining the amount of work to be done to achieve desired results. *How to guide and to judge constitute the therapist's problem while the patient's task is that of learning through his own efforts to understand his experiential life in a new way.* [italics added] Such reeducation is, of course, necessarily in terms of the patient's life experiences, his understandings, memories, attitudes and ideas, and it cannot be in terms of the therapist's ideas and opinions. (In Rossi, 1980d, p. 39)

Note again the *cooperative* emphasis of the Ericksonian approach. Responsibility is mutually assumed: The client is responsible for actually making the changes, the therapist for creating an appropriate context for uninhibited explorations. In doing this, the therapist assumes that

(1) the client has the requisite intelligence and resources to develop both trance and therapeutic changes, but that (2) habituated patterns of expression (e.g., conscious processes, beliefs, motor acts) limit access to these resources. The therapist thus works to join the client's patterns in order to enable the client to dissipate a frozen attachment to them, thereby enabling autonomous unconscious process to generate transformational change. This general approach is captured by a comment Erickson would frequently make to a subject:

> Your conscious mind is very intelligent . . . but your unconscious is a lot smarter . . . and so I'm not asking you to learn any new skills . . . I'm only asking you to be willing to utilize the skills you already have, but do not yet fully know about.

This general attitude allows the hypnotherapist to cooperate with full integrity. Rather than imposing programs and processes, the therapist respects and utilizes the client's patterns, while also emphasizing the client's highly underrated potentialities. This enables the client to become an active participant in the change process, invariably making the therapeutic work both easier and more rewarding. Rather than worrying about the exact solution that some ignorant or sick individual needs to be *given*, the hypnotherapist wonders how he or she can cooperate with the client's unique and highly intelligent unconscious processes to develop the desired experiences. As Erickson would say:

> Everybody's got their own style . . . their own rate . . . their own unconscious needs . . . and so I'm interested in which particular way *you* will find best suits *you* as an individual.

By operating from such a context of integrity and respect, the truly impressive number of possibilities becomes apparent to the therapist.


### THE HYPNOTHERAPIST'S COMMUNICATIONAL PROCESSES

Integrity allows but does not guarantee therapeutic success. It creates a context which the hypnotherapist must then utilize by cooperating in an effective and compelling fashion. To do so, the therapist assumes that the *process* ("how") of communication is often more important than its *content* ("what"). For instance, the way in which I say no to someone will often have more impact than the two-letter word itself. Depending on variables such as previous experiences and present nonverbal communications, the listener might interpret me as saying, for example, "Maybe tomorrow," or "Keep trying," or "Don't ever ask me that again," or "I'm really not sure." In other words, meaning is context-dependent and nonverbally conveyed, especially in the intense interpersonal context of hypnotherapy. The client's responsiveness is greatly influenced by the therapist's communicational processes. As such, this section will identify some of the most important aspects of these processes.

### The Experience of Interpersonal Trance

Many educated members of the western world assume that intelligent action requires conscious thought. This is not always true; in fact, creative and effective behavior sometimes necessitates an *absence* of analytical interventions. This is sometimes the case in the hypnotherapeutic context, where the therapist must remain "tuned" to the client's ongoing experience. Conscious mediations tend to interfere, since *one cannot attend to external information to the extent that he or she is oriented primarily to intrapersonal computations* (e.g., images, internal dialogues, theories, etc.). By having to "stop and think," the therapist severs sensory connections with the client. This shuts down access to the most important informational source — the client's ongoing responses — and disengages any synchronized rhythms (which, as we will see later in the chapter, is the basis for rapport and hypnotic responsiveness). In addition, extensive conscious processing will inhibit the creative unconscious processing needed to generate various hypnotic communications.

Thus, the Ericksonian hypnotherapist sometimes sets aside conscious processes to absorb all attention in the client. In this process, the therapist does not "go inside" to think and is not distracted by extraneous external cues. *The primary contents of the therapist's consciousness are the client's ongoing behaviors.*

This general state has been addressed by numerous writers (e.g., Erickson, 1966b, 1977; Epstein, 1984; Freud, 1909, 1912; Rogers, 1985). For example, Ellenberger (1970) noted:

In 1912 . . . [Freud] introduced the principle of free-floating attention: the analyst, far from concentrating too intensively on the utterances of the patient, should trust his "unconscious memory"; he should not take abundant notes. . . . He should not speculate about the causes and structure of the case until he was well advanced: 'Go on without definite intention,' Freud advised. (p. 519)

To elaborate this often ignored or misunderstood emphasis by Freud, a handful of his statements on the matter may be instructive:

> Suspend ... judgement and give ... impartial attention to everything there is to observe. (Freud, 1909, p. 23)

> [The technique] ... is a very simple one. As we shall see, it rejects the use of any special expedient (even that of taking notes.) It consists simply in not directing one's notice to anything in particular and in maintaining the same "evenly suspended attention" (as I have called it) in the face of all that one hears. ... It will be seen that the rule of giving equal notice to everything is the necessary counterpart to the demand made on the patient that he should communicate everything that occurs to him without criticism or selection. If the doctor behaves otherwise, he is throwing away most of the advantage which results from the patient's obeying the "fundamental rule of psychoanalysis." The rule for the doctor may be expressed: "He should withhold all conscious influences from his capacity to attend, and give himself over completely to his "unconscious memory." Or, to put it purely in terms of technique: "He should simply listen, and not bother about whether he is keeping anything in mind." (Freud, 1912, pp. 111–112)

> Experience soon showed that the attitude which the analytic physician could most advantageously adopt was to surrender himself to his own unconscious mental activity, in a state of evenly suspended attention, to avoid so far as possible reflection and the construction of conscious expectations, not to try to fix anything that he heard particularly in his memory, and by these means to catch the drift of the patient's unconscious with his own unconscious. (Freud, 1923, p. 239)

> To put in a formula: he must turn his own unconscious like a receptive organ toward the transmitting unconscious of the patient. He must adjust himself to the patient as a telephone receiver is adjusted to the transmitting microphone. Just as the receiver converts back into sound waves the electric oscillations in the telephone line which were set up by sound waves, so the doctor's unconscious is able, from the derivatives of the unconscious which are communicated to him, to reconstruct that unconscious, which has determined the patient's free associations. (Freud, 1912, p. 115)

> For as soon as anyone deliberately concentrates his attention to a certain degree, he begins to select from the material before him; one point will be fixed in his mind with particular clearness and some other will be correspondingly disregarded, and in making this

selection he will be following his expectations or inclination. This, however, is precisely what must not be done. In making the selection, if he follows his expectations he is in danger of never finding anything but what he already knows; and if he follows his inclinations he will certainly falsify what he may perceive. It must not be forgotten that the things one hears are for the most part things whose meaning is only recognized later. (Freud, 1912, p. 112)

The phenomenological experience of a similar type of "externally oriented trance state" has been lucidly described by the psychiatrist, Arthur Deikman (1963, 1966). Deikman emphasized the tremendous value of what he called the *deautomatized experience*, wherein a person temporarily casts aside the "shell of automatic perception, of automatic affective and cognitive controls in order to perceive more deeply into reality" (in Tart, 1969, p. 222).[3] He found that most individuals could learn to develop such a state by focusing attention on some external object, then gradually relinquishing the customary modes of analytical thinking and perceiving (Deikman, 1963). Deikman (1966) proposed five principal features of the deautomatized state: (1) *intense realness* (e.g., a "fresh vision" in which everything is seen as if for the first time); (2) *unusual sensations* (both in internal imagery and cognitions, and in external perception); (3) an experience of *unity* in which the normally perceived separation of "self vs. others" dissipates; (4) *ineffability* (i.e., the inability to verbally describe the experience to others); and (5) *trans-sensate phenomena* (i.e., the experience goes beyond the normal sensory modalities, ideas, and memories).

Interestingly, Deikman's subjects reported having experiences laden with the "trance characteristics" reported in Chapter 2 (e.g., timelessness, attentional focus, effortlessness). However, Deikman argues that this deautomatized experience differs from the hypnotic experience in that the former is more "ineffable, profound, uplifting, and highly valued" (in Tart, 1969, p. 219). Although such qualities may not be generally present in traditional hypnotic experiences, they frequently characterize the "generative autonomy trance" under discussion here.

This state has also been addressed by Carl Rogers:

---

[3]As Deikman (1966) pointed out, Hartmann (1958) originally proposed the concept of *behavioral automatization* to describe habituated modes of action. Gill and Brenman (1959) then derived the concept of *deautomatization* in discussing processes for "undoing" these externally goal-directed, automatized structures.

When I am at my best as a group facilitator or a therapist, I discover another characteristic. I find that when I am closest to my inner, intuitive self, when I am somehow in touch with the unknown in me, when perhaps I am in a slightly altered state of consciousness in the relationship, then whatever I do seems to be full of healing. Then simply my *presence* is releasing and helpful. There is nothing I can do to force this experience, but when I can relax and be close to the transcendental core of me, then I may behave in strange and impulsive ways in the relationship, ways which I cannot justify rationally, which have nothing to do with my thought processes. But these strange behaviors turn out to be *right*, in some odd way. At those moments it seems that my inner spirit has reached out and touched the inner of the other. Our relationship transcends itself, and has become a part of something larger. Profound growth and healing and energy are present. (1985, p. 565)

The observations of Freud, Deikman, Rogers, and others (Asante, 1984; Katz, 1982; Richeport, 1982) relate profoundly to the interpersonal hypnotic orientation of Milton Erickson. In emphasizing the primacy of unconscious intelligence, Erickson observed:

Too many psychotherapists try to plan what thinking they will do instead of waiting to see what the stimulus they receive is, and then letting their unconscious mind respond to that stimulus. (In Gordon & Meyers-Anderson, 1981, p. 17)

. . . underneath the diversified nature of the consciously organized aspects of the personality, the unconscious talks in a language which has a remarkable uniformity . . . so constant that the unconscious of one individual is better equipped to understand the unconscious of another than the conscious aspect of the personality of either. (Erickson & Kubie, 1940, p. 62. Reprinted in Rossi, 1980c, p. 186)

If I have any doubts about my capacity to see the important things I go into a trance. When there is a crucial issue with a patient and I don't want to miss any of the clues I go into trance. . . . I start keeping close track of every movement, sign, or behavioral manifestation that could be important. (Erickson & Rossi, 1977, p. 42)

Erickson thus emphasized an *externally oriented interpersonal trance state* as valuable for effective hypnotherapeutic work. There are many ways to develop such states. One procedure can be summarized as follows:

*1. Ensure comfortable seating positions.* Both hypnotist and subject should be seated comfortably, facing each other (3–5 feet apart). Your physical presence is your major communicational instrument as a hypnotist; you want to make maximum use of it.

*2. Go inside for a few moments.* Identify and relax any sources of physical or emotional tension. Any unnecessary tension will make it difficult for the hypnotist, and consequently the subject, to develop the flexibility and "flowing feeling" needed to creatively adapt to ongoing processes.

*3. Attentionally focus on the subject.* Note breathing patterns, body posture, muscular tension, emotional state, and so forth.

*4. Breathe comfortably and easily.* Although you don't want to be lethargic or inattentive, you do want to be relaxed and absorbed in the subject. As will be repeatedly emphasized, irregular or constricted breathing makes it near impossible to remain fully externally oriented; conversely, proper breathing promotes the relaxation and confidence needed to effectively interact (especially when one is initially uncertain or scared). If possible, synchronize your breathing with that of the subject. As the next chapter discusses, synchronized breathing generally enhances the therapist's ability to effectively interact with the client. Exceptions to this are when clients are emotionally upset and thus breathing either very shallowly and restrictedly (e.g., if scared or withdrawn) or very quickly and irregularly (e.g., if agitated); adopting such patterns will often trigger similar self-devaluing emotional states.

*5. Establish eye contact.* Many hypnotherapists find it best to look only into one of the subject's eyes, since gazing into both often creates a disorienting feeling which distracts from the hypnotist's concerns. Maintain this eye contact as much as possible, setting aside the need to blink, look away, or access internal thoughts. (The altered state usually resulting from this process will be discussed in a moment.)

One particularly effective technique for maintaining eye contact is to focus the left eye as if looking *through* the subject's left eye (about a foot behind it). This tends to absorb attention on the hypnotist, thereby successfully depotentiating conscious processes. Meanwhile, the hypnotist's right eye focuses about a foot in front of the subject, so that peripheral vision can now detect movements made by any part of the subject's body. Thus, the technique enables the hypnotist to simultaneously carry out two important tasks: absorbing the subject's attention and continually gathering information about ongoing behavioral responses. Although the procedure may sound unusual, I strongly encourage you to try it out before dismissing it. It's not that difficult to learn and can produce impressive results.

6. *Allow effortless mental processes.* Let any thoughts or images "drift" through your consciousness. Don't try to logically figure out something or to concentrate on any one aspect of the situation. This may be difficult and confusing at first, but just keep breathing and focusing on the subject. Before long something of interest will usually happen.

7. *Let yourself speak freely and easily.* This may also be hard to allow yourself to do initially, but just let the words come out of your mouth. You will soon discover that you can communicate quite intelligently and creatively in this fashion.

Therapists following this procedure typically find themselves in an *externally oriented interpersonal trance.* Phenomenological experience usually alters: tunnel vision, motoric inhibition, "body tinglings," and other trance characteristics commonly develop. This may be slightly disorienting at first but is no cause for alarm; it is simply a temporary (maybe five minutes) "transition period" from conscious to unconscious processing. If the therapist continues to comfortably breathe and externally orient to the client (perhaps making small talk at the same time), a state of unusual perceptual and cognitive clarity will often emerge. The therapist may have the paradoxical experience of feeling totally connected to the client, yet at the same time feel detached and impersonally involved. It's as if part of the self becomes totally immersed in experientially relating with the client, while another part dissociates and observes the ongoing interaction. This difficult-to-describe, "a-part-of-yet-apart-from" state allows the therapist to be compassionate and yet dispassionate. Rather than being mired in processes of effortfully trying to figure things out, the therapist tunes into unconscious spontaneity. Observational abilities seem greatly enhanced; thoughts, often in the form of metaphorical images, just seem to "pop up"; appropriate communications just seem to develop.

This empathic state was further described by Rogers (1980):

> An empathic way of being with another person has several facets.
> It means entering the private perceptual world of the other and
> becoming thoroughly at home in it. It involves being sensitive,
> moment by moment, to the changing felt meanings which flow in
> this person, to the fear or rage or tenderness or confusion of what-
> ever that he or she is experiencing. It means temporarily living in
> the other's life, moving about in it delicately without making judg-
> ments; it means sensing meanings of which he or she is scarcely
> aware, but not trying to uncover totally unconscious feelings, since
> that would be too threatening. . . . To be with another in this way
> means that for the time being, you lay aside your own views and
> values in order to enter another's world without prejudice. In some
> sense it means that you lay aside your self; this can only be done
> by persons who are secure enough in themselves that they know
> they will not get lost in what may turn out to be the strange or
> bizarre world of the other, and they can comfortably return to their
> own world when they wish. (pp. 142–143)

During all of this, the client will also be significantly affected by the
therapist's unwavering absorption. Alterations in body sensation (e.g.,
catalepsy, tingling, warmth) often develop. Eye fixation commonly develops, frequently followed by tunnel vision and other trance-ratifying
phenomenological alterations. The development of these and other trance
characteristics serve to depotentiate any conscious processes inhibiting
experiential participation. Some clients will consequently feel in deep
rapport with the therapist; others will grow uncertain and slightly
anxious, then usually "retreat" into trance; *most will be in a state of
heightened responsiveness*. The hypnotherapist can utilize this state
to introduce appropriate hypnotic communications.

An interpersonal trance state is not always achieved readily. This
may reflect inadequate practice: months of regular practice may be
needed to develop the ability to easily slip into the state; the skill must
then be regularly exercised to be maintained. Besides practicing in the
clinical context, you might work with a friend or colleague who observes
and signals (with, say, a light tap on the shoulder) every time you shift
out of an externally oriented trance (via restricted breathing, postural
shifts, breaking eye contact, etc.). Or you can practice by looking in a
mirror and experimenting with self-hypnotic inductions. This might
sound a bit strange, but many people find it to be quite effective. Besides, you'll get to know yourself a little better if nothing else.

Interpersonal trance may also be inhibited by the therapist's beliefs about the unconscious mind. Most of us have been taught that unconscious processes cannot operate in a coherent and intelligent fashion. We have also been taught that meaningful action only occurs through effortful conscious direction. This discourages development of an interpersonal trance, since there is little trust in unconscious generativity. These limiting and fallacious assumptions can be identified and transformed through various procedures described later.

Finally, difficulty in developing or maintaining an interpersonal trance state may be due to "unacceptable experiences" accessed while interacting with the client. To reiterate, such experiences typically bring about discomfort in the hypnotist, manifested by restricted and arrhythmic breathing, lack of eye contact, tightening of musculature, and so on. In short, these experiences inhibit the flexibility, external orientation, and acceptance needed by the therapist to develop interpersonal trance. To temporarily allay such experiences, therapists can systematically move through the seven-step procedure described above. However, remember that they must eventually be handled after the session is completed, or they will constitute an increasing problem.

Once an interpersonal trance is developed, it need not be maintained for the entire therapeutic interaction. Conscious analytical processes are complementary strategies for understanding a particular case. In my own work, I typically spend the first 10–15 minutes gathering information through conscious discussion with the client (see Chapter 5). I then shift into interpersonal trance, arousing only after the trance work has been completed, some 30–90 minutes later. Finally, I employ conscious processes during the 10–15 minutes of concluding communications.

The point here is that the frequency and style of developing interpersonal trance states will vary for each therapist. Even Erickson, who had an amazing ability to operate productively in an externally oriented trance for hours, sometimes didn't use it. In discussing this and other autohypnotic experiences with Ernest Rossi (Erickson & Rossi, 1977), Erickson commented:

> *E:* In doing experimental hypnotic work with a subject in the laboratory I would notice we were all alone. The only thing present was the subject, the physical apparatus I was using to graph their behavior, and myself.
>
> *R:* You were so focused on your work that everything else disappeared?

*E:* Yes, I discovered I was in a trance with my subject. The next thing I wanted to learn was could I do equally good work with reality all around me or did I have to go into trance. I found I could work equally well under both conditions.

*R:* Do you tend to go into autohypnosis now when you work with patients in trance?

*E:* At the present time *if I have any doubts about my capacity to see the important things I go into trance.* [italics added] When there is a crucial issue with a patient and I don't want to miss any of the clues I go into trance.

*R:* How do you let yourself go into such trance [sic]?

*E:* It happens automatically because I start keeping close track of every movement, sign, or behavioral manifestation that could be important. And as I began speaking to you just now my vision became tunnel-like and I saw only you and your chair. It happened automatically, that terrible intensity, as I was looking at you. The word "terrible" is wrong; it's pleasurable.

*R:* It's the same tunnel vision as sometimes when one does crystal gazing?

*E:* Yes. (p. 42)

Interestingly, Carl Rogers (1985) described similar experiences of letting his unconscious processes direct therapy at times. In commenting on an intuitive response he made during a therapy session that had no rational relevance to preceding conversation, he observed:

> I have come to value highly these intuitive responses. They occur infrequently . . . but they are almost always helpful in advancing therapy. In these moments I am perhaps in a slightly altered state of consciousness, indwelling in the client's world, completely in tune with that world. My nonconscious intellect takes over. I know much more than my conscious mind is aware of. I do not form my responses consciously, they simply arise in me, from my nonconscious sensing of the world of the other. (p. 565)

In summary, therapeutic communications can be facilitated immensely by the therapist's entry into an interpersonal trance wherein full experiential attention is given to the client. This state is especially useful for depotentiating the conscious processes of both therapist and client, thereby enabling the development of a deep experiential rapport.

*Therapeutic Trances*

Both participants consequently become more willing and able to allow their unconscious processes to operate in an autonomous and creative fashion: the therapist's to guide and supervise the client, the client's to transform his or her experience. Since interpersonal trances are, in the present view, so essential to effective Ericksonian work, we will explore them in greater detail in the chapters ahead, especially in relation to how the therapist can use them to reduce uncertainty and to generate effective hypnotic communications.

## Be Flexible

Once the therapist has "tuned in" with the client through hypnotic processes, this rapport must be maintained. To reemphasize an earlier point, *hypnotherapeutic effectiveness requires flexibility*. The therapist needs to continually tailor communications to the client's unique situation. This requires the development of a synchronized rhythm in which the therapist closely observes and participates in the client's ongoing processes, thereby allowing the generation of communications (techniques) that appropriately utilize them.

Of course, the hypnotherapist's assessments will not always be accurate. In this sense, I highly recommend your distrusting your perceptions (while trusting the deeper Self). Your techniques and strategies will frequently not produce their intended effect. This presents no problem whatsoever: *if a technique doesn't work, use another one*. There are really no mistakes in hypnotic interchange. Every communication will produce an outcome; all outcomes are utilizable. By remaining flexible, the therapist can utilize any behavioral response, no matter how bizarre or unexpected it may seem.

This sort of flexibility strongly characterized Erickson's work. I once heard him describe psychotherapy as "a process where two people get together to try to find out what the hell one of them wants." On another occasion I observed him working in a marvelously creative way with a hypnotherapeutic client. I assumed that his sophisticated strategies had to be generated from complex conscious computations, and was thus determined to identify the exact thought processes he used. After the patient left, I poised pencil on paper and resolutely began to interrogate him.

"Do you make a lot of pictures?"
"No," he slowly but firmly stated.
"No pictures," I muttered, crossing that category out on my sheet. "OK, do you have a lot of internal dialogue?"

"No," he again convincingly replied.

"OK. No internal dialogue. . . . Let me write that down here. . . . OK. . . . Well, do you have kinesthetic sensations? You know, feelings in your body, that sort of thing?"

"No."

I was beginning to get both suspicious and confused. "Let's see, no pictures, no internal dialogue, no kinesthetic sensations. . . . Hmmm . . . Well, Milton, I don't understand. How do you know what to do?"

"I don't know. . . . I don't know what I'm going to do, I don't know what I'm going to say. . . . All I know is that I trust my unconscious to shelve into my conscious that which is appropriate. . . . And I don't know how they're going to respond. . . . All I know is that they *will*. . . . I don't know why. . . . I don't know when. . . . All I know is that they'll respond in an appropriate fashion, in a way which best suits them as an individual. And I become so intrigued with wondering exactly *how* their unconscious will choose to respond. And so I comfortably await their response, knowing that when it occurs I can accept and utilize it."

He paused, his eyes twinkling. "Now I know that sounds ridiculous . . . *BUT IT WORKS*!!"

An important point here is that the hypnotherapist never really knows just exactly how "it" will work. Unfortunately, many clinicians have difficulty accepting this and too often become mired in rigidly using the same approach for everybody. For example, a psychiatrist attending one of my weekend workshops watched with fascination as I used a handshake interruption technique (see Chapter 7) to induce deep trances in several highly responsive demonstration subjects. Appearing at another workshop some three years later, the psychiatrist confided to me that although he had been periodically using hypnosis since the previous workshop, only about a third of his patients were "hypnotizable." Inquiry revealed that the major induction technique he used was the handshake interruption technique since, as he noted, "It was the best induction technique I ever saw."

This may seem like an extreme example, yet it is not that different from the more common situation in which a therapist always applies the same technique (whether it be a trance induction, relaxation, gestalt, psychoanalytic, etc.) None of these techniques is inherently ineffective; it's just that using them indiscriminately will guarantee a significant number of failures (often branded as "resistant" clients). A technique may be incredibly effective with a client at one point but not at another; a therapeutic strategy that works for many clients may not work well for a particular individual. Thus, a more generative approach is to appreciate the client's patterns of self-expression as the "techniques" to be used as the basis for any therapeutic explorations. In other words, the client's individual model is the "theory" or model from which distinctions of change emerge. The therapist must be flexible and adaptive. This not only makes the therapist's work more effective; it allows him or her to enjoy the work.

*Communicate Meaningfully*

The hypnotherapist's major task – assisting clients in generating more self-valuing ways of being – is achievable to the extent that clients are willing and able to explore unconscious processes. Facilitating this motivation and response potential requires *meaningful* communication; that is, the hypnotherapist conveys a sense of importance and immediacy to fully absorb attention and stimulate hypnotic responsiveness.

This does not mean that authoritative or overpowering communications are needed; in fact, such behaviors may be highly ineffective. Because meaning depends on context, the actual behaviors will vary. For example, a client's reports of sexual frigidity were accompanied by her overriding need to understand everything in precise logical terms. To establish rapport, I initially presented her with a logical sequence of facts and figures that convinced her of the need to trust and cooperate with me. While maintaining this serious intellectual demeanor over the next 4-5 sessions, I gradually began to make puns and act "lightheartedly," especially when the patient began to address her problems. This frustrated her pattern of being coldly analytical about her experience. As expected, she eventually became quite confused, at which point I immediately assumed an intense and focused look, then softly but compellingly instructed her to "let go of everything and drop into trance."[4] As anticipated, she softened and tears welled up. Accordingly, I shifted into a soft and supportive approach to guide her through some integrative changes.

Thus, depending on the situation, an effective delivery style may involve being serious, humorous, angry, and so forth. Constant throughout such variability is the therapist's underlying sense of focus and purpose. Unwavering orientation to the client conveys that nothing else

---

[4]This pattern of interrupting a dominant pattern to produce a state of uncertainty, which is then immediately utilized to develop hypnotic processes, is a highly effective one. We will explore in detail its value during trance inductions in Chapter 7.

is important at the present time, and that it is both safe and appropriate to fully respond. The client thus finds it difficult *not* to participate meaningfully.

In developing the skill to communicate meaningfully, the therapist soon comes to realize that the "how" of hypnotic communication is usually more important than the "what." As an experiential example, take a statement like "What a nice thing to know that you can fully relax now." Communicate it at least five times, to yourself (e.g., using a mirror or tape recorder) or to another person or to several different people. Each time you do so, change your nonverbal communication. Employ a quick and choppy delivery one time, a dull and uninvolved demeanor the next, then a convincing and intense style, and so on. By experimenting in such ways, the powerful influence of nonverbal behavior in social interactions will readily become apparent.

Because meaningful communication is essential to successful hypno-therapeutic work, each of the remaining chapters has something to say about it. As a preview, three important aspects might be briefly mentioned here.

*1. Intensity.* The Ericksonian practitioner must be capable of communicating with dramatic intensity. He or she should be able to completely absorb a person's attention, then convey experiential ideas in a way that sounds and looks like what is being communicated is highly relevant and important. At the same time, rapport and trust need to be maintained with the clients, and the therapist thus cannot come across as dominating or harsh. As such, the most effective delivery style is often one that is compelling while supportive, powerful yet gentle, challenging but compassionate.

*2. Rhythm.* All living processes are distinguished by rhythm. Rhythm is expressed at many levels – from simple behaviors like breathing patterns, eye blink rates, and body movements to more complex patterns such as manic-depressive shifts, interactional arguments, and rest/work cycles (see Leonard, 1978). Effective communication (establishing a "common-unity") is enabled by synchronicity of rhythms. Thus, the Ericksonian practitioner continually calibrates to ("gets in tune with") client rhythms. He or she might speak slowly to the depressed person, quickly to the excited individual; speed rhythms to disorient a client, slow them down to bore or calm a client. Tonal inflections are usually timed to the client's breathing exhalations (or inhalations, as in hand levitation methods where the upwards inflections emphasize the desired lifting up). These and other techniques are discussed in the next chapter.

*3. Congruency.* Meaning is conveyed through many behavioral parameters – voice tonality, body posture, facial expression, and so on. A person's communication is *congruent* when the outputs from these various channels are consistent with each other. Although the Ericksonian therapist occasionally uses intentionally incongruent behaviors to disorient a client (Chapter 7), most effective communication requires congruency. Thus, the therapist should usually not, for example, sound bored while talking about something exciting; nor would it be advisable to offer relaxation suggestions in a tense and shrill voice, or talk to an age-regressed person like a rational adult.

Rather, all expressions should support each other. For example, the voice should inflect downward when the subject is instructed to "drop deeper into trance"; the therapist looks and sounds more serious when starting to discuss an important topic; he or she speeds the pace of delivery when telling a story about somebody experiencing growing confusion. This congruency lends a convincing and compelling tone to hypnotic communications, thus making it more likely that they will be accepted and acted upon. In fact, it could argued that most hypnotic influence occurs at a nonverbal level.

## Be Confident

This may sound easier said than done. To successfully utilize the processes outlined in this section, you need to believe in your ability to hypnotically communicate. Again, you needn't always know the exact content or process of what you are going to do. In fact, setting aside the need to consciously plan or predict is sometimes the key to dissipating worries and other distractions. Most importantly, it allows you to experientially join the client, such that thinking become *interpersonally* based; that is, the therapist benefits by receiving "suggestions" from the unconscious processes of both his or her self and the client. Because this therapeutic process is achievable only when experiential rhythms and psychological security are present, the therapist needs to monitor and continually ensure these conditions. Furthermore, some hypnotherapists find it useful to hold in mind a few simple ideas or themes to elaborate on during such hypnotic explorations. But rather than dictating beforehand how these ideas will be specifically realized by the client, the therapist learns to trust unconscious process to utilize the situation in a creative fashion.

Again, this is not to say that planning and other analytical processes are unnecessary or never useful. Rather, the suggestion here is that such processes are often insufficient, and that "controlled spontaneity" processes that emphasize unconscious creativity are valuable tools employed at times by the Ericksonian hypnotherapist. Developing this "controlled spontaneity" does not entail a mindless abandonment of rigor or coherence. On the contrary, it requires the full presence and awareness of the therapist, a task that involves intensive ongoing training and commitment. Underlying this commitment is a confidence in the integrity and potential creativity of unconscious processes. This is a basic idea the Ericksonian therapist communicates to clients. Thus, if the therapist doesn't experience such confidence in his or her own unconscious processes, clients will be hard pressed to develop it in their own lives.

As therapists increasingly trust their unconscious processes, they also deepen their confidence in clients' potentials. In realizing such confidence, the therapist relieves debilitating pressures created by erroneously assuming responsibility for generating another person's experience; in communicating it, the therapist stimulates clients to be more willing and able to assume responsibility. This generally enhances therapeutic success.

For example, a client entered hypnotherapy with me in a sorry state. She had spent a majority of her 40 years institutionalized in orphan homes and later in mental hospitals. Without going into detail, the hypnotherapy proved to be a long and arduous struggle for her. But she stuck with it and, after many months, had accrued some major transformations. When we reviewed the therapeutic course of events, she emphasized several times that the most powerful thing I had done was to communicate an unwavering belief in her ability to operate in an intelligent and self-supporting fashion. She noted that virtually everybody in her life, *especially* mental health professionals, had always explicitly or implicitly communicated that she was forever doomed to be an undesirable and miserable failure. Naturally she came to accept this dictum for the most part.[5] She was thus initially shocked and con-

---

[5]This is an excellent example of how "hypnotic" suggestions are frequently offered in an unwitting fashion. Specifically, repetitive evaluations given to a person constitute an "induction" which creates and/or stabilizes a particular state in that person. For example, the person who is continually told he should feel depressed about an event will often develop such a response. (This metaphor can be expanded to view "personality" as a "trance state" maintained by repetitive sensory/motor correlations [inputs and outputs] with the environment [e.g., friends/enemies] and memory.) The important point here is that the therapist's prognostic statements are especially influential as naturalistic hypnotic suggestions.

fused when I communicated otherwise. After spending several months
fervently trying to deny this possibility, she was forced to consider it.
This eventually led to her being tremendously willing to cooperate with
me, and to experiment with new ways of being, both in and outside of
the hypnotherapeutic context. In short, her trust in me and belief in
herself motivated and enabled the gradual development of long-desired
changes.

All of this is not to say that confidence is all that is needed to develop
dramatic changes; successful therapy generally requires much more.
Nor is it to say that the therapist should be continually cheery-eyed and
optimistic. A therapist may at times experience little confidence in self
and others; at other times, he or she may deliberately communicate a
lack of confidence as a playful therapeutic ploy. The point here is that
out of a general context of confidence can emerge a positive cycle wherein increased confidence begets increased effectiveness, which begets
increased confidence, and so on. Greater therapeutic success typically
follows in the footsteps of such a process.

An important question thus becomes: How can you develop full confidence as a hypnotic communicator? For now, four possibilities can be
cited.

*1. Engage in personal trance training.* This will provide an appreciation of how naturalistic trance is, and how intelligent and autonomous
the unconscious can be. It can also furnish a good feel for various
hypnotic phenomena. The trance experiences may be developed using
self-hypnosis, another hypnotist, or trance exploration groups with
colleagues and friends. (An excellent resource book for use in trance
exploration groups is Masters and Houston's (1972) *Mind Games.*) Operating as the subject can yield valuable insights about effective hypnotic
communication (e.g., speaking generally, using certain rhythms). Self-
hypnosis is sometimes more difficult to fully develop at first, especially
with individuals having little previous trance experience and/or much
internal dialogue. It may therefore be best to start by spending several
sessions with a hypnotherapist and continuing to practice by using self-
hypnosis.

The therapist should realize, in exploring trance, that not everybody's
trance experiences will be similar. As an illustration, I might confess
that the first years of my hypnotic investigations included repeated
arguments with a close colleague (Paul Carter) about the "true" nature
of trance. Since most of my trance experiences were highlighted by
impressive visual imagery, I assumed that was what trance was all

about; the feelings dominating Paul's trance experiences led him to argue otherwise. Interestingly, these limiting beliefs were confirmed by our respective subjects: my subjects tended to report visual imagery, whereas his tended to report more feelings. We were much chagrined upon finally realizing that our "resistant" subjects were people who had difficulty visualizing (my recalcitrants) or deeply relaxing (his clients). In short, our personal biases severely limited the trance experiences of both ourselves and our clients. By eventually realizing the arbitrary nature of these assumptions, we were able to overcome these limits.

*2. Experientially cooperate with clients.* The hypnotherapist invites personal involvement in trance through his or her own experiential participation. In this regard, I find the following principle tremendously valuable as an ethical and practical guide:

> *Do not ask, direct, or expect clients to do or experience anything hypnotically until you as the therapist have experientially demonstrated to yourself and to the client your own willingness and ability to do the same.*

In other words, *respond to your own suggestions before asking clients to do so.* Generate the general state within yourself, then invite clients to participate in it in their own fashion. As Erickson (1964b) noted:

> I soon learned during the process developing that technique (hand-levitation) that I almost invariably would find my hand lifting and my eyelids closing. Thus I learned the importance of giving my subjects suggestions in a tone of voice completely expressive of meaningfulness, expectation and of "feeling" my words and their meanings within me as a person. (In Rossi, 1980a, p. 344)

Experiential cooperation can unmire therapists from thinking ruts. It can also enhance observational abilities and facilitate the generation of creative responses unmitigated by conscious mediation. This often sets into motion the earlier-mentioned cycle of increased confidence/ increased effectiveness.

*3. Anticipate and appreciate that most techniques will "fail."* Many aspiring hypnotherapists become unduly concerned about whether clients will respond successfully to a specific technique. Breathing becomes restricted and rhythms disjointed as the therapist anxiously applies a technique in hopes of "success." This approach leads to major obstacles, for sooner or later the client will not respond as expected. When therapists are fixated to specific techniques, these unexpected responses mean that client and/or therapist has "failed" in some way.

The Ericksonian practitioner generally finds little utility in such "win-lose" frames. Interested in cooperating rather than controlling, he or she does not impose but suggests experiential *possibilities* to clients. Of the many possibilities, you can be fully confident that only some of them will be *actualized*. That is, perhaps 90% of your techniques and suggestions will not elicit deep experiential responses; a person will selectively orient to those few ideas most personally meaningful and develop them experientially. You cannot predict precisely which suggestions will be most relevant; as in any meaningful interaction, you never quite know how the other person will respond.

Realizing that most techniques will "fail" (to elicit the expected response) can be quite a relief. Each and every response made by the client – regardless of its relation to the "suggested" response – can be fully appreciated as important feedback about the unique values of that person. Also, therapists can shift attention to a more general and inclusive level, experientially realizing that sooner or later, in one way or another, *the person will respond hypnotically*. The therapist thus becomes deeply absorbed in wondering exactly how and when *hypnotic responses will occur*. Holding in mind a general idea, the hypnotherapist elaborates many specific possible ways a client might choose to respond. Again, it is assumed that the client will "fail" to respond hypnotically to most of these suggestions, but will eventually respond meaningfully to at least one of them.

*4. Practice, practice, practice.* There is no substitute for practice! Like any skill, effective hypnotic communication results from rigorous training. Practice whenever, however, and with whomever you can; the more variety, the better. Recruit willing friends and volunteers. When they're not available, devise other training methods, such as recording and reviewing your sessions, writing down various inductions, looking into a mirror while hypnotically communicating, imagining a subject sitting in the chair in front of you. (This latter technique is derived from Erickson's (1964b) "My friend John" technique, discussed in Chapter 7.) As you learn various hypnotic techniques and principles, begin to notice how they occur in "nonhypnotic" contexts, especially in the psychotherapeutic domain. Pay particular attention to how you already utilize many hypnotic techniques without designating them as such. As you do, begin to amplify and extend the hypnotic responses that such communications elicit.

These and other training procedures are more thoroughly explored in the following chapters. Important to mention here is that therapists will usually develop full confidence in both their own and their clients' hypnotic abilities only after engaging in multifarious practice. This is not say that 20 years are required; the devoted and flexible individual can *experientially* realize in much less time that both therapist and client are highly intelligent beings capable of impressive hypnotic learnings. Buoyed with this confidence, therapists can artfully operate in the various ways described in this chapter, thereby placing them well on the road to being a generative hypnotherapist.

## GENERAL PRINCIPLES

In a paradoxical way, the effective Ericksonian practitioner is flexible but systematic, unpredictable yet coherent, creative while orderly. This is partly due to a reliance on heuristics rather than algorithms; the Ericksonian therapist is guided by general principles rather than standardized techniques. This section overviews the most important of these principles.

The most elementary principles of effective hypnotic communication, as defined by Erickson (e.g., 1952, 1959, 1964d, 1965; Erickson & Rossi, 1979), are:

(1a) *Accept the person's reality.*
(1b) *Utilize the person's reality.*

*Accepting a reality* means that you assume and congruently communicate that *what a person is doing is fine: it is exactly what you would like the person to be doing at the present time*. This does not mean that the therapist necessarily agrees with a client's choices, or personally feels they are "good" or "right." Rather, the therapist refrains from *wanting* or *needing* to immediately impose understandings or strategies, instead acknowledging fully that the client's present experience is *valid*; it doesn't need to be denied, hidden, rationalized, or otherwise dissociated. This acceptance aligns therapist with client, thereby encouraging the client's self-acceptance. Since self-devaluing dissociation is central to most psychological problems, this is an essential first step in the change process.

This is especially true with behavior or experience traditionally branded "sick" or "deviant." As Erickson (1964d) noted:

> There are many types of difficult patients who seek psychother-
> apy and yet are openly hostile, antagonistic, resistant, defensive,
> and present every appearance of being unwilling to accept the ther-
> apy they have come to seek. This adverse attitude is a part and
> parcel of their reason for seeking therapy. . . . Therefore, this at-
> titude should be respected rather than regarded as an active and
> deliberate or even unconscious intention to oppose the therapist.
> Such resistance should be openly accepted, in fact, graciously ac-
> cepted, since it is a vitally important communication of a part of
> their problem and often can be used as an opening into their de-
> fenses. . . . The therapist who is aware of this, particularly if well
> skilled in hypnotherapy, can easily and often quickly transform
> these overt seemingly uncooperative forms of behavior into a good
> rapport, a feeling of being understood, and an attitude of hopeful
> expectancy of successfully achieving the goals being sought. (In
> Rossi, 1980a, p. 299)

Thus, accepting behavior allows it to be therapeutically *utilized*. To do this, the therapist generally conveys to the client that "What you are doing right now is exactly that which will allow you to do (X)." The therapist assumes that the (specified) desired state will follow natural-ly from the present state, and thus generates communicational strat-egies based on aspects of the client's reality (e.g., present behavior, be-liefs, limits, assets, memories). For example, I began to develop rapport with a Catholic client by sharing stories of my own Catholic upbring-ing. To motivate a penny-pinching client who at the outset of therapy was (unnecessarily) worried about bankruptcy, I noted that he would be charged half the normal fee if therapy was successfully accomplished within a specified period. Another client seeking hypnotherapy exhibit-ed an intense need to do the opposite of whatever was suggested. Orders were therefore given that he remain out of trance at all times; as antici-pated, he began to "sneak" into trances, which gradually were deepened and therapeutically utilized.

In each of these cases, client idiosyncrasies were utilized to enlist ex-periential cooperation. Practical details about such strategies are delin-eated in the next chapter; important here is that these principles of ac-cepting and utilizing behavior are applied continually by the Ericksonian practitioner. They are not "one-shot" deals; they refer to an ongoing behavioral process in which the therapist moves through a reiterative cycle of observing, accepting, and utilizing client responses.

To emphasize this, Bandler and Grinder (1975) discussed Ericksonian principles in process-oriented terms:

(2a) *Pace all behavior.*
(2b) *Lead behavior.*

*Pacing* communications feed back the client's expressions; they add no new content to the interchange. Their major purpose is to enhance rapport (i.e., reduce differences and thereby develop trance) between therapist and client. This enables the client to be more trustful and cooperative, and the therapist to be more understanding.

The extreme form of pacing is complete mimicry of ongoing behavior. As might be expected, this can produce discomfort in the person. While occasionally desirable and always utilizable (see Chapter 7), it is often unnecessary. To avoid arousing such anxiety, the therapist generally needs to be a bit more subtle. The next chapter explores how the therapist needn't pace *all* aspects of the client's reality, just some key ones; also discussed is how pacing can be accomplished *indirectly* through either verbal or nonverbal channels.

It is often best to pace outside of a client's conscious awareness, since the goal of hypnotic communications is to facilitate the autonomy of unconscious generative processes. The therapist therefore needs to operate in a natural and "nonmanipulative" fashion, for the client will otherwise grow suspicious and uneasy. This demeanor is more easily attained when one realizes pacing as an extremely pervasive, general, and naturalistic phenomenon. For example, most people intuitively recognize two conversationalists in deep rapport with each other by observing their bodies move in harmonized rhythms; the effective speaker develops a "feel" for the audience and acknowledges their position (e.g., beliefs, feelings) before attempting to convince them of anything; adults usually dramatically alter mannerisms when speaking to a child; religious rituals typically involve rhythmic chanting or dancing. These examples illustrate how pacing produces greater rapport and understanding. By observing them and countless other instances, one begins to realize that *pacing is essential for effective communication: it establishes a "common-unity" context in which autonomous systems can cooperate within an experientially unified field.*

In addition to pacing, the Ericksonian practitioner also *leads* by introducing distinctions (e.g., behaviors) different from, but consistent with, the client's present state, and which move towards a desired state. The actual goal state is variable – it may be an experience (e.g., relaxation, anger, trance), a simple behavior (sitting in a chair, talking about one's feelings), a complex behavior (e.g., carrying out a homework assignment, establishing transformational changes), and so on.

Regardless of its content, successful leading requires adequate pacing. Specifically, failure to elicit a desired response is usually due to any of three possibilities. First, sufficient rapport may not be present: the client perhaps doesn't trust or feel "in tune" with the therapist, and consequently will not follow suggestions by the latter. Second, leading communications may specify some experience or behavior(s) too different from the present state; thus, the client may be *willing but unable* to oblige the therapist. For example, the statement "You're reading this book and therefore can go deeply into trance right NOWWW!!!" is mildly stated, too much of a lead for most readers. Hence, a series of intermediary steps generally need to be sequenced. Third, the specified state may be inconsistent with the client's experience, values, or beliefs. In such cases, the client may be *able but unwilling* to follow directives.

The point here is that a paucity of pacing ensures a paucity of successful leading. This is especially true in the beginning stages of an interchange (e.g., hypnotic inductions), where much more pacing than leading is required. But remember that pacing is needed at all stages of communication, especially when the client seems unwilling or unable to follow therapeutic directives. The Ericksonian practitioner thus continually adapts communications to (a) develop and maintain rapport, (b) proceed at a rate appropriate to the individual client, and (c) respect the needs and understandings of the client.

This critical idea might be clarified via a musical analogy. Imagine the human body as a musical instrument, and behavior as a song or melody played by that instrument. It is the task of the music instructor (*therapist*) to enhance the ability of students (*clients*) to play their instruments. The instructor first listens to the student play his or her instrument, closely noting individual style, strengths and weaknesses, interests, and so on. The instructor then picks up his or her own instrument, tunes it to the student's (*develops rapport*), then starts to play the same melody or song (*pacing*). As a "groove" is developed with the student, new notes are here and there interspersed, and changes now and again suggested (*leading*); yet always is there the return to the student's basic rhythm (*return to pacing*). In this way, the instructor enables students to slowly develop their own inherent skills.

Of course, the student will not always be willing or able to follow the instructor's leads. This is especially likely if the two instruments are out of tune with each other, or if the musicians (therapist and client) are playing in a different key (*lack of rapport*). Or the instructor may be shifting too abruptly (*leading too quickly*) into a new song, rhythm, or style (e.g., blues to jazz); or introducing some new style (e.g., Flamenco music) that is totally unappealing to the student (*leading inappropriately*). Whatever the case, the effective instructor astutely observes difficulties encountered by the student, then adapts to handle them (*returns to pacing*).

This metaphor suggests some of the rhythmic, ongoing, interpenetrating, and complementary nature of pacing and leading. It also serves to introduce a third major principle of effective communication:

(3) *Resistant behavior is a statement that the therapist needs to pace some further aspect(s) of the client's experience.*

This does not mean that the therapist is "wrong" or a "failure," but simply that communications need to be adjusted. In other words, the Ericksonian practitioner assumes that all experience is valid and utilizable, then behaviorally paces and leads towards the desired state. The therapist doesn't know exactly when or how the goal will be reached, only that a continuous rhythm can be established wherein patterns are observed, accepted, and utilized to unfold a unique trajectory from present to desired state. Along this unpredictable path to change, the therapist will undoubtedly encounter various obstacles and barriers. Rather than trying to plow straight through them or label them in derogatory and devaluing fashions, the therapist simply acknowledges and adapts to them. Thus, the client's eccentric response patterns are not rejected as "bad" or "sick"; on the contrary, they are accepted as those enabling the development of desired states (e.g., hypnotic experiences, therapeutic changes).

Of course, every therapist will periodically experience difficulty completely accepting and utilizing client patterns. That's fine. You can dissipate such impasses by pausing, orienting internally, then asking yourself, "How can I utilize this behavior?" *Do not attempt to influence clients until you experientially feel that their experiences are both valid and utilizable.* By so operating, you soon realize that clients are not incompetent or belligerent; each simply has a unique style of cooperating (cf. de Shazer, 1982). Hypnotherapeutic interaction accordingly becomes a fascinating process of identifying that particular style of cooperating and consequently exploring how it can be utilized to develop the desired state(s).

Given the general and cross-contextual nature of pacing and leading, this process can occur in many ways. In the hypnotic context, utilization principles can be expressed in a more specific form:

(4a) *Pace and depotentiate conscious processes.*
(4b) *Absorb and amplify unconscious processes.*

These principles contain the essence of effective hypnotic communication. They assume that many difficulties, whether in developing trance or handling life challenges, result from engulfment by habituated conscious processes. The Ericksonian practitioner thus seeks to depotentiate recurrent conscious processes and to enable previously inaccessible resources to be actualized. To do this, clients are aided in setting aside conscious processes to tune into unconscious (i.e., experiential, paradoxical, nonlinear) processes. To circumvent possible objections ("resistances"), an indirect approach is often used.

For example, a client whose incessant internal dialogue inhibited trance development was told to count backwards from 1000 to 1 by threes during the induction process. Another client desiring hypnosis was a medical doctor beset with an overwhelming need to try to rationally understand everything. To distract and fixate his conscious attention, I instructed him to "very closely observe *all and only* the behaviors" of another person with whom I would demonstrate the induction process. However, all of my inductions concentrated on indirectly pacing and leading his ongoing behavior into trance. In a third instance, a client was "bored" into trance via several hours of dull stories spiced with indirect trance suggestions.

It is no coincidence that these examples all involve hypnotic inductions. Indirect communication is usually most needed at this phase, since it is here that the client is essentially asked to set aside attachment to conscious processes. Of course, it is sometimes necessary to be indirect during other hypnotherapeutic phases as well. For example, a client nearing the end of her therapy was terrified about meeting her father, whom she had run away from as a child. In trance she was given posthypnotic suggestions that her fears would steadily increase as she drove to his house the next day until, upon finally arriving, she would be so overwhelmed and exhausted that she would drop deeply into trance. A state of inner peace coupled with external responsiveness would then develop and remain throughout the afternoon encounter. Briefly stated, she handled the meeting with her father remarkably well.

These examples suggest a few of the many possibilities. More specific strategies for determining how and when to be indirect are detailed in the coming pages. For now, we can conclude with a final principle:

(5) *Use indirect communication to the extent that a client's conscious processes might object or otherwise interfere with the development of desired changes.*

Stated obversely, indirectness is not necessary to the extent that the client is in trance, since (by definition) conscious processes will not be dominant at such times.

## SUMMARY

This chapter overviewed the general approach followed by the Ericksonian hypnotherapist. The first section focused on the therapist's integrity, emphasizing both the vital necessity and benefits of fully respecting the unique personality and situation of each client. To do so, the therapist identifies and assumes responsibility for the intent and specific outcomes of therapeutic communications. This integrity is maintained in various ways, including (1) identifying and handling personal limits, (2) generally being nonevaluative while hypnotically interacting, and (3) allowing clients to generate their own experiences.

The second section outlined general communicational processes. It was suggested that the hypnotherapist can achieve success by (1) staying externally oriented in an interpersonal trance, (2) remaining flexible, (3) communicating meaningfully (e.g., with intensity, rhythm, and congruency), and (4) remaining confident in both self and client.

The final section overviewed basic utilization principles. The continual application of these principles is emphasized by the process terms of pacing and leading. These principles suggest that the traditional concept of resistance is better viewed as behavioral feedback indicating a need for further pacing by the therapist. The hypnotic application of these principles often assumes the form of pacing and depotentiating conscious processes, while accessing and utilizing unconscious process. Finally, indirect communication is needed to the extent that conscious processes interfere with therapeutic developments.

# CHAPTER 4

# *Cooperation Strategies*

The last chapter outlined the context, processes, and principles distinguishing the approach of the Ericksonian hypnotherapist, especially emphasizing the cooperative principles of appreciating and utilizing the "realities" of the client as the basis for hypnotic and therapeutic developments. In this approach, the underlying intention is to expand the domain of self-valuing expressions while preserving (i.e., not taking away) client values. Relationship between complementary structures (e.g., subject/object, self/other) is seen as the basic unit of both interpersonal and intrapersonal interaction, and the feedback loop is appreciated as the process of information flow connecting complements.

In this view, self-expression always involves three domains: (1) intentions (injunctions or commitments), (2) biological rhythms and patterns, and (3) psychological frames or structures (to represent and express patterns). In typical goal-orienting states, frames — for example, plans or strategies — usually dominate the conscious mind, while intention and nonverbal realities take up the peripheral — that is, surrounding unconscious — field. Problems are seen to develop when these three domains become condensed into a frozen (i.e., *invariant*) constellation such that a person becomes insensitive to context shifts and biological rhythms. Thus, the same response is made time after time, oblivious to changing realities.

The Ericksonian practitioner appreciates the problem as the solution, realizing that the same structures expressed in diverse fashions with biological rapport in self-valuing contexts can be generative. Thus, the hypnotherapist uses cooperation principles to (1) create a self-valuing context in which a person is receptive to the environment (e.g., the therapist) and to new ideas, (2) depotentiate conscious frames and, (3) reunite information patterns with biological rhythms ("mind" with "body"). To accomplish this, the therapist expresses the very same structural patterns dominating the client's experience. This expands intrapersonal loops containing the client to an interpersonal circle involving therapist and client; that is, pacing dissipates differences between inner and outer, thereby collapsing the information boundaries rigidly dissociating the former from the latter.[1] This allows receptivity to new ideas and exploration of new ways of being.

This chapter details specific ways whereby these cooperation principles can be applied. The first section discusses how verbal and nonverbal techniques of pacing and leading can absorb and direct the client's ongoing awareness. The second section explores how to observe and utilize the minimal behavior cues indicative of a person's internal experience (i.e., level of trance, emotional state, and representational systems). The final section illustrates ways to "cooperate" with idiosyncratic patterns such as symptom phenomena, expressive style, general metaphors in thinking, skills and assets, and the structure of the behavioral problem.

## UTILIZING DIRECT OBSERVATIONS

One aspect of client experiences that often needs to be utilized is externally oriented awareness — body position, attentional gaze, orientation to environmental stimuli, verbal statements, and so on. This is generally the simplest case of pacing and leading because such external phenomena are directly observable. Thus, the therapist needn't try to infer or guess the client's internal state, and consequently can be more accurate.

External awareness can be utilized in many ways. This section identifies basic patterns of verbal and nonverbal pacing and leading and discusses how they can be applied directly or indirectly.

### Verbal Pacing and Leading

The syntax of effective hypnotic communication has been discussed by various Ericksonian-oriented investigators (Erickson, Rossi, & Rossi, 1976; Erickson & Rossi, 1979; Bandler & Grinder, 1975; Lankton & Lankton, 1983; Hartland, 1971). Basically, it involves linking leading statements to pacing statements so the former seem to follow undeniably from the latter. This can be done in the *conjunctive* form of "X and

---

[1] In other words, an information boundary can only exist ("ex"-"stande," to stand out from) when differences are perceived between the two sides of the boundary (Brown, 1979). When the therapist assumes the client's patterns, the latter's fixation to a frame dissipates. This allows the client to reunite at a deeper (deframed) level of Self where generative resources are available. Thus, pacing collapses information boundaries to enhance the sense of self-autonomy.

X and X and X and Y," where X=pacing statements and Y=leading statements. For example:

(1) You're sitting in that chair,          (pacing statement)
(2) and you're looking at me,              (pacing statement)
(3) and you're breathing easily,           (pacing statement)
(4) and I'm talking to you,                (pacing statement)
(5) and you can begin to relax.            (leading statement)

Or it can be done in the more *disjunctive* form of "X or X or X or X but Y." For example:

(1) I don't know whether you'd like to continue to
    look at the floor,                          (pace)
(2) or whether you'd like to look at me,        (pace)
(3) or again look at the floor,                 (pace)
(4) or perhaps adjust into a more comfortable po-
    sition,                                     (pace)
(5) but I do know that your unconscious can de-
    velop a trance in a manner that best suits *you*
    as an individual.                           (lead)

In both forms, the first four statements simply describe the directly observable, ongoing behavior of a hypothetical subject. As Erickson, Rossi, and Rossi (1976) noted, this pacing of undeniable realities sets up a "yes" response pattern. This receptive state is then utilized to introduce the leading communication.

A third syntactical structure for effective hypnotic communication is the adverbial clause:

*General Form*                          *Example*

(1) Since X, then Y                     Since you're sitting in that
                                        chair, you can begin to relax.

(2) While X, then Y                     While you're getting comforta-
                                        ble, you can begin to recognize
                                        that your unconscious can begin
                                        to develop a trance.

(3) When X, then Y                      When you hear my voice, you
                                        can remember this feeling of
                                        comfort.

(4) After X, then Y          After you've positioned yourself comfortably, your unconscious can begin to express itself in an appropriate fashion.

To apply these structures effectively, the therapist assumes an appropriate nonverbal delivery style. To reiterate, *the client will generally be unwilling or unable to respond hypnotically to someone who appears tense, manipulative, contrived, uninterested, unconvincing, and so on.* The best results are therefore often obtained when the therapist (a) shifts into an externally oriented trance, (b) establishes a synchronized rhythm with the client, (c) speaks in a meaningful and absorbing fashion, and (d) remains sensitive to the client's continually changing responses.

Furthermore, the content of the verbal forms should not be inappropriate or offensive to the client. To reiterate, more pacing than leading statements are usually needed, especially in the initial stages. Also, statements should generally, though not always, be permissive (e.g., "you *can* do this) rather than authoritarian (e.g., "You *will* do this," "You *must* do that"), since many clients automatically rebel against the latter style.

Successfully actualizing these processes is much easier when one recognizes their pervasive presence in everyday situations. Everyone, for example, has received or issued verbalizations such as:

"Since you're going into the kitchen, will you get me a cup of coffee?"

or

"Oh, by the way, as long as you're doing that, why don't you . . . ?"

or

"Would you like to hear the story now or later?"

Note that these directives usually work best when offered in a naturalistic and permissive fashion. The effective therapist simply utilizes these same communicational processes, but with more awareness and intensity.

These and related points can be illustrated through some brief examples of therapeutic applications of external pacing and leading.

*1. Securing agreements.* A major goal in the initial phases of a therapy is to secure a commitment to the change process. The following transcriptional excerpt illustrates how pacing and leading may contribute to this goal.

| *Abbreviated Transcript* | *Commentary* |
|---|---|
| (1) OK . . . now we've been talking for a while, so I'd like you to listen to a few things I have to say about what I've heard so far. | (1) This first sentence shows that the therapist can also pace *past* behaviors (e.g., the immediately preceding conversation), then lead by framing the desired behavior (e.g., the client listening) as a logical consequence of the past behavior. This simple "Since X, then Y" form is commonly used by effective communicators. |
| (2) Now when you came in here today, you sat down in that chair, and you began to share a variety of different things. . . . You told me that things haven't been going right for a long time, and that you've paid a heavy emotional price as a result. . . . Your job and personal relationships have deteriorated because of these difficulties. | (2) Now the therapist continues to pace by descriptively feeding back the client's immediately preceding expressions. This simple process is often invaluable in producing at least three important outcomes. First, it secures and absorbs a person's attention. As brief experimentation will quickly demonstrate, it's very difficult *not* to pay attention to someone who is completely pacing your ongoing behavior. Second, the person will typically feel understood and will consequently develop more trust, rapport, and motivation to participate. Third, if dramatically delivered, the description of the major problems will tend to elicit corresponding experiences in the client. Clients will usually feel motivated to reduce this unpleasant state of emotional arousal and, as we will see, will consequently be highly responsive to hypnotic directives. |

(3) Am I correct? (Client responds affirmatively)

(3) On the surface, this simple question seeks to verify the accuracy of the previous pacing statements. More important, it also implicitly asks the client to acknowledge that his life isn't working. This is generally a necessary first step to change. Parenthetically, this lead also emphasizes a highly important fact: *purely descriptive pacing often implicitly leads.* In the present case, for instance, a small subset of the ongoing behavior is selected out and described in a way that highlights the problems; but the therapist could just as easily have selected out behaviors that created a different "reference structure." Thus, in general, selective pacing can "frame" reality in different ways. As we will see, this is a subtle and hence highly effective form of leading.

(4) All right, fine. And so I want to ask you an important question, and I don't want you to respond off the top of your head. I want you to really think about it, because the right answer might be "yes," or it might be "no"; only you know for sure.

But before I ask the question, I want to say that I think there is hope for you, that you can make those changes, but that it will be difficult, it will be rough, it may even be a bit painful at times. You'll probably feel uncomfortable at times, have a few relapses along the way, think it not worth the effort . . . but if

(4) The therapist now leads by seeking a commitment to the therapeutic process. Several points about external pacing and leading can be made from this simple example. First, in most hypnotic work the subject's awareness is gradually oriented to internal processes within 5–10 minutes, at which point any further comments on external affairs will be unnecessary and often distracting to the subject. However, there are some exceptions to this, such as when the internally-oriented (e.g., eyes closed) subject behaviorally indicates a physical discomfort or orientation to outside noises.

you stick with it, I really think you can make those changes. But it's up to you to decide if you're really ready to give up all of your pain, your suffering.

And so the question I want you to closely consider is this: Are you willing and ready to commit yourself to developing the desired changes?

Second, the leading should be introduced gradually, often with a good deal of redundancy. In fact, a bit too much pacing often has the favorable effect of producing "response potential" in the subject. Third, a person's future behavior can also be paced. Such *future pacing* should be general enough to include any possible outcome, each of which can then be linked to success. For example, the present transcript frames relapses, giving up, discomfort, etc., as part of the therapeutic process.

*2. Inductions.* External pacing and leading is often very useful at the outset of a hypnotic induction. It serves to absorb attention, which is normally scattered about on various external realities, in a way that establishes a synchronicity of rhythm between therapist and client. This rapport and absorption can then be utilized to direct the client to experientially explore internal processes (i.e., develop trance), as represented in the following:

| Attention Shifting About | → | Attention Focused (on Hypnotist) | → | Attention Focused Internally |

For example:

*Example*

(1) All right, now you're looking at me and now you're moving about, trying to find a comfortable position in which you can begin to go into trance . . . and as you do, you can begin to simply notice whatever is occurring in your ongoing awareness. . . .

*Commentary*

(1) After pacing several obvious behaviors (looking and moving), the therapist leads by defining the shift as leading into trance. These statements are then used to direct (lead) the client into a state of general self-awareness.

(2) You're probably aware of a variety of different things . . . and whether it is the sound of my voice, the cars outside, the activity of the tape recorder, or the movement in the room, that's not important. . . .

(2) Plausible external contents of external awareness are now paced. Note they are stated as possibilities, since the therapist really can't be sure if the client is actually thinking about them. (Again, telling clients they are aware of something they aren't may dissipate rapport.) Also, note that the pacing of possibilities implicitly leads by directing the client's awareness to these various objects; i.e., the client is now following the therapist's directives.

(3) What is important is that you can begin to recognize that you can begin to attend to the need to attend to your own internal needs.

(3) The preceding pacing statements are now utilized to cross over (lead) to internally oriented awareness.

(4) Whether you're sitting in that chair, or listening to my voice, or noticing your own increasing comfort, that's not important either . . . because your unconscious can experience the development of trance in a variety of ways. . . .

(4) After introducing the leading statement, the therapist now falls back to pacing. This illustrates the important pattern of pace/pace/pace/lead, pace/pace/pace/lead, etc.; i.e., each time the therapist leads, he or she immediately goes back to pacing and then closely observes the client's responses. If the client appears to be following the directives, this new state is now paced/paced, paced/led, etc; if he or she remains in the same state, more pacing or different leading statements are introduced.

Also, note that the statements again pace possible external awarenesses, and then lead by defining any of these awarenesses as appropriate for the development. In other words, *whatever a person is doing can allow him or her to develop a trance.*

(5) You can go into a trance with your eyes open, or you can close your eyes and drop deeply into trance. And I don't know which way will be best for you as an individual. . . .

(5) These statements illustrate the common and effective technique of following general statements with specific examples. This is an explicit pace; it is also an implicit lead, as it defines the specific (eyelid) behavior in terms of the general lead (trance-inducing behaviors).

(6) Because your eyelids are open, but then blinking . . . open . . . and then blinking again . . . up . . . and then down again . . . open . . . and then closing all the way down so easily . . . *nowww*!!! . . . and drop deeply into trance.

(6) The hypnotherapist now zeros in on the client's eyelid behavior. Pacing (e.g, mentioning "blinking" immediately *after* the subject's eyes actually blink) is followed by leading (e.g., mentioning "blinking" before it occurs, and then pausing until it does). When delivered with a compellingly meaningful and appropriate rhythm (e.g., timing) this technique is incredibly effective.

(7) And what a nice thing to know that with each breath that you take, you can drop deeper into trance . . . with each breath, breathing in so much comfort . . . and with each exhalation letting go of any need to hold on to any unnecessary needs. . . .

(7) After eye closure is obtained, the client's observable breathing patterns are utilized to further pace and lead into trance. At this point, the induction usually shifts gradually away from commenting on external realities, since they are now probably out of the client's awareness.

Of course, not all interactions will run as smoothly as the above example; some clients will be less willing or able to straightforwardly cooperate. As we will see, however, the same basic communicational forms can be successfully applied in more challenging cases, albeit in a modified fashion.

*3. "Nonhypnotic" therapeutic interactions.* Behavioral pacing and leading can be effective in any therapeutic interaction, regardless of whether formal hypnosis is involved. For example, a young married couple began arguing heatedly during a couples counseling session. Since neither was really listening to the other, the therapist intervened with the intent of reconnecting them with the "here and now." He interrupted them, paced Cathy by assuring her that he would attend to her momentarily, and then turned to Bob and said:

| *Excerpts from Transcript* | *Commentary* |
|---|---|
| (1) *Therapist:* OK, let's stop for a minute. How are you feeling, Bob?<br><br>*Bob:* She doesn't understand me.<br><br>*T:* You think she doesn't understand you. And would you like her to understand you?<br><br>*B:* Well, of course.<br><br>*T:* OK, fine. So are you willing to try something that might allow her to understand you?<br><br>*B:* Well, I don't know. . . .<br><br>*T:* You don't know if you would like her to understand you?<br><br>*B:* Well, no, I do want her to understand me. But. . . .<br><br>*T:* (interrupts) OK, so you want her to understand you; so are you willing then to try something out, something very simple and painless?<br><br>*B:* Yeah. . . . | (1) In this first step the therapist begins by simply pacing Bob's verbal statements, and then leads by connecting them to an unspecified behavioral task ("doing something different"). Bob hedges a bit, so pacing is reintroduced, and then more forcefully linked (Since X, then Y) to a willingness to try something new. |
| (2) *Therapist:* OK, great. So all I'd like you to do right now is just stop for a moment and look at me . . . that's right . . . just | (2) The client's nonverbal behavior is now more directly utilized. The hypnotherapist starts with eye contact, paces it for a while, |

look at me for a moment . . .
that's fine . . . and as you continue to look at me, I'd like you
to become aware of the fact that
you haven't been breathing too
much . . . so what I'd like you to
do is begin to breathe deeply
and comfortably . . . that's right
. . . in and out . . . in and out . . .
and simply begin to notice that
with each breath you can feel
more secure, more relaxed, more
at ease . . . can you feel that? . . .
(Bob nods head affirmatively)

. . . OK, now this increased comfort can allow you to do a lot of
things, because what seemed so
terrible and overpowering before
can now seem a bit more manageable . . . and so what I'd like
you to do now is simply look at
your wife again . . . and as you
do . . . that's right . . . as you do,
I want you to again take a deep
breath and relax . . . and I want
you to do the same, Cathy . . .
and Bob, as you breathe in that
comfort and relaxation, realize
that in a moment I'm going to
ask you to tell Cathy how you
feel inside. . . .

(3) And as you begin to do so,
you're probably going to begin
to feel a bit upset at first . . .
that's to be expected, but we
know now that when you feel
that upset beginning to develop,
you can recognize it as a cue
that you're not breathing . . . and
that cue will allow you to stop
again and take a breath. . . . Now
I'm going to help you to do this
at first . . . so go ahead right

leads to breathing awareness
and then breathing changes,
which is then defined as leading
to internal comfort. After Bob's
internal state is paced and developed for a while, it is utilized
to lead him back into external
contact with his wife, although
now in a different way.

(3) Future pacing is now used to
define possible difficulties as
part of the therapeutic process.
Leading communications then
frame stress as a momentary
state which will lead to relaxed
breathing. To ensure this, the
therapist paces by acting as a
guide during the first few trials.

now and just look at her and
begin to talk about how you feel
inside . . . that's right. . . .

*4. Indirect Applications.* The illustrations thus far presented have
involved relatively direct communications. Sometimes, however, the
therapist needs to speak more indirectly, for example, by using metaphorical stories to induce or utilize a trance state. The following transcript, excerpted from the middle of an indirect induction, indicates how
this might be done. (The previous 30 minutes had been spent absorbing
the subject's attention, then inducing a light trance.)

| *Example* | *Commentary* |
|---|---|
| (1) . . . And the passengers on that cruise voyage spent much of the day *looking* out over the water, *listening* to the lapping of the waves, *feeling* the rhythms of the boat rock back and forth, back and forth . . . *slowly* moving into deeper and deeper territory . . . | (1) This is an indirect pace of the client being a participant in the trance induction ("passenger on trip"), listening to the therapist's voice (the "lapping waves"), which was rhythmically shifting back and forth. The final clause is an indirect lead into a deeper trance. |
| (2) . . . and the air was so wonderful to *breathe in* . . . the environment so secure and peaceful . . . that many of the passengers, sitting ever more comfortably on the deck, began to *let go* of all their worries, all of the tension, and simply began to *increasingly relax*, realizing that there was no need to do anything except to attend to the need to attend to their own internal needs . . . | (2) Essentially, this is an indirect suggestion that the client's breathing (pace) will lead to increasing relaxation. |
| (3) . . . and as night began to fall . . . (that's right) . . . slowly but inevitably down . . . the sea was no longer visible, although the sound of the lapping waves | (3) The client's spontaneous eye closure is paced as "night falling"; this is then connected to continued rapport with the therapist's voice ("waves lap- |

could still be heard . . . and no longer feeling the glare of the sun, the reclining passengers began to thoroughly enjoy the cool, delightful evening . . . a light on the deck was turned on after a while, but then shut off again . . . and it stayed off for a while . . .

(4) . . . and before long the captain suggested that it was *time to go inside* . . . the passengers began to slowly *head down* below the deck, gradually becoming absorbed in various activities . . . this absorption was momentarily interrupted by the surprising sound of a ship's horn blowing . . . but the captain came on the speaker, reassuring everyone that it was just the sound of another ship passing peacefully in the night . . . and so the absorption in those internal activities began to grow once again. . . .

ping"). Next, the client's slight discomfort at the therapist's unrelenting eye contact is paced (glare of sun) and then used to lead to further relaxation. Finally, the subject opened her eyes momentarily, which was paced and then led as a light turning on and off.

(4) The therapist ("captain") now leads with trance suggestions ("go inside"). The subject's downward head movement is paced and this led to further trance (absorption below the deck). The subject displayed a startle response to a phone ringing in the next room; this was paced (ship horn blowing) and then led (captain reassures) to further absorption.

In summary, these various examples illustrate that verbal pacing of external realities typically involves describing the past, present, or future behavior of the subject. The general purpose of such communications is to absorb attention and acknowledge present experience, thereby creating a rapport allowing therapeutic explorations. If the therapist speaks in a relaxed but meaningful fashion, this can often be accomplished in a relatively short time. The gradually introduced leading communications can be *explicit* (e.g., "since you're sitting in that chair, you can relax"), or more *implicit*, such as when observable behavior is described within a particular framework (e.g., "the comfort of sitting in a chair"), or when a certain aspect of the client's behavior is selectively paced. The pacing and leading statements can be direct or indirect (e.g., metaphorical); they can also be general or specific. Whatever the case, the therapist should generally deliver them in a permissive yet absorbing style.

*Nonverbal Pacing and Leading*

The therapist also *nonverbally* paces and leads the client's ongoing behavior in various ways. For example, the upper panel of Figure 4.1 represents the process of *direct mirroring*, whereby the therapist adjusts some or all behaviors to *identically* match those expressed by the client. This might mean breathing at the same rate, assuming the same body posture or facial expression, and so on. Direct mirroring can be done fully (matching every output) or partially (selectively aligning with one or two outputs).

The lower panel of the figure illustrates the more indirect process of *cross-behavioral mirroring*, whereby the therapist feeds back some behavioral patterns of the client, *but in a different channel*. For example, the therapist might subtly nod his or her head each time the client blinks, or tap a finger every time the client exhales. Because cross-behavioral mirroring is more complex, it is done selectively (i.e., one or two channels at a time).

Like verbal pacing, the major purpose of nonverbal pacing is to develop rapport. To reiterate, the Ericksonian practitioner uses his or her body like an instrument, tuning and playing it in synchronized rhythm with the client's. Generally speaking, this alignment is a necessary condition for therapeutic success. Without it, the client will often be unwilling or unable to trust and cooperate fully. This restraint is frequently well justified, as the "unaligned" therapist will generally have difficulty in understanding, much less responding effectively to, the client's ongoing experience. In short, nonverbal pacing enables both therapist and client to participate in the hypnotic interaction more effectively.

Nonverbal leading can be used to gradually shift paced behavior toward some desired state. For example, the therapist might begin to overload the client's conscious processes by speaking in a quicker, louder, and more arrhythmic fashion (see Chapter 7). Or to calm down an excited client, the therapist might first pace by assuming a similarly quick and breathless speech rate, then lead by gradually slowing it down.

As is discussed in Chapter 7, this overload technique is generally not advisable if the person is extremely agitated. Not only will this tend to make the therapist uncomfortable, but it may also further agitate the client, sometimes to the point of physical violence. Thus, it is more appropriate in such cases to use indirect (cross-behavioral) pacing.

As part of an induction procedure, the client's body posture, espe-

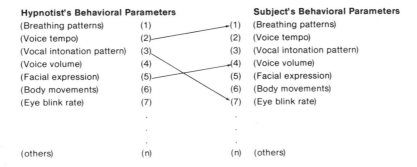

Figure 4.1. Partial list of nonverbal channels involved in pacing and leading, with examples of direct and full, direct and partial, and indirect and partial mirroring

cially breathing patterns, might be mirrored while his or her eye blink rate is gradually increased. Or a particular emotional state (e.g., relaxation, sadness, anger, happiness) might be elicited via a voice tone and/or facial expression congruent with that emotion.

In this dancelike interaction, it is generally not critical that every behavioral channel be continually monitored. What's important is to sense when rhythms of therapist and client grow dissonant, because that is when behavioral adjustments are needed. Such rhythmic discords are not uncommon, since another person's responses can never be perfectly predicted. However, the sensitive therapist who remains tuned in to the client can quickly detect them through various sensory channels. For example, he or she may *feel* out of tune with the client, or experience the client pulling away, or *see* the client respond in an unexpected (e.g., tense) fashion, or perhaps *hear* emotional changes in the client's voice. Most of these unanticipated dissonances are minor and are best regarded as helpful cues indicating the need for behavioral adjustment.

Sometimes, however, *rhythmic* adjustments will be insufficient. This is usually evidenced by the therapist feeling increasingly confused or upset, and/or perceiving the client as growing "resistant" or otherwise uncooperative. As previously noted, this usually means that the therapist's general approach needs to be modified. Keeping in mind that the specific alterations will depend upon the particular situation, three communicational variables frequently requiring adjustment might be cited.

*1. General demeanor.* The therapist may come off as extremely manipulative, or perhaps look guilty or apologetic when applying a technique. These seemingly opposite responses are related in several ways. First, underlying both is the fallacious assumption that the intent of pacing and leading is to *control* another person. This belief strongly threatens the integrity of both therapist and client, thereby limiting chances of therapeutic success.

Second, in both cases the therapist will typically be self-conscious in pacing and leading attempts. This typically results in a choppy, interruptive rhythm. For example, the therapist might consciously try to think of a "good technique," awkwardly attempt to apply it, then closely watch to see if it worked. By thus doing something *to* rather than *with* the client, the latter will feel more like an object than a unique person.

The client, usually quite sensitive to all of this, will often be momentarily confused, then look to the therapist for explanation. At this point, the flexible therapist can transform the situation by stopping, relaxing, and reconnecting with the client. Unfortunately, it is here that the unseasoned therapist often makes the regrettable mistake of trying to deny or distract from the obvious. To make matters worse, he or she usually does it in a tense and self-conscious fashion. Regardless of actual intention, this will, to put it mildly, discourage the client from fully trusting the therapist.

The general point here is that the therapist needs to be relaxed but focused while utilizing pacing and leading techniques. Although therapy requires being indirect at times, therapists should never lie to clients. The intent is not to "put one over" on the person, but to fully support him or her.

Appreciation of this cooperative attitude can be deepened by observing the pervasiveness of nonverbal pacing and leading in everyday interactions. Examples abound: two people strolling down the street, synchronized in gait; two lovers sitting at a table, harmoniously mirroring each other; a cheering crowd beginning to clap together, then gradually speeding up the tempo until a crescendo is reached; two dancers facing each other, alternately following, matching, and leading the other in dance steps. To be sure, the participants in these situations do not call what they are doing nonverbal pacing and leading; in fact, they are rarely consciously aware of being engaged in such processes. Yet it is precisely these principles and processes that the Ericksonian practitioner uses. Again, what is sometimes different is that the therapist applies them with a specific purpose (e.g., trance), with awareness, and usually with greater focus and intensity. In realizing nonverbal pacing and leading as completely naturalistic, the therapist can utilize it effectively. Unburdened by the erroneous belief that he or she must do something totally new, the therapist is free to become absorbed in gently guiding nonverbal processes already in effect.

*2. Level of directness.* Therapists can sometimes be too direct. This may involve, for example, being overly obvious in attempts to, say, mirror body posture, mimic voice qualities, or lead into trance. Clients who become consciously aware of this will typically grow self-conscious, as evidenced by an interruption in ongoing behavioral rhythms (breathing, body posture, voice tone, eye gaze, etc.).

Therapists can usually handle this without difficulty, as long as they remain comfortably in tune with clients. To reiterate, clients will generally become really angry or upset only if the therapist responds to their self-consciousness by becoming upset (e.g., embarrassed, angry, confused). Thus, therapists should first check and, if necessary, modify their breathing, body posture, eye gaze, and so on.

If the client is fully aware and/or particularly upset about some technique, direct comments about intention are usually needed. For example, the therapist might begin with one of the following openers:

(a) Would you like to know my intent here? I'm trying to help you develop a trance. . . . How much do you think you'd like to do that? . . . All right, how much do you think you'd be willing to help me then? Fine, now. . . .

(b) Why am I doing that? Because I'm trying to understand you. And sometimes it's hard for me . . . because I really don't know exactly what you need, and I'm interested in discovering that. So one of the ways I try to understand another person's reality is to find some way of connecting that's comfortable for both of us.

Most of the time, remarks as brief as these will generally suffice, as long as therapists remain undefensive and honest. Sometimes they are best delivered with a playful sense of humor, since this can loosen up the clients; other times it is more suitable to respond in a soft but serious fashion. The important point is to communicate nonverbally an acknowledgment and full respect for the person as a unique individual. When this is done, unexpected difficulties become fully utilizable.

Since it is frequently desirable in hypnotic work to bypass conscious processes, one appropriate utilization would be to nonverbally pace and lead less obviously. At first, this generally means less of it; after a while, the therapist might reintroduce it, but in a more indirect (i.e., cross-behavioral mirroring) fashion.

At other times, the therapist might more effectively utilize by becoming *more* direct. A common instance of this is when the therapist exercises full mirroring (Panel A of Figure 4.1, p. 112) at the beginning of an induction. Many clients respond by growing increasingly self-conscious. Although some try to distract the unwavering mirroring of the therapist, most eventually develop attentional absorption. This usually creates further uncertainty; the client will typically either begin to "retreat" into trance or become even more transfixed on the therapist. In either case, it is fairly easy to then direct the client into trance (see Chapter 7).

Again, this sort of technique will succeed only if delivered within a context of respect and trust. The therapist doesn't try to goad or force the client into something; he or she simply aligns with the client's behavior, thereby depotentiating the client's dominating conscious processes and enabling generative change processes to unfold.

Finally, therapists can sometimes be too *indirect*. Pacing or leading might be so obscure that the client doesn't perceive it, consciously or unconsciously. For example, the therapist will probably not be too effective if pacing consists entirely of, say, tapping a foot every sixth time the client exhales, since such a minor pattern would be trivial compared to the many others operating. Generally speaking, the therapist should therefore make sure that (1) the client's attention is absorbed, and (2) nonverbal techniques synchronize with some prominent (though not necessarily conscious) behavioral rhythm of the client.

*3. Insufficient pacing or inappropriate leading.* In most practical applications, nonverbal pacing and leading create a gradual, rhythmic, but nonlinear progression toward some desired state (e.g., trance). To reiterate, leading communications should be (1) preceded by, and interspersed with, sufficient pacing, and (2) consistent with the client's present experience, as well as his or her values, beliefs, capabilities, and so forth. In other words, the therapist should not try to get the client to do something he or she is not ready or willing to do. For example, a client may not want to enter trance just yet, in which case the therapist might wait a bit; or perhaps the client finds it difficult to relax, whereupon the therapist might first nonverbally lead toward greater tension and then eventually towards relaxation. In short, the therapist adjusts the pace and behavioral goals of nonverbal pacing and leading to the client's experiential realities.

*Some Clarifying Remarks*

We have thus far sketched how a person's external awareness can be paced and led through verbal and nonverbal communications. Before concluding, several important points should be clarified.

*1. Verbal and nonverbal pacing and leading are usually simultaneously operative.* One common application is the complementing of verbalizations with congruent nonverbal communications. For example, the therapist might verbally describe a gradual progression towards relaxation, while concurrently relaxing nonverbal expressions; or talk about developing a particular emotion (e.g., happiness) while communicating that emotion through emotional voice tone and facial expression; or when, say, seeking hand levitation, deliver suggestions to "lift up" with an upward vocal expression and time them to the client's breath inhalations. When done in a natural (not exaggerated) fashion, this general process of utilizing multiple behavioral channels to access a state can be quite powerful.

Verbal and nonverbal communications can also be combined to pace and lead indirectly. For example, the therapist can distract the client's conscious processes with a seemingly relevant verbal discussion, while simultaneously accessing the unconscious through nonverbal channels. As we will see, this is a common and highly effective strategy for hypnotic communication.

*2. The type of behavioral pacing and leading thus far described— gradual, permissive, and adaptive—is not always appropriate.* Chapter 7 details, for example, how it is sometimes more effective to deliberately interrupt the client's rhythms or to directly challenge his or her position. These "shock" or "confusion" techniques serve to dislodge the person from conscious processes, thereby permitting the development of alternate, more nurturing ways of being. Such techniques are successful because they still pace and lead, *but at a higher level*; that is, they support the desires of the individual to develop more choices in life.

*3. These techniques will be powerfully effective only if applied intelligently and coherently.* The hypnotherapist uses techniques to accomplish therapeutic goals. As repeatedly emphasized, he or she must be flexible and adaptive to do this. However, *this is not to say that all the therapist does is follow the direction of the client*; in fact, the effective hypnotic operator also redirects behavior in systematic ways (e.g., towards trance or therapeutic change). Unfortunately, many practitioners, particularly novices, sometimes forget this and become hopelessly lost in chasing the client through a labyrinth of mental processes. This is quite understandable: the Ericksonian practitioner works in a flexible fashion, never really knowing exactly how processes will lead to the desired state. Consequently, you will occasionally find that, much to your dismay, the client has been leading you in circles.

The therapist can often recognize this by feeling frustrated or confused or by sensing the client as dominating or controlling the interaction. At this point, it is wise to "regroup": take a few moments to orient internally and "center." Once relaxed, you might ask yourself: "What is this person doing again and again? (That is, what invariant patterns is the client fixated in?) How can I join and appreciate these patterns as those that will lead us to the desired state?" Once a sense of appreciating the client's loop has been developed, reorient to the client and begin anew.

It is important that therapists do not become overly upset (e.g., ashamed, angry, confused) upon realizing they have been "lost" in the client's processes, as this will only bog down progress further. Appreciate it as a common occurrence that can be easily transformed when properly acknowledged. In fact, it can often have the extremely beneficial effect of modeling for the client how failure or confusion can be effectively handled and transformed. In any case, it teaches the therapist that behavioral pacing and leading must be used permissively but directively, flexibly yet systematically. If applied without awareness, the processes can limit rather than expand the therapist's choices and effectiveness; if used with awareness, they are magnificent tools for generating an unlimited number of satisfying experiences.

   *4. The content of effective utilization is forever changing.* Pacing and leading are relationship principles; they are prescriptions for cooperating with ongoing patterns. Hence, whether or not a technique constitutes pacing or leading is reflected entirely in the client's response; the technique cannot be defined independently from the relationship. The therapist thus proceeds, in T. S. Eliot's (1963) words, with "hints and guesses, hints followed by guesses" (p. 213). The success of the technique is signaled by the deepening experiential absorption of the client. Then, since the client's experience is changing, the technique must be modified anew. Thus, that which is effective pacing one moment is usually inappropriate soon afterwards. The therapist must continue to modify communications with the changing experience of the client. To know what to do, the therapist remains absorbed with the client; that is, the client's patterns are the therapist's contexts of communication. Again, this bespeaks of the need for an interpersonal trance.


### INFERRING AND UTILIZING INTERNAL PROCESSES

   Because Ericksonian strategies are based on ongoing processes, the practitioner must be able to assess accurately what the client is actually experiencing, especially in terms of (a) level of trance, (b) general emotional state, and (c) any conscious processes interfering with the trance experience. This section explores how this can be done through observation of minimal cues.

### *Minimal Cues*

   To reiterate, *minimal cues* are subtle, usually unnoticed, changes in a person's ongoing behavior. They are products of *ideodynamic processes*, which automatically translate ideas into dynamic expressions.

Thus, when I think about a happy event, I begin to *look* a little happier; when I revivify an anxious experience, my breathing again begins to restrict and my pupils dilate. *Ideodynamic responses usually are intensified in trance states.*

Table 4.1 lists some minimal cues typically important in hypnotic work. To appreciate their value, we might briefly immerse into the delightful world of Sherlock Holmes. In the following passage – a wonderful illustration of the detective's "science of deduction" – Holmes and Dr. Watson have been spending a lazy afternoon reading newspapers in their London flat. Holmes interrupts Watson's daydreaming with a statement implying that he had been "reading" the doctor's train of thought. We pick up here with Watson's incredulous response (in Doyle, 1905):

"Do you mean to say that you read my train of thoughts from my features?"
"Your features, and especially your eyes. Perhaps you cannot yourself recall how your reveries commenced?"
"No, I cannot."
"Then I will tell you. After throwing down your paper, which was the action which drew my attention to you, you sat for half a minute with a vacant expression. Then your eyes fixed themselves upon your newly framed picture of General Gordon, and I saw by the alteration in your face that a train of thought had been started. But it did not lead very far. Your eyes turned across to the unframed portrait of Henry Ward Beecher, which stands upon the top of your books. You then glanced up at the wall, and of course your meaning was obvious. You were thinking that if the portrait were framed it would just cover that bare space and correspond with Gordon's picture over there."
"You have followed me wonderfully!", I exclaimed.
"So far I could hardly have gone astray. But now your thoughts went back to Beecher, and you looked hard across as if you were studying the character in his features. Then your eyes ceased to pucker, but you continued to look across, and your face was thoughtful. You were recalling the incidents of Beecher's career. I was well aware that you could not do this without thinking of the mission which he undertook on behalf of the North at the time of the Civil War, for I remember your expressing your passionate indignation at the way in which he was received by the more turbulent of our people. You felt so strongly about it that I knew you could not think of Beecher without thinking of that also. When a moment later I saw your eyes wander away from the picture, I suspected that your mind had now turned to the Civil War, and

TABLE 4.1
A List of Some Potentially Important Minimal Cues

| Kinesic Cues | Paralinguistic Cues | Linguistic Cues |
|---|---|---|
| 1. *Eyes* (e.g., eye contact/aversion, blink rate, eyelid flutter, pipillary dilation, accessing cues, fixation/tracking movements, tears, "twinkling," eye muscle twitches, wide open/half closed, "hard/soft" gaze) | 1. *Voice tone* (e.g., harsh/soft, nasal/resonant, flat/excited, high/low, whining, shrill/pleasant, "throaty/choked up") | 1. *Predicates* (e.g., visual, auditory, kinesthetic, general, ambiguous) |
| 2. *Cheeks* (e.g., flattening, twitches, tightened jaw, blushing/paling, symmetry/asymmetry of sides of face) | 2. *Speech tempo* (e.g., hesitations, pauses, quickening/slowing, fast/slow) | 2. *Organ language* (e.g., "get off my back," "you're a pain in the neck," "that makes me sick to my stomach") |
| 3. *Lips* (e.g., coloration changes, size changes, pursed lips, slight smile) | 3. *Intonation pattern* (e.g., monotone/variable, rhythmic/arrhythmic, regular/irregular, upwards/downwards) | 3. *Conceptual metaphors* (e.g., "life is war," "time is money") |
| 4. *Forehead* (tense/relaxed, furrowed eyebrows, frown, eyebrow lift) | 4. *Voice volume* (e.g., loud/soft, increasing/decreasing) | |
| 5. *Neck* (e.g., tightening, pulse rate evident, swallowing) | | |

TABLE 4.1 (continued)

6. *Head movements* (e.g., "cocked ear," subtle ideomotoric nods or shakes, obvious volitional nods or shakes, head dropping down to chest during trance, rearing back/leaning forward)

7. *Shoulders* (e.g., tense/relaxed, hunched, raised)

8. *Hands* (e.g., folded, clenched/relaxed, twitching—especially during hand levitation procedures, still/active, nervously fiddling)

9. *General muscle tonus* (e.g., tense/relaxed)

10. *Body posture* (e.g., leaning forward/back, directed towards/away, folded arms of legs, reclining, erect, stretching)

11. *Breathing pattern* (e.g., regular/irregular, from stomach/chest, rapid/slow, interrupted, restricted, "integration sighs")

12. *Lower body* (e.g., tapping foot, crossed legs)

when I observed that your lips set, your eyes sparkled, and your hands clinched, I was positive that you were indeed thinking of the gallantry which was shown by both sides in that desperate struggle. But then, again, your face grew sadder; you shook your head. You were dwelling upon the sadness and horror and useless waste of life. Your hand stole toward your old wound, and a smile quivered upon your lips, which showed me that the ridiculous side of this method of settling international questions had forced itself upon your mind. At this point I agree with you that it was preposterous, and was glad to find that all my deductions had been correct."

"Absolutely!", said I. "And now that you have explained it, I confess that I am as amazed as before."

"It was superficial, my dear Watson, I assure you. I should not have intruded it upon your attention had you not shown some incredulity the other day. But the evening had brought a breeze with it. What do you say to a ramble through London?"

(pp. 423–424)

Rest assured that one needn't possess the extraordinary incisiveness and acumen of Sherlock Holmes to be effective. However, it is wise to observe several points indicated by the passage.

Most important, *reading* of minimal cues requires close observation. Here again we find the need for an externally oriented state. Specifically, the therapist fully orients attention to the client in a relaxed, uncritical, but intent fashion, then looks for subtle but informative *changes* — "differences that make a difference" (Bateson, 1972, p. 272). For example, the therapist might notice that, upon introducing a particular topic, the client manifests restricted breathing, or increased muscle tension, or increased pupillary eye dilation, and so forth.

Many people initially have difficulty in detecting minimal cues. This is due partly to cultural training. The child looking intently at the stranger is repeatedly scolded not to stare; in most situations, the person fully attending to another individual elicits anxiety, even hostility, from that individual. Thus, we generally learn to refrain from looking at another person in any close, intense, or prolonged fashion.

Therapists need to regain this choice. To do so, they might start with some simple observational exercises. A fairly easy one is to restrict observation to only one or two cues (see Table 4.1) in a person's behavior. This might be practiced in social situations where you are not an active participant, thereby enabling all attention to be placed on the cues in question; for example, nearby conversationalists at a party or coffee shop might be discreetly scrutinized.

Generally speaking, a relaxed, externally oriented state will enhance observational abilities. In this regard, conscious processes (e.g., internal dialogue) are usually best set aside. This is sometimes difficult, especially when you worry about whether you'll really be able to detect the minimal cues, or what you'll do if you actually see them. Inevitably, this fear of failing leads to a self-fulfilling prophecy, as it disenables full attention to the minimal cues. To allay such worries, attentional training exercises such as those described in Chapter 3 can be practiced.

As the ability to detect several cues becomes refined, the scope of observation can be expanded. In particular, the task of detecting *configured patterns of cues* might be initiated. To do this effectively, develop an externally oriented trance, then focus your eyes about a foot in front of the person in question.[2] As previously noted, this will enable a more holistic viewing of the person's behavior. Thus, the person's hands may be observed to move in rhythm with speech tempo; facial blushing may accompany tightening in the neck and restricted breathing; a smile may occur with a clenching of the fist. Observing such patterns will be much easier when you do not try to immediately interpret them! Simple description is initially most appropriate; accurate interpretation develops gradually thereafter. It takes time to refine long-dormant observational skills, so exercise plenty of patience during these training processes.

Once observed, minimal cues can then be interpreted. The sensitive practitioner can grow remarkably adept at inferring internal experience from minimal cues. Some inferences are straightforward, such as when a general emotional state (e.g., happiness) is expressed. As Ekman (1972, 1980) has shown, certain facial expressions – such as the "happy smile" – indicate the same emotion in all cultures.

Still, meaning ultimately depends upon context. A cue might mean one thing about one person, another thing about a second person. When this critical point is forgotten, faulty conclusions are likely to be the result. Interestingly, this is sometimes more apt to occur with veteran practitioners than with novices, as the former sometimes grow "cocky" about their abilities.

A rather amusing example of this occurred some years ago when I was leading a professional training group. The topic of the evening was minimal cues, and I was using a volunteer to demonstrate various

---

[2]The optimum focus point is actually a function of the distance between observer and observed. For example, it will be more than a foot in front of the observed if the distance is, say, ten feet; but certainly less if the distance is a foot or so.

points. I asked him to close his eyes, "go inside," and recall a happy memory. As he did, I commented on various minimal cues he began to manifest, such as deeper breathing, a facial flush, and relaxation of cheek muscles. I especially noted the prominent swelling and reddening in his lips. Knowing he was romantically involved with a woman, I assumed on the basis of previous experience that he was recalling an amorous encounter. Thus, I reoriented him back to the room, then dramatically paused before smugly asking, "Would you like to talk about how wonderful that kiss really was?" He looked at me quizzically and stated: "Kiss? What kiss? I was eating a red-hot pepperoni pizza with some friends. It was so hot it burned my lips, but it sure was good!" The chagrin suffered was well worth the lesson learned.

Thus, it is wise to rely upon additional sources of information. The Holmes passage (see p. 000) illustrates how one interpretational aid is the *immediate context*. Each of Holmes' deductions follow from previous ones, as when he interprets Watson's gaze at the wall on the basis of his preceding fixation on the general's picture. A second aid in inference is the therapist's knowledge of the client's history. This is also aptly demonstrated in Holmes' utilization of his knowledge of Watson's mental associations between General Beecher and a Civil War incident.

Even the best inference aids will sometimes lead you astray. Thus, while trusting fully your ability to freely generate hypotheses, you should always doubt their validity before checking them out with the client. This can be done in various ways, depending upon which aspect of the person's experience is being utilized and for what purpose. The remainder of the section explores three aspects central to hypnotic work: (1) level of trance, (2) emotional state, and (3) cognitive strategies.

### Behavioral Indicators of Trance

Since hypnotized persons usually do not move around or talk extensively, level of trance is best monitored through minimal cue observation. The most common trance-indicating cues are listed in Table 4.2. Although people in an internally oriented trance usually exhibit most of these cues, considerable individual differences obtain. One entranced person might look extremely relaxed, while another might seem to be in a "frozen" and suspended-like state. However, a given individual will often display similar patterns of minimal cues across trances. Thus, it is usually not too difficult for the therapist to learn to recognize a particular client's trance level. In addition, the therapist need not rely

TABLE 4.2
Some Common Behavioral Indicators of Trance

1. If eyes open: lessening or loss of blink reflex; eyelid fluttering
eye fixation;
pupilary dilation;
lessening of eye tracking movements;
spontaneous eye closure

2. Lack of physical movement

3. Verbal inhibition

4. Muscular relaxation

5. Breathing changes: from stomach;
slower and more regular rhythm

6. Slowing of pulse rate

7. Slowing of heart rate

8. Smoothing (flattening) of facial muscles (especially in cheeks)

9. Lessening or loss of orienting response (e.g., to noises in room)

10. Changes in facial coloration (either lighter—suggesting more dissociative states—or redder—suggesting more kinesthetic relaxation)

11. Time lag to respond (e.g., in talking or moving)

12. Spontaneous ideomotoric behavior (e.g., finger twitches, hand levitation, eyelid flutter)

exclusively on minimal cues. Other trance assessment techniques include ideomotor signaling and posttrance discussion.

These minimal cues can also be used for the equally important task of recognizing when a person is coming out of trance. For example, the reappearance of behaviors such as swallow responses, eye opening, spontaneous talking, body movements, furrowing of the brow, and orienting responses typically indicates a lightening of trance. The therapist need not be alarmed or disappointed at this common development, but should acknowledge and utilize it. For example, it is often best to discontinue any deep trance work, since the client is no longer in one, and to shift back to induction techniques. This is more thoroughly addressed in Chapters 5 and 6.

## The Client's Emotional Experience

The therapist also needs to monitor the client's general emotional state (stress, relaxation, sadness, etc.), particularly its intensity.[3] This is especially important during trance processes, where much of the work involves accessing and utilizing emotional states. In orienting to emotional states exact details are not always critical: It is often sufficient to recognize the state as being unpleasant, pleasant, or neutral. Unpleasant emotions are often evidenced by interrupted breathing, facial flushes, muscle tension, eye tearing, asymmetry in the right and left sides of the face, and so on; pleasant emotions are frequently accompanied by more relaxed and steady breathing, sighs, smiling, "looks of satisfaction," left/right facial symmetry, flattening of facial muscles, and so forth.

These sorts of cues generally indicate the client's emotional response to a particular topic. For example, one client may look very tense when his wife is mentioned, thereby suggesting the presence of a conflict in the relationship; another client may look serene when a backpacking trip is described, thus indicating a source of pleasure. The therapist can use this information in various ways; he or she may want the client to continue (intensify) or discontinue (detach from) the emotion, depending upon the situation. For illustration, three possibilities can be briefly cited:

*1. The "fishing in the dark" technique.* This is a modified version of a technique of the same name reported by Erickson and Rosen (1954), in which the hypnotherapist, unaware of the hypnotized client's specific unconscious conflict(s), urges the client to "feel it, FEEL IT" until the specific conflict is accessed, whereupon it is therapeutically utilized. The technique resembles the game of "20 questions." Specifically, the therapist seeks to access some state in the client by initially mentioning a series of very general topics, gradually narrowing the topics according to the client's minimal cue responses. This might involve accessing pleasant experiences as a means to induce trance, as in the following example:

---

[3]In this regard Ekman (1965, 1980), on the basis of his research, argues that the head–face area carries information about the *type* of affect (joy, sadness, etc.), while the body cues primarily reflect the *intensity* of that affect.

| *Example* | *Commentary* |
|---|---|
| As you're sitting there, what a nice thing to know that trance is an enjoyable and naturalistic experience, not unlike many you've had before . . . and so your unconscious can draw upon those pleasant memories to develop a trance . . . and I don't know which ones your unconscious will select . . . it's really not important which ones they are. . . . Whether you remember an enjoyable picnic with friends . . . (pause) . . . or the experience of being so deeply lost in lazy dream reveries . . . (pause) . . . or perhaps the memory of happily driving along a country road . . . (pause) . . . or the wonderful feeling of being in love with another person . . . (pause) . . . that's right . . . it's not important which one you continue to develop, because you can learn to appreciate yourself in trance in many different ways. . . . | Here the therapist starts out with a general pacing (external behavior) and leading (internal awareness) statement. This general comment is then compared (i.e., linked) to common enjoyable experiences. This not only frames trance in naturalistic terms, but also seeks to elicit the experience. After each possibility is mentioned, the therapist pauses and looks expectantly (for 3–5 seconds) at the client, thereby encouraging the accessing. It should be noted that this process will only work if the person's attention is fully absorbed. In this particular example, the client exhibited little response to the first several topics, but reacted to the romance generality with blushing, glazed eyes, smile, relaxed musculature, etc. Accordingly, the therapist continued by talking about trance as a process in which one really appreciates oneself. Thus, the client's strongly positive association to romance was utilized as the basis to develop trance. Of course, this may not have been appropriate for another client. Again, the client's world model should always be considered. |

This same simple strategy can be used for the hypnotherapeutically important task of accessing dissociated experiences in the client:

| *Example* | *Commentary* |
|---|---|
| And there's an experience that you've been avoiding for a very long time now . . . trying not to | The therapist again starts out very generally; however, he sounds very congruent and spe- |

think about . . . but that experience has been creating a lot of
trouble for you . . . and it's not
important whether that experience involves your relationship
with your wife . . . (meaningful
pause) . . . or with your children. . . . . . (pause meaningfully)
. . . or with your job at work . . .
(pause meaningfully). . . . What's
more important is that your unconscious has the ability to access, explore, and transform
that experience . . . that's right
. . . and so as you breathe in and
out, you can continue to feel
that experience. . . .

cific. Of course, virtually everyone avoids some kind of experience; thus, the client will
generally have no problem in accessing a particular experience.
In this case, the client exhibited
some muscular twitches and restricted breathing when his
work was mentioned. The topic
was therefore continued, with
the client becoming increasingly
tense. The tenseness was utilized to induce a trance in which
the problem was then therapeutically explored. As it turned
out, he desperately wanted to
quit a job he found tremendously unsatisfying.

This general-to-specific progression constitutes an excellent strategy
for utilizing the client's prominent experiences as the basis for hypnotic
explorations. The therapist mentions possibilities; the client nonverbally
indicates their relevance. I often observed Erickson use sophisticated
versions of this strategy. Interestingly, some people would declare him
"psychic" for apparently being so uncannily accurate at pinpointing the
key experiences in their lives. More likely, Erickson was exercising his
remarkable abilities to (1) speak generally but sound specific and (2)
closely observe minimal cues. We will later return to this "fishing in the
dark" technique in Chapter 6.

*2. Confusion techniques.* A person's conscious processes often interfere with the development of trance or hypnotherapeutic changes. Accordingly, the Ericksonian practitioner often uses confusion techniques
to depotentiate these processes. As Chapter 7 explores in detail, these
confusion techniques all share a similar sequence of steps, each introduced only after certain minimal cues have been observed. Specifically,
an initial step – pacing conscious processes – is finished once the person
looks comfortable and secure. The next step – confusing the processes
through interruption or information overload – is complete when the
person begins to look perplexed or disoriented. The following step –
amplifying the confusion – works to increase the state of uncertainty
and is finished when the person looks absolutely bewildered. The final
step – utilizing the confusion – involves communication designed to re-

duce the unpleasant state of uncertainty by offering an alternative (e.g., trance).

In short, this strategy involves a sequence of communications intended to amplify either a pleasant (the first and last steps) or unpleasant (the middle two steps) emotional state. Thus, at each step the therapist generates communications based on close observation of minimal cues. When a particular communicational context or process elicits the desired emotional response, it is continued; if not, different communications are tried.

*3. Hypnotherapeutic procedures.* To effectively carry out hypnotherapeutic procedures the therapist closely observes and adapts to the client's emotion-indicating minimal cues. Many of these procedures share a general two-step strategy. In the first step – accessing the problem state – hypnotic communications selectively pace and lead (amplify) minimal cues indicative of an unpleasant emotional state as described above. This step is not complete until the client appears absorbed in the unacceptable experiences associated to the problem state. The second step – guiding the client's unconscious to transform the experiences – shifts to communications that encourage and reinforce pleasant emotional states. Very important, this step is over only when the client's minimal cues indicate that an integration has occurred (e.g., a deep sigh, left/right facial symmetry, muscular relaxation).

This important task of recognizing and interpreting emotional cues is not always easy, even in the simplified case of dichotomizing responses into pleasant and unpleasant categories. The cues are sometimes subtle, and thus difficult for even the trained observer to observe. For example, one of the few cues indicating deep stress in one client was an increased pulse rate in his carotid artery. At other times, the cues will be idiosyncratic. For example, one very shy client would generally remain extremely still during trance work; but when she would need to withdraw for a while, her left hand would unconsciously signal by ideomotorically twitching. At still other times, the cues will be ambiguous. For example, rapid and shallow breathing for one client signaled a sense of losing control, which required therapeutic assurances; for a second client, the same signal typically indicated the beginning of an integration process, which needed little hypnotherapeutic guidance.

The Ericksonian practitioner therefore learns the specific patterns of each particular client. Once the abilities to observe closely and to adapt flexibly have been developed, identifying key patterns can be effectively accomplished in different ways. For example, one simple way to test hypotheses about the possible meaning of some minimal cues is to continue with hypnotic communications designed to pace and develop further what is believed to be the client's internal experience. Thus, the entranced person who seems to respond pleasantly upon the mention of, say, the joys of family life can be offered further elaboration on this topic. If he or she remains in rapport and in fact seems to grow happier, the intuitions regarding the emotional state will be generally supported; if he or she responds indifferently or adversely, the inaccuracy of the intuitions should be strongly suspected, and general pacing of the person's process therefore reintroduced. (Keep in mind, however, that with trance subjects there often is time lag between suggestion and response; thus, the hypnotist should wait a little while before concluding a lack of response.) In any case, conclusions can be further checked by posttrance inquiries.

Sometimes, however, the therapist might feel that things cannot wait that long. For example, many practitioners grow anxious when they do not know the content of some intense emotional experience spontaneously developed by the client. Although such information is often not needed and may even distract the therapist, it can occasionally be helpful. In such instances, the client might be asked to briefly *describe* (not evaluate or explain) the experience. If the person is still in trance and in close rapport with the therapist, a hypnotherapeutic procedure to utilize the emotional experience can be promptly introduced. Otherwise, the client can be reoriented from trance and the trance experience discussed, after which other hypnotherapeutic procedures might be introduced.

## Utilizing Representational Systems

People generally do not consciously attend to their entire experience at a point in time. Instead, they select out certain aspects for conscious "representation." For example, you are probably orienting to your visual system in order to read these words. But as I mention it, you may begin to tune into various sounds in the external environment. Or perhaps you may now begin to notice a growing feeling of relaxation or start to wander down a trail of internal dialogue. Absorbed in any of these experiences, you will tend to orient to one modality (visual, auditory, kinesthetic) more than others.

Grinder and Bandler (1975) referred to these conscious modes of processing as *representational systems*. They claimed that most individuals have a *most highly developed* or *most highly preferred* representational system. That is, some people think primarily in visual images;

others rely primarily on auditory imagery (e.g., internal dialogue); still others favor kinesthetic imagery (i.e., feelings).[4] In the present view, people are capable of using any representational system in a given situation (see, e.g., Richardson, 1969). Furthermore, all systems function together as an integrated whole within generative states of experiential unity (e.g., trance). However, conscious strategies tend to differentiate (dissociate) representational systems, such that one becomes focal (figure) as the others recede to peripheral (ground or unconscious) awareness. This differentiation presents no problem if one remains relatively flexible, allowing modality dominance to shift as the situation warrants. This process was noted by Albert Einstein in a letter he wrote to Jacques Hadamard (reported in Ghiselin (1955):

> The words or the language, as they are written or spoken, do not seem to play any role in my mechanism of thought. The physical entities which seem to serve as elements in thought are certain signs and more or less clear images which can be 'voluntarily' reproduced and combined. . . . The above elements are, in my case, of visual and some of muscular type. Conventional words and other signs have to be sought for laboriously only in a secondary stage, when the mentioned associative play is sufficiently established and can be produced at will. (p. 43)

It is the chronic (i.e., invariant) favoring of a modality that stifles creative responses, for successful living requires balanced use of all systems. Thus, not only will the academician who comes to rely heavily on auditory representations while ignoring other systems have difficulty in interpersonal situations (e.g., affective interchanges), but also his or her professional work will likely suffer. Habitual favoring of a single representational system is especially true of psychotherapy clients; in fact, I think it is sometimes one of the major limits responsible for their problems.

Perhaps most important, such inflexibility makes it extremely difficult for a person to communicate effectively with another person using a different representational system. Thus, the therapist wishing to develop rapport with the conscious mind should use a person's currently dominant representational system. This requires development of all of one's representational systems, as well as the ability to identify and adapt to another person's primary system.

---

[4]This is certainly not a novel hypothesis, having been proposed by various psychologists over the past century. For an historical review, see Richardson (1969).

*1. Predicates.* Grinder and Bandler (1975) proposed that a primary representational system is revealed by the type of predicates (verbs, adverbs, adjectives) a person predominantly uses. Specifically, the visualizer will mostly use "visual" predicates (e.g., "see," "focus," "flash"); the auditory will rely more on "auditory" predicates (e.g., "talk it out," "sounds good," "rings true,"); and the kinesthetic will speak with more "feeling" predicates (e.g., "grasp," "heavy," "lighten up"). Grinder and Bandler further suggested that a person's conscious processes could be effectively paced by employing the same type of predicates. The following example briefly illustrates how this might be done with a highly visual person:

*Therapist:* And what are your interests here?
*Client:* Well, you *see*, I guess I should make a few things *clear*. But it's hard. Everything is a little *fuzzy* to me. I just can't seem to *focus* on what *looks* to me like a real *blind spot* in my experience.
*Therapist:* All right, let me *see* if I'm *clear* about what's happening. The *picture* I'm getting from you is that you'd like to *shed a little light* on some *dark* area of your experience, so that things would *brighten up* and *clear up* a bit.
*Client:* Yeah, that's right. You really seem to *see* what I'm saying. That's sure different from the last therapist I saw. I just couldn't seem to *see eye to eye* with him. He seemed *blind* to what was going on with me. All he kept talking about was that I needed to express my feelings about things. I really couldn't relate to what he was saying.
*Therapist:* I think I can *see* what you're saying. Well, now that that's all *cleared* up, let's *focus* on some of the things I think are going to be important here. I think the first thing to do is to develop a general *frame of reference* for *looking* at some of the *cloudy* issues in your life.

Similar pacing techniques can be applied to the other representational systems. However, things will not always be so cut and dry. Sometimes, for instance, the predicates will be ambiguous (e.g., *clear* could be auditory or visual) or general (e.g., *aware, experience, know*). In such cases the therapist might seek clarification by, say, asking: "How specifically are you aware of that? Do you feel it, or see it, or talk about it inside?" At other times, a person's utterances will contain a mixture of different types of predicates. For example:

Whenever I begin to sound myself out on this problem, I try to come to grips with the realities staring me in the face, but then things start to look real fuzzy and I feel real down.

The therapist might pace the pattern:

So when you talk with yourself about getting in touch with how things look, you get weighted down by the lack of clarity.

Or, if this is too difficult, the therapist can speak *generally*

So you become aware that things become very difficult for you when you try to investigate the problem.

Besides these simple examples, representational system predicates can be utilized in many other ways.[5] For example, Grinder and Bandler (1975) describe how pacing and leading techniques can be used to develop an individual's different representational systems. Specifically, individuals are first paced with instructions to imagine a scene (e.g., sitting on a beach) in *only* their primary representation system. They are then gradually led to include other representational systems, starting with the next most developed and ending with the most deficient system.

For example, say a person is highly auditory, can develop kinesthetic imagery fairly well, but is impoverished at visualizing. He or she might be asked first to hear the sounds of being at the beach (e.g., the roar of the pounding surf, the cries of the gulls, the laughter of the children). Once this is successfully accomplished, kinesthetic imagery might be added (e.g., the hot sun against your back and face, the feel of sand between your toes, the cool breeze blowing against your face). If the person has difficulty actualizing these leading suggestions, auditory imagery is reintroduced (i.e., return to pacing); successful actualizations can be utilized by leading into, say, olfactory imagery (e.g., the smells of the salt water, the fresh sea air). After several minutes the person is again asked if he or she is able to develop such imagery. If not, he or she is paced back into the other representational systems for a while; if so, visual imagery can now be introduced (e.g., "As you hear the sounds, and feel those enjoyable feelings, just imagine what those waves look like . . . perhaps the image will be consciously imperceptible at

---

[5]These applications have been clearly discussed by various other members of the Bandler/Grinder group. For example, Grinder and Bandler (1975) present various exercises to sharpen one's skill in detecting predicates; Bandler and Grinder (1979) discuss its general therapeutic applications; Bandler, Grinder, and Satir (1976) apply it to couples therapy; Gordon (1978) applies it to therapeutic metaphors; and Dilts, Grinder, Bandler, Delozier, and Cameron-Bandler, (1979) incorporate it into their system of Neurolinguistic Programming.

# 134 *Therapeutic Trances*

first . . . but with each breath you take, each sound you hear, it can become a bit more clear, a bit more apparent . . . "). By continuing to pace and lead the client's responses in this "two steps forward, one step backward" fashion, the therapist can help gradually develop the deficient representational system.

Representational system predicates can also be used during hypnotic inductions. Chapter 6 describes, for example, how the kinesthetic client might be offered "progressive relaxation" inductions, or the visual client given "guided imagery" processes. Chapter 7 discusses how confusion techniques often involve interrupting or overloading the client's primary representational system, thereby depotentiating trance-inhibiting conscious processes.

*2. Physical distance/breathing/voice tone.* The interdependency of these three minimal cues merits considering them together. Preferred *physical distance* refers to the point at which one person is most comfortable talking to another person.[6] Sitting inside this preferred distance may stimulate anxiety in the person; sitting too far outside it can diminish the experience of "close contact" that enhances hypnotic responses. Preferred physical distance will vary among individuals; the therapist can identify it for a given client by discreetly and casually moving forward while conversing about some innocuous topic. At some point the client will tense slightly (e.g., in body posture and breathing), thereby indicating that the preferred physical distance has been violated. The therapist can then establish the optimum distance by moving back just a bit. As we will see in Chapter 7, it is sometimes appropriate to remain slightly inside the boundary, thereby creating an arousal state in the subject which can be therapeutically utilized.

Much of the variance of this pattern, as well as the other two noted above, can be explained in terms of representational systems.[7] For example, primarily kinesthetic persons will be most sensitive to their bodily feelings, since it is here that the important information resides. They will thus generally breathe from deep in their stomachs and consequently will often appear relaxed, with even muscle tone. Stomach breathing will provide a rhythmic quality to the speech tempo. Finally, kinesthetics will generally want to feel "in touch" with people, and thus will usually have a preferred physical distance of 2–3 feet.

---

[6]This notion of preferred physical distance is a central topic in the field of *proxemics*, the study of perception and use of space. For an overview of the field, see Hall (1968).
[7]Another major variable is culture; different cultures have different preferred physical distances for conversational exchange (e.g., see Hall, 1983).

To the visualizer, however, somatic information is less important; in fact, it is often interfering. For example, visualization processes will often be interrupted by physical movements or by touch. Thus, to reduce such potential interference, the habitual visualizer often remains still and breathes shallowly from the chest. Consequently, the voice tone will sound more "crisp" and choppy, sometimes getting shrill. Because visualizers want to "get a good look at things," they often prefer to communicate from a distance of 3–4 feet.

The auditory person also tends to neglect somatic information. While "thinking" (i.e., engrossed in internal dialogue), the auditory will not move around too much. Being centered in "the head," breathing is often shallow and irregular, and from high in the chest. This will make the voice sound nasal and monotonic. Often preoccupied with language and conceptualizations, the auditory will frequently not be too interested in close interpersonal contact, and thus prefers a seating distance of 3–5 feet.

*3. Accessing cues.* This last pattern is a bit more complex than the others. *Accessing cues* are the eye movement patterns people exhibit when they "stop to think." For example, everyone has observed persons responding to a question by shifting their eyes, say, up and to the left, then mumbling something like, "Hmm. . . . let's see." Day (1964, 1967) was the first of various researchers to propose that the direction of the eye gaze indicates which representational system is being used. Grinder, Delozier, and Bandler (1977) later discussed the therapeutic applications of these behavioral patterns. Specifically, they suggested that the therapist could, by asking a series of particular questions, identify which representational system a person was orienting to by observing accessing cues. Some sample questions are listed in Table 4.3, note that each question presupposes the use of a particular representational system (e.g., color implies visualization).

Before asking each question, the therapist should ensure that the client is in a "cleared out" state — that is, relaxed, looking straight ahead, and unengaged in any particular mode or train of thought. The client can be informed that he or she need not look at the therapist (as this will interfere with spontaneous accessing), that he or she can simply pay attention to *internal* responses, letting happen whatever happens. The question is then asked and the person's eye movements duly observed. After 5–10 seconds, the procedure is repeated with a different question.

The right column of Table 4.3 lists the typical accessing patterns reported by Grinder et al. (1977). These descriptions are from the person's point of view; for example, "up and left" means to the client's left,

TABLE 4.3

Sample Questions to Identify Correlations of Accessing Cues with Representational System

| Accessing Modality | Type of Accessing Questions | Common Accessing Cue (Eye Direction) |
|---|---|---|
| Visual Eidetic ($V_e$) | What color are your mother's eyes?<br>What was I wearing the last time you saw me? | Up and left, or eyes defocused and straight ahead |
| Visual Construction ($V_c$) | Can you imagine your mother with purple hair?<br>Can you see two geometric patterns beginning to move together? | Up and right |
| Auditory Tonal ($A_t$) | Can you remember hearing a few bars of the melody of a favorite song?<br>Can you remember hearing the alphabet song? | Middle left |
| Auditory Digital ($A_d$) | How do you know when you are having internal dialogue?<br>Go inside and have a discussion with yourself about something meaningful. | Middle right |
| Kinesthetics (K) | Can you remember a time you really felt sad?<br>Can you remember the feeling of a cold shower in the morning? | Down and right |

the therapist's right. As they rightfully caution, these patterns are generalizations that will not obtain for every client. However, *a given person will usually manifest similar accessing patterns over time.* Thus, the therapist who determines that a client is, say, accessing feelings while looking down and to the right can rest fairly well assured that it means the same thing when displayed at a later date.

Because accessing cues are displayed so frequently by the open-eyed client, they constitute a valuable informational source to the therapist. They give clue not only to the person's most highly preferred system, but also to the presently dominant system. For example, one client predominantly exhibited "up and left" accessing patterns, which I discovered indicated that she was visualizing (her primary system). However, whenever she had doubts or objections about what I was communicating, her eyes would shift down and to the right; I learned this meant she was engaging in internal dialogue. Thus, the appearance of these latter cues signaled the need for more pacing. Depending upon the situation, this was handled in various ways. It was sometimes more appropriate to ask her directly about any objections she had; at other times, such as when telling a therapeutic metaphor, I would pace more indirectly by (1) using more auditory predicates and (2) metaphorically addressing her general objections within the story itself.

Utilizing accessing cues is not always as straightforward as this. Of particular relevance is that the *initial* accessing cues, evidential of what Grinder et al. (1977) called the *lead system*, do not always indicate the dominant representational system. The lead system is used to retrieve a memory. It is generally very brief in nature (1–2 seconds), frequently operates out of awareness, and often involves a different modality than the primary representational system. For example, I might respond to a question about how I'm getting along with my wife by briefly glancing up and to the left to *visually access* some experience shared with her, then shift down and to the right as I describe in detail my *feelings* for her. Thus, my lead system would be visual, but my primary representational system would be kinesthetic. If someone wished to pace my conscious processes, they should thus disregard the initial (visual) cues, paying attention instead to the more extended secondary (kinesthetic) cues.

However, the lead system is sometimes quite relevant to the therapist interested in how a client repeatedly accesses the same (problem) state. For example, one client, a professional man with excellent credentials, had been unable to obtain work for several years because he would "fall to pieces" at any job interview. In a role-playing situation designed to examine this process, I asked him to enter the room as if arriving for a job interview. When he did so, a remarkable change came over him: he looked up and to the left, his body noticeably slumped, his breathing grew irregular, and his facial muscles began to twitch nervously. When asked what was happening, he could only report a "feeling of horrible failure." I therefore asked him to repeat the process, meanwhile casually positioning myself near the door. As he stepped into the room this time, his eyes again shifting up and to the left, I moved in quickly, gently took hold of his arm, then directed him to "stop, close your eyes, and look very closely at *that there now!*"

As we will see in Chapter 7, this rapid pattern interruption usually creates a state of high hypnotic responsiveness which can be immediately utilized, as in this situation. As he complied with the instructions, the client exhibited shocked surprise, then reported becoming aware of a forgotten scene involving a bitter argument with his last boss. Of special importance was his boss furiously yelling at him, claiming that "you'll never get another job as long as I live!" In the client's state of extreme stress and uncertainty, he uncritically accepted this message as a powerful posthypnotic suggestion, then forgot about it. However, the experience would be unconsciously reactivated whenever he went for a job interview, though he would be consciously aware only of the kinesthetic component. Through hypnotherapeutic age regression strategies he was able to develop alternate response strategies.

As earlier noted, this process of uncritically accepting evaluations or injunctions as naturalistic "posthypnotic suggestions" is not uncommon. It is especially likely to occur when (1) the person is in a state of extreme stress (see Chapter 8), and (2) the "suggestion" is made by an individual accorded importance or authority (e.g., boss, therapist, parent).

This common unconscious process of accessing limiting experiences can also be utilized with a different strategy: rather than bringing the lead system into consciousness, the therapist might interrupt it, thereby disenabling the access of the experience. For example, a student sought to improve her public speaking skills. Investigation disclosed that, upon beginning to speak, she would unconsciously access "down and left," which would activate her mother's voice repetitively telling her "you'll never make it." I arranged for her to talk in a small training group. But as she stood up to make her presentation, I positioned several people next to her. One was to touch her stomach every time her breathing became restricted; another was to whisper "look outside" each time she displayed her chronic accessing cues. Although this interruption of her lead system was initially frustrating to her, she soon learned to speak without accessing. Other techniques for therapeutically using this general strategy of interrupting cues are presented in Chapter 7.

## COOPERATING WITH GENERAL IDIOSYNCRATIC PATTERNS

We have thus far seen how the principles of pacing and leading can be applied to externally oriented awarenesses and to ongoing internal processes. This section overviews how the principles can also be used with the client's more enduring strategies, beliefs, habits, and so forth. These general patterns are often not directly evident from a single behavior, but need to be abstracted from multiple observations. We will consider brief examples of five such patterns: (1) symptoms as trance phenomena, (2) idiosyncratic expressive style, (3) recurrent conceptual metaphors, (4) skills and assets, and (5) the problem pattern.

### Symptom Phenomena as Trance Phenomena

Chapter 2 noted how trances can be self-valuing or self-devaluing and how symptom phenomena are phenomenologically equivalent to hypnotic trance phenomena. In this view, both types of trances are characterized by ideodynamicism and paradoxical (both/and) logic; the major differences are in *context* (e.g., value of intention), biological *rhythm* (symptom trances have arrested rhythms), and *variability* (the content of self-expression generally changes in generative trance but remains invariant in symptomatic trances). Thus, a major cooperation strategy involves creating a self-valuing (interpersonal) context in which clients can synchronize their nonverbal rhythms, then discover how to express the symptom processes hypnotically in many self-valuing ways. That is, symptoms are defined as general hypnotic abilities, then expressed in trance in many new ways.

This utilization strategy process can be described in four steps:

1. Identify autonomous expressions in symptom complex.
2. Relanguage expressions as general abilities.
3. Hypnotically express abilities in multiple ways.
4. Integrate expressions back into symptom complex.

An example of this strategy is presented in Figure 4.2. The first column indicates the general name ("binge eating") that a client used to describe her symptom complex. The second column shows a few autonomous

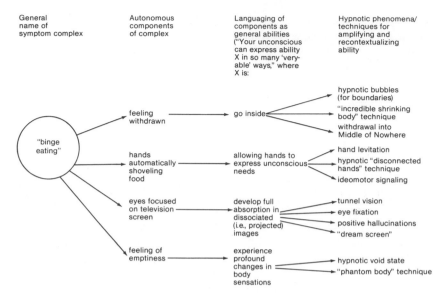

Figure 4.2. An example of identifying, relanguaging, and hypnotically recontextualizing elements of a symptom complex

components (that is, individual elements) of the symptom complex identified by the client as recurrently present. Thus, the experience of an eating binge for this individual included feeling withdrawn, hands shoveling food automatically to mouth, eyes focused on the television screen, and a feeling of emptiness. (This is merely a representative sample of her complex elements; a more elaborate set can and usually should be developed for each client.) The third column shows how these various elements can be languaged in terms of general abilities that each human being needs to have available. The fourth column suggests hypnotic phenomena that embody these general abilities, such that their development can be used to symbolically access, differentiate, and recontextualize the expressions bound within the frame of the symptom complex. Thus, the client is experientially encouraged to "do more" of their symptom complex expressions, but within different contexts (and hence with different values).

This cooperation strategy exemplifies the Ericksonian assumption of hypnosis as a process of communicating meaningful ideas. The symptom complex is seen as a condensed structure containing multiple experiential ideas. This frozen constellation is dysfunctional in that it allows no variation in idea expression; that is, the same structure is actualized time after time, regardless of changing values in the ongoing situation. At the same time, it is seen as a valid attempt at integration. Thus, the hypnotherapist develops trance to *deframe* the condensed ideas and *reunite* a person with biological rhythms, then introduces hypnotic processes to promote new ways of expressing the key ideas. The ideas are thus preserved by amplifying the ways in which they are expressed; no attempt is made to control or limit the client. Rather, clients are encouraged to "do their symptoms better," that is, to learn to express them in many new ways.

## Idiosyncratic Expressive Style

A person's unique identity is expressed in many ways – walking and speaking style, habits, clothing, mannerisms, and so on. The observant therapist can utilize these idiosyncrasies for therapeutic gains.

For example, Erickson (1955) described one patient who rather convincingly insisted that she would commit suicide if things didn't improve after three months of therapy. She complained bitterly about her many defects, the most outstanding being an unsightly space between two upper front teeth. Erickson judged her claims to be grossly exaggerated; although her appearance was indeed disheveled, he observed her to be an attractive and graceful woman. After a month of unsuccessful therapy, Erickson discovered she was attracted to a fellow employee in the office where she worked. She would secretly observe him on his frequent trips to the drinking fountain but ignored the several overtures he made.

With this knowledge in mind, Erickson spent the next month indirectly maneuvering the patient to (1) gradually develop a new wardrobe and hairstyle, and (2) learn to squirt water through her gapped teeth. Utilizing her pessimism, Erickson was able to spend the next several sessions securing her agreement to take "one last fling." Specifically, she was to dress up and have her hair done, go to work, wait near the drinking fountain, fill her mouth with water when the fellow employee approached it, spray him with water, and giggle and "run like hell." She followed the instructions, to which the "victim" responded by running after her and "punishing" her with a kiss. This led to further interchanges: water fights, then romantic dinners, and finally marriage. Needless to say, her therapeutic development proceeded rapidly during this time.

Such utilizations do not always have to involve the client's "defects" and can often be much simpler. For instance, Bartlett (1977) described how she first met Erickson as a student in one of his training seminars:

142   *Therapeutic Trances*

At the end of the day we all filed past the faculty, shaking their hands. As I reached Milton, he smilingly said, "Greetings to a fellow Badger," and I realized that he also had been graduated from the University of Wisconsin Medical School and was thus offering a bond of affinity. His very special gift of perception enabled him to recognize immediately this rather diffident person and simultaneously put her at greater ease for the rest of the seminar. (p. 7)

The person's speaking style might also be utilized. For example, while working with drug-abusing adolescents I assume their unique slang and also their "laid back" style. Of course, this should only be done if the therapist feels comfortable and competent at it; otherwise, a "reverse effect" will typically result.

The pacing of speech style can also be used more confrontively. For example, one woman seeking better interpersonal relationships would often shift to a whining voice that would, to put it mildly, alienate all those around her. To join her patterns, I began to shift into a similar, even more offensive, tone whenever she slipped into it. When she realized what I was doing, she initially became defensive and angry. But by remaining gentle and playful and clarifying my intent with her, she became willing to learn alternate choices. Over several months, her whining gradually lessened. Whenever she would reintroduce it, I would usually respond with more of the same. She would usually graciously accept this as a cue to "recenter" herself.

A final example is that of a client who was overwhelmingly placative in manner. She was continually offering unnecessary and inappropriate apologies. To get the therapeutic "ball of change" rolling, I utilized this pattern by "confiding" my worries that the therapy might fail due to *my* deficiencies. I further "confessed" that this would cause me great humiliation and embarrassment with my peers, then apologized for bringing up the issue. As expected, she became extremely motivated to make the therapy a success. After some initial progress had been made, I shifted my strategy to amplify her apologetic pattern, then to include other, more self-valuing ways of expressing it.

### Recurrent Conceptual Metaphors

The previous discussion of how predicates indicate representational systems was one illustration of how language gives clue to a person's internal experience. A more complex instance of this relationship is the metaphorical concepts used in verbal communications. This topic has been elegantly explored by the psycholinguists Lakoff and Johnson (1980) who observe:

The human conceptual system . . . is fundamentally metaphorical in character. That is, it contains metaphorical as well as nonmetaphorical concepts, and the metaphorical structure is extremely rich and complex. *Metaphorical concepts* are those which are understood and structured not merely on their own terms, but rather in terms of other concepts. This involves conceptualizing *one kind* of object or experience in terms of a *different kind* of object or experience. (p. 195)

The clinically relevant point here is that the particular metaphorical concepts used by a person suggest basic structures governing his or her thinking processes. For example, consider the metaphorical concept INTERACTION IS BATTLE, which would yield the following sort of statements (adapted from Lakoff and Johnson, 1980):

1. I'll beat this guy at his own game.
2. You approach life with a defeatist attitude.
3. He defended himself well against the verbal assault.
4. Everyone's got an Achilles heel.
5. I'll shoot down every one of that guy's claims . . . it'll demolish his battle plan.
6. We've got to attack this thing head on.

To communicate effectively with someone who recurrently uses such related metaphors, the therapist might employ phrases like: "We're interested here in mobilizing your internal resources," "Hypnosis is a process of learning to exercise full command over yourself," "Let's tackle this problem," "You're fighting for your dignity and self-respect here," "It's time you made peace with yourself," or "Win in the game of life."

Another common metaphorical concept is TIME IS A VALUABLE COMMODITY:

1. That decision cost me a year of my life.
2. I can't give you any of my precious time.
3. I spent hours thinking about this.
4. I've got to budget my time better.
5. I've squandered and wasted my time.
6. We had a profitable time together.

Appropriate pacing of the client strongly expressing this concept might include statements like: "Let's look at the high cost of maintaining the problem," "If you spend a little time practicing this, it'll really pay off with some valuable dividends," or "You've invested so much time in this . . . you can't abandon it now."

To identify these general themes, the therapist should be patient and relaxed, yet remain attentive to the person's verbalizations. The metaphor patterns may not always become immediately apparent; thus, it is sometimes useful to mull over a session afterwards, thinking about the various expressions used by the client. A tape recording of the session can certainly help in this task.

It may also be useful to visualize the literal value of client utterances, either during or after the session. These images may be quite bizarre and often humorous, as with the phrases "I'm all tied up," "This burns me up," "I'm up in the air about this whole thing," "It's a dog-eat-dog world," "Get off my back," "I made an ass of myself," and so on. Regardless, they are usually extremely informative about the nature of a person's experience.

*Skills and Assets*

Therapeutic strategies will usually be more effective when they utilize the client's special artistic talents or occupational skills. For example, one client was a successful corporate president who suffered from intense internal conflicts. Part of the therapeutic strategy involved having him, while in trance, imagine himself at a "board meeting" where all the different "parts" of himself were present. He was directed to utilize his position as "chairman" to solve the various disagreements among the "board members." This was done over several sessions and produced favorable results.

Another client, an excellent musician and song writer, was mired in deep depression. At each weekly session, he was assigned the homework of writing a song. On the first few occasions, he was instructed to write only songs that dolefully lamented his sad situation. Subsequent assignments specified that while the first half of the song was to be commiserative, each verse in the second half was to contain "no more than two" possible solutions to the posed problems. Combined with other therapeutic work, this led to meaningful changes.

A similar application was made with a client who was an excellent athlete. Investigation disclosed that he was most confident and secure while "working up a sweat." Thus, he was assigned the homework of jogging every other day in a park near his home, during which time he was to explore his problems through processes I outlined. This worked out so well that he began to jog daily.

Finally, the client's skills can also be utilized during trance inductions. For example, one therapist exercised excellent technique in hypnotizing others, but could not experience trance himself. Discussion revealed that he believed trance to result from the hypnotist "tricking" the subject. He didn't conceptualize this in terms of oppressive domination, but rather as a good-natured battle of the wits. Unfortunately, his familiarity with hypnotic techniques precluded him from ever "losing" as a subject. The mild satisfaction gained from these "victories" was far outweighed by his severe disappointment in not experiencing trance.

Discussions aimed at correcting his misconceptions were only mildly successful; while willing to change his conceptual understanding, he still was not able to allay the internal dialogue that neatly categorized each hypnotic communication. I thus proceeded by telling him that he could self-hypnotically induce himself into a trance with a new "exotic" technique. Specifically, he was to close his eyes and then, as I began the induction, imagine himself giving me minimal cues as to what I should be hypnotically communicating. Thus, instead of me putting him into trance, he would subtly direct me to direct him. Although we both laughed at the obvious "trickery" of the strategy, his intense desire to experience trance enabled him to use the strategy as a means of putting his hypnotically sophisticated conscious processes to good use. In short, he developed an enjoyable trance experience. As Erickson said of such techniques: "I know it sounds ridiculous . . . *but it works!*"

### The Problem Pattern

The client's behavioral symptoms can also be beneficially utilized. For example, Haley (1969) described how Erickson worked with an institutionalized psychotic who had paranoid delusions of being Jesus Christ. Erickson introduced himself to "Christ," complimented him on his reputation as a carpenter, then assigned him construction work at a nearby hospital wing. Only later were other therapeutic techniques introduced.

The client's dysfunctional processes can also be utilized in less spectacular ways. For example, an extremely heavy woman approached me for therapeutic assistance in losing weight. Because correlated with this problem seemed to be many others (e.g., socialization skills, assertiveness, family problems), the weight problem was not directly addressed until several months of intensive therapy had modified some of these other problems. In then exploring her relationship with food, the familiar "binge" pattern was discovered. Specifically, she would try desperately to diet, then find herself launching periodic raids on the local convenience store, which ultimately ended in the feverish consumption of fruit pies, soda pop, candy, and so forth.

As part of the cooperation strategy, the client was induced into light trance and gravely informed she was doing things in a "half-assed" way. Noting that this obviously was not working, I secured her promise to follow my instructions. (This was after rapport had been built over months of therapy; without such rapport, she probably would not have agreed to this or the other instructions described below.) I described in elaborate detail how, two weeks hence, she was going to have to have the biggest binge of her life, involving an "all-time raid" on the convenience store. To prepare for it properly, she was dutifully to walk down to the store three times daily. Each time she was to think only of the delectable goodies that were soon to be hers, *as she walked around the store several times and then on back home.* Her initial response was one of horrified confusion, but a promise was a promise. I told her to return on the day of the binge before it occurred, and then dismissed her.

She complied with the instructions with several slight "failures." But almost nightly she would call me, relating her tremendous fear about the upcoming binge and then desperately pleading that I nullify the agreement, to which I responded with a polite refusal. As she arrived for the scheduled appointment, she was a nervous wreck. I promptly induced a trance and then, after some preliminary comments, told her that I'd decided the choice would be hers: *she could either take the binge or leave it.* Her initial surprise was followed by great relief: *she would leave it.* After emphasizing that *she* had made the decision, she was roused from trance and dismissed.

To explain briefly, the woman really did not consciously believe that she could lose weight but harbored tremendous fears of gaining even more weight. The behavioral instructions absorbed both of these realities, *thereby distracting her conscious mind from realizing that she was developing the new choice of walking down to the store and coming back empty-handed.* The accomplishment of this behavioral reality enabled further therapeutic work to transform other aspects of her dysfunctional eating patterns successfully.

With another client desiring weight loss, a similar cooperation strategy was applied. The client continually "nibbled" at assorted "junk foods" throughout the day. I bought large amounts of such food and placed them in my office. During the next several sessions I would periodically (about every 10 minutes) offer her a cracker, a potato chip, a candy bar, and so on, politely prodding her to "nibble away" freely. This was done in an apparently friendly and casual fashion, but in a way that invariably interrupted our discussion.

The purpose of this strategy was to experientially access her uncon-

scious habit within our interpersonal context. It certainly was successful in this sense. Over maybe 20 food offerings, she initially became
embarrassed (to which I apologized, feigning ignorance of what was
happening), then angry (to which I responded similarly), then confused
and uncertain, at which point a trance was induced and hypnotherapeutic procedures involving age regression introduced to reorganize the
accessed structures.

In closing, it should be noted that the descriptions of these few cases
are selective. They are intended merely to provide a general sense of how
the therapist can cooperate to transform problems into solutions. As
later chapters will make clear, these utilizations alone rarely constitute
a complete therapy. For example, it is often necessary to spend at least
several sessions securing the client's trust; also, the changes initiated
by such strategies frequently need to be consolidated via other therapeutic procedures.

## SUMMARY

This chapter detailed ways to apply cooperation principles in the hypnotic context. The simplest cases of verbal and nonverbal pacing and
leading, involving utilization of externally directed awareness (e.g., environmental stimuli, physical behavior) were first outlined. Observing
minimal cues to infer and utilize internal experience (e.g., level of trance,
emotional state, conscious modes of thought) was next discussed. Finally, the value of utilizing general idiosyncratic patterns (e.g., symptom
phenomena, expressive style, conceptual metaphors, skills and assets,
and problem patterns) was noted. These general applications form the
basis for the Ericksonian practitioner's strategies and techniques. The
rest of the book investigates how they are used in preparing for trance
(Chapter 5) and inducing and utilizing trance (Chapters 6–8).

# CHAPTER 5

# *Creating a Context for Therapeutic Trance*

Like therapy, a hypnotic induction is designed to stimulate some meaningful changes in a person's experiential realities. In the Ericksonian approach, this involves utilizing the present realities of the client as the basis for all such changes. Thus, the Ericksonian practitioner sets out to identify the idiosyncratic values and patterns peculiar to the client system, then works to preserve these basic values while expanding the range and flexibility of their expression. This chapter overviews how this cooperation principle can be applied in the initial phase of preparing for therapeutic trance. The first section identifies questions that can be used in developing a model of how a client creates his or her world of experience, and suggests ways in which this gathered information can be utilized for a variety of hypnotherapeutic purposes, including attentional absorption, motivation enhancement, hypnotic induction, developing trance phenomena, and presenting therapeutic ideas. The second section explores how trance may be introduced into the therapeutic context.

### ASKING QUESTIONS: CONSTRUCTING A MODEL

To appreciate how a client generates his or her experience, the therapist usually introduces at the outset, along with other diagnostic techniques, a set of questions. These diagnostic questions are never neutral or "objective": they are guided by, and subsequently reflect, the underlying views of therapy held by the therapist (cf. Haley, 1976). Among other functions, such questions serve to mark out basic distinctions around which the therapeutic exploration is organized. That is, they operate as indirect suggestions, orienting and structuring the attention of both therapist and client around certain ideas and frames.

148

A rather striking example of this phenomenon occurred at a major conference on psychotherapy. One meeting involved a supervision panel consisting of four therapists, each from a different therapeutic orientation. When an audience member presented a case description for each therapist to comment upon, the questions and ideas suggested by each member differed remarkably. The behavior therapist asked questions designed to develop a desensitization hierarchy, the psychodynamic therapist inquired about past events, the family therapist suggested investigation of family relations, and so forth. Starkly plain was how the different questions asked by each therapist were instrumental in developing different "reality" representations.

Given that the reality perceived is generated in part by the questions asked, the therapist should be clear about the premises guiding his or her questions. In the Ericksonian approach, one such premise is that orienting more to the future than the past generally provides greater opportunity for therapeutic change. Thus, questions will tend to direct clients towards exploring how resources or potentials will be applied to further development of the self-system.

A second premise is that solutions are contained within problems; that is, what a person is presently doing is the basis for transformational changes. To best implement this idea, the language used to describe the present (problems) should be the same as that used to describe the future (solutions). Traditionally, this has not been the case: clinical language typically employs pejorative (i.e., denoting social undesirability) diagnostic terms in representing a problem, such that a startling discontinuity exists between the present ("bad") state and the future ("good") desired state. In the present view, using different languages for the problem and solution states makes it difficult to apply the key principle of utilization in appreciating how solutions are contained in the problem. Consequently, the Ericksonian therapist strives for neutrality in problem representation, such that the pattern description could be desirable or undesirable (i.e., a solution or a problem), depending on the quality and context of its expression. For example, the process of expressing anger is neither "good" nor "bad"; its value depends on how and when it is expressed.

A related premise is that *hypnosis is an excellent model for describing the construction of an experiential reality.* As we saw in Chapter 2, the language of hypnosis can be used to describe both the development of a hypnotic trance and the development of a symptomatic problem state. In this view, an orientation to a problematic process is an orientation to a naturalistic "hypnotic induction" already in effect, i.e., to an interactional sequence of experientially absorbing ideas (behaviors, cognitions, affects, etc.) that has the effect of inducing ("leading in" to) an altered state of consciousness characterized by trancelike characteristics (cf. Ritterman, 1983). As we will see, this allows the hypnotic induction and other therapeutic communications to be fashioned directly from the "problem induction" employed by the client.

Thus, the general question pondered by the Ericksonian hypnotherapist is:

   1a. How does the client construct experience such that stability is
       achieved?

This question seeks to identify the fixed values and strategies a person uses again and again in his or her experience. The answers lead to contemplation of the complementary question:

   1b. How can the fixed values of the present be used to generate new
       ways of being?

For therapeutic purposes, alternative phrasings of this central question include:

   2a. How does the client induce self-devaluing trance states in him/
       herself?
   2b. How can we use those same patterns as the means to create self-
       valuing trance states?

   3a. How does the problem remain the problem?
   3b. How can the ways that the client maintains the problem be used
       to generate solutions?

To investigate these general queries, it is assumed that people organize their experience within an associational network of values. This complex organizational system contains distinctions ("ideas" about relationships) from a variety of different areas of a person's life. The Ericksonian therapist utilizes a variety of different areas of this network, including the following:

   1. Social identity
   2. Intention
   3. Problem induction sequence
   4. Symptom complex

5. Invariant role players
6. Beliefs
7. Skills and resources

The remainder of this section explores how to identify the fixed values operating in each of these areas, and suggests ways to vary these values to enable more flexible and context-sensitive self-expression.

*Social Identity*

A person's sense of identity develops and is maintained via relationships within social communities. Thus, therapeutic communications should be sensitive to the various values characterizing a client's social identity. To ascertain these values, questions can be directly asked regarding:

1. Family system
2. Childhood home(s)
3. Age
4. Marital status
5. Education
6. Occupation
7. Friendship networks
8. Religious orientation
9. Ethnic class
10. Previous therapy

To save time and allow preparation, I often ask clients prior to the first session to send me a letter containing written information about these categories, along with any other information they find relevant. These responses can be elaborated and clarified during subsequent sessions with the person.

A major value of such information is in providing a sense of how a person views the world and their position in it. This constitutes a starting point for therapy, and is a major basis by which the hypnotherapist decides how trance is to be presented and developed, how motivation is developed, what stories are told, the degree to which indirect communication is used, and so forth. In short, the therapist works to convey to the client the following message:

I'm hearing from you that you have a variety of different values which make you unique. (These values might be mentioned.) I'm also hearing that you would like to express yourself in some new ways, without being rigidly constrained by certain understandings about these values. And so I'm not going to ask you to give up any of those values. In fact, I think it is important that you hold onto those values as we explore how you can develop in a "very-able" way those styles and ways of being that express those values according to the present needs and challenges of the self.

Thus, the values are respected as the stability allowing for change. For example, a Filipino-American woman, born and raised in the Philippines, was referred to me for hypnotherapy. The presenting problem was that she was experiencing recurrent states of paralysis and anxiety while her husband was away on business trips. Her social identity suggested that a "chaperone" be present during intense hypnotic work; thus, a female Asian therapist was enlisted as a co-therapist for such work.

With another client, a man whose social patterns included a repeated quitting of jobs, it was anticipated that the same identity pattern might be actualized in therapy, i.e., he might quit when progress began to occur. To absorb this pattern, I explained to him that his therapy would be intense, requiring a great deal of individual initiative in terms of withdrawing and exploring his "real needs" at key points during the therapy. When he insisted he was ready, I emphasized that this "individuation therapy" would require him to be an "equal partner" in "employing" a sense of judgment in selecting certain times for him to fully consider ending the therapy and beginning anew. Specifically, I would select two times each week, as would he, to withdraw and "experientially consider" (via self-hypnosis strategies I taught him) how he could really "let go fully and securely" and explore his real needs at that time. In short, his social strategy of "exiting" was incorporated as a hypnotic process within the therapy. Such strategies are straightforward ways of respecting and absorbing the symbolic means by which a client maintains an identity in the world.

In closing, it should be emphasized that in identifying and utilizing social values, the therapist should not be shackled by them. While social values are utilized as a major means to absorb and work with client patterns, they should not be confused as "being" the client. The Ericksonian therapist recognizes the client as a person whose potential extends far beyond social constraints. By fully connecting with the social values with which a person identifies, experiential processes can be developed wherein an appreciation of a deeper sense of Self emerges. Thus, supporting a pattern while connecting with the deeper essence of the person allows the person to expand that pattern.

*Intention*

The present view assumes that meaningful action flows from coherent intention. That is, intention ("holding in" consciousness) is a central means by which an idea—a basic premise, primary distinction or injunction, organizing theme or principle, motivation, etc.—translates into experience via actions, perceptions, cognitions, emotions, and so forth. In hypnotic terms, intentions are the "simple ideas" (Erickson, 1952) that operate (usually implicitly) as "hypnotic suggestions" to initiate ideodynamic (i.e., unconscious) expression. Like all artifacts (tools), an intention can generate new ways of being as well as maintain old ways, depending on how it is used. It is therefore important that the therapist be clear, at least in his or her own mind, about the intentions of the client (and subsequently of the therapist) in the therapeutic endeavor. To accomplish this, the therapist pursues the general question:

*What new choices in your relationships would you like to develop?*

In exploring this inquiry, the therapist soon discovers that intentions can be represented and expressed in many ways. For example, they can be positive or negative, describing what a person wants or doesn't want. Many clients emphasize what they don't want—"I don't want to feel this way anymore," "I don't want to worry so much," and so forth. Such negative intentions may work temporarily to inhibit some undesirable pattern, but are generally insufficient for generating new patterns. In other words, positive intention reflects the primary processes of generative expression, while negative intention signals the secondary process of conscious regulation (i.e., inhibition or constraint). Although both are thus essential, positive intention is especially important when new expressions are the chief concern. Thus, the therapist works to recognize negative intention as well as to identify positive intention: "I want to be able to feel in a variety of different ways," "I want to communicate with my husband and maintain a feeling of comfort," and so forth.

Intentions can also be represented either in constructive or destructive terms. Constructive intentions involve generating some new state of being which allows potentials to be actualized; they involve the "growing" of new expressions and experiences. Examples are:

1. I would like to develop new ways of experiencing sexual interest.
2. I want to respond to my father in ways that are satisfying for me.
3. I want to experience autonomy in my life.

Destructive intentions have to do with obliterating, dissociating, or otherwise denying identification with certain aspects of one's experience. For example:

1. I want to get rid of my mother's voice always talking inside of me.
2. I want to blast away any doubts I have.
3. I want to forget about my past completely.

In problem states, intentions are often represented in destructive terms, i.e., in terms of reducing the set of available self-expressions by excluding unpopular members. Since any recurrent experience has become part of the self-identity (especially when denied), such efforts are indeed ultimately self-destructive. For solution states, the hypnotherapist thus works to include constructive representations of intention such that a therapeutic goal is to expand the range of available self-expressions.

It might be further noted that destructive intention is past-oriented; that is, by prescribing getting rid of experiential processes that occurred in the past and still linger on, it primarily orients to the person's past. On the other hand, constructive intention focuses on the future, i.e., on realizing the unactualized potentials of the present by doing something new.

Finally, intentions also vary in terms of how much they are tied to specific frames. Intentions are general suggestions or injunctions to satisfy some condition or premise identified with the self; frames and strategies are the interactional structures designed to realize them. While thus distinct, intentions often get condensed (i.e., confused or merged) with frames, such that certain images, plans, actions, and so on become rigidly associated with an intention. A person may thus believe that, say, being heard requires shouting other people down. This invariant binding of intention (e.g., being heard) to frame (shouting at other people) tends to create problems, since the changing field of experience requires sensitivity and variability in frame usage; otherwise, intentions go unactualized and problems crop up as a person attempts to apply "more of the same" frame (cf. Watzlawick, Weakland, & Fisch, 1974). In the present approach, this problematic state of affairs is transformed by first formulating intention independent of images and other frame elements. For example,

1. I want to be able to experience sensations in a comfortable and secure way.
2. I want to have choices about how I interact with doctors.
3. I want to relate to food in different ways.

Represented at this abstract a level, an intention does not specify how experience is to be structured. Trance inductions are then used to further "deframe" a client's attentional field, so that his or her creative unconscious processes can be invited to restructure frames according to the present needs of the self.

To summarize thus far, the Ericksonian hypnotherapist works to develop intention in positive, constructive, future-oriented, and deframed terms. This is not to say that negative, destructive, past-oriented, or frame-bound descriptions are attacked or actively discouraged, for to do so would be to reinforce exactly those distinctions. Rather, each pair of descriptions is seen as a complementarity: postive/negative, constructive/destructive, past/future, frame–constant/frame–variable. As in any complementarity, one side is marked as primary when action (i.e., distinction) is to occur (cf. Varela, 1979).[1] In problem states, the markings are usually fixed in the following way:

*Intention often represented in problem context as*:

NEGATIVE/positive
DESTRUCTIVE/constructive
FUTURE-ORIENTED/past-oriented
FRAME-INVARIANT/frame-variable

The therapist accepts and paces these markings while working (leading) to markings more conducive to new ways of being:

*Intention represented in solution context as*:

POSITIVE/negative
CONSTRUCTIVE/destructive
PAST-ORIENTED/future-oriented
FRAME-VARIABLE/frame-invariant

Thus, the therapist works to fill out each complementarity, then moves (at a rate appropriate to the client) to emphasize the solution-oriented sides of each pair. Within this new context, the old representations take on new values.

---

[1] A perhaps simpler example of this is the "inhaling/exhaling" complementarity dynamic underlying "breathing." Although both are essential, one is marked (i.e., emphasized) at one point in time, then the other becomes dominant. The proposal here is that problems occur when one side of the complementarity is always emphasized. This sets up an imbalance which the unconscious will attempt to rectify by introducing the other (deemphasized) part in a dissociated way.

As a final note, it should be acknowledged that some clients are unwilling or unable to identify their exact intentions. Therapists can respond in such cases in a variety of ways. One excellent method is to identify the person's intention as "wanting to identify my intention," then using trance as a process for experiential exploration and identification of the intention. Thus, the unconscious is designated as the agent for discovering and revealing the needs of the self.

Another method is to simply identify the experiential outcomes of the client's recurrent problem pattern as intentions. For example, a client reported that he wanted to "get rid of" his anger because it was "destructive." When asked to identify the intention in positive terms, he reported being unable to do so. I thus asked him to elaborate on some of the experiential effects of his angry outbursts. These outcomes included:

1. Relief and relaxation (after the outburst)
2. A sense of distance between him and his wife
3. A sense of identity with his father
4. An altered state of consciousness where things "just happened"

As is commonly the case, inquiry disclosed that these outcomes were not achieved in other experiential contexts. Thus, each outcome was identified as a frame-variable intention to be expressed in multiple ways during hypnotherapeutic exploration.

Intentions can be clarified in other ways as well. I have sent some clients home with instructions to return when they develop some sense of awareness of their intention in the therapeutic endeavor. With other clients, I have left them sitting in my office for 15–30 minutes, giving them an opportunity to clarify their interests. Whatever the method used, a major goal of the hypnotherapist, especially in the initial stages, is to stimulate clients toward thinking about how they would like to further develop as achieving human beings.

*Problem Induction Sequence*

To reiterate, the presenting problem can be thought of as a rigid interactional sequence with predictable outcomes (cf. Haley, 1976). A major characteristic of this "induction loop," which tends to operate in both the interpersonal and/or intrapersonal domains, is that it repeats itself. Thus, the therapist can determine induction sequences by seeking descriptions of patterns that tend to happen again and again in the client's experience. The general question to pursue is:

*At those times when you experience the problem, what is the exact sequence of processes that you go through?*

Figure 5.1 shows induction sequences obtained in three different cases. Again, each of these loops can be appreciated as a hypnotic induction ("leading in") sequence that has the effect of creating a trancelike state (i.e., the symptom). More specifically, trance usually develops when an automatized sequence moves into a reiterative "oppositional" loop, such as in the first example where the woman finds herself bound in the "worry/don't worry" cycle. With each spin of the "vicious cycle," the (usually self-devaluing) trance can be observed to deepen, such that expressions become increasingly nonvolitional and paradoxical in nature. During this time, many additional trance characteristics discussed in Chapter 2 (perceptual alterations, time distortion, nonrational logics, and so on) develop rather rapidly. As the examples in Figure 5.1 suggest, this trance-induction cycle often culminates in the emergence of self-devaluing trance phenomena: feeling very small and then leaving home, hallucinatory voices along with frozen fear, depression, and so

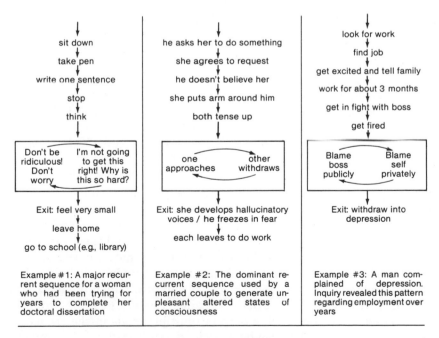

Figure 5.1. Examples of problem inductions

on. Such symptoms can thus be seen as attempted solutions for double-binding loops (Gilligan, 1985).

By recognizing where in the sequence the looping between opposites begins to reiterate, the therapist identifies key points where self-devaluing trances develop. This knowledge can be used as the basis for hypnotic induction and therapeutic change. For example, an initial session with the client claiming writer's block (Example #1 in the figure) included suggestions for her to (1) sit down, (2) take hold of a pen, pencil, and notepad supplied to her, (3) focus intensely on the sensations in her hand and her orientation to the paper, (4) develop automatic writing of only a single letter when she was ready, (5) stop (after she completed a letter), (6) develop a dissociated state of being in the "middle of nowhere" with just my voice and a growing sense of security, (7) feel small yet secure, and (8) find a psychological "home" where she could be "right" (write) "with and for herself and her present needs." Thus, the very sequence used to induce a self-devaluing process of "going away" (accompanied by hapless feelings of pity and disgust) was used to promote a therapeutic trance involving "going away" to a secure context where meaningful changes could be developed. By using the problem structure as the basis for hypnotherapeutic induction, the therapist ensures that the resulting trance will be relevant to the problem. The therapist's concern during this time is improving the quality of the client's experience within this structure; to achieve this, biological rapport, psychological security, and other processes covered in subsequent chapters are of the utmost importance.

In determining induction sequences, a number of further points are relevant. First, the therapist can orient to loops at different levels of abstractness. Although the examples in Figure 5.1 are somewhat sketchily drawn, more concrete and detailed descriptions are often useful for purposes of hypnotherapeutic induction. For example, more detailed associations for the dissertation writer included stopping (the writing), feeling tight, pulling elbows in, jaw tightening, and back hunching. Each of these more minute cues constituted both a signal to the therapist to note when the pattern was being accessed during hypnotic work, and a possible hypnotic suggestion useful in accessing and then restructuring the symptomatic pattern. For example, one sequence of suggestions repetitively interspersed during the hypnotic state included directives to stop, feel tension develop in the chest and jaw, hunch the back, and then drop deeper into a security-accessing trance. Thus, the sequence was accessed and then redirected via multiple trials in the trance.

Second, a problem loop can be described in terms of multiple modalities of experience—behaviors, cognitions, emotions, sensations, images, perceptions, and so on (see Gilligan, 1985). It is assumed that while *something* is happening in each of these modalities, a person is often oriented to only some of them. By "fleshing out" a description in multiple modalities, the therapist identifies a rich set of possible areas to hypnotically orient attention. For example, inductional communications might shift from motoric expressions to sensations to perceptions to images, and so forth. Shifting attention across modalities in this way is a means of deframing and restructuring attention, which is the essence of effective hypnotic communication.

Third, a person will tend to have more than one invariant behavioral sequence. However, it is often most effective for the therapist to work with a single dominant sequence at a time, shifting to others as flexibility is gained in the current one.

Fourth, the therapist may use a variety of methods to determine an induction sequence. One technique I use frequently is having the client(s) "pantomime" out the problem sequence. That is, I'll ask them to nonverbally demonstrate, without any words (but perhaps including sounds), the sequence they tend to circulate through again and again. This method cuts through the verbal descriptions that sometimes make it difficult to discern exactly what is going on that needs to be made more flexible. Also, experimentation will reveal that varying the nonverbal way this pattern is expressed (e.g., the timing of shifts, speed of execution, grace of movement) can enhance the quality of its expression.

For example, I will sometimes use light trance to slow down an induction loop and intensify involvement in it. Thus, a binge eater may be asked to repetitively pantomime out the process of lifting hands to mouth; after a while, hypnotic suggestions may be used to slow the pattern down and ask the person to detach partially from it, whereupon the hypnotist can add further suggestions to modify the images, cognitions, and other experiential processes associated to the sequence. Thus, the sequence is first paced to develop hypnotic absorption in it, then modified to develop a new relationship to it.

Finally, even if an interactional sequence is not used as the therapeutic unit of focus for hypnotic communications, it can be used for related purposes. For example, the therapist's knowledge of a self-devaluation sequence will allow intervention at its initiation. One client, for example, began a sequence of deep withdrawal and self-beratement by an intense frown, followed by eye glazing, shoulder tightening, and turned-in shoulders. To shift the quality of this sequence, the therapist gently but firmly called the client's name each time the frown began to develop. After further interpersonal connections were developed via hand holding and instructing the client to keep his eyes open, the therapist proceeded to acknowledge the need for withdrawal, while elaborating how this could be done with comfort and while remaining in an interpersonal field.

A related application derives from appreciating that opposition of some sort is present in every interactional sequence. In a repetitive sequence, the fixed oppositional elements signal "splits" (i.e., dissociated states) within the constructed reality of the client. While the relationship between these polarities can be changed by hypnotically enacting the entire induction sequence, other hypnotic methods may also be used to stimulate therapeutic change (see Gilligan, 1985).

*Symptom Complex*

For some hypnotherapeutic applications, problems are best thought of as fixed induction sequences; for others, it is more useful to consider them as symptom complexes, i.e., as associational networks with fixed (i.e., context-insensitive) relationships. A major difference between induction loops and symptom complexes is that the former features the lineal concepts of time and sequence. Because these concepts play a less prominent role as trance deepens (and a more fluid, non-sequential state obtains), sequences may be a better language when lighter trances are used.

To determine a symptom complex, the hypnotherapist asks the general question:

> *When you experience the problem, what are all the behaviors, images, sensations, cognitions, emotions, perceptions, and other associations that tend to be expressed?*

Figure 5.2 illustrates one symptom complex developed via this general question; this complex was derived from a woman seeking relief from pain in her breast area following a mastectomy. She was asked in a light trance to simply report the different images, sensations, cognitions, and so on that came to mind when she thought about her removed breast. As the figure shows, a variety of idiosyncratic distinctions were thus identified to be accessed *as an undifferentiated family of associations* whenever she contemplated her relationship with the removed breast. Needless to say, trying to deal with this complex of emotional values all at once proved too formidable a task for her, and thus she sought therapeutic assistance.

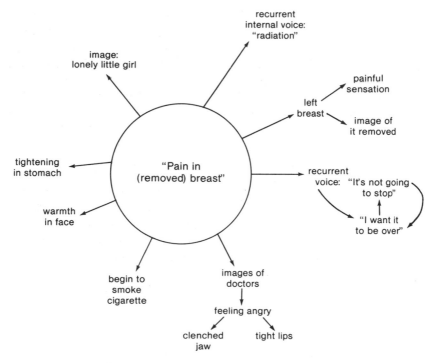

Figure 5.2. An example of a symptom complex

Thus, each distinction in a symptom complex is like an individual in a dysfunctional family system: it has become bound in an unchanging network of relationships, such that no differentiation (i.e., individuation) of identity can occur. That is, a symptom complex is like an "undifferentiated blob," where all the distinctions are condensed (or collapsed) into a larger unit. (This concept is akin to Bowen's "undifferentiated group ego mass.") Activation of any of the complex cues accesses the entire complex in a predictable way, and problems consequently result. Thus arises a major task of the hypnotherapist: to reorganize and make more flexible the relationship among cues in the client's associational network of ideas, such that the frames (i.e., complexes) formed in a situation are responsive to the shifting environmental cues of that situation.

For this task, trance has therapeutic value in several major ways. First, it unbinds the attachment of the self to its expressions; that is, a person in trance can feel "a part of yet apart from" ongoing phenomenological experience, such that observation without interference is possible. Second, trance loosens the connections between associational elements of a frame, such that an individual element can be experienced within multiple associational frames. For example, one segment of the hypnotherapeutic work accomplished with the above client involved multiple associations to the key cue word of "radiation": different stories, images, and fantasies interspersed among other hypnotic communications emphasized all the different relationships the self could develop to "radiation" (e.g., of the sun, of sensations in the fingertips, of a baby's face). In this way and others, defining the members of a symptom complex can lead to their "deframing" (i.e., differentiation) via hypnotic processes; when this happens, new relationships can begin to develop.

In developing a symptom complex representation, the therapist should first ensure that the client is experientially absorbed enough to allow associations to autonomously surface. The therapist can then gently guide the process by continuing to reiterate the general question, "What else do you become aware of in the modality of (images, cognitions, etc.) when you think about the problem?" Some clients will "draw blanks" for certain modalities, thus indicating possible areas of dissociation. In such instances, further experiential absorption may be useful in eliciting the material, though such deeper trance work is usually best done only after rapport and mutual experience with trance has been accomplished.

*Invariant Role Players*

As an interactional sequence, the problem induction necessarily involves two or more players enacting opposing roles. These actors may be present interpersonally (as real people) or intrapersonally (as imaginal figures). Since therapeutic communications are designed to improve the relationship of these complementary players, it is important for the hypnotherapist to know:

1. *Who is physically present again and again when the problem occurs?*
2. *Who is imaginally present again and again when the problem occurs?*

The information gained from these questions reveals who needs to be included and paced in hypnotic communications. For example, a woman seeking relief from "anxiety attacks" disclosed that her husband was usually around when she experienced them. As Panel A of Figure 5.3 illustrates, "woman plus husband" was identified as the structural coupling (i.e., the relationship unit) to be addressed. Since the husband was physically present when the problem occurred, the therapist requested

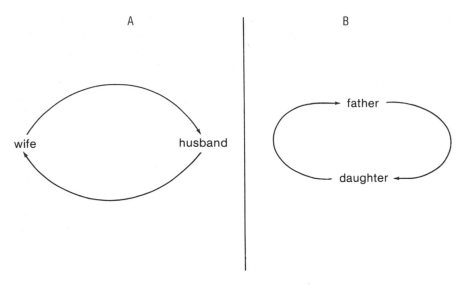

Figure 5.3. Structural couplings: Complementarities as relationship units

that he also be physically present for the treatment process. When he initially balked at directly participating in hypnotic experiences, the husband was instructed to watch closely and "relate according to his own needs" as hypnotic work was directly accomplished with his wife. By offering indirect suggestions to him along with direct suggestions given to the wife, a meaningful trance was developed in both participants. As is commonly the case when such a method is used, the husband asked a few sessions later to be directly included in the hypnotic work.

With another client—the woman seeking to complete her dissertation (see p. 157)—it was discovered that images of her father lecturing her were invariant in the symptom complex. As panel B of Figure 5.3 shows, "daughter with father" was identified as a major relationship unit to be hypnotically addressed. Because this relationship transpired (at the time of treatment) mostly in the woman's imaginal processes, it was decided that effective changes could develop by seeing her alone.[2]

---

[2]I have generally found it essential to work with all interactional players when they are actively involved in dependent relationships—e.g., with teenagers living at home, spouses living together. The hypnotherapeutic treatment of families is discussed by Ritterman (1983) and Lankton and Lankton (1986), and of couples by Gilligan (in preparation).

A major idea here is that invariant relationship sequences are memorized information patterns held by each individual. That is, they are fixed instructions for interacting in certain relationships in predetermined ways. Although a person may be explicitly identified with only one side of the pattern, his or her behavior is governed by the dynamic underlying both sides; thus, both sides must be actively addressed by the hypnotic communications. This can be done by having both (or all) sides actually present, or by hypnotically absorbing a person with both sides. In either case, therapeutic trance can play a major role. As we saw in Chapter 2, entranced individuals can develop experiential states in which they are "a part of, yet apart from" a relationship. This enables a person to shift points of view, and even hold contradictory points of view simultaneously. Furthermore, therapeutic trance reconnects the figure (i.e., psychological structures) with its field (i.e., biological context); *this seems to be a necessary condition for lasting change.*[3] Shifting a person from a rigid attachment to psychological structures to a secure absorption in biological context enables transformational changes to occur in the symbolic structures.

To facilitate these changes, the hypnotherapist should be aware of the identities of each side of the conflict, what their pattern and content of their communication content is, how each side would respond to a given hypnotic idea, and so on. In then offering hypnotic ideas, the therapist keeps in mind that he or she is speaking to at least two complementary "parts" of the person simultaneously. Methods for pacing and leading this relationship dynamic are numerous. One way is symbolic stories: the hypnotherapist offers anecdotes featuring interactions between characters that are analogous to the problem dynamic of the client (see Chapter 6). Another method is for the therapist to congruently enact one part of the dynamic, such that the client takes up the other. As we will see in Chapter 7, this may involve, say, playing the role of pessimist better than the depressed client, so that the latter begins to protest and thereby shifts into the complementary role ("things aren't

---

[3]Regarding reconnecting figure (structure, symptom, or identified patient) to field (context or family) as a necessary condition for change, it is interesting to note that family therapy and Ericksonian hypnotherapy pursue the same goal in different ways. Although both are interested in the *context* in which a symptom occurs, family therapy tends to orient to the social context (family), while hypnotic therapy often focuses on the organismic context. In the present view, the psychological field of the family is a unified *system* as is the biological field of the organism; either can give rise to generative change. Consequently, it may be best to attend equally to biological and psychological contexts in working to transform a system.

that bad"). By then shifting to the opposite role, the therapist begins to guide the client through a series of role reversals leading to an experiential valuation of both sides of the dynamic; this enables a systemic integration via trance to then occur (see Chapter 7). Another method involves shuttling a person in trance through an experiential identification of the characters involved in the dynamic, then suggesting that he or she let go and "let the unconscious develop an integrating and mutually supporting relationship between the two parts."

Whatever the method used, the therapist proceeds from the assumption that the client(s) is stuck in a relationship dynamic involving unchanging character roles interacting in unchanging ways. Furthermore, the client is usually clinging to one side of the dynamic while rejecting the other, thereby sustaining the conflict. By identifying the characters and their response strategies in the invariant dynamic, the hypnotherapist can structure experiential explorations to pace the dynamic and lead it to more balanced and complementary expressions.

As a final note, it should be emphasized that the relationship players may not always be represented by persons. They may be symbolic "parts" of a person, represented with fantasy symbols, voice dialogues, images (e.g., of animals), and so forth. Although it is quite appropriate to work with these parts as they appear, it is generally assumed that the fixed dynamic arises from and reflects the real interpersonal challenges faced by the client. Thus, while the hypnotherapist frequently works with symbolic and imaginal figures, such work should ultimately be connected with real relationship challenges in the interpersonal domain.

## Beliefs

Beliefs function as powerful induction techniques that structure a person's ongoing experience. When rigidly held, they strongly constrain the range of self-expression, thereby encouraging problems to develop. For example, a person who steadfastly anticipates rejection in a job interview will tend to exhibit exactly those behaviors essential to inducing self and others into enacting that outcome; furthermore, that person's perceptual, emotional, and cognitive processes will be structured by the dominant belief, leading to a conviction that "the reality" held no other possibilities but failure. In this way, invariant (i.e., context-insensitive) beliefs constitute hypnotic inductions used to maintain a problematic state. Accordingly, the hypnotherapist seeks to explore the general question:

*What fixed beliefs do you hold relevant to the problematic experience?*

In pursuing this general inquiry, some specific questions include:

1. How/where/why/with whom did the problem develop?
2. What are the changes of the problem being solved?
3. What would happen if you didn't have the problem?
4. What parts of the problem should be talked about? not talked about?
5. How does the problem continue to be created?

Related questions concern beliefs dominant while the problematic behavior is being enacted. Specifically, clients can be directed to imagine themselves in the problem situation and then asked (in regard to that situation) such questions as:

1. What do you believe about what other people want from you?
2. What do you need?
3. What is going to happen?
4. What can you say or do? not say or do?

Responses to these questions reveal the premises by which a person unconsciously structures attention and activates behavior patterns to fulfill a "prophecy" about an event outcome. Thus, beliefs in a problem state function as regulators by which a person continues to do the same thing; accordingly, in the utilization approach, they are used as justifiers for doing something different. That is, whereas a problem is held in place by the belief

Since X is true, then I have no choices but (the problem state),

in the utilization approach, the therapist communicates:

Since X is true, then many further choices can begin to develop.

Thus, the belief is not challenged but utilized as a springboard for the development of new ways of being. For example, let's take the above case of the person who believes rejection was immanent in an interview situation. The person represents a belief as:

The experience of rejection will occur, and it will lead to an undesired state.

The hypnotherapist thus identifies a major therapeutic idea to be hypnotically communicated as:

The experience of rejection will occur, and will lead to a variety of desired states.

An example of how this therapeutic idea might be communicated hypnotically (after light trance has been developed) is as follows:

... And so your unconscious can develop and affirm your ability in relationships in a variety of different ways. For example, you have the ability to talk to others, to a variety of different others in a variety of different ways. You learned to talk as a baby, you continued to talk as a child, as a young adult, in so many ways. And so as time passes, your understanding of relationships and how to present yourself begins to alter in accord with the *changing sense of self*. And so in learning to converse, you developed multiple relationships regarding the acceptance and rejection of an idea out of hand. You learned to accept certain beliefs and reject other beliefs . . . and so now you can reject any need to attend to anything but that sense of how that rejection will grow in terms of how it will be experienced and responded to according to the needs of the present self . . . in trance you can explore certain acceptances and certain rejections . . . because in that preview of that interview you can explore how many different ways – and I don't know and you don't know consciously how *many* different ways – you will, can, *are* discovering when, where, and how to experience rejection in ways that are *satisfying to the self* . . . the rejection of a tendency to restrict breathing . . . an acceptance of the ability to *breathe comfortably* . . . *a rejection of unnecessary tension* . . . *an acceptance of deserved experiential security* . . . a rejection of knowing in detail how specifically you will enjoy that interview . . . an acceptance of the discovery of unconscious guidance supporting you . . . a rejection of wanting to go too fast or too slow . . . an acceptance of your own rhythms, your own ability to *proceed comfortably* . . . a rejection of having to remember my specific words . . . an acceptance of your *integration* in the dreams tonight and tomorrow. . . .

Thus, the client's dominant theme of rejection is accepted, balanced with its complement of "acceptance," and hypnotically elaborated in terms of the many self-valuing ways it will be experienced. In short, the themes of the problem state are the themes of the solution state. Of course, the themes are translatable into solution states only when the client is in an experientially receptive state. Thus, the presentation of these recontextualized ideas is successful to the extent that rapport and absorption have been developed in the interpersonal relationship.

A major idea here is that a belief is simply a hypothesis or "suggestion" about how things may be, and that its adaptive value rests on the ability of the self to (1) modify the hypothesis according to shifting situations and (2) respond to the predicted event in a variety of creative ways. To do this, a person must be sufficiently detached from the belief to recognize its double-edged value. When a belief is held as absolute, a person's behavior will consequently be rigid and problematic. To develop solutions, the person's attachment to the belief can first be loosened by joining it hypnotically, then modified by amplifying the possible responses it can stimulate. In this way, the belief is not directly challenged; rather, the self is encouraged and allowed opportunities via hypnotic guidance to develop a more flexible relationship to it.

A related idea is that the more rigidly attached a person is to a value, the easier it is to shift their relationship to that value, as long as that fixation is not directly challenged. Thus, the hypnotherapist continually contemplates the koan, "How can change occur by encouraging more of the same and then some?" Beliefs are appreciated as the means by which both problems and solutions develop, and the hypnotherapist thus uses how the former are created to enable the latter to emerge.

*Skills and Resources*

A person's ability to change rests on the willingness and ability to actualize his or her resources and skills. As we saw in Chapter 4, the Ericksonian therapist therefore explores the general question:

*What skills, resources, or abilities has the client developed?*

This can be phrased in a variety of different ways:

1. What do you do well in your life?
2. What do you really get absorbed in?
3. What hobbies do you have?
4. With whom do you have special connections?
5. What do you do when you really need to "let go" and take a break?
6. What do you do a lot of in your day-to-day existence?

The responses can be listed as possible resources for hypnotic communications. For example, the following are lists developed in initial sessions with three different clients:

*Client #1 (Male, 13, diabetic)*
shooting basketballs
thinking about flying airplanes
listening to rock music
withdrawing from parents
playing video games

*Client #2 (Male, 35, college professor)*
photography
love of pets
intense concentration
ability to shift states rapidly
teaching
ability to withdraw

*Client #3 (Female, 30, pregnant)*
relationship with husband
knitting
reading
music
driving a car
walking on a beach
worrying (i.e., thinking extensively about the future)

In each instance, the therapist can contemplate how these resources may be combined with some problematic experience to enable a reorganization of that experience. The assumption is that in problem states, the self experiences little connection to essential resources. The resources may either be *outside* (i.e., functionally dissociated from) the problem frame (e.g., the person may lose his/her ability to ask for what he/she wants) or operating in a rigid self-dissociated manner *within* the frame (e.g., the person may only ask for what he/she wants in a shrill, ineffective manner). In both cases, the rigidity of the frame allows no new movement from outside or within its boundaries. The induction of therapeutic trance allows a "deframed" context wherein resources from multiple contexts can be accessed and integrated:

PROBLEMATIC EXPERIENCE + RESOURCES = POSSIBLE SOLUTIONS

For example, problem/resource pairings made in the case of the young diabetic boy (Client #1) included:

| *Specific problem area* | + | *Possible resources* |
|---|---|---|
| shooting insulin ⟷ | | shooting basketballs comfortably |
| checking blood sugar ⟷ | | checking free throw percentage |

spacing out ⟵————————————⟶ air pilot fantasy
sense of future ⟵———————————⟶ tuning to rhythms, anticipating
changes

Each resource description thus serves as a possible frame for therapeutically addressing key aspects of the problem situation in indirect and hypnotic ways. Thus, metaphors of shooting basketballs comfortably were used to address the comfort of shooting insulin; stories of checking free throw percentages and keeping tabs of numerical consistencies were used to suggest regular monitoring of glucose levels; and so forth. As Figure 5.4 illustrates, each of these problem/resource connections is made in multiple ways, thereby ensuring the weaving of many new associational pathways between states. *By thus reorganizing problem descriptions within solution frames and balanced biological contexts, the hypnotherapist allows solutions to begin to emerge.*

Before concluding, it should be noted that some clients maintain that they have little resources. Furthermore, the ways they have of presenting themselves sometimes convince therapists that they are correct in

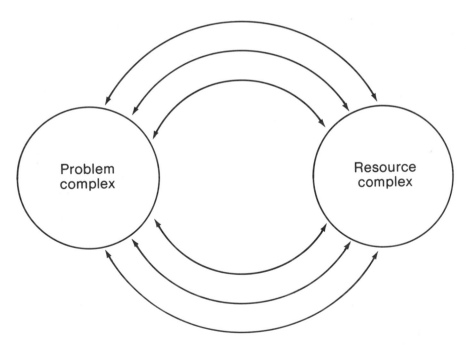

Figure 5.4. Establishing multiple pathways of connection of resources to problems

their assertions. However, resources can always be found in different areas. One is the problem area: it takes profound skill to maintain the same way of being over long periods of time. Thus, the tendency to withdraw can be appreciated and utilized as the ability to go inside and protect the self when needed; the therapist's valuing of the state and interpersonal connection with the client during such processes enables the skill to be reframed experientially in terms of its value.

Second, resources can be found in basic developmental processes: learning to read, write, walk, talk, withdraw, focus, eat, and so forth. Erickson frequently used these basic experiential learnings shared by all as bases for addressing specific developmental challenges faced by a client, perhaps reflecting his own learnings in which no resources seemed to be available (e.g., when he needed to learn to walk again). He emphasized:

> As we go through life we learn a great many things by experience. We learn things by experience we do not even know that we learn. ... In hypnosis one makes use of all these experiential learnings in order to direct and organize the patient's behavior. (In Rossi, Ryan, & Sharp, 1983, pp. 161–162)

By joining a person in areas where resources are available, other resources soon begin to be actualized as progress continues.

In summary, the task of the Ericksonian hypnotherapist is to join a person's reality in order to expand it. To accomplish this, the therapist first identifies the values a person uses in creating their experience. These values may be identified in many aspects of a person's orientation to relationships: social systems, intentions, interactional sequences, symptom complexes, specific role or person attachments, beliefs, and skills and resources. In the present view, each value is a "technique" by which a person generates a reality; it is a fixed constant in the associational network of "mind" by which a client generates, experiences, and maintains a reality. When this reality has become invariant and problematic, the rigid attachment to its underlying values must be loosened to enable new "vary-able" representational structures to develop. By identifying and joining the fixed values, the Ericksonian hypnotherapist is then able to make them once again "vary-able," i.e., capable of changing according to the shifting needs of ongoing experience. Thus, the techniques used to maintain problems are the techniques used to generate solutions.

In working to identify and utilize client values, the hypnotherapist should remain flexible. The hypnotherapist gathers information over time, using a variety of methods. With some clients, it may be useful to have them write down information between sessions, to increase their participation and save therapy time. With most clients, it is valuable to intersperse questions with experiential work, such that one complements the other. As we will see in the next section, it may be useful for the therapist to, say, use the information from one question to develop an experiential hypnotic response, then introduce a next question as the basis for further hypnotic explorations. In this way, the hypnotherapist succeeds in maintaining an interpersonal absorption as the context for inquiry, thereby ensuring that the responses reflect the actual experiential values of the client.

Finally, it should be noted that experiential values can be identified in many ways. For example, Gilligan (1985) has described how hypnotic observation strategies (Chapter 3) may be used to gather information, and also how diagnostic inquiry can be based on identifying psychological splits that form the basis for problem binds. In short, the techniques cited here are suggestive and not exhaustive; other questions and strategies may be included as the therapist pursues multiple paths of inquiry to identify those ways of being constant for a client.

## INTRODUCING TRANCE

Besides gathering information during the initial phases of hypnotherapy, the hypnotherapist also introduces trance processes to the client. Accomplishing this task enables communication to occur within an experientially receptive field, thereby increasing the possibility that meaningful changes can transpire. Trance can be introduced in many ways; this section outlines six aspects of the process:

1. Creating a conducive environment
2. General discussion of trance
3. Light naturalistic development of trance
4. Refractionation methods
5. Modeling trance
6. Trance training

### Creating a Conducive Environment

Trance is an experience in which a person surrenders to his or her deeper experiential self, allowing unconscious processes to express themselves in a therapeutic fashion. Because this process involves letting go of muscle-bound orientation reactions to some degree or another, trance may be more easily developed at first if (1) the physical environment is perceived as safe and comfortable and (2) unanticipated noises or other stimuli (phones, traffic, etc.) are minimized. Comfortable chairs with firm back support should be provided, and a protective environment created. I usually recommend that clients sit in an upright position, having found horizontal positions less advantageous for accessing and integrating habitual client patterns within the trance state. However, discomforts or various other conditions may suggest that other positions (lying, movement) be introduced as alternatives.

If noises (e.g., traffic) are unavoidable, trance may certainly still be developed, assuming that the therapist is willing and able to fully absorb the client's attention. You can probably recall events wherein full absorption in an interpersonal relationship was developed within a noisy social situation. I remember sitting in Milton Erickson's office, then later listening to tapes of the session; to my amazement, it was only then that I really noted the loud traffic and various other noises – phones, other people talking in the next room, for instance – that filtered through his office. Thus, the therapist's willingness to orient to the client with full intensity and a sense of comfort and safety will allow the client to do likewise. Should the client react to unexpected stimuli along the way – for example, by startling – such disruptions can be appreciated as small opportunities to take a short break, then reconnect to the interpersonal relationship for further hypnotic explorations.

In short, the hypnotherapist works to create a physical environment wherein the client can feel sufficiently safe to let go of conscious monitoring and allow hypnotic explorations. Although comfort and minimal external stimuli can contribute significantly to developing this safe environment, the therapist's own comfort and absorption in the client's experiential realities are ultimately the most important factors.

## General Discussion of Trance

Both client and therapist enter the therapy situation with ideas about what does and does not constitute hypnosis. Since the ideas held by the client often differ from those of the therapist, some time should be devoted to straightforward discussion of this issue. I usually start by asking a person what they think of when they hear the word hypnosis. Replies typically emphasize processes such as losing control, blacking out, doing strange things, relaxing, hearing only the hypnotist's voice, being programmed, instant changes, and amnesia. Needless to say, such associations will make it difficult for the client to fully participate in the naturalistic development of a therapeutic trance. Thus, I usually emphasize my own associations to hypnosis. Although the way in which this is done depends on the client, I typically convey directly that first and foremost my intention is one of respecting and valuing the person's integrity. I continue by discussing how I see trance as a powerful means by which security can be developed, such that a sense of "center" (self, control, peace, acceptance, etc., are alternative words) can be pleasurably realized. Further elaboration discloses that this can be achieved in many different ways, and that the present situation is an opportunity to discover the way best suited to the particular needs, values, and styles of the client. I note that the experience of trance can vary: sometimes the client will hear me, sometimes not; sometimes my voice will be in the forefront, sometimes in the back; the client may keep his or her eyes open or closed, or a combination thereof; trance may be developed immediately or in the next session, for several minutes or hours on end; and so forth. I reiterate that the important question is how to develop the security and trust needed to let experience develop in accord with client needs. I then often ask the client to let me know about major values, concerns, considerations, and so on, so that I can best adapt my style of communication.

Another major idea I introduce in regard to trance is that of mastery. Emphasis is placed on trance as an opportunity to master experiential processes that may be "out of control" for the person. Examples are often used to elaborate how problems may be explored and solutions discovered within the security of trance.

In discussing of ideas about trance, it should be appreciated that hypnosis is but one of many languages describing a very naturalistic and potentially therapeutic experience. Many alternatives exist and should be used to adequately convey that the major intention of the therapy is to connect the client with experiential processes in a safe and productive fashion, such that desired changes can occur. With a dancer, for example, hypnotic processes were introduced and developed in terms of "experiential movement" through different "expression patterns"; with a computer programmer, emphasis was placed on "letting programs run without hitches," "rearranging patterns of nesting and sub-nesting," "input/output rearrangements," "experiential interfaces," and so forth; and with an experimental psychologist, the "terms of entrancement" focused on multimodal learning (via parallel processing, probabilistic responding, random patterning, multivariate experiences, bell curves of internal dialogue activity, and so on). Thus, the therapist encourages hypnotic experience via terms and expressions most suitable to the individual client.

*Light Naturalistic Development of Trance*

While talking about trance is important, it is equally essential that some experiential developments complement the conceptual exchange, since it is very difficult to convey the essence of trance through words alone. I usually seek to elicit at least a brief, light trance state within the conversational flow, such that the client can develop a sense of what is being talked about. This elicitation process is usually best accomplished in an informal, naturalistic fashion, such as by experiential shifts in the therapist's nonverbal communication. As Chapter 3 outlined, the therapist can move through a step-by-step process of orienting hypnotically to the client, thereby using nonverbal leading techniques (e.g., breathing rhythmically, focusing interpersonally) to initiate trance. The major purpose in using this nonverbal method is to absorb and reorganize the client's nonverbal patterning, so as to develop an experiential rapport for further conversation. This allows symbols to be exchanged in an experiential (i.e., organismic) field, which is the basis for unconscious learning.

In addition to using nonverbal shifts, the therapist also uses associational symbols personally relevant to the client to stimulate light trance. This may involve childhood associations – like favorite ice cream, first pair of sneakers – or current relationships, such as ways in which the client has of "letting go" or "unwinding." As will be detailed in the next chapter, the basic technique is one of accessing and amplifying the various associational elements of a meaningful relationship while maintaining interpersonal absorption; this creates a therapeutically powerful state wherein the client may feel the paradoxical sense of participating in an interpersonal and intrapersonal relationship simultaneously. To develop and maintain this state, the therapist must cooperate with the unique rhythms and rates of the client, a process akin to a delicate dance.

*Refractionation Methods*

The balancing of rational and hypnotic discourse is an excellent way to enable clients to learn about trance in a naturalistic fashion. This sequential movement between talking and experiencing trance can be developed through *refractionation* methods, which involve having the client go a little bit into trance, come out and talk for a while, go back into trance (a little deeper this time), come out and talk some more, go back in (a little deeper), and so forth. Thus, the therapist might spend an hour alternating between 5-minute periods of talking and 5-minute periods of trance experience, with each trance slightly deeper than the preceding one.

Refractionation methods are advantageous in a variety of ways. They allow clients to learn how to easily shift in and out of trance, a skill that will be useful in everyday living challenges. They enable clients to explore trance gradually, thereby making it a safer experience for many individuals. Refractionation processes also allow both therapist and client to mutually educate each other in a naturalistic fashion: for example, clients can ask questions and communicate what went on in response to hypnotic communications, while therapists can use the time to emphasize certain ideas about trance relevant to the experience. The next round of trance can then utilize and incorporate these responses to develop the personal experience of trance a little further.

Refractionation methods also allow the therapist to orient more to the breadth than the depth of trance. Instead of a "deeper, deeper, deeper" approach in which little attention is paid to accessing the client's major problem and resource strategies within the trance, the therapist can concentrate on introducing different themes and modalities across successive trances. By moving gradually and distributing attention widely over multiple modalities, the therapist avoids going too fast down one path of development; this enables a stronger interpersonal connection, and allows the client to develop a general appreciation for the fact that there is no set way to achieve or experience trance and that many relevant aspects of one's life experience can be included. The therapeutic value of this realization cannot be understated.

In using refractionation, the rate of shifts between waking and trance states should be timed according to client responses, especially nonverbal regulator cues. One client may maintain hypnotic absorption for 5 minutes, another for 5 seconds, a third for 10 minutes, a fourth for 20 seconds; all will indicate the intrusion of conscious participation by (arrhythmic) muscular shifts. The hypnotherapist can appreciate these cues as signals to reabsorb the subject's attention in the interpersonal field, shift attention to some other topic to allow the conscious mind to participate in its analytical strategies *while remaining in tune with the therapist*, then gradually shift attention back to hypnotic experience via a different route.

In a recent session, for instance, four different trances were developed with a client during a 90-minute session. The first occurred when the client showed an emotional absorption while talking about his dogs. This topic was elaborated ("the feeling of petting a dog," "the security of acceptance by that puppy") and nonverbal communication shifted to guide the client into a light trance. When after about two minutes he furrowed his brow and adjusted his position, I adjusted (verbally and nonverbally) by inquiring when he first became aware that he had a skill with numbers. (He was an accountant.) I thought this question of early awarenesses could be developed into a naturalistic age regression technique, but he indicated a confusion and uneasiness as we talked further about childhood learnings. Thus, I oriented back to the present interpersonal relationship by shifting my nonverbal communication and addressing him by name. We talked for about 10 minutes about difficulties he had in childhood, with special care taken to keep him out of trance for a while.

In beginning to elaborate again on how he could enjoy developing his hypnotic skills, I pointed out that he could count on a lot of things in the present relationship, and that his eyelids might be a good place to start. I further noted that his eyelids blinked "now and again," and that he could count the number of times his unconscious communicated with me by "blinking his eyes and expressing other channels as well." I added that he should keep his eyes open during the time, even as other changes might develop. Proceeding in this way (this technique is detailed in Chapter 6), another trance was developed and further ideas about security and trance were introduced. When muscular regulation again appeared after about 5 minutes, I complimented him for knowing when "enough is enough for now," then shifted my communication to a waking state style while inquiring about hobbies he had. After several minutes, I inquired about how he felt during the previous ten minutes, and we discussed some of the trancelike processes that he experienced.

A third trance developed when I started shaking his hand while talking about social patterns, then gently left it suspended as I talked about trance as an opportunity to let his unconscious work independently of normal limitations (see Chapter 7). A final trance unfolded via eye fixation along with suggestions for perceptual alterations in the hands. This 10-minute trance, during which eye closure developed, concluded with the hypnotic suggestions:

> ... And so in integrating all of the explorations you have accomplished here today, what a nice thing to know that you can take great satisfaction in learning further in the coming days and weeks ahead all of these ways and then some to allow your unconscious to make those perceptual, behavioral, and mental alterations best suited to allow the present needs to be recognized and satisfied in a fashion appropriate to the needs of the entire self. ...

Gently adjusting my position, I noted that he could rejoin me when he was ready. In the final 15 minutes, we talked generally about the different feelings experienced during the various naturalistic trances, with my emphasis on "there's a lot more where that came from" and the importance of feeling secure and safe in the interpersonal relationship.

Thus, a series of mini-trances were developed within an initial therapy session. Each trance unfolded naturally from the conversational flow between therapist and client; each trance involved a sustained interpersonal connection as well as an intrapersonal absorption; and each trance was concluded when the client's cues indicated a need for reorientation of some sort. Furthermore, each trance was used to seed a variety of simple ideas within an experientially receptive field: ideas about the nature of trance, the safety and security that could characterize the experience, the therapeutic success that lay ahead, the potential autonomy of the unconscious, and so forth. Finally, straightforward conversation was sandwiched between each trance, to allow both therapist and client to learn more about how to participate in the therapeutic encounter.

As a further comment, it should be noted that in using methods involving fairly frequent shifts across topics or experiential states (e.g., trance/waking), the hypnotherapist can achieve an underlying continuity by the sustained absorption of the interpersonal connection. That is, the hypnotherapist moves from topic to topic but continues to appreciate experientially the self that remains constant throughout the variability. Without this unitary orientation, the client will likely become confused or feel uncomfortably fragmented. Thus, the relationship context provides the glue to hold all of the different ideas together.

## Modeling Trance

In introducing trance processes, the therapist may discover that the client is unwilling or unable to directly participate as the focal subject of attention. This is understandable, given the concerns of trust and security that often are dominant at the outset of therapy. Following the general Ericksonian principle of focusing indirectly when direct approaches are unsuitable, the therapist might proceed by modeling trance via another person or persons. The client can be asked to *not* participate directly, a suggestion often stimulating trance development via vicarious identification with the model.

Modeling trance can be accomplished in a variety of ways. First, the therapist might demonstrate self-hypnosis, a strategy particularly appropriate when the client may see the therapist in an authority position. Second, spouses or partners might be used; this is often useful when working with couples, where often only one person can fully experience trance at a time. Third, family members may be utilized, such that an "identified hypnotic subject" (IHS) is designated in the family; this method capitalizes on the fact that hypnotic processes often occur naturally in family systems (see Ritterman, 1983; Lankton & Lankton, 1986). Fourth, trained subjects unrelated to the client may be used; this was a technique Erickson often applied. Fifth, the therapist might use a version of Erickson's (1964b) "my friend John" technique, in which the therapist responds to a client's unwillingness or inability to experience trance by shifting attention to an imaginary person seated next to the client and proceeding to do a trance induction on this imaginary other.

Sixth, related techniques involving puppets or other props might be used. Such techniques may be especially delightful for children, though adults can also benefit from them. For example I had a client holding three stuffed bears while I communicated hypnotically to each of them; this playful process enabled the man to develop a meaningful trance involving childlike resources. Finally, stories about others may be used. This is a central technique in the Ericksonian approach, in which the therapist hypnotically describes events (e.g., trance development) that involved other people at other times. As we will see in the next chapter, this storytelling method can be quite effective in allowing clients to participate in their own way.

In using symbolic others to indirectly invite participation in hypnotic processes, the therapist remains tuned to the interpersonal relationship. While the topic of conversation is shifted away from the client, the underlying focus remains on the client's ongoing responses.

*Trance Training*

The preparation phase for hypnosis involves the beginning of each session, as well as the beginning sessions of a therapy. In the latter, it may be useful to formally train the client in a variety of hypnotic processes before specific problems are addressed. This is especially the case when direct focus on the problem area tends to threaten the client. For example, I recently worked with a woman who had been sexually molested as a child. Her involvement in the experience was still intense, and she felt little trust in her inner abilities. I therefore spent much of the initial five sessions with her primarily focused on me (an "external" connection), while developing a variety of hypnotic phenomena useful for problem solution — e.g., hypnotic "shields" (for boundary delineation), secure dissociation, affect/perception dissociations, and so on. In short, the developed phenomena were a means of indirectly developing the needed resources without directly addressing the problem context. Once these phenomena had been mastered, we gradually focused upon the relationship issues involving the development of new choices.

In addition to having the client learn specific hypnotic phenomena, the trance training period can also enable an increasing appreciation of trance as a context for security, self-exploration, and mastery of psychological skills. Each trance is an opportunity to get to know one's self at a deeper, more intimate level; thus, a series of self-valuing trances can go a long way in boosting self-esteem and confidence in everyday living.

## SUMMARY

The initial phase of hypnotherapy includes the complementary processes of (1) gathering information about how a client generates and maintains a reality and (2) introducing the experiential and naturalistic process of therapeutic trance within the interpersonal field. The first process seeks to identify invariant aspects of the client's experience, including social matrices, intentions, problem induction sequences, symptom complexes, skills and abilities, and beliefs. These and other values, which can be gathered in many ways, constitute the basis for the therapist's techniques and strategies. In a formal sense, the client's values are seen as technical means by which altered states of consciousness are developed; the cooperation principle directs the therapist to join with these naturalistic techniques in order to expand their range of self-expression.

In introducing trance processes, the therapist continues to adapt to client values and responses while assuming responsibility for creating an environment wherein the client can safely and fully absorb in an experiential process. Part of this involves ensuring a comfortable physical environment, though a much larger role is played by the integrity and presence of the therapist. Straightforward discussion about hypnosis and trance, complemented with brief naturalistic opportunities to experience trance, constitute a major part of the initial education process. Various modeling techniques and refractionation methods contribute to further development of experiential learnings about trance, as can formal training in hypnotic phenomena. In short, the therapist seeks to absorb the client in a flexible interpersonal rapport, such that the therapeutic value of trance is realized in a naturalistic fashion.

# CHAPTER 6

# *Associational Strategies for Developing Therapeutic Trance*

Following the initial phase of creating a context, the hypnotherapist works to stimulate therapeutic trances. In terms of a single session, this induction phase involves shifting from waking state to trance state, and may last anywhere from 5 to 60 minutes. In terms of a multiple session hypnotherapy, it may consist of a training period of 2–8 sessions in which the client learns to easily develop trance states (cf. Erickson, 1948).

This chapter explores ways in which these therapeutic processes can be achieved. The first section briefly reviews the notion of trance as naturalistic and then outlines three basic principles of hypnotic induction. The second section explores various accessing techniques useful for experientially unfolding therapeutic trances within the interpersonal context.

## DEVELOPING TRANCE NATURALISTICALLY

To develop therapeutic trances, the Ericksonian operator recognizes trance as a naturalistic experience involving the same basic psychological processes prominent in waking state experience. For example, age regression is an extreme version of memory revivification; amnesia is a special case of forgetting; hallucinations are very vivid imaginings; posthypnotic suggestions are unconscious associational learnings; hypnotic dreaming resembles the nocturnal dreams we have many times each night in our sleep. A major difference is that trance greatly intensifies experiential involvement in these basic psychological processes, sometimes to the point where we forget that our "as if" world is just a simulation. Also, trance loosens other mental constraints, such as the rigid and fixed ways we typically relate to time and space. In short, in trance critical faculties become temporarily suspended and experiential absorption is heightened, thus permitting complete immersion in an experiential reality (cf. Shor, 1962). When a person feels protected and secure, absorption in hypnotic realities can be highly therapeutic, as this enables new ways of thinking and being.

That trance is naturalistic means that it should be conceptualized as representing one end of a continuum of experiential involvement, *not* as an artificial state discrete from other psychological experience. Most subjects *gradually* shift into the internally oriented, effortless, and imaginal style of processing that characterizes trance (Chapter 2); trance is *not* an "all or none" phenomenon in which the subject abruptly goes "over the edge." The specific progression of experiences leading into trance will be unique for each individual. Some subjects may grow more alert initially, then want to talk for 5–10 minutes, then develop eye fixation before going into trance; others may immediately relax, develop trance, but then come out within 5 minutes. *Each person needs to discover his or her own style and rate of going into trance: the hypnotist's task is to guide and facilitate that discovery process.*

Thus, it is *not* the hypnotist's task to "put the subject under." This way of conceptualizing an induction is not only insulting to the subject's intelligence and capabilities, but also burdens the hypnotist with the impossible-to-fulfill responsibility of creating another person's reality. Hypnotherapists need not and should not attempt to impose understandings and experiences on clients; they need not even try to get subjects to imagine various things. Trance is much easier induced by eliciting and utilizing the naturalistic experiences (e.g., memories), resources, and processes already available to individuals. To do this, the Ericksonian hypnotherapist first creates a context where clients are both willing and able to set aside normal conscious processes and explore new ways of being. Naturalistic communications are then used to immerse clients in experiential realities conducive to both trance development and personal growth.

To generate effective hypnotic inductions, I find it useful to keep three principles in mind. The first is to *secure and maintain attentional absorption.* In short, the hypnotist must garner the subject's attention, which is usually shifting among changing external stimuli, and direct it in some way. Any number of fixation stimuli can be employed – a thumbtack on the wall, the subject's thumbnail, the monotonous drone of the hypnotist's voice, the hypnotist's eyes, a metronome, a mantra, counting numbers, and so on. (I have a strong preference for developing eye fixation with clients, as it creates an interpersonal absorption that enhances the experiential participation of both therapist and client. However, some individuals find other fixation techniques work better for them.) Once experientially absorbed, attention is maintained via verbal and (especially) nonverbal pacing and leading.

A second principle for induction is to *access and develop unconscious processes*. This involves using *associational strategies* to access experiential responses. This chapter discusses some major techniques for accomplishing this goal, including asking autobiographical questions, telling stories, giving general instructions, and recognizing and ratifying trance responses.

The third principle is to *bypass and depotentiate conscious processes*. Underlying this principle is the assumption that the primary obstacle to trance in willing subjects is the efforting and rational processes that characterize waking states. To the extent that this is the case, the Ericksonian operator applies *dissociational strategies* which induce trance by pacing and then depotentiating the trance-inhibiting conscious processes. Major methods for doing this include boredom, dissociation, metaphorical stories, distraction, and confusion. The bulk of the next chapter is devoted to this latter strategy, as it is the most developed and sophisticated and often the most effective of the methods.

These three principles are interdependent. Generally speaking, the hypnotist starts an induction by absorbing the subject's attention, then applies the second and third principles in a complementary fashion. Associational strategies are introduced to immerse the absorbed subject in trance, while dissociational strategies are added when the subject experiences difficulty in doing so.

## ACCESSING TECHNIQUES

The most naturalistic and graceful strategy for inducing trance is to create a feedback loop of communication in which trance-relevant experiences and processes are accessed and then utilized. The basic method is to offer communications which initiate a *search process* (see Erickson & Rossi, 1981; Lankton, 1980) whereby subjects experientially examine their internal processes to derive personal meaning from the communications. For example, the subject asked to remember a pleasant time will often access (perhaps not consciously) various memories before settling on a particular event. This search process loosens up mental processes and encourages a more inward orientation; also, by *ideodynamic principles* (Chapters 1 and 2) the subject will begin to develop the feelings and other experiential aspects of the trance-relevant accessed experience. The Ericksonian hypnotist simply identifies generally (e.g., by observation) what the subject has accessed, paces it, then introduces communications to stimulate further search processes. Thus, the general intent within the feedback loop interaction is to access a sequence of trance-relevant experiences which produces a trajectory from waking state to trance.

There are many accessing techniques useful in this regard. This section explores nine methods: (1) asking questions; (2) embedding suggestions; (3) presupposing trance responses; (4) speaking generally; (5) telling stories; (6) using already-developed associational relationships; (7) developing new associational correlations; (8) pacing and leading representational systems; and (9) framing and ratifying hypnotic responses.

## Asking Questions

Many types of questions can be used to initiate search processes and access trance experiences (see Erickson & Rossi, 1979; Bandler & Grinder, 1975). For example, *attentionally absorbing questions* are ideal communications for beginning a naturalistic induction, as they enable a smooth transition from casual conversation to the induction. The hypnotist might start, for instance, by asking common social questions ("How's the weather?" "Have any difficulty getting here?" "Are you feeling comfortable?") and then shift to inquiries regarding innocuous external stimuli ("How do you like this watch?" "What do you think of my new bookcase?" "Where did you get that nice outfit?"). Upon achieving rapport and securing the subject's attention, the hypnotist can gracefully shift to *memory-accessing questions* which elicit trance responses. These questions may concern trance-relevant experiences; for example:

1. How do you feel when you're really relaxed? Can you remember such a time?
2. Can you remember a time you felt very secure?
3. Can you remember how it feels to take a nice warm shower or bath when you're tired?

Similar questions might address experiences that exemplify naturalistic trance phenomena. For example, naturalistic age regression processes might begin with questions such as:

1. Did you have a nickname as a child?
2. Where did you grow up? How many bedrooms did your house have?
3. Can you remember what your mother's voice sounded like when she was nice to you?

Or the memory-accessing questions might directly address previous trance experiences:

1. When was the deepest trance you've ever been in?
2. How do you know you're beginning to develop a trance?
3. Can you remember the last time you were in trance?

Of course, the subject with no formal trance experience can be presented with trance-relevant questions (1–6) or asked to speculate:

1. What do you think it would be like to develop a light trance?
2. Can you describe some of the phenomenological changes you might experience in developing trance?

The hypnotic effect of memory-accessing questions depends largely on *how* they are asked. If presented straightforwardly in a normal situation, they obviously will not catapult a person into trance. Their trance-inducing effect occurs to the extent that (1) the subject is experientially oriented and attentionally absorbed and (2) the hypnotist asks the questions in a meaningful and expectant fashion. To fulfill the first condition, time to prepare the subject must be allotted *before* asking the question(s); to satisfy the second condition, the hypnotist must allow time *after* the question for the subject to experientially access a trance response. Even when these conditions are met, however, the question may not be relevant to the subject's experience; thus, the hypnotist might proceed with at least several lines of questioning before discovering one to which the subject is hypnotically responsive.

In my own work, I use questions to initiate trance extremely often. I usually include innocuous questions in an opening 5–10 minutes of casual conversation designed to elicit rapport and an experiential, self-referential style of processing. I gradually shift to memory-accessing questions. While asking such questions, my nonverbal processes begin to slow down and generally become more focused (while still relaxed). (This nonverbal leading technique tends to slow the subject down and encourage nonanalytical, self-referential processing.) Before asking a question, I pause for a second or two, looking meaningfully and expectantly at the person to build response potential. After the question is delivered, usually in a soft and slow fashion, I pause another second or so, looking even more expectantly at the subject (while often very subtly nodding my head). For each question asked, I closely observe the person's responses. When the subject begins to exhibit trance-indicative cues (Table 4.2, p. 125), I intensify my slowed and meaningful demeanor before asking another question. Once the subject is clearly entranced – good signs of this are an absence of the saccadic (back and forth) eye movements which generally accompany conscious processing, motor inhibition, and inhibition or latency in verbal response – I typically shift into techniques (e.g., rhetorical questions, or the generalities or stories described later in the section) that enable the subject to stop responding verbally and go all the way into trance.

There are numerous ways in which responses to memory-accessing questions can be expanded upon to develop trance fully. One especially effective technique is to ask subjects to describe in detail their previous experience in developing a trance – or, for inexperienced subjects, what they imagine it would be like – and then feed back each statement, ostensibly for the purpose of ensuring that you're just keeping track of things. For example:

*Hypnotist:* Have you ever before been in what you would consider to be a deep trance?
*Subject:* Yes.
*Hypnotist:* Can you describe what things were like as you began to develop that deep trance?
*Subject:* Well, I was sitting in the chair . . .
*Hypnotist:* Sitting in the chair . . .
*Subject:* . . . looking at the hypnotist's eyes . . .
*Hypnotist:* . . . looking at the hypnotist's eyes, that's right . . .
*Subject:* . . . and I listened to what he was saying and began to relax . . .
*Hypnotist:* . . . listening to the hypnotist's voice and relaxing comfortably . . .
*Subject:* . . . and my vision started to blur . . .
*Hypnotist:* . . . blurring of the vision. . . .

This sort of interchange can be continued until trance is reaccessed. The technique is particularly nice in that it essentially directs the client to outline an induction sequence appropriate for him or her as an individual. The hypnotist then simply uses absorbing communications and reinforcing suggestions (the verbal feedback) to enhance the trance-inducing ideodynamic processes – that is, thinking about an experience tends to revivify that experience – already set into play. This shifts responsibility for developing trance to its rightful place – the client – and thus bypasses the common possibility that the hypnotic induction will reflect more the therapist's than the client's preferred style of trance development.

Besides questions that are innocuous, absorbing, or memory-accessing, the therapist can also use *rhetorical questions*. Such questions serve the dual function of occupying conscious processes and instigating unconscious search processes. They are particularly useful during trance-deepening phases of the induction, when the client has his or her eyes closed and is no longer talking. The following induction excerpt exemplifies how rhetorical questions might be used:

> (After a light trance has been induced) . . . And trance can develop in so many ways . . . and I wonder, *How deeply will you go into trance? . . .* and *how much can you let yourself relax completely? . . . .* and you really can discover at your own rate and pace exactly how trance will unfold for you . . . and as you do, I wonder, How will your unconscious express itself? Will it simply share with you a variety of unexpected and yet so secure and educational hypnotic realities? Will it let the hand lift up independently, as a way of letting you know that it really can operate autonomously? And will you, can you, won't you, aren't you going down now even deeper? What a nice thing to know that you can discover all of those things and then some. . . .

Although such questions are relatively innocuous, they invite the person to explore various trance possibilities, and thus constitute effective hypnotic suggestions in and of themselves (Erickson & Rossi, 1979). The questions are generally delivered in a slow, rhythmic, and meaningful demeanor to maximize the client's responsivity to them. Sometimes, though, a quicker tempo is used to overload the conscious processes of individuals having difficulty in letting go into trance. For such clients, the content of the rhetorical questions might also be more disorienting, or it might pace possible internal dialogue in which the person is mired. For example:

> . . . And you can go into trance *or not* in so many different ways . . . your conscious mind can hear me here and really needn't interfere with the autonomous development of unconscious processes . . . your conscious mind may wonder, What techniques is he going to use? What is he *really* saying? Is it going to happen? Will it, why, why not, won't it happen now? And your unconscious can

continue to wander as the conscious wonders . . . And flowers
bloom in the spring and leaves fall in the autumn and your breathing goes in and out . . . *And yet what is the natural complement
to a waking state?* Some say sleep . . . *And yet what is the complement of a rigidly rational state,* where internal dialogue continues on and on and on? . . . Some say trance . . . but you really
should discover these things first hand . . . *And what does it mean
to have a FIRST hand?* . . .

This sort of conversational induction is an excellent way to pace and
depotentiate conscious processes while accessing unconscious processes,
and is explored in depth in the following chapter. Noteworthy here is
the central role that rhetorical questions can play in such inductions.
   Another class of interrogative includes *tag questions.* For example:

1. And you *really* would like to go into trance, would you *not?*
2. And you probably can't get yourself fully comfortable, can you?
   (with upwards inflection)
3. And it really is all right to relax, is it not?

Tag questions are nice ways to pace opposing parts of a person – e.g.,
a part that wants to go into trance and a part that wants to stay out.
As Bandler and Grinder (1975) point out, the linguistic "deep structure"
of tag questions contains both the positive and negative meanings of
the statement. It also takes a relatively long time to understand such
questions, thus making them an effective means for occupying conscious processes (Erickson & Rossi, 1979).
   Two other types of questions – *embedded questions* and *conversational postulates* – might be briefly mentioned (cf. Bandler & Grinder,
1975). The former are actually statements containing implicit questions.
For example:

1. And I wonder how easily you can begin to go into trance.
2. And I'm curious as to what you would like to do right now.

By social convention, such statements request that the listener respond
*as if* they are questions, and thus constitute an indirect form of communication. Conversational postulates are questions which are actually
directives:

1. Can you place your hands on your lap and your feet flat on the
   floor?

2. Won't you seat yourself comfortably?
3. Could you describe to me how deep a trance you would like to develop?

As can be observed, conversational postulates are permissive and indirect ways to issue directives and are thus valuable to the Ericksonian practitioner.

To summarize, many types of questions can be used in hypnotic communication: absorbing questions, innocuous questions, memory-accessing questions, rhetorical questions, tag questions, embedded questions, and conversational postulates. These questions can be applied for different purposes, including gathering information, developing rapport, issuing directives, absorbing attention, pacing conscious and unconscious processes simultaneously, eliciting memories (especially trance-relevant ones), deepening a trance, and overloading. Regardless of the type or intent of the question, the therapist must pay considerable attention to nonverbal delivery style, as it determines to a great degree how and how much the client will experientially respond.

## Embedding Suggestions

Milton Erickson had a remarkable ability to convey indirect suggestions by interspersing them unnoticeably within a set of statements (see, e.g., Erickson, 1966a). One major way he did this was by nonverbally marking out certain messages by shifting the tempo, volume, or intensity of his voice, or by postural or facial expression changes.[1] These *embedded commands*, as Bandler and Grinder (1975) termed them, were subtle enough to bypass conscious recognition yet sufficient enough to affect unconscious processes. In my own work, I have found embedded suggestions one of the simplest yet most powerful techniques for delivering indirect communications.

An embedded suggestion can be verbally expressed in a variety of ways. The general procedure for forming one is simply to identify the suggestion you want to convey and then embed it within a larger linguistic context. In the following examples, suggestions to develop trance (in italics) are embedded straightforwardly within simple sentences:

---

[1]Erickson's deft ability to use subtle vocal changes to elicit hypnotic responses was made all the more remarkable by the fact that he was tone deaf and thus relied mainly on kinesthetic feedback from his throat to explore and refine this powerful ability.

1. There are a number of ways to *begin to drop into trance*, Denise.
2. One of the things you might consider is how easy it is to *develop a state of comfort*.
3. And you really can *relax fully*, Martha.

The suggestions can be made more indirect by shifting the subject's conscious attention onto some other time, place, or person. For example, the hypnotist might talk about somebody else:

1. And Peter really had a nice way of sitting down and letting himself *drop into trance*.
2. . . . And so I went home and let myself *feel warm and comfortable all over*. . . .

A special kind of embedded command – *direct quotes* (Bandler & Grinder, 1975) – might be given in this way:

1. And I said to Mary, "*Why not let your unconscious begin to do the work for you?*"
2. And Hank turned around and he said, "*I really think it's time to go into trance*."

A related indirect strategy is to talk very generally:

1. And a lot of people discover that in developing the ability to *drop comfortably into trance*, they learn so much about themselves.
2. And each person has their own style of beginning to *relax* and let the unconscious respond freely and hypnotically.

As illustrated by the many italicized examples contained in the rest of the book, these analogically marked suggestions can be used extensively. Any number of nonverbal channels can be used to mark out the messages – facial expression, vocal shifts, postural cues, and so forth. The general strategy is to use a different nonverbal pattern for the embedded suggestion. For example, you might be speaking at a relatively normal tempo and intensity, then shift to a slower and softer delivery to convey the embedded suggestion, perhaps pause a moment or so to let the message "sink in," then reassume immediately the "normal" nonverbal style. The embedding should not be so dramatic that it is obvious to the person's conscious mind, but it should also be significant enough to be unconsciously detected. Experimentation is needed to find the balance point between these two considerations.

Because embedded suggestions are subtle nonverbal communications that generally bypass conscious detection, one is sometimes left with doubts when rationally considering their potential effectiveness as hypnotic techniques. Thus, I strongly urge you to experiment with the technique before judging its value. I think you will find that most people are surprisingly responsive to embedded suggestions, especially when their message is consistent with a person's needs and understandings.

My understanding of why embedded suggestions work is that they utilize information-processing strategies central in unconscious comprehension but peripheral to conscious attention. Specifically, the former uses a great deal of *analogical* information – differences that make a difference, as Bateson (1979) would say – while conscious understanding relies heavily on *digital* (e.g., verbal) information (cf. Watzlawick, Beavin, & Jackson, 1967).[2] The use of embedded suggestions therefore follows the hypnotic utilization principle of bypassing conscious processes while accessing unconscious processes.

This utilization strategy can be applied in the simple ways described above as well as in more complex fashions. With regard to the latter, Erickson sometimes fashioned an entire therapy by interspersing embedded suggestions within elaborate discourses on topics unrelated to the problem. A classic example is his work with a dying cancer patient, "Joe," who was wracked with intolerable pain and impervious to even massive dosages of narcotics (Erickson, 1966a). At the request of a close relative of Joe's, Erickson agreed to explore the possibility of hypnotic pain control, then discovered that Joe strongly disliked even the word hypnosis. Forced therefore into seeking ways to work indirectly, Erickson used Joe's lifelong occupation as a florist as the conversational topic for absorbing the patient, while interspersing embedded commands for trance and pain control. The following excerpt (with embedded suggestions in italics) gives a flavor of the comments:

---

[2]With regard to neuropsychological processes, a speculative account of why embedded suggestions work can be made in terms of a hypothesized core brain orienting response which occurs whenever incoming information differs significantly from the immediately preceding input (see Pribram, 1971). In this model, developed by Sokolov (1963), the mechanisms of the core brain – especially those regulating the thalamus, hypothalamus, and amygdala – are constantly sampling environmental input. When an informative (i.e., novel or unexpected) input is sampled, an automatic orienting response releases all information being processed to attend to it. Hence, a change in the patterned vocal delivery will "clear" the system to enable full attention to the new pattern (i.e., the embedded suggestion). That an embedded suggestion receives greater attention and is processed distinctly from the other incoming "items" means that it will be "learned" better – i.e., have more effect – than other communications (see Glass, Holyoak, & Santa, 1979).

Joe, I would like to talk to you. I know you are a florist, that you grow flowers, and I grew up on a farm in Wisconsin and I liked growing flowers. I still do. So I would like to have you take a seat in that easy chair as I talk to you. I'm going to say a lot of things but it won't be about flowers because you know more than I do about flowers. *That isn't what you want.* Now as I talk and I can do so *comfortably*, I wish that you will *listen to me comfortably* as I talk about a tomato plant. That is an odd thing to talk about. It makes one *curious. Why talk about a tomato plant*? One puts a tomato seed in the ground. One can *feel hope* that it will grow into a tomato plant that *will bring satisfaction* by the fruit it has. The seed soaks up water, *not very difficult* in doing that because of the rains that *bring peace and comfort* and the growing to flowers and tomatoes. That little seed, Joe, slowly swells, sends out a little rootlet with cilia. Now you may not know what cilia are, but cilia are *things that work* to help the tomato seed grow, to push above the ground as a sprouting plant, and *you can listen to me Joe* so I will keep on talking and *you can keep on listening, wondering, just wondering what you can really learn.* . . . (Erickson, 1966a; in Rossi, 1980d, pp. 269–270)

These sorts of embedded suggestions, greatly elaborated upon in a repetitive yet totally absorbing fashion, were continued until Joe was clearly hypnotized, whereupon posthypnotic suggestions for continued pain control were subtly included. Briefly stated, the suggestions were effective and Joe developed enough pain relief and physical strength to move back home. About a month later, Erickson spent a day with Joe – ostensibly for social reasons – during which he embedded more therapeutic suggestions in the same indirect fashion. Joe's relief from pain continued until his quiet death some three months after the original visit from Erickson.

In discussing this and other cases, Erickson (1966a) stressed the importance of (1) establishing an appropriate relationship, (2) recognizing and utilizing the patient's strong desire to change, (3) respecting and utilizing the needs and characteristics of the individual, and (4) speaking meaningfully enough to hypnotically absorb and maintain attention. These points apply of course to any therapeutic situation. When they are observed, embedded suggestions are powerful indirect techniques for eliciting unconscious responses; when they are not, such suggestions – or any hypnotic techniques, for that matter – are likely to be rejected by the person's unconscious processes.

## Presupposing Trance Responses

*Presuppositions* are ideas implicitly assumed to be true in a statement. All statements contain a number of presuppositions. In hypnotic inductions, they can be used by focusing the subject's attention on how, when, where, or with whom a hypnotic response will occur, thereby indirectly conveying the assumption that *a hypnotic response will occur* (Bandler & Grinder, 1975; Erickson & Rossi, 1979). As Figure 6.1 illustrates, hypnotic presuppositions elaborate specific possibilities while assuming the general hypnotic response.

This is a major difference between traditional hypnosis and Ericksonian hypnosis. In the former, the hypnotist focuses on giving specific suggestions – e.g., hand levitation; in the latter, the hypnotist orients to a general class of hypnotic responses – e.g., body dissociation – and waits and wonders as to which specific possibility the subject will select to develop. This latter method bypasses "resistance" and encourages the subject's unconscious processes to be more active in the hypnotic processes.

One way to offer hypnotic presuppositions is in the form of questions:

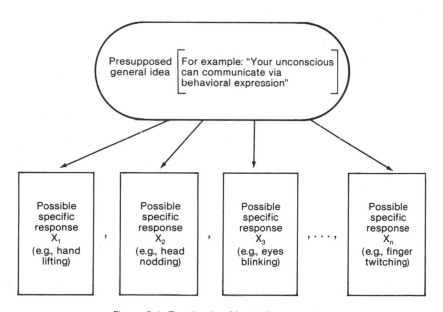

Figure 6.1. Two levels of hypnotic suggestion

1. How deep a trance would you like to go into?
2. Would you like to *go into trance now* or in five minutes?
3. Would you like to *go into trance* sitting in this chair or that chair?
4. And do you know how easy it is to *let your unconscious do it for you*?
5. Do you think you'll *go into trance* better sitting or lying down?

Note how embedded suggestions (in italics) can be interspersed within such queries.

Hypnotic responses can also be presupposed within statements:

> And I really don't know exactly how you will *begin to develop a trance*. . . . You can go into trance with your eyes open or closed . . . you can go into trance thinking consciously about how you can't . . . you can go into a light trance, a medium trance, or a deep trance . . . and so I'm wondering which way will be best for you . . . and whether you *drop all the way into trance immediately* or wait a while is not that important . . . what's more important is your own ability to discover the way of developing a trance that best fits you as an individual . . . some people prefer to *relax* a bit, shift down into trance for a while, then come back up before going all the way back down. . . . Others prefer to wait a few minutes and then *drop deeply down*, all the way down, at once . . . others prefer to go in and out, back and forth, up and down, until at some point in time they *go down and forget to come back up for a while*. . . .

All of the above statements presuppose that trance will indeed be experienced. In addition, they help bypass any relationship struggle by (1) providing the subject with the "illusory freedom" (Kubie, 1958) to choose which response to make and (2) never suggesting trance directly. They also provide a wealth of information about trance which enables clients to be aware of the many possible experiences, thus reducing the chances they will become stuck in one way of trying to experience things.

Presuppositions can be applied similarly when a hypnotic phenomenon is being suggested:

1. And I wonder whether your right or your left hand will begin to lift first.
2. And I don't know whether you will go back to the sixth grade, or the fourth, or even sooner . . .
3. And we can both wonder as to when your unconscious will begin to lift that finger up . . .

4. And in your sleep tonight, I don't exactly know which dream your unconscious will select to continue to integrate these learnings.

These are simple statements that presuppose a *specific* phenomenon will develop. The hypnotherapist might be more general and elaborate, especially when a specific response is not immediately elicited. The following example shows this might be done with the more general phenomenon of body dissociation:

And what a nice thing to know that in trance your unconscious can respond independently, autonomously, and intelligently . . . and you can enjoy the security of those experiences and the learnings you can derive from them. . . . Your unconscious can respond and express itself in so many different ways . . . and so I don't know and you don't know exactly how your unconscious will express its autonomy. . . . But I do know that it has the naturalistic ability to handle your physical activities in a variety of valuable fashions. . . . For example, your unconscious usually controls your breathing, which can be so *easy and comfortable* as it continues to automatically go in and out, in and out, in and out . . . and your unconscious controls your heart rate and your pulse rate . . . and when you really enjoy a good run, your unconscious is taking care of the process of automatically lifting the legs up and down, up and down, in that pleasurable, rhythmic fashion . . . and in trance, that general ability of your unconscious can also be experienced in a variety of different ways . . . *and so I really don't know how your unconscious will physically express itself* . . . perhaps by lifting a hand up . . . easily . . . comfortably . . . nonvolitionally . . . up [this is said with upwards inflections] . . . perhaps it will be the right hand or the left one or a combination thereof . . . perhaps it will start with just a finger twitching . . . perhaps the hand jerking . . . but some people think more holistically and prefer to let the unconscious lift the entire arm and hand up . . . others discover it pressing down, so heavy that it seems to be a part of yet apart from the rest of your body. . . . Others find themselves operating independently of their entire body, delighting in seeing it over *there* while hearing me *here* . . . and whether it's your finger, your hand, your arm, your whole body is not that important . . . and whether they press down or lift up, get heavy or lighten up, or remain the same is not important either. . . . what's important is your uplifting and unfolding discovery of the ability of your unconscious to operate in its own way . . . and so why not let it surprise you with that autonomous body . . . and I wonder *what* that surprise will be, and when and how it will happen. . . .

These statements illustrate an excellent strategy for eliciting any hypnotic phenomenon:

1. Start by generally emphasizing the value and intelligence of the unconscious.
2. Identify the general form of the phenomenon – e.g., body dissociation, age regression, amnesia – as an example of unconscious capabilities.
3. Give naturalistic examples of this general phenomenon (usually more elaborate than the above example).
4. Shift to specific hypnotic manifestations of the phenomenon, covering all possibilities.
5. Suggest that the subject's unconscious select the particular manifestation most appropriate for the subject.
6. Accept and build upon whatever responses occur.

This strategy frames the suggested phenomenon as a beneficial, naturalistic, and familiar process, thereby enhancing greatly the probability that the client will be willing and able to respond. Again, it also presupposes that *something* hypnotic is going to happen.

As will be discussed later, there is sometimes a time lag between suggestion and response. In such cases, the hypnotist might state the suggestions in various ways and then shift to a different topic while keeping an eye out for the suggested phenomenon to develop. If and when it does, it can be ratified and further developed.

It might be further noted that the hypnotherapist can cover all possibilities while biasing the chances that a particular one will occur. For instance, in the above example hand levitation might have been more heavily weighted – so to speak – by offering more examples of hands lifting up autonomously (e.g., standing on a bus, raising a hand in a classroom), reiterating the hand levitation suggestions more, embedding suggestions only for this response, using upwards inflections timed to inhalations to give a "lifting" feeling, and so forth.

Of course, presupposing a response does not guarantee its occurrence. The therapist must speak meaningfully enough so that the client is absorbed experientially, thus heightening response potential while inhibiting the critical faculties that might logically analyze the statement(s). In addition, the presupposed response must be consistent with the situational and personality needs of the individual. For example, a deeply troubled client would probably be *unable* to respond positively to the suggestion to make deep, lasting changes either today or tomorrow. Similarly, a person would likely be *unwilling* to follow a directive to commit an antisocial act "either today or tomorrow." Of course, there are many less extreme examples; the point is that pacing and leading principles need to be observed if presuppositions are to be hypnotically effective.

Presupposing responses can be accomplished in more ways than those described here. For example, they can used to ensure that a subject will carry out homework assignments. For instance, with an entranced client whom I wanted to sit in a restaurant and observe others, I emphasized for 15-20 minutes how she had to *randomly* select the to-be-observed individuals. She was so perplexed in wondering about why it had to be random that she had no time to question whether she should be doing such a thing in the first place. With another client, a man suffering from migraine headaches seemingly related to an inability to express resentment, I gave posthypnotic suggestions that he would awaken in the middle of the night with "all the pain in the world" in his *left arm*. I adamantly insisted that it be the *left arm* and no other part of his body, so much so that he responded (as expected) by reporting he had awoken with severe pain in his *right shoulder* (and none in his head). In both these cases, the presupposed general response was made peripheral (i.e., unconscious) by focusing the subject on a particular aspect of the response. Of course, this general strategy can also be applied within hypnotic inductions.

*Speaking Generally*

The Ericksonian practitioner often speaks generally while *sounding* quite specific. This pattern stimulates listeners to derive the specific meaning best suited to their personal understandings and needs. This serves many valuable functions—for example, it shifts the burden of responsibility onto the client; it enables the therapist to offer effective guidance without needing to know the exact content of a person's experience, thereby reducing chances of imposing (possibly misfitting) strategies onto the client; it encourages the accessing of meaningful associated experiences (a major goal of associational inductions); and it provides valuable information about what's important to the client. In short, speaking generally is an essential part of the Ericksonian approach.

There are various ways to speak generally but sound specific. For example, *general event referents* can be used:

"that particular time long ago"
"an unexpected yet pleasant surprise"
"the deepest trance you've ever experienced"

"a very happy time from long ago"
"trance"
"a very satisfying feeling"
"those learning experiences of relevance"
"that unfinished, unpleasant experience that you've avoided for so
long"

*General verbs* can also be used: learn, experience, allow, develop,
involve, explore, recognize, become aware of, begin, discover, and so
forth.
*General noun referents* are also available:

"that young child within you who has been hiding for so many years"
"a particular person"
"a very good friend"
"an old enemy who has been haunting you"
"that person you really want to be close to"
"your first grade classroom"
"those deep aspects of yourself that can aid in the process of discovery"

Each of these examples constitutes a general, indirect way to suggest an experiential search through memory for a specific person, place,
event, object, or process. When spoken with conviction within the hypnotic interchange, these generalities immerse the client in internal search
processes culminating in the access of a particular referent. Because the
accessed referent will be different for each individual, using generalities
is an excellent way to respect the unique processes of each individual.

Generalities can be used for many hypnotic purposes. One application
is *accessing trance-related experiences* within an induction. In fact, an
induction might consist entirely of generalities, delivered meaningfully
enough to sound as if they are referring especially to key personal
experiences of the client. The following induction segment illustrates
this possibility (with the commentary questions pointing to the extreme
generality of the referents).

| *Induction Segment* | *Commentary* |
|---|---|
| All right, now all I would like you to do is find *that particular position* which is most comfort- able to you as an individual . . . | which position? |
| and as you *allow* yourself to | allow how? |

begin to shift into *that position*,     which position?
what a nice thing to know that
you can recognize that *a trance*     which trance?
state can be *developed* in *so*     developed how? which ways?
*many different ways* . . . because
trance is *a learning experience*,     experience what learnings?
and you've had so many *differ-*
*ent learning experiences* be-     which experiences?
fore . . .

    you've had *experiences as a*
*young child*, as a growing boy,     which experiences? how young?
as a maturing man, and you will
continue to have *experiences of*
*a specific nature* throughout     which experiences? what nature?
your entire life . . . and what a
nice thing to *know* that you can
*utilize* a trance state to *explore*     know how? utilize how?
*past learning experiences*, and     explore how? which past learn-
*allow* your unconscious to *create*     ing experiences? allow how?
a variety of *experiences impor-*     create how? which experiences?
*tant and valuable* to you as an     important how? important how?
individual . . .

    and so why not let yourself
securely *explore* in a very per-     explore how?
sonal fashion how *absorbing and*     absorb and interest how?
interesting it can be to *drop into*     drop into trance how? know how?
*trance* and get to *know yourself*
at a *different level of experience*     which level?
    . . . and so just *allow* yourself     allow how?
to discover *that particular style,*     which style? which rhythm?
*rhythm? that particular rhythm,*
*that particular rate* of develop-     which rate? suitable how?
ing a trance that is most *suita-*
*ble* for you as an individual. . . .

    These sorts of general and permissive suggestions enable individuals
to derive the specific trance-relevant meanings best for them. This
places the hypnotist in the proper role of merely guiding and supervising
the subject's trance development (Erickson, 1952). It also bypasses the
potential "resistance" which often occurs when specific suggestions are
(1) delivered in too direct or overbearing a fashion or (2) simply inappropriate for the individual's unique needs and understandings.

    Generalities can also be used to *pace a person's ongoing internal*
*experience*. As noted in Chapter 4, the hypnotherapist often needs to

know only the client's trance depth and the type of intensity of emotional processes; at the same time, the therapist must communicate *as if* he or she is aware of the specific content of the experience, for otherwise clients may feel insufficient rapport and thus be unwilling to fully let go. Ideal for this purpose are specific-sounding generalities based on the client's nonverbal behavior. For example, the subject who appears to be developing a pleasant hypnotic experience might be told:

> . . . That's right . . . and just allow yourself to continue to develop that experience, knowing that your unconscious can provide you with the security and guidance to become even more fully immersed in that enjoyable and supportive experience . . . and I don't know and you don't know where that experience will lead . . . but I do know that you can let yourself fully explore it. . . .

Such statements could be modified appropriately if minimal cues indicate that the client is coming out of trance, accessing an unpleasant experience, finding something funny, and so on.

Relatedly, a third application is to *pace external stimuli during trance* – for example, a telephone ringing, plane flying overhead, children playing outside. The subject immersed in trance may or may not have oriented to these noises. To play it safe, the hypnotist can generally pace them by saying something like:

> . . . And you become aware of a variety of different things in trance . . . and what a nice thing to know that you can let those awarenesses come and go, secure in the understanding that they all can enable you to become ever more immersed in trance. . . .

Such statements pace any external stimuli in the subject's awareness, but do not force orientation to unattended stimuli. As such, they are preferable to specific statements, which run the risk of disrupting the absorption of the person unaware of the stimuli.

Another application of generalities is as *filler material* insertable when the hypnotherapist runs out of things to say, or when he or she wants to provide the client with the opportunity to develop some accessed experience or generally explore hypnotic realities for a while. During such periods, speaking generally (e.g., about the intelligence and autonomy of the unconscious or the benefits or security of trance) is entirely appropriate. It provides the hypnotist with "breathing room" to assess which direction is best to proceed in, and enables the subject to experience the enormous benefits possible from specific trance explorations guided *not* by the hypnotist but by his or her own unconscious. Permission to use generalities as filler material often brings great relief to the many trainees worried and burdened by the erroneous idea that they must spew out a continuous stream of specific, relevant suggestions for the entirety of an induction. Everything you say as a hypnotist *does not* have to be profound or incredibly relevant; if it simply *sounds* meaningful (and if your intent is clearly to support the person), the subject's unconscious can often take care of the rest.

Generalities can also be employed to *"bridge"* topics in a smooth fashion. Often this simply requires general phrases such as:

... And so the unconscious can respond in a variety of different ways ... I'll give you another example. . . .

... And those things happen in other ways. . . . For example. . . .

As Figure 6.2 indicates, such statements enable the hypnotist to make transitions to virtually unrelated topics, especially since the hypnotized subject will generally be uncritical of the logical relations between top-

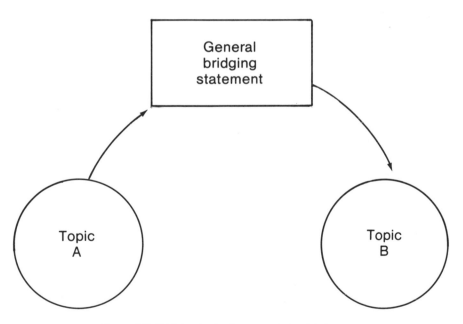

Figure 6.2. Bridging topics in conversational inductions

ics. They are particularly valuable in beginning and ending metaphorical stories used during the induction (as discussed in the section on telling stories).

In the bridging technique, the general strategy is to use a general characteristic shared by the to-be-connected topics as the crossover point. For example, say I wanted to bridge from talking about a child-hood classroom experience to getting into an argument as an adult. I might say something like:

> And among other things, those many learnings accrued as a child included understandings about the many different ways people relate to each other . . . and those understandings were important, because people really can interact in so many different ways, some pleasant and some not. For example, people sometimes argue. . . .

Thus, the shared characteristic of "ways of relating" forms the middle term in the specific-to-general-to-specific bridging process. Because of the vast array of possible shared characteristics, using general statements as crossover communications is usually an easy task.

Relatedly, a sixth possibility is to use generalities to set forth general "themes" that serve as frames of references to integrate various hypnotic communications. Themes I commonly employ include:

1. Trance is naturalistic.
2. Trance is a learning experience.
3. Trance is an opportunity to get to know yourself at a different level of experience.
4. Trance is a secure place you can always use to support yourself.
5. The unconscious is intelligent.
6. The unconscious can operate autonomously.
7. Your unconscious is an ally.

Besides serving some of the above-mentioned functions (e.g., filler communications, bridges, general instructions), elaborated comments on these themes can play a major role in the critical hypnotherapeutic task of teaching the client to trust and utilize trance experiences and unconscious processes. As such, I make it a point to intersperse them liberally throughout an induction.

A final possibility is to use general statements for *diagnostic purposes*. This can be done with a modified form of the "game of 20 questions" in which the therapist starts by absorbing the client's attention and then, using an intensely meaningful delivery, mentions various experiences of potential therapeutic importance. For example:

And there are certain experiences in your life that cry out for special attention . . . experiences you feel especially insecure about . . . and whether they involve your wife . . . (pause several seconds) . . . or your work situation . . . (pause again) . . . or your children . . . (pause) . . . is not that important . . . what's important is that your unconscious can assist you in dealing with them. . . .

The pause after each specific topic allows the activation of any relevant experiences. This accessing process can be intensified by looking probingly and expectantly at the client; this also enables detection of minimal cues indicating an emotional (i.e., self-relevant) response to a presented topic. The absence of such cues suggests that the topic is not therapeutically critical, in which case another one might be mentioned.[3] The presence of emotional cues (e.g., changes in breathing, facial coloration, pupillary dilation) indicate that the topic is therapeutically relevant in some way. To gain more specific information (while intensifying the accessed experience), the therapist can reiterate the process of mentioning various possibilities, this time focusing only on the responded-to topic. Thus, if a client given the above example responded emotionally when his wife was mentioned, the hypnotist might continue by saying:

. . . And a relationship between a husband and a wife can be very complicated at times, and can go wrong in so many different places . . . the sexual relationship . . . (pause meaningfully) . . . the social aspects . . . (pause) . . . arguments over the children . . . etc.

In this way, the hypnotherapist can gradually hone in on some particularly relevant experience and utilize it accordingly.

This "game of 20 questions" is an effective technique for rapidly accessing experiential issues central to a client's problems. It is especially valuable with clients unable or unwilling to report such information, as it bypasses the intellectual involvement of the conscious mind. Of course, its range of application extends beyond accessing problem issues. For example, it can be used to probe which childhood associations (e.g., a nickname, a pet or playmate, a teacher) will best absorb a person in an age regression process, or which styles of trance development might be best for a person. In all these situations, the therapist (1) offers general possibilities, (2) observationally identifies ones that elicit emotional responses, then (3) narrows the scope of discussion to

---

[3]This assumes, of course, that the hypnotist has the subject adequately absorbed and is speaking compellingly enough so that the subject *would* access emotional responses if there were any related to the topic.

them. This process is reiterated until the client is hypnotically immersed in some specific experience.

In conclusion, speaking generally enables a person to derive unique meanings from hypnotic communications. Its many applications include inducing trance, pacing internal or external awarenesses, bridging topics, serving as filler material, setting themes, and accessing key experiences. For generalities to be effective, they must be delivered meaningfully and expectantly to an experientially absorbed subject.

## Telling Stories

Chapter 1 noted how unconscious processes tend to represent and comprehend ideas more metaphorically than conscious processes. The Ericksonian hypnotherapist therefore utilizes symbolic and metaphorical communications — especially those which stimulate self-referential processing — to encourage unconscious processing. In this regard, a major Ericksonian technique is to tell stories which are metaphorical in that (1) the content of the story does *not* refer to the subject but (2) some major aspects of the story (e.g., the characters, events, themes, goals) are relevant to the subject's experience. Thus, the client fearing trance might be offered an anecdote about *somebody else* who faced and successfully overcame such difficulties; the person overeager to go into trance might be told a story about a marathon runner who burnt himself out too quickly or a man who suffered from premature ejaculation; the individual desiring a pleasant regression experience could be presented with tales about class reunions or common childhood experiences. That such stories do not *directly* reference the subject makes it difficult to consciously "resist" them, but their relevance encourages the automatic activation of similar experiences. This is a pervasive naturalistic process; for example, a typical response while listening to a friend casually describe a vacation trip to Hawaii is to revivify memories of *your* vacation to Hawaii or some place similar, or to think of some related personal experience(s). This self-referencing strategy is actually quite functional. As Bower and Gilligan (1979) reported, items learned by associating personal experiences to them are much better remembered than items learned with other major learning strategies. As such, stories are excellent indirect techniques for bypassing the conscious mind while accessing unconscious processes.

In terms of the therapeutic relationship, stories can be seen to provide a third focus point, thereby expanding an unstable dyad to a balanced triad. Specifically, Panel A of Figure 6.3 represents the therapist as one

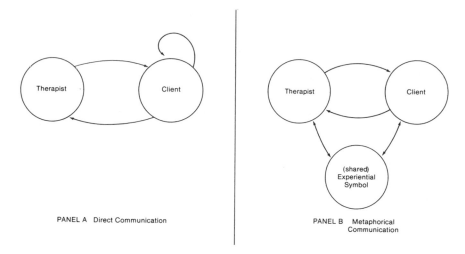

Figure 6.3. Structural differences between direct and indirect (metaphorical) communication

point of reference and the client as another. In direct communication, the subject of reference is either therapist or client; Panel A indicates the latter choice as the more typical one in traditional therapy, and shows how this creates a self-referential loop back onto the client. That is, the client must operate simultaneously at a private, experiential level and a public, behavioral level. This tends to facilitate self-consciousness (e.g., anxiety, inhibition, defensiveness, self-monitoring).

Panel B represents how indirect communications (e.g., stories) bypass this potential imbalance by introducting a third point of reference, one that is neither therapist nor client. As the arrows indicate, this meta-phorical referent enables the client to participate experientially in the interpersonal domain in a discrete (i.e., safe) and balanced fashion. Meta-phorical stories, then, constitute an experiential circle of overlap in which both therapist and client can operate as "a part of yet apart from" the experiential process.

Metaphorical stories can be used for various purposes in the hypnotic setting; this section focuses on their utilization during inductions. One general strategy for inducing trance via stories is to mold the story to aspects of the client's experience (e.g., interests, concerns, ongoing be-havior). In this approach, the hypnotherapist first identifies the thera-peutic intention for telling a story (e.g., to absorb attention, develop trance, elicit a trance phenomenon). With this basic interest in mind, the therapist might then generate possible stories by shifting into an interpersonal trance and letting images and associations flow in and out of awareness as hypnotic interaction occurs with the client. From this wealth of unconscious productions an appropriate image can be selected – for example, one that relates to the client's situation, will sufficiently absorb attention, is not too similar in content to the client's situation (because conscious awareness of the parallels invites conscious interference), does not end in a disastrous state (e.g., a story about a nuclear war is not too utilizable), will not trigger emotional responses unrelated to the desired response (e.g., don't try to induce a trance in a socialist by extolling the greatness of Ronald Reagan).[4] This image can then be unfolded into a story befitting the intention and circumstances of the present situation.

A good way to begin a story is with a general theme or idea. For example:

1. And trance is naturalistic, involving psychological processes which occur in a variety of different situations. . . . For example. . . .

2. And the unconscious really can operate independently. . . . For example. . . .

3. And trance is a learning experience . . . and we've all had so many different learning experiences. . . . For example. . . .

4. Now before you go into trance, here's a story you should really contemplate. . . .

5. And what does all of this have to do with trance? Well I'll illustrate the point I want to make with a story. . . .

The story can then be delivered, with the content adjusted to fit the client's experience. For example, certain themes can be repetitively emphasized, or the client's behavioral responses metaphorically paced. How the story is developed depends partly on its purpose within the induction. It might be used to bore or distract the client's conscious

---

[4]It is almost unavoidable that at some point during hypnotic elaborations the therapist will unwittingly violate an emotional value held by the client. This will be evidenced by arrythmic shifts in the client's muscular and breathing patterns (as part of a withdrawal from the therapist), and usually can be handled by a straightforward utilization (e.g., an apology). Clients are generally very forgiving (as long as the therapist's intent is clear), and such pattern interruptions provide excellent diagnostic information (see Gilligan, 1985).

mind, thereby clearing the way for trance development.[5] Or it might *reframe* the client's understandings or concerns in a positive way, thereby motivating the person to develop trance. The story can also be used to access trancelike experiences in the client. Of course, an induction might include all these applications. For example, a man was eager but apprehensive about experiencing trance. His mentioning of a keen interest in outdoor activities triggered the following metaphorical induction:

| *Induction* | *Commentary* |
|---|---|
| All right, Fred, now it's important that you don't go all the way into trance just yet . . . it's very important that you hold on for as long as is appropriate. . . . And so before I even ask you to fully experience a trance, I'd like to share with you a story about a boating experience I had. Now | The story is prefaced with statements which (1) pace the trance inhibitions while (2) presupposing trance will occur. |
| I've always wanted to go out sailing in the bay, and I mentioned this to a friend of mine, Peter, and Peter immediately mentioned that his business partner, Dave, happened to own a beautiful yacht which he kept down at the Marina, and which they were planning to go out sailing on that Saturday . . . | The subject had been referred to me for trance by a mutual friend. The invitation to the "new boating experience" is a metaphorical reference to this. |
| Peter promptly invited me along, saying he was sure it would be all right with Dave . . . I began to experience some trepidation, some hesitation, some concerns about sailing out in the bay, but I figured they'd just go away . . . or at least I hoped they would | The subject's anxiety about trance is paced, along with his desire to experience it. |

---

[5]In this regard, boredom was a favorite technique that Erickson employed with recalcitrant subjects in his final years. As he once told me, "If they won't go into trance any other way, I'll *bore* them into trance."

... and so I quickly assented to his offer ... I made all the necessary arrangements for the trip ... (I proceeded for about 10 minutes to describe various details of this preparation process.) But upon arriving at the Marina that Saturday, I felt myself in the grips of a nervous anxiety ... I didn't know what might happen, I was afraid of not being on the solid land to which I was accustomed ... but I boarded the yacht, and Dave was waiting there along with Peter ... and Peter seemed like a nice enough fellow who knew what he was doing, and so I knew it was appropriate to *feel at ease* because the captain was competent ... but that didn't happen all at once, of course ... we had a cup of coffee, talked about mutual interests, and were able to establish some rapport ... and so after a while I was still nervous but willing to go ahead with it. ... The captain told me to *just sit comfortably*, that there was *no need to move or talk*, that I could simply let him do all the work, and I could devote myself fully to the scenery, fully allowing myself to *enjoy the experience* ... but as he talked to me, I still felt somewhat nervous. .... He was an astute observer, and so he noticed this and said to me: "Now I'm sure you've got a lot of expectations about what you'd like to get out of this trip. ... And I'm sure you might be a little excited ... and maybe a little scared about going into this. ... But that's normal ...

This detailing was done to further distract and bore his conscious mind, thereby "lulling" him into a more experiential "daydreaming" type of processing.

The subject arrived that morning feeling nervous about the possibility of losing "grounding" with his normal support systems. There was nobody else in the office. Such mismatching of information is added to ensure that the story isn't too obvious.

The subject seemed to like me, and appeared to relax a bit after a while. Embedded suggestions to relax are offered, along with assurances of my competency.

The subject stirred a bit at this point, seemingly in reaction to my preceding statement. His need to not fully let go is paced. The subject's attention was by now pretty well absorbed, and so embedded suggestions for trance are given.

The remaining nervousness of the subject is still paced.

I was looking intently at the subject, who had developed tunnel vision, as I gave these direct quotes for trance development.

| | |
|---|---|
| I'd suggest you just stay with those feelings . . . *breathe fully, freely, and comfortably*, and notice how they can begin to change. . . . Now I'll handle all the steering and protect you from any danger . . . all you need to do is *relax and feel* the undeniable immersion into a *pleasant state begin to develop so easily.*" | The subject is instructed to let go of conscious control, and is assured that he is protected. |
| And so I began to let myself really *enjoy the trip* and *let go and learn about these new ways of being.* . . . | Further embedded suggestions for trance are given, as the subject is now developing a nice trance. |

I continued the story for another 10 minutes or so. During this time I metaphorically described various trance experiences by generally noting some of the enjoyable experiences available on a sailing trip. I also included various dialogue as a means of pacing and leading the subject's internal dialogue. In addition, ongoing responses were paced indirectly. For example, the subject's head nodding from side to side was paralleled with comments about how the pleasant rocking of the boat by the wind provided such a secure and enjoyable feeling.

To complete the trance, I described the conclusion of the trip and how we got back to shore. I included direct quotes stating, "It's time to come back now . . . time to reorient to the mundane world once again." This served to reorient the subject. He opened his eyes, smiled, stretched, yawned, then smiled again. He reported becoming so absorbed in hypnotic explorations after a while that he was no longer aware of hearing my voice. After about a half hour of discussion, he was dismissed.

In using such metaphorical stories, keep in mind that the process is far more important than the content. The best story in the world will not elicit hypnotic responses unless the listener implicitly recognizes *and accepts* that it is appropriate to respond personally to a story. For example, your willingness and ability to become absorbed experientially in a story told by a good friend in a casual situation would probably be far greater than if the same story was told in roughly the same way by a stranger in a busy business situation. Similarly, persons in the hypnotic setting may be *unwilling* to open up and access personal experiences if they don't trust the hypnotist; or they may be *unable* to become experientially absorbed, often owing to (1) nagging internal dialogue which constantly questions things or (2) a noncompelling delivery style employed by the hypnotist (e.g., a dry and somber monotone). Thus, the hypnotist must first establish an adequate context and then accompany the story with communications that adequately pace the subject's responses and are meaningful enough to secure and maintain attentional absorption.

By attending to these variables, the hypnotist will find that stories can play a major role in the induction process. In addition to their above-described value in pacing conscious processes while accessing unconscious responses, applications include many of those described in the preceding section on generalities – for example, as "filler" material, to reframe processes, to emphasize general themes, and to identify therapeutic issues with the modified "game of 20 questions." Stories are also tremendously valuable in eliciting specific trance phenomena. In this regard, an excellent training exercise is to generate 10 naturalistic examples of each hypnotic phenomenon – that is, common everyday experiences involving the psychological processes represented by a phenomenon. For example, think of 10 times when you surprisingly forgot something ("amnesia"); or experiences resembling hand levitation or arm catalepsy (standing on a bus, holding the telephone, raising a hand in class); or incidents of "age regression" (going back home for Christmas, seeing an old lover, looking at a photograph). At a general level, this task reveals trance phenomena as naturalistic processes; perhaps more than anything else, this way of conceptualizing trance responses is critical to mastering Ericksonian approaches.[6] At a specific level, a highly effective way to educe a phenomenon is to follow general statements with some of the generated examples. For example, the hypnotist could begin to elicit age regression by saying:

> And what a nice thing to know that the unconscious can operate creatively in so many different ways . . . you can explore a variety of different experiences in such a secure fashion . . . and so what

---

[6]To reiterate, much of Erickson's understanding of trance came from naturalistic experiences (Erickson & Rossi, 1977). For example, a major strategy he used to recover physically from the total paralysis induced by an adolescent polio attack was to single out a small group of muscles (e.g., his right index finger) and then revivify childhood experiences in which those muscles were active (e.g., swinging on a tree). By intensely absorbing himself in the memory for extended periods, he usually could produce ideomotoric movement in the target muscles. Eventually, he regained mobility in most of his body. This and other examples of how Erickson spontaneously used hypnotic processes in his own life (see Erickson & Rossi, 1977) provide some insight into his remarkable ability to develop and apply naturalistic techniques, such as metaphorical stories, in his hypnotic work with others.

a nice thing to know that your unconscious can surprise you by calling to mind an experience from long ago, an experience you've long forgotten . . . and we've all had that pleasant surprise of a long-forgotten memory before. . . . For example . . . (tell story).

In this strategy, the generalities develop a general framework for regression, and the stories then reference specific examples which emphasize the phenomenon as a naturalistic and familiar psychological process. The stories also provide the subject with the time needed to develop the phenomenon. And by ideodynamic principles – which, remember, are enhanced in trance – the specific memories activated by the stories will tend to revivify the referenced phenomenon. Thus, such stories are excellent techniques for indirectly developing hypnotic phenomenon.

## Using Associational Anchors

Modern psychology began with simple theories of association which assumed that a response related to a stimulus through experience will tend to *automatically* be elicited upon presentation of the stimulus (see Hilgard & Bower, 1975). While associational theories have become much more sophisticated and diversified, especially with the recent rise of cognitive psychology, the basic concept of associational bonding is still central to most learning theories. In the hypnotherapeutic context, triggering associational responses is a major method used to induce trance. This section discusses how to identify and use *previously developed associations*; the next section addresses *therapist-developed anchors* (i.e., associational cues).

To start with, we may consider all experience in terms of relationships between elemental ideas. Figure 6.4 illustrates experiences as associational networks tagged with digital markers (i.e., language). Each associational complex is a multiple-cue, multiple-modality gestalt, perhaps best considered as an event structure. The value (i.e., the meaning) of the experiential unit is derived from the relationship gestalt among the multiple cues and indicated by the markers tagged to it. A person's life history may be represented as a complex network of different interrelated associational complexes bonded by shared stimulus cues and higher-order gestalts (e.g., abstracted meanings).

For our present purposes, a major point is that the utilization approach emphasizes hypnotic communications based on the naturalistic use of a person's associational values. Of course, it is impossible to *not* utilize these associational values, since all understanding is based on

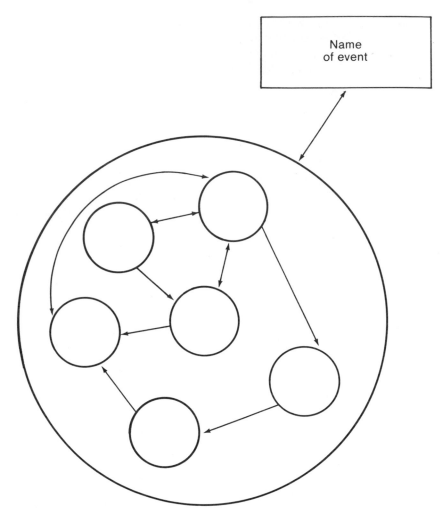

Figure 6.4. Generalized schema representation of an experience as an associational complex

them. The therapist's task is to identify those verbal and nonverbal cues that elicit experiential responses from the client, and then to use them as the basis for therapeutic explorations. A number of points are relevant in this regard:

*1. An evocative stimulus can occur in any experiential modality.* That is, a cue may involve a sensation, a visual image, a feeling, a body posture or movement, a perception, a word or phrase, a person, etc.

*2. Associational stimuli are generally idiosyncratic.* For example, one woman accessed a sense of security upon thinking of her childhood stuffed animals; another woman felt incredibly pleasant and childlike when "fudgicles" were mentioned; a man felt serene and complete when he thought of his darling two-year-old daughter. Of course, some evocative cues are more collectively shared: the alphabet song, childhood nicknames, a pat on the head, and so forth.

*3. An accessed response may be pleasant or unpleasant.* For example, discussing horses with one woman accessed her satisfaction of riding her champion horse; for another woman, it revivified the awful pain felt when her horse died of starvation; for a young man it triggered a frightening memory of being nipped by a belligerent pony. In hypnotic inductions, it is often preferable to access pleasant responses when initially training a client to experience trance, thereby emphasizing trance as a secure and safe context for self exploration. Thus, the therapist might use casual conversation to identify emotional responses to various associations and then use those evocative of pleasant states to develop trance. (Of course, such probing might trigger unpleasant responses, to which the hypnotist can respond by pacing and then leading to something else. The exception to this is when the response is rather strong and thus not easily dissipated, in which case it can be utilized as the basis for developing and utilizing a therapeutic trance. This is further discussed later on.)

*4. A variety of trance-related responses can be accessed by associational stimuli.* To identify associational responses, a number of questions can be offered in an absorbing fashion, with the experiential responses carefully observed. Examples of typical questions include:

- What sorts of activities really allow you to feel pleasurably absorbed? Movies? Books? Watching sports? Work?
- What do you do for relaxation?
- What especially pleasurable associations come to mind when I ask you to think of pleasurable childhood memories?
- What were your favorite games as a child?
- What relationships are especially valuable to you?

Through interviews including questions such as these, a number of different associational values can be identified. Recently, for example, I identified during an initial session with a client the following experiential associations.

*Experiential absorption*
- reading the newspaper in the morning
- listening to jazz music
- looking in my eyes

*Relaxation*
- meditation
- going for a walk after dinner
- receiving a massage

*Security*
- confidence in mountain climbing abilities
- confidence in relationship with wife ("Alice")
- holding his baby daughter ("Tina")

*Childhood state (age regression)*
- childhood nickname of "Bud"
- playing Scrabble with his brother
- watching cartoons

*Naturalistic dissociation*
- watching movies
- sitting in class on Friday afternoon
- driving his car long distance

These stimuli constitute evocative cues enabling direct access to the client's experiential tapestry of life resources. They can be utilized for many purposes, including hypnotic induction. Using the associational values obtained in the above case, the following suggests how the different identified cues could be woven into a naturalistic induction based on the subject's values and associations.

| *Example* | *Commentary* |
|---|---|
| (i) And now Charlie, I'd like to have you look here and continue to look here even as you *there* continue to *hear* me *here* and see me *here* from you *there* with the discovery developing of so many different secure alterations in orientation even while maintaining, in fact deepening, that security of Self . . . that's right . . . because Charlie, trance is an experiential process, a process of security, a process of learning, a process of comfortable development of a state for | The association of absorption while looking in my eyes is used to secure attention within an interpersonal and intrapersonal framework while providing a ground for offering initial statements about trance. As in most trances, I emphasize security immediately, since I find this to be an outstanding concern of most individuals. The emphasis on "here" and "there" is used to distinguish the interpersonal context as the context for trance. |

the Self in the Self by the Self
for the Self with the Self. . . .

(ii) . . . and with the Self you can
realize, Charlie, that trance is an
opportunity for secure revivification and meaningful reorganization of learnings . . . learnings
and values that are resources
and will be resources for the rest
of your life . . . and you've got so
many different resources, so
many different learnings, so
many different possibilities, so
many different ways to develop
a trance . . . that's right . . . and
so you really can enjoy discovering that ability, even now developing further that letting go,
and finding that secure and
meaningful trance state unfolding from within . . . with the
confidence of climbing that
mountain for the Self and with
the Self, Charlie . . . of obtaining
a secure foothold for Self expression . . . with the security of
knowing the feeling of a baby's
eyes, Charlie . . . with the comfort of walking after a good
meal shared with a family . . . all
those values and then some . . .
in a trance you can enjoy those
values and then some, with the
security and letting go of meditation expressed in the natural
rhythms of Self. . . .

A basic idea ("trance is a secure
context for reorganization") is
experientially introduced. The
identified associations of mountain climbing, baby's eyes,
walking after dinner, and meditation are interspersed straightforwardly to stimulate relaxation
and security responses. The in-
clusion of multiple associations
helps also to disperse attention
widely and discourage the lineal,
sequential cognitive processing
of the conscious mind.

(iii) . . . and you can let that security of trance unfold in so many
different ways . . . you can discover the ability of your unconscious to operate autonomously
in accord with the needs of entire Self . . . and whether reading
a paper . . . whether listening to

Further associations (reading
paper, jazz, my eyes, baby's
eyes, massage) are seeded as the
general message of deeper expression of unconscious processes is offered.

jazz . . . whether looking in my
eyes or the eyes of a baby
daughter . . . you can feel that
confidence, like a massage
through and in and from the
secure Center of Self . . . and the
massage is the message, Charlie
. . . you can feel it . . . the tension
letting go . . . the associations
unfolding . . . the deeper Self expressing . . . you can feel it. . . .

(iv) . . . and you can feel those
natural rhythms of the Self
which grew as a Bud, which
were present as you learned to
arrange and rearrange elemental
learnings and understandings in
complex relationships . . . Big
A's and little A's . . . Big B's and
little B's . . . Big brothers and
little brothers . . . and fitting
them together in new ways . . .
spelling your name . . . and the
Scrabble of finding new expressions . . . "i" after "e" except. . . .
and holding the Q (cue), wondering and waiting when "u" (You)
will follow . . . and finding in a
trance – that's right, a little bit
deeper – that elemental learning
of a Bud growing . . . of a cue (Q)
followed by You (U) . . . and so
trance really is an opportunity
for an organization and reorganization of the values and learnings of Self in accord with the
present needs and understandings of the Self. . . .

Childhood associations (learning
the alphabet, spelling your
name, big brother, playing
Scrabble, the nickname of "Bud")
are used to elaborate a major
theme of Ericksonian hypnotherapy, namely, that trance is a
context for reorganization of
elemental learnings.

(v) . . . and so you can feel so
many different things, all generated from that security of Self
. . . because you know those
pleasurable and secure values of

An association to security (his
wife "Alice") is used to introduce
a dissociational state of hypnotic exploration unconstrained
by time/space coordinates.[7] The

Alice in Wonderland . . . and you can enjoy that wonderland with Alice . . . and so why not let go even more and explore that wonderland of different experiential associations . . . in that security of Self where you can operate independently of time and space constants . . . where time and space can alter in accord with the needs of the entire Self . . . time and space as variables . . . time changing, as when you experience that absorption of watching a movie . . . or sit in a lecture listening to the instructor drone on full bore . . . or drive so far and so long in that auto . . . hypnotic state of mile after mile . . . the scenery changes, Charlie . . . space changes . . . time is changing . . . you can feel it . . . and watch and feel and know and treasure those unfolding values of the Self as you drop even deeper now into that secure Middle of Nowhere. . . .

dissociation associations (absorbing movies, boring lecture, "auto-hypnotic" trip) are used to further develop this "Middle of Nowhere" or "Center of Self" state, which is a context central in hypnotherapeutic work.

The above example is one of many ways that associations can play a major role in hypnotic communications. Any of these associations might be elaborated in depth (e.g., through stories), depending on the subject's responses and the goals of the hypnotherapy.

*5. Associational responses can be accessed directly or indirectly.* Again, the basic idea is that experiential learnings are represented as associational complexes of multiple elements in multiple modalities. To access certain responses (e.g., emotional experiences of absorption or security), one need only identify idiosyncratic cues related through

---

[7]This unbounded dissociational state should only be introduced when the hypnotherapist is confident that the interpersonal and intrapersonal relationships are sufficiently balanced to allow free-floating exploration. With deeply insecure clients, for example, more boundaries are needed at the outset.

experience to these responses. The strength of the associational relationships will vary, of course. A relatively direct accessing of desired
responses can be made by selecting strongly related cues and straightforwardly inserting them within hypnotic communications, as in the
above example. A more indirect accessing of responses can be accomplished by selecting weakly related cues and presenting them in unrelated contexts. A beautiful illustration of this is described by Erickson (1964b):

> Perhaps a very simple and easily understood example can be
> given to clarify this type of accumulation of minimal cues leading
> to a specific response. The rest of the family was out for the
> evening. I was ill but comfortably seated in a chair. Bert, aged
> 17, had volunteered to remain at home to keep me company
> although there was no such need. A casual conversation was ini-
> tiated by Bert in which he mentioned the rush and turmoil of
> getting everybody dressed and fed and everything packed for a
> past vacation trip to northern Michigan. . . . Next he mentioned
> the fishing, the catching of frogs and frog-leg dinner, the beach
> dinner, and the sand that the smaller children managed to sprin-
> kle over every item of food, and the albino frog at the abandoned
> quarry we had found.
> Next he described in vivid detail the turmoil of getting every-
> thing out of the summer cabin, the oversights, the hunting for
> misplaced items, and the wandering off of the smaller children and
> the hurried search for them, the locking-up of the cabin, and the
> hungry tired state we were in when we arrived at Wayne County
> General Hospital near Detroit where we lived.
> At this point, a vague notion passed through my mind to sug-
> gest to Bert that he might take the car and visit some friend, but
> this idea vanished as Bert laughingly told of how his brother
> Lance particularly liked Grandma Erickson's fried chicken on the
> way back to Michigan from Wisconsin. With much laughter, he
> recalled another occasion in which his small brother Allan had
> amused everybody, and especially Grandma and Grandpa Erick-
> son with his "bulldozer" pattern of eating, that is, holding his plate
> up to his mouth and systematically using his other hand to shove
> the contents of the plate slowly and steadily into his mouth.
> Again, this time a clearer idea came to mind of suggesting that
> Bert take the car keys and go for a ride so that I could enjoy
> reading, but I forgot it as I recalled my father's amused comment
> on the absolute efficiency and speed of Allan's method of eating.
> While we were laughing about this, Bert mentioned the trip to
> my brother's farm and six-year-old Betty Alice's long solemn ex-

planation to three-year-old Allan's worried inquiry about how the mama chickens nursed their babies, that chickens were not mammals and only mammals nursed their young. While we were laughing about this, a third time the thought came to mind of offering the car for the evening, this time most clearly, and I recognized why. In every item of reminiscences, Bert was speaking of pleasant and happy memories based each upon the driving of the car. Yet not once had he actually said the word "car," the nearest he came to that was to say "packing up," "trip," "went to see," "way out to the old quarry," "down to the beach," "on the way back to Michigan from Wisconsin," and the trip to my brother's farm, and not once did he mention the word key — locking-up the cabin was as close as he came to that.

I recognized that situation at once and remarked, "The answer is 'No'." He laughed and said, "Well, Dad, you'll have to admit it was a good try." "Not good enough, I caught on too fast. You overemphasized trips in the car. You should have mentioned the picketing of Ned's place, where our car was serviced, Ed Carpenter from whom I bought the car, the ice-fishing trip which was in Emil's car but did involve an automobile. In brief, you restricted yourself to a constant indirect mention of pleasure trips, always in relationship to us, it was always in our car. The inference to be drawn became too obvious. Do you really want the car?" His answer was, "No, I just thought I'd get a little fun out of getting you to offer me the car keys." (In Rossi, 1980a, pp. 358–359)

Comparing this example to the preceding one, one can see its more indirect nature. Generally speaking, more indirect accessing is desirable to the extent that the client's conscious processes may interfere with receptive experiential processing.

*6. Associational elements should be utilized at a rate and pace appropriate for the individual client.* Since the general purpose of introducing associational cues is to access experiential responses, it should be kept in mind that the degree to which a client is willing and able to become fully absorbed in his or her tapestry of experiential learnings will vary. With a recent client, for example, I had great difficulty identifying many pleasant associations. She grew up in Europe during World War II and had terrible childhood experiences. Her reports indicated that her adult life was not much better: she married a violent alcoholic, felt depressed much of the time, had difficulty finding work, and had few friends. With such individuals possessing a paucity of learnings marked as valuable, I usually refrain initially from attempting to access specific memories and instead focus on absorbing the person in an interpersonal trance involving experiential orientation to me. Once security associations have been developed with me, I then slowly guide the client through the unpleasant associational responses that have come to dominate them.

## Developing Associational Relationships

Besides utilizing existing associational values, the hypnotherapist can develop new associational bondings for therapeutic purposes. This enables the therapist to influence how, what, and when experiential associations are evoked. To establish associational bondings effectively, the following five principles should be observed.

*1. Interpersonal absorption and trust.* Meaningful associations are always established within a context. Thus, it is important that the experiential context distinguishing the client's state should include the hypnotherapist if the latter is to successfully establish associational cues. The therapist should therefore absorb the subject's attention before attempting to anchor any experiences, and secure trust and rapport.

*2. Uniqueness.* The most effective "anchor" cues will be those not already tagged to other experiences in a person's experiences. For example, a normal handshake would probably not be a good tag to associate to some experience, since it already is connected with many other experiences. Thus, the best cues are usually those associated to the hypnotherapist, either innocuous (e.g., a meaningful touch on the knee) or unusually unique (e.g., a deeply meaningful look).

*3. Clearing.* At the time of the associational bonding, no other experience should be prominent in the subject's consciousness. Thus, the subject should be experientially absorbed (e.g., entranced) before and while the associational tagging is made.

*4. Timing.* Experiential associations are best developed when the anchor is presented at the height of experiential accessing. A simple way to ensure proper timing is to use accessing techniques to elicit a desired experience. While a technique is being utilized, the therapist should carefully observe the nonverbal minimal cues characterizing the subject's response (e.g., breathing pattern, facial coloration, muscle tonus). Shifts in these parameters reflect experiential accessing, at which point the associational tag is best introduced.

*5. Conscious bypassing.* This principle assumes that in the hypnotic context, associational tags are best developed independent from conscious mediation by the subject. Conscious mediation will typically impose the subject's frames between the experience and the tag, thereby defeating the purpose of such bondings in the hypnotic context. To effectively bypass conscious participation, it is often best to have the subject in at least a light trance. Another approach is to distract the subject in one representational system (Chapter 4) – for example, the input system they tend to most selectively use consciously – while tagging an accessed experience in another modality.

To apply these principles, the therapist might begin by ensuring that the subject is "cleared out," that is, absorbed fully and experientially in the interpersonal process. This can be accomplished straightforwardly by looking meaningfully at the subject, absorbing his or her attention, and asking gently that he or she simply orient internally. The hypnotherapist then utilizes some accessing technique (e.g., any outlined in this chapter); for example, the person might be asked to remember an experience characterized by comfort and security, and to indicate with a head nod or finger lift when the experience has been accessed. When the person signals accordingly, the therapist introduces the cue. For example, he or she might reach over and touch the subject's knee in a particular fashion; or emphasize softly the phrase "*that* experience of security"; or perhaps use a distinctly different tone of voice (that is congruent with the accessed experience). The selected cue thereby becomes tagged to the experience of comfort, such that its presentation will elicit the experience at a later time. If it does not, a review of the above principles will allow further efforts to succeed.

Of the many clinical applications of developing associational bonds, a few especially relevant to the hypnotic context will be mentioned here.

*1. Induce trance.* Trance can be developed by associationally tagging certain ongoing behavior of the subject as trance-inducing. An excellent example is the "blink synchronization" technique, which involves associating the eyelid blinking responses of the subject to the development of trance. Since blinking is automatic, naturalistic, and usually unavoidable, its gentle utilization invariably leads into trance. A somewhat indirect version of the technique involves describing some behavior (other than blinking) in terms of "up" and "down" motions, while synchronizing these directional terms to the actual blinking patterns of the subject. This is best implemented during a "casual conversation" induction, as represented by the following example:

| *Example* | *Commentary* |
|---|---|
| (i) . . . And there's a lot of ways you can develop and experience a trance. . . . you can *drop all the way down into trance* . . . and then *come up* for a while. . . . (pause to await next blink). . . . and then *drop down* again, and back *up*. . . . and drop *down*, and come back *up*. . . . | This first step indirectly paces the eyeblink responses of the subject. The words "drop down" are stated when the subject blinks, and the words "come up" immediately follow the eyelids opening again. In this way, the blink is paced and tagged as connected to trance activity. Also, "down" is delivered with a downwards inflection, "up" with a rising inflection. |
| (ii) . . . And you begin to find the rhythm that best allows you to experience an increasing depth of security and experiential absorption . . . so whether it is *up* or *down* at a slow rate, or whether you come *up* and then *down, up*. . . . and down. . . . *up* and *down* in an increasingly effortless and autonomous fashion. . . . | The hypnotherapist begins to gradually lead the subject's blink responses by introducing the words "down" and then waiting for the blink to occur. This is an indirect suggestion to increase the rate of blinking while simultaneously defining it to be an indication of trance development. The hypnotherapist may choose to further pace and lead the blink response with his or her own blinking responses. |
| (iii) . . . Until at some point in time as you go *up* and *down, up* and *down, up* and *down* . . . that's right . . . *up* and *down* . . . and then *go down into trance* all the way and stay down for a while, *dropping all the way into trance NOWWWWW!!!!* | Once the blink rate speeds up and is synchronized with the hypnotherapist's pace (oftentimes evidenced by an eyelid flutter response), blinking can be further accelerated to depotentiate conscious processes. Tonally marked embedded suggestions to drop fully into trance can then be offered.<br><br>    If the subject does not develop eye closure, the hypnotherapist can utilize by simply noting that " . . . and what a nice thing to know that you can go |

> deeply into trance with your
> eyes open or closed" and then
> continue with other strategies.

The blink synchronization technique can be utilized in a slightly
different way with a subject "trying" to remain out of trance. A more
direct challenge can be offered:

> ... And you can be able to go into a trance with your eyes open
> or you can *close your eyes and drop into trance* ... and it's really
> not important whether you open your eyes, or close them and open
> them again ... that's right ... and then close them ... (pause to
> wait for closure) ... and open them again ... and then close them
> again ... (pause to wait for closure) ... and open. ... and blink up
> and down ... (wait for blink) ... up and down ... (wait for blink)
> ... up and down ... that's not important ... what is important is
> that your unconscious can learn to develop a secure and meaning-
> ful trance with your eyes open, or it can *close your eyes and drop
> into trance NOWWW!!!*

In both versions of the technique, the hypnotherapist defines the
blinks as indications of trances, uses head nods to reinforce every blinking response, and intersperses verbal comments such as "that's right"
and "deeper ... all the way down." Combined with the hypnotherapist's
genuine absorption in the subject, these techniques work effectively to
develop trance.

Of course, the subject could always respond by not blinking, in which
case he or she may be encouraged to keep the eyes open as long as
possible. The hypnotherapist can then develop absorption through casual conversation with the open-eyed subject. The determination to not
blink will generally result in one of two responses: (1) the eyes will begin
to blink involuntarily sooner or later, whereupon their expression can
be utilized as an indication of trance onset; or (2) the eyes will remain
in an unblinking state, whereupon they will develop a cataleptic state
leading to hypnotic responses (especially body catalepsy, tunnel vision,
and body sensations). Thus, the hypnotherapist can appreciate all responses as roads into trance, and wait comfortably to discover which
the subject prefers.

*2. Reinduce trance.* In a multiple session hypnotherapy, associational
cues can be used to anchor and then reinduce trance states. This saves
time, provides continuity across trance experiences, and enables the

therapist to elicit hypnotic states indirectly and promptly. Many techniques can be used in this regard. For example, the hypnotherapist might use a different tone of voice or a different facial expression (if the subject's eyes are open) as the subject begins to develop trance. In later sessions, the cue(s) can serve to trigger reentry into trance.

Voice tonalities make especially good anchors in the hypnotic context, since subjects often have their eyes closed (making visual cues impractical) and are oriented internally (making physical touch potentially disruptive). Also, most individuals are not very aware consciously of, but are quite unconsciously responsive to, voice tonalities. I often will utilize up to five different voice tonalities to associationally tag client experiences.

Many other anchors are possible, of course. For example, the subject might be asked to assume a particular posture—for example, feet flat on the floor, hands unfolded on lap, eyes oriented to a certain stimulus—for trance development. Another possibility is to assign a name to the trance state, and then use it to develop later trances.

A potential problem in using reinduction anchors is that the therapeutic quality of the resulting trance may not be as great were more extensive techniques utilized. That is, some clients need special attention and a significant amount of time to hypnotically "surrender" to themselves. Such clients may respond to techniques instructing them to rapidly enter trance by doing so in an impersonal and hence nontherapeutic fashion. (A good example of this is stage hypnosis, where the trance states that some volunteers rapidly develop can hardly be said to be intimate.) Reinduction anchors, like all hypnotic techniques, should thus be utilized with sensitivity to the parameters of the therapeutic relationship—for example, the needs of the individual client. Reinduction anchors augment but do not replace other aspects of the therapeutic process.

*3. Security anchors.* As Erickson (1952) emphasized, the hypnotic subject must be protected and made secure at all times. Associational tags can ensure that resources of safety and security are readily available during hypnotic explorations. I routinely spent a good deal of time in initial trance explorations with a client developing and anchoring experiences of security. Because anchors are probabilistic recall cues (i.e., a given cue will not always work), I generally develop multiple security associations for a client, especially if traumatic experiences are likely to surface during hypnotic explorations. This redundancy in anchoring helps ensure the therapist's ability to access security contexts as and when needed.

Security anchors are especially useful when hypnotically revivifying unpleasant experiences. For example, a reputable jeweler suffered the misfortune of being seriously threatened by hoodlums interested in stealing valuable jewels from her. Absorbed deeply in a trancelike state of panic and fear, she hid the jewels where, as she noted, "nobody would find them." This generalization unfortunately proved accurate, as she developed amnesia for where she hid them.

It was three years later when she sought assistance from me. Inquiry disclosed that several attempts to recover the memory with other hypnotherapists failed due to an overwhelming terror that gripped her whenever she tried to remember. Several sessions of hypnotic training found her to be an excellent subject. In one trance I asked her what would allow her to recover the lost information. She replied that she would need "some strong support, and a real feeling of safety." Accordingly, I assisted her in hypnotically accessing a time when she felt quite secure and supported. Since she had indicated that holding her hand would be especially helpful, I anchored that experience to a hand squeeze from me, noting that she could squeeze my hand whenever she needed more security accessed.

The rest of the session was spent practicing evoking the security experience via the hand squeeze. I interspersed posthypnotic suggestions to the effect that she would feel somewhat frightened, but that she could be pleasurably surprised discovering that "such fear will activate the friends and supportive resources available in the palm of your hand." (I'd squeeze her hand gently when saying this.)

In the next session, I held her hand as trance was reinduced. Hypnotic suggestions emphasized that she could very comfortably enjoy "that deepening feeling of security and safety" as she "drifted pleasurably in the Middle of Nowhere with me, the voice and the hand with you"; that different images would come and go; that one image would especially intrigue her, for it would be "a safe gift, a surprising treasure, a shiny present that you can open in the present, at your own rate and pace, in your own style, knowing you can stop along the way for an extra hand as is appropriate." An image of the jewels appeared after a while and with several "pauses that refresh" (i.e., security accessing) along the way, she recalled where she had hidden the jewels. Thus, the associational bonding of the resource state enabled her to reexperience an unpleasant situation in a way she could handle.

"Security anchors" can be developed in any modality; they may be words, images, sounds, feelings, and so on. One consideration in selecting such anchors is how prominently they involve the therapist in the foreground of the client's experience. While the ultimate goal of therapy is to enable the client to access and utilize resources independently from the therapist, many clients have not actualized this ability at the outset of therapy. For example, clients traumatized by deeply violent incidents are often unwilling or unable to fully let go in trance. To the extent that this is so, I will develop security anchors that are more connected to me, thereby allowing the client to utilize me as a "cooperating" guide. These anchors experientially enable the *interpersonal* context to contain (i.e., support) the client's intrapersonal domain, so that the additional resource of the therapist is readily available to the client. Thus, clients might be instructed to keep their eyes open while in trance; or their name might be periodically called softly; or other anchors might be used that connect the (revivified, potentially traumatic) experience of "then" with the self-valuing relationship of "now." When such an approach is used, the progress of the therapy is revealed by the increasing reliance of the client on intrapersonal anchors rather than those tied to the therapist.

*4. Separate "parts" or psychological states.* A major task of any therapy is that of differentiation, that is, distinguishing psychological "parts" or states in a personality complex to enable their autonomous functioning within an integrated whole. Associational anchors can facilitate this task in various ways. For example, they can be used to distinguish the desire to go into trance from the desire to stay out of trance. Erickson, for instance, would sometimes ask clients to sit in one chair and access all their "resistances" in *that* chair, and then move them to another chair for trance. Thus, the different chairs would serve as anchors to separate out different psychological motivations.

Similarly, the introduction of the terms "conscious mind" and "unconscious mind" into the therapeutic conversation is a means of distinguishing the goal-oriented, analytical processing of the client from a more holistic and experiential processing style. Once distinguished, this "conscious/unconscious" anchoring can be developed further. For example:

- Your conscious mind can wonder what will happen, and your unconscious mind can wander experientially and experimentally.

- Your conscious mind can listen carefully to my words, while your unconscious can respond fully according to your own needs.

- Your conscious mind can entertain doubts and dialogue . . . your unconscious can develop undeniable and meaningful expressions.

Through such means, the two modes of psychological functioning can be encouraged to operate side-by-side in a noninterfering fashion.

Anchors can also be used to differentiate enmeshed members of a couple or family system. With one couple, for example, I started by seating them on either side of me. Differential pointing, postural shifts, voice tones, and expressions were used in communicating to them, each cue modality emphasizing and anchoring the differences between them. As their attention became experientially absorbed by my hypnotic communications, two "Care Bears" lying on the office floor climbed into my field of awareness. Placing one stuffed animal in the lap of each person, I had them attentional fixate on their "bear (bare) essence." Hypnotically presented stories about the bears elaborated on the difficult relationship each "bear essence" had experienced because no humans had been available to give them each an autonomous self-context. In short, the care bears were used as anchors to distinguish and develop the self-autonomy of each spouse.

5. *Integrate "parts" or psychological states.* Balancing the need to differentiate is the need to *integrate* complementary parts into systemic wholes. Anchors can also be advantageous in this regard. One application for integrating unpleasant or incomplete experiences is the "collapsing anchors" technique described by Bandler and Grinder (1982). In this procedure, an unpleasant experience is first accessed, anchored, and checked (via reintroduction of the anchor). Second, the client is asked to access a pleasurable experience that seems to be the opposite (i.e., complement) of the unpleasant one; this is also anchored (with a different cue) and then checked. Next, the client is assisted in developing a light trance independent of either state, whereupon the two anchors are "fired" simultaneously, often resulting in a meaningful integration experience of the "positive" and "negative" states. Finally, the efficacy of the procedure is checked by firing off the original unpleasant anchor. A new emotional valence should be the result; otherwise, the procedure needs to be repeated.

For example, a client entered therapy with complaints of sexual inadequacy. In a light trance, he accessed the unpleasant high school experience of being impotent with his girlfriend in the back seat of his car; this was anchored with a touch on the left knee. Suggestions to access an opposite "positive" experience revivified the joyful memory of buying a new car;[8] this was anchored with a touch on his right knee. Further suggestions directed him to "let go" and "clear out," and a light

---

[8] As may be inferred, it is difficult to predict which experience the subject will unconsciously generate as a complement. In the present case, the idea of "emotions while in cars" was apparently used as the fulcrum to generate the complements.

trance was reinduced in which both knees were touched simultaneously to fire both anchors at once. Amidst intense body sensations ("flashes," "spinal rushes"), a new experience emerged: the client discovered himself looking at the battery of a new car and connecting the "positive" and "negative" battery cables to set off a euphoric and dazzling "integration rush." Investigation of the "unpleasant experience" anchor revealed that it now stimulated the integration experience. Thus, firing two "opposing anchors" simultaneously gave birth to a third integration anchor.

To summarize, the therapist can develop anchors for many purposes. Successful development of anchors depends on (1) interpersonal absorption, (2) uniqueness of cue, (3) the subject being in a "cleared" state, (4) timing, and (5) conscious bypassing. Anchors can be effectively used in many aspects of the hypnotherapeutic process, including induction of trance, reinduction of trance, development of security anchors, separating out psychological parts, and integrating psychological parts. Multiple anchors are often appropriate, especially when psychological security is a central consideration. Anchors can be developed for previously or newly developed experiences; generally speaking, the most effective use of anchors involves utilizing already-established anchors along with therapist-established anchors. Finally, the therapist can utilize expressions spontaneously generated by the client as anchors.

### Pace and Lead Representational Systems

Representational systems were described in Chapter 4 as the cognitive modalities people use in processing information. It was noted that individuals sometimes favor a particular representational system – auditory, visual, or kinesthetic – in a given situation, a possibility verifiable by attending to verbal and nonverbal behaviors. In terms of inductions, a dominant representational system can be paced by emphasizing imagery congruent with it, then led by gradually introducing other imagery modalities. To do this effectively, it is useful to recognize that general communications constituting an induction can be expressed in different representational systems.

For example, the following induction excerpt starts in the visual modality and then includes the other systems:

> Now you're sitting there and looking at me . . . and so what I'd like to do is share with you some of the various ways that you can allow yourself to continue to *look at me* for as long as possible while also developing the opportunity to *explore* the realities of *your uncon-*

*scious.* . . . Because as you're sitting there, it is possible to take a look at a variety of different things. . . . Because while your conscious mind is very intelligent, your unconscious is a lot smarter . . . it can identify fuzzy areas of your experience and begin to put them in a proper *focus*, an appropriate framework, a valuable perspective. You can see yourself in a lot of different ways in *trance* . . . and your unconscious can shed some light on and clarify those experiences which have been difficult to look at . . . and as you *drop deeply into trance*, you can recognize a lot of other things as well . . . for example, you've experienced a trance in situations before where you haven't really recognized it as such. . . . Everybody, for example, has taken a long ride in a car and entered into a state of autohypnosis along the way . . . and driving on a country road on a sunny day, and with the scenery all around . . . but your mind *beginning to drift* . . . just allow yourself to take in all those wonderful and pleasant images . . . and as you do, feeling so comfortable, so relaxed . . . and what a nice thing to know that you can attend to only those needs important to attend to, feeling at ease and listening to your unconscious more and more. . . .

The same general induction could be modified for the kinesthetically oriented subject:

And as you *sit comfortably* in that chair and allow yourself to begin to orient in a way most pleasurable for you as an individual, what a nice thing to know that you can not only recognize and *enjoy* your present state of *comfort*, but you can also *feel quite secure* in beginning to develop the undeniable awareness that those feelings can begin to alter in a pleasant and enjoyable fashion . . . because in a trance state you can feel a lot of different things . . . most of all, you can *feel secure and very absorbed.* . . . absorbed in allowing yourself to begin to get more and more in touch with your unconscious abilities to *support and appreciate yourself* in so many ways . . . and what a nice thing to know that you can feel so accepted, so appreciated, so relaxed . . . because trance is an opportunity to really give yourself a big hug . . . it allows you to totally *let go* and experience a lot of different things . . . and so as you *drift easily* but ever *deeper into trance*, you can recognize that with each breath you take, you can *let go even more* . . . breathing in *comfort* and *relaxation*, and breathing out any discomfort . . . and devoting yourself to a sheer comfort, a special warmth and softness . . . and in a trance, your unconscious can shift and move through a variety of different experiences . . . you can *trust your unconscious* to come to grips with any insecurities . . . but for *now*

just enjoy that *trance* and let your unconscious share with you that
special feeling of being close with yourself ... perhaps like a special
experience from long ago, when you felt totally supported, very
touched by the humanity from within ... and as you do, you can
hear the words that go with it ... and any visual images associated
to it ... people from the past ... sounds from then. ...

And for individuals more oriented to their auditory systems:

And trance really is a process of tuning in and listening to your
unconscious, because your unconscious really does have so many
things of importance to say ... and so as you hear the sound of
my voice, you can simply allow yourself to become absorbed in
what's really important for you as an individual ... and whether
you consciously attend to my voice or your own or a combination
thereof really isn't that important ... because of more importance
is your gradually increasing dialogue with your unconscious ...
your own ability to tune in and attend to those aspects of Self that
are important to you as an individual ... because trance is a process of learning ... and you've had so many different learnings
before, all of which you can call on as allies. ... And so as you
simply *let your unconscious unfold those hypnotic experiences* in
its own way, its own style, at its own rate, you may wonder as you
listen to the drone of my voice: When is he going to get to the
point? What is he saying? Because listening to any lecture, where
the speaker just goes on and on, it's hard not to *drift off into your
own special world* ... your own special daydream where you can
be all alone with yourself ... all alone with yourself and a voice ...
and my voice can stay with you, though you really don't need to
attend to it ... you can attend to the sounds of silence which can
envelop you as you let your unconscious call to mind some experience from the past that was particularly pleasant ... and hearing
the voices, the sounds, the melodic strains, the pleasant tones ...
and all the feelings that go with it. ... And what kind of feeling
does listening to a favorite piece of music bring? ... And what
does that favorite musician look like? ... And it's such a nice thing
to allow yourself to become pleasurably engrossed in hypnotic realities. ...

In each of these inductions, the subject is attentionally absorbed and
then asked to recognize the unconscious as a powerful ally, to allow
trance to develop, and then to access a pleasant experience. The revivified memory is used to cross over to other sensory modalities.

The ability to address different imagery systems is important, because a failure to pace a dominant system often results in an unsuccessful induction. For example, most standardized inductions don't address internal dialogue, and thus are ineffective with subjects inundated with it. Similarly, hypnotists who use mostly visual imagery do not work well with subjects who are not visually oriented. To be effective, then, the hypnotist needs to recognize and accommodate individual differences in cognitive styles, making sure that hypnotic communications are phrased in imagery modalities appropriate to the subject.

### Framing and Ratifying Hypnotic Responses

A final method for accessing and developing trance states is the framing and ratifying of ongoing responses as hypnotic expressions. This involves verbally and nonverbally emphasizing various client responses as leading to trance deepening and greater unconscious autonomy.

*1. Framing responses.* This technique involves singling out various behaviors and describing them as evidence of the development of ideodynamic processes (i.e., the growing ability of your unconscious to operate autonomously in your own behalf). In applying this technique, keep in mind that the utilization principle assumes that virtually *any* behavior can be used to develop trance. One class of behaviors that lends itself to hypnotic framing is the relatively unconscious automatic behaviors that characterize ongoing processes – for example, breathing, blinking, and posture. Framing such responses can be accomplished via comments interspersed during a conversational induction. For example:

| Subject's Ongoing Responses | Hypnotist's Interspersed Framings |
|---|---|
| Finger moving slightly | " . . . That's it . . . and your unconscious can *move* into a deeper trance and *indicate* those growing preferences for creative autonomy. . . . " |
| Breathing in and out | "That's right . . . your unconscious can take in and let go, expand out back and forth, and follow that rhythm into a deeper trance. . . . " |

| | |
|---|---|
| Eyes blinking | "And you can go into trance with your eyes *open* or *closed*, open or closed . . . closing them to *blink*, opening them to see and *watch perceptual alterations* . . . closing them to rest . . . and letting your unconscious have all the rest. . . . " |
| Eyes unblinking | "That's it . . . and your unconscious can *focus* meaningfully and securely on those issues, *watching* the perceptual changes while feeling the growing security and absorption. . . . " |
| Posture adjustment | "That's right . . . and you can *move* into so many different states in developing trance . . . make so many *adjustments* . . . *shift* orientations in so many different secure ways. . . . " |
| Sigh | "That's it . . . and you really can let go of unnecessary concerns and devote yourself fully to your own security and unfolding actuality of hypnotic realities. . . . " |

In each instance, a relatively innocuous ongoing response is marked out as reflecting hypnotic development. When emphasized in a nonverbally meaningful fashion, this tends to intensify experiential involvement in the response, thereby deepening its (newly) designated function as a hypnotic phenomenon ("appearance").

For this technique to succeed, the therapist must appreciate these responses as indeed being hypnotic in nature. This is best accomplished in an interpersonal trance wherein the therapist can experientially focus on simple responses as potential trance phenomena, then wonder how and when these responses *will* manifest ideodynamic and experientially absorbing properties. As Erickson noted:

> It is your attitude toward the patient that determines the results you achieve. . . . Whenever you want any hypnotic results with your patients, you had better mean what you say. . . . Your total

experience should teach that you are not asking anything of your patients that is beyond their abilities. When you give a suggestion to a patient, you'd better keep in mind, "I *know* this patient can develop an analgesia – I *know* this patient can develop an anesthesia – I *know* this patient can develop amnesia." (In Rossi, Ryan, & Sharp, 1983, p. 125)

Thus the effectiveness of the technique depends on the willingness and ability of the therapist to nonverbally realize and convey the expressions as potentially hypnotic. That is, the therapist not only describes but also *experiences* the trance-related nature of the behaviors. Hypnosis is thus not "just a way of talking"; it is a means by which generative, self-valuing experience is created.

Hypnotic framing can also be applied to symptomatic expressions. To reiterate, symptom phenomena closely parallel hypnotic phenomena, with a major difference being the contexts in which they occur. By appreciating the ideodynamic nature of symptom expressions as illustrations of unconscious autonomy, the therapist begins to recontextualize such expressions as therapeutically "value-able." Symptoms can thus serve as the basis for naturalistic trance development. For example, a woman sought assistance in regard to how she related with her husband. She would develop intense jealousy whenever her husband looked at another woman, even when watching television. Her "jealousy induction strategy" – the invariant behavioral patterns she utilized to induce the symptom trance – included intense eye fixation and subsequent tunnel vision; in other words, she demonstrated a tremendous ability to develop hypnotic perceptual alterations. Framing this skill as evidence of her general ability to let her unconscious mind operate autonomously in her own behalf, I utilized it as the means to develop trance and offer hypnotherapeutic ideas.

Thus, the client's symptom induction strategy is also the basis for the induction of therapeutic trance. Again, the difference in the *value* of the strategy emerges from the relationship context in which it occurs. The therapist is responsible for ensuring a state of security, a sense of biological rhythm (e.g., continuous breathing, relaxed muscles), and a self-valuing intention; the client supplies the induction strategy; therapist and client then cooperate to differentiate the induction strategy so that it could be used to achieve many different goals.

*2. Ratifying hypnotic responses.* This technique is closely related to framing, the major difference being that it acknowledges responses already framed (implicitly or explicitly) as hypnotic. One class of behaviors utilizable in this regard is the trance-indicative behaviors listed in Table 4.2 (e.g., motor inhibitions, verbal inhibition, breathing alterations, smoothing of facial muscles, eye blink changes). As these cues develop, the Erickson hypnotist ratifies them with simple statements, such as "That's it . . . you really can let your unconscious respond in your own behalf. . . . " This lets the client know that the therapist is sensitive to the experiential shifts, thereby enhancing the trust and rapport in the relationship; it also reinforces and tends to deepen the hypnotic responsiveness of the client.

Related to the spontaneously developing indicators of trance are hypnotic responses suggested by the hypnotist. These suggestions can be of a wide variety (e.g., eye closure, relaxation, finger signaling, experiential absorption), and there may be a time lag between the suggestion and the response (Erickson, 1952). When a suggested response does occur, however, it should be simply yet immediately acknowledged as evidence of the growing autonomy of unconscious generativity.

## SUMMARY

In the present view, hypnotic induction is a cooperative endeavor in which hypnotist joins and utilizes the processes by which the subject is already creating experience. Within this experiential feedback loop, the hypnotherapist first works to create a context where the subject is able to set aside normal conscious processes and explore new ways of being. Naturalistic communications are then used to immerse the subject in experiential realities conducive to both trance development and therapeutic change. Among the many accessing techniques utilizable in this regard are: (1) asking questions; (2) embedding suggestions; (3) presupposing trance responses; (4) speaking generally; (5) telling stories; (6) using associational connections; (7) developing associational anchors; (8) matching and then shifting representational systems; and (9) framing and ratifying responses.

# CHAPTER 7

# *Depotentiating Conscious Processes: Confusion Techniques*

Using just the associational strategies described in the preceding chapter will be insufficient for subjects who are willing to go into trance but are unable to set aside their conscious processes to do so. These *willing but unable* subjects, who comprise at least half the clinical population, may have incessant internal dialogue, or be constantly oriented to internal imagery, or perhaps be continually distracted with kinesthetic sensations. To depotentiate these trance-interfering processes, the Ericksonian hypnotherapist uses various *dissociational strategies*. One such strategy is *boredom* — for example, the hypnotist might tell story after story to wear down the person's conscious "resistances." A second dissociational strategy is *distraction* — for example, the subject might be asked to count backwards from 1000 to 1 by 3's, or verbalize the alphabet forwards while visualizing it backwards (i.e., saying "A" while seeing "Z," saying "B" while seeing "Y," etc.), or simply attend to some attentional stimulus during the induction (preferably one the person is already intrigued with). A third dissociational strategy is to induce dissociation through, say, ideomotor techniques.

A fourth strategy — and the one this chapter mainly focuses on — is *confusion*. The first section discusses generally the intent and structure of confusion techniques. The next two sections detail specific confusion techniques involving *interruption* and *overload*, respectively. The final section discusses clinical issues involved in applying confusion techniques.

235

### THE NATURE OF CONFUSION TECHNIQUES

Confusion techniques are essentially communications that disrupt a person's conscious processing strategies, thereby enabling the development of experiential trance processes. Following the cooperation principle, *confusion techniques utilize whatever the client is doing to inhibit trance or other therapeutic developments as the basis for inducing those developments.* As Erickson (1964a) noted:

> Clinically, it is of much value with patients desperately seeking therapy but restricted and dominated by their clinical problems and uncontrollable resistances which prevent the initiation of therapy. Once these resistances are circumvented, there is then the possibility of securing the patient's cooperation in correcting both his clinical problem and dissipating the resistances. . . . (Confusion techniques) have many times effected exceedingly rapid hypnotic inductions under unfavorable conditions such as . . . in persons interested but hostile, aggressive, and resistant.
> . . . One should bear in mind that these patients are highly motivated, that their disinterest, antagonism, belligerence, and disbelief are actually allies bringing about the eventual result. . . . (In Rossi, 1980a, pp. 284–286)

Thus, for example, with a client who continually fidgets during a trance induction, the therapist might encourage exaggeration of the movement by having the client switch from chair to chair in the office, increasing the rate of switching until the person exhibits a disorientation that can be utilized to secure a trance. Or with a client who continually looks to the therapist for guidance, the latter might sit silently and give no guidance whatsoever, thereby interrupting the trance-interfering pattern. As the bulk of the chapter discloses, there are many different confusion techniques; important here is that such techniques are naturalistic communications that disrupt rigid mental sets.

Confusion techniques are based on the following assumptions:[1]

1. There are many automatic and predictable patterns in a person's behavioral processes;

---

[1] These assumptions are consistent with the two-factor theory of emotion, which distinguishes between physiological arousal and a subsequent psychological attribution and interpretation of that arousal in terms of the social context (see Mandler, 1975; Schacter & Singer, 1962; but also see Marshall, 1976; Maslach, 1977).

2. Disruption of any of these patterns creates a state of uncertainty dominated by undifferentiated arousal (e.g., confusion);

3. Most people strongly dislike uncertainty states and are hence extremely motivated to avoid them;

4. The arousal will increase unless the person can attribute it to something ("this happened because . . . ");

5. As uncertainty increases, so does the motivation to reduce it;

6. The person who is highly uncertain will typically accept the first viable way by which the uncertainty can be reduced (e.g., suggestions to drop into trance).

Based on these assumptions, most confusion techniques follow the basic steps listed in Table 7.1. The first step—*identifying the pattern(s)*—can be accomplished in many ways. Because there are so many patterns in human behavior, an excellent exercise is to jot down as many patterns as you can identify and then work from there. These patterns can be social ones; for example, something as simple as a handshake involves one person extending a hand, the other person responding in kind, the two hands shaking and then releasing after a second or so, and then (usually) a step backwards and some talk. Other social patterns include saying "hello" at the beginning of a conversation, "goodbye" at the end, "good morning" in the morning, and so on; men not wearing dresses (except in Scotland and perhaps San Francisco); clients paying therapists and not vice versa; clients telling their troubles to therapists and not vice versa; in a conversation, one person speaking at a time;

TABLE 7.1
Steps in Applying a Confusion Technique

1. Identify pattern(s) of expression

2. Align with the pattern (and the person)

3. Introduce confusion via interrupting or overloading the pattern

4. Amplify the confusion

5. Utilize the confusion

listeners usually nodding their heads to speakers from time to time; the speaker making comments relevant to the established context of conversation; the speaker generally using proper grammar. These few examples suggest the phenomenal number of patterns that can potentially serve as the basis for a confusion technique.

Besides general social patterns, the hypnotist might also identify patterns idiosyncratic to a given individual. These might be certain habitual movements, such as brushing the hair back when in stress, looking down when depressed, moving around when excited, looking away when confused. Or they might be related types of responses, such as arguing or agreeing when emotionally uncertain, changing the topic of conversation when confused, blaming or placating or sounding superrational when feeling threatened. They could be rules based on social identity, such as a man never yells at a woman, one should always be polite and never raise one's voice, people shouldn't comment on a person's "negative" experiences. Again, there are many, many different possibilities.

Once patterns have been identified, the therapist begins to *pace* in order to generate an appropriate context for successfully applying a confusion technique. At its most general level, this involves creating some sort of rapport so that the client realizes that the therapist's intent is to support. In other words, the therapist operates from the assumption that the primary purpose of using confusion is to disengage a person from rigid attachment to conscious processes, thereby enabling more intimate and self-valuing ways of being. Thus, the person is respected as being much more than a behavioral pattern, and confusion is introduced as a method to enable an appreciation of this deeper essence. Operating from a context of respect is absolutely critical to the therapeutic success of a confusion technique, for the individual who feels crassly manipulated or taken advantage of will not benefit from the effects of confusion. Naturalistic experimentation in various social contexts (e.g., restaurants, airports, casual conversations) will quickly reveal that although it is rather easy to temporarily confuse a person, it is much harder to utilize that confusion in any significant way. Persons feeling unsafe and unprotected will pull away from the operator to reestablish some sense of equilibrium. However, individuals feeling supported will be willing and able to go with the confusion and see what experiential states (e.g., hypnotic realities) unfold from it. Thus, the operator's attitude and nonverbal communications before, during, and after the presentation of confusion play a major role in the response to the technique.

Besides the general pacing of the relationship, the therapist also paces the specific pattern(s) to be absorbed by confusion techniques. This might simply involve activating the pattern in a normal way (e.g., reaching out to shake someone's hand as a way to start the handshake pattern, or complimenting and encouraging some idiosyncratic pattern the subject is wrapped up in).

Following adequate pacing, the hypnotist initiates the third step of *introducing confusion*, either by *interrupting* some pattern or *overloading* it. Most of the chapter is devoted to specific techniques for accomplishing this. Briefly, interruption techniques are short, quick pattern disruptions that are frequently used before any formal induction is introduced; usually, the hypnotherapist needs to use at least several interruption techniques to adequately confuse an individual. On the other hand, overload techniques are longer communications often best utilized during a formal induction.

The immediate response to a well-delivered confusion technique is typically bewilderment and uncertainty. This natural reaction is the one most of us make when, say, a friend says something to us that is completely unexpected and incomprehensible. In such situations, we immediately try to understand what happened, usually looking to the speaker for some sort of explanation. In that the speaker usually apologizes and explains, or looks guilty and confused, the confusion is usually lessened. However, the Ericksonian practitioner using confusion continues to act in a completely congruent and meaningful way at this point, thereby serving to *amplify the confusion*. This fourth step is extremely important, as it is here that confusion techniques differ markedly from the not uncommon occasions when spontaneous communications produce unplanned confusion.

The fifth and final step is to *utilize the confusion* once it reaches what appears to be its apex. It is important to recognize that nonutilized confusion will eventually backfire on the operator, for at some point uncertain individuals require some certainty or closure or they will leave the context. As discussed above, it is at this point that the person will be willing to accept something very simple that reduces the confusion — for example, the simple and gentle suggestion to drop into trance.

In implementing these five steps of a confusion technique, it is important to recognize that they will not always work according to plan, especially when first trying them out. Sometimes a technique will need to be modified or abandoned altogether, depending upon the subject's ongoing responses. Regardless, *all responses are utilizable*. The person who grows angry and feels resentful might be offered sincere apologies along with statements regarding the intent of the communications. The person partially confused might be provided even more confusion, especially of different varieties. Subjects who giggle or laugh might be complimented on their fine ability to keep a sense of humor and encouraged to begin to use it as a way of letting unconscious responses develop even more. In short, the Ericksonian therapist closely monitors and adapts to the client's responses. Keep this in mind as you read in the next two sections about some of the many confusion techniques of interruption and overload, respectively.


## INTERRUPTION TECHNIQUES

As noted above, interruption techniques are naturalistic communications that disrupt the way in which an individual is inputting, accessing, representing, or communicating information. This can be done in any of the major cognitive modalities, that is, auditory, visual, or kinesthetic. To illustrate, this section details a variety of interruption techniques effective in disrupting these different modalities. The techniques described are (1) meaningful nonsequiturs; (2) syntactical violations; (3) inhibition of motoric expression (the subject's or the hypnotist's); (4) interrupting accessing cues; (5) the handshake induction; and (6) polarity plays.

### Meaningful Nonsequiturs

A communication is always comprehended in terms of its context. For example, a listener will usually understand a verbal statement in terms of its relation to those preceding it as well as the nonverbal communications accompanying it. A statement totally irrelevant to or not following from the established context is known as a *nonsequitur*. The listener will usually be taken aback and surprised by a nonsequitur, then respond to this automatic interruption of language patterns by trying to figure out what the heck the speaker meant. In the typical case, the speaker will acknowledge the "mistake" by clarifying or apologizing, thereby quickly reducing any uncertainty generated by the nonsequitur. If, however, the nonsequitur is delivered meaningfully in a manner implying it is a perfectly sensible and in fact rather important statement, the listener will typically continue to search (in vain) for the "real" meaning of the utterance. This is especially true when the listener respects the speaker and assumes he or she is speaking sensibly and seriously, as in the therapist/client relationship. The longer a person tries to grasp some sense in the nonsequitur, the more uncertain he or she will become. This building response potential can often be utilized after 3–5 seconds by the hypnotherapist softly but emphatically suggesting that the subject drop into trance.

A nice illustration of how such a naturalistic technique works is offered by Erickson's (1964a) description of one of his first discoveries of the effect of meaningfully-delivered nonsequiturs:

. . . One windy day as I was on my way to attend the first formal seminar of hypnosis conducted in the U.S. by Clark L. Hull at the University of Wisconsin in 1923, where I reported on my experimental work and graduate psychology students discussed my findings, a man came rushing around the corner of a building and bumped hard against me as I stood bracing myself against the wind. Before he could recover his poise to speak to me, I glanced elaborately at my watch and courteously, as if he had inquired the time of day, and I stated, "It's exactly 10 minutes to two," though it was actually closer to 4:00 p.m., and I walked on. About a half a block away, I turned and saw him still looking at me, undoubtedly still puzzled and bewildered by my remark.

I continued on my way to the laboratory and began to puzzle over the total situation and to recall various other times I had made similar remarks to my classmates, laboratory mates, friends, and acquaintances and the resulting confusion, bewilderment and feeling of mental eagerness on their part for some comprehensible understanding. Particularly did I recall the occasion on which my physics laboratory mate had told his friends that he intended to do the second (and interesting) part of a coming experiment and that he was going to make me do the first (and onerous) part of the experiment. I learned of this and when we collected our experimental material and apparatus and were dividing it up into two separate piles, I told him at the crucial moment quietly but with great intensity, *"That sparrow really flew to the right, then suddenly flew left, and then up and I just don't know what happened after that."* While he stared blankly at me, I took the equipment for the second part of the experiment and set busily to work and he, still bewildered, merely followed my example by setting to work with the equipment for the first part of the experiment. Not until the experiment was nearly complete did he break the customary silence that characterized our work together. He asked, "How come I'm doing this part? I wanted to do that part." To this I replied simply, "It just seemed to work out naturally this way." (In Rossi, 1980a, p. 259)

When I met Erickson almost 50 years later, his ability to use this spontaneously discovered technique for hypnotic and therapeutic purposes was rather refined. One of my most memorable and educational experiences with him occurred early in my training with him. I was very determined to figure out and learn everything Erickson did, and rather naively assumed that the only way to do this was to try to rationally analyze *everything* that happened. Eventually I settled smugly into the erroneous assumption that since Erickson was a "master of metaphor," every one of the many stories he told was "really" describing the ongoing activities of someone in the room listening to the story. I thus constructed a mental "metaphor translation" machine whereby I would listen closely to a story and then immediately "recognize" which present participant it was "really" about.

This rather limiting preoccupation of mine did not escape Erickson's attention. One day he started telling a series of "obviously" metaphorical stories, thereby setting into action my "metaphor translation" machine. But rather suddenly he interrupted a story by looking intently at my right hand, pointing at it, then uttering in a most surprised and incredulous fashion, "Isn't that your *left* hand not lifting? . . . Yet? . . . Now!!??" My recollection of the experience is still rather hazy. I remember first injecting the statement into my "metaphor machine" to try to figure out whose hand he was really talking about. After several unsuccessful attempts had intensified my confusion, I experienced the room begin to "swim about" while my right hand began to involuntarily float upwards. I found myself looking right into Erickson's eyes as he said, "That's right, close your eyes and drop into trance NOW!!!" To understate my response, I did so at once. He then added, " . . . and let your unconscious do the learning for a while." And I did that also. This rather intense experience of involuntarily dropping into trance not only was a "first hand" experience of a nonsequitur interruption technique, but it also led to the eventual realization that relying on conscious computations for learning the Ericksonian approach is pitifully inadequate.

Note that this simple yet sophisticated technique followed the confusion steps of *identifying a pattern* (translating stories), *pacing the pattern* (by absorbing me in the story), *interrupting the pattern* (by presenting the nonsequitur), *amplifying the confusion* (by continuing to look intently for about 5 seconds), then *utilizing the confusion* (by simply suggesting that I close my eyes and drop into trance). Note also that the nonsequitur's effectiveness as a confusion technique was aided by (1) its target being a dominant trance-inhibiting conscious pattern and

(2) the added use of a sharp incongruency (pointing to the right hand and talking about the left) to enhance the confusion. Additionally, Erickson's demeanor in presenting the statement was utterly serious and meaningful. In applying similar interruption techniques, the hypnotist should bear these points in mind.

I have experimented extensively with this technique and found it remarkably effective for most subjects. Of course, you need to modify the technique according to the situation and the subject's response. For example, you might gently lift the hand of a relatively responsive subject — either the hand you're pointing to or the one you're talking about — as you note that the hand isn't lifting yet, thereby adding considerably to the confusion. (The lifted hand can usually be made cataleptic rather easily, and consequent utilizations then undertaken.) Or you might introduce a flurry of additional nonsequiturs or other confusion techniques to amplify the confusion of an only partially confused individual. Or with a person who doesn't seem confused at all, you might — *while remaining confident and meaningful* — continue by saying something like, "But, of course, why should we expect it to . . . my God, I think I really have been working too hard. Have you ever had that feeling? . . . " and then switch the topic. Again, let the specific dynamics of the technique unfold in response to the interactional responses.

Also, you should not expect to elicit a full trance with a single nonsequitur. Oftentimes the latter serves the simple but exceedingly valuable purpose of loosening up the client a bit, thereby enhancing the effectiveness of further, more elaborate induction techniques. In these cases, the therapist delivers the nonsequitur remark, then rapidly reassumes the topic of conversation or shifts to a new one. Relatedly, nonsequiturs can depotentiate a train of thought a client is mired in, thus enabling the introduction of new ideas. For example, recently I interrupted the self-pitying discourse of a client by listening and nodding understandably for a while, then saying with the utmost seriousness, "You know, John, geese don't fly south in California. It really can be an entirely different state." John froze momentarily with confusion, his eyes quickly dilating, then asked me to explain my remark. I suggested cryptically but gently that it was best for him to comprehend it in his own way, encouraged him to think about it for a while, then changed the topic. As happens with most individuals in this sort of situation, these remarks catapulted the client from his mental rut, thus making it possible to proceed with interactions of a more therapeutic nature.

Nonsequiturs can also be used to depotentiate conscious computations during an induction. For example, the hypnotherapist might interperse cryptic remarks into a conversational induction as in the following excerpt:

> And you can experience many things in a trance. . . . *Blue Max!!!*
> . . . *What does it mean to have a Blue Max*?? . . . and other things
> as well . . . and you can let your unconscious do it for you *because
> your hands are in your laps and your shoes are tied* . . . and so why
> not drop deeply into trance.

To reiterate, such nonsequiturs will have maximal hypnotic effect when (1) they are delivered meaningfully (2) by a speaker assumed and expected to speak rationally and relevantly (3) in a context where the listener trusts the integrity of the speaker. To assess the accuracy of these points, experiment naturalistically with nonsequiturs in various situations while employing different delivery styles. For example, you might answer the phone with the question, "Is Bill there please?"; wait several seconds before saying softly, "That's right . . . and you can close your eyes and relax as soon as you hear the phone hanging up"; then hang up the phone. Or the next time a waiter or waitress asks for your order in a restaurant, you might with the utmost seriousness request "three spare tires, hold the jack," wait 3–5 seconds (to let the confusion build), then lift the person's hand up. In spontaneous field utilizations such as these, the person will often become immobile, with eyes glazed, unblinking, and dilated, for 5–10 seconds. He or she will typically then recover and look to you in astonishment. If at this point you smile in a way that communicates that you're doing something *with* the person rather than *to* him or her – that is, your intent is to support rather than ridicule – the person usually will express thorough enjoyment with the proceedings. (If you do not communicate this supportive intent, either nonverbally or verbally, the person will often become angry with you, and rightfully so.) Receptivity in such situations, however, will rarely extend to the point where an extended trance can be developed. These constraints will demonstrate how significantly the factors of perceived intent and situational context affect responses to meaningfully delivered nonsequiturs.

## Syntactical Violations

Besides the pragmatic rules governing conversations (e.g. speak clearly, speak relevantly, speak in turn), there are many syntactic rules. As Chomsky (1957, 1965) has so elegantly argued, natural language speakers share a set of intuitions about the grammatical well-formedness of an utterance. Thus, when we encounter an ill-formed statement — say I tell you, "It is then store for because feel I" — we generally feel momentarily interrupted and confused before wondering if the speaker is on drugs, playing some game, simply crazy, doesn't speak English well, and so on. The correct answer is usually not difficult to discern. However, imagine that none of these attributions explain the grammatical violation — that is, the speaker conveys (e.g., through nonverbal meaningfulness and congruency, and preceding and subsequent statements that are grammatically well-formed) that he or she is coherent, sane, undrugged, English-speaking, responsible, and well-intentioned. In such a situation, the listener will typically grow more uncertain and confused and look to the speaker for some communication that will reduce the uncertainty. As in any confusion technique, it is at this point that the hypnotist utilizes the subject's response potential by offering hypnotic suggestions.

There are a variety of ways in which syntactical violations can be used advantageously in the hypnotic context. One particularly effective technique is to use key words in the middle of a sentence to overlap into an entirely different statement. For example:

1. . . . and the rain was coming down and all of a sudden I felt a *drop right down into trance.*

2. . . . and when I go to Germany, I always like to have a *translator (trance later), John, or trance now, John, trance now all the way down. . . .*

3. . . . and what does it mean when someone says that you can be as quick as a *blink the eyes . . . that's right . . . again . . . and again . . . and down now all the way. . . .*

4. "Isn't that your *watch very carefully as your eyelids slowly move over your eyes and you close them down into trance very easily now. . . .*

Thus, hypnotically utilizable syntactical violations can be generated by (1) selecting words that have more than one meaning, at least one of which is relevant to trance development (e.g., drop, translator, blink, and watch); (2) forming a statement in which the key word appears at the end of the statement in its trance-unrelated sense; (3) forming another statement in which the key word appears in the beginning of the utterance in its trance-related sense; and (4) connecting the two statements together, with the key word used once as the overlap.

The effect of delivering these somewhat bizarre statements hinges greatly on the preceding statements, the nonverbal delivery, and the subsequent utilization by the hypnotist. In this regard, an extremely useful training technique is to identify and practice those nonverbal expressions and movements in your behavior that elicit absorption, surprise, "meaningfulness," and other psychological responses relevant to interruption techniques.

However, to reiterate, even a well-delivered interruption technique will not always induce a prolonged trance. But the hypnotist who remains confident and congruent will generally have little difficulty utilizing the subject's reaction. In terms of the present technique, a common effect will be to absorb the subject's attention in a manner conducive to further hypnotic communications. Such communications might involve straightforward pacing and leading (e.g., of the eye blinks). The hypnotist might continue with suggestions for tunnel vision. For example:

> That's right . . . and you can look at me . . . and in looking at me you can appreciate and enjoy your unconscious ability to develop that secure *absorption* in the continuing process of seeing me *here* while enjoying that perceptual fogging developing even a little more pleasurably all around *here* now. . . .

Such statements are usually best delivered somewhat rapidly but very meaningfully, so as to maintain both the confusion and the absorption.

### Inhibition of Motoric Expression

A prevalent but usually unnoticed pattern in human interaction is the small motoric adjustments (e.g., postural shifts, tapping, head nodding) that conversational participants frequently make. A major function of such movement is to maintain conscious processing in an externally oriented fashion. This can be demonstrated through simple naturalistic observation—e.g., note that such movements often lessen when a person becomes absorbed in internal thought—or through experimentation. For example, note what happens if you or somebody else completely stops moving for more than a minute (the typical result will be increased internal absorption, usually accompanied by reduced or distorted perception of external stimuli).

The hypnotic relevance of this is obvious—namely, an interesting induction technique is to interrupt motoric movements. This can be done in several ways, one of which is to restrict the subject's movements. (As noted previously, the spontaneous occurrence of motoric inhibition is good evidence of a developing trance.) In fact, Erickson would frequently suggest to subjects at the outset of an induction:

> You don't have to move . . . and you don't have to talk. . . .

Such simple immobility suggestions can then be bolstered by attentional fixation (and thus motorically immobilizing) techniques. For example, Erickson would often continue with suggestions for visual fixation and tunnel vision:

> . . . and what's behind me is not important . . . what's to the left is not important . . . what's to the right is not important . . . what's important is your internal experience. . . .

When delivered in a compelling and absorbing fashion, such communications tend to inhibit movement, thereby interrupting a major way in which conscious processes are automatically maintained. This greatly enhances the success of subsequent induction techniques.

This simple method is especially useful with clients mired in conscious computations making trance development virtually impossible. For example, a client entered my office and began to complain bitterly about virtually anything he could think of. After several unsuccessful attempts to politely interrupt him, I began to show great interest in his complaints, agreeing with him and then actually encouraging him to intensify his complaints. Once this secured his attention and rapport, I said to him, intensely:

> All right, Bill, it seems to me you've got an awful lot to be upset about. Your wife doesn't understand you, your boss doesn't understand you, your kids don't understand you . . . in short, you've got it real tough, and you don't know what to do. And you're here because you'd like to know how to handle those situations, how to be able to get these people off your back and make them understand you. Is that correct?

As these statements essentially encapsulated his torrent of complaints, he was forced to agree. I thus continued by telling him I had listened closely to what he had been saying, that now I wanted to say something in response that was very important, and that since he was willing to try something different I wanted him to sit in his chair and *respond only nonverbally*. I repeated this last statement several times, emphasizing that he would want to respond verbally, that he would feel compelled to say something, but I wanted him to respond *only* nonverbally. His desperation and my somber and insistent tone ensured his complicity. As I began to talk, he struggled mightily against chiming in. I utilized this by telling him that he should hold tightly onto the chair and sit up very straight in it in order to keep his solemn promise. This led quickly to a rigid and frozen posture enabling the rapid development of trance via metaphorical stories and interspersed hypnotic directives. In short, the motoric restriction method interrupted both his verbal and non-verbal patterns, thereby permitting therapeutic work to take place.

Like most of the confusion techniques in this chapter, I learned this method from Erickson. He emphasized that the technique was especially useful with individuals feeling a compulsive need to continually talk and understand their experience rationally. Haley (1973) described a case of Erickson's which illustrates this beautifully. A superrational academic couple sought therapeutic assistance for what they referred to as their three-year "frustration of philoprogenitive desires"; that is, they had unsuccessfully attempted to conceive a baby. After building appropriate response potential and securing their agreement to participate in "experimental therapy" involving "psychological shock," Erickson instructed them to sit silently and grab tightly onto their chairs to brace themselves for the "shock." He demanded that they not talk all the way home following the administration of the shock therapy, despite the fact that they would probably be overwhelmed with various thoughts and feelings. After dramatically building up even more response potential and repeating in their academic language everything they had told him, Erickson suddenly said, "Now why in hell don't you fuck for fun and pray to the devil she doesn't get knocked up for at least three months. Now please leave" (in Haley, 1973, p. 166). To abbreviate, a phone call late that night revealed they couldn't even wait to get to the bedroom by the time they had driven the 40 miles home; they did "it" on the living room floor. As Erickson explained, these shocking instructions combined with the restriction on their verbal and nonverbal communicational patterns to unfetter a tremendous amount of repressed erotic thoughts, and led to the development of a more natural sexual relationship.

*Interrupting Accessing Cues*

Other motoric movements that are sometimes useful to interrupt are the accessing cues described in Chapter 4. As noted, these cues are typically used to initiate conscious cognitive strategies. Since such strategies inhibit the spontaneity of therapeutic trance explorations, their interruption can clear the way for hypnotic developments. For example, a client having difficulty experiencing trance would continually shift his eyes down and to the right, an accessing cue that I discovered correlated with a strong tendency to analyze every suggestion offered. As this verbal analysis disenabled the effortless processes of hypnotic experience, I interrupted them by simply asking the subject to fixate upon my eyes during the induction. Each time he started to access in his traditional way, I called his attention back to me. In this way, it was possible to induce a trance.

There are a variety of other ways in which accessing cues can be interrupted. Touching a person (e.g., on the arm or knee) typically works quite effectively. Waving one's hand subtly (e.g., as if moving to brush back your hair) generally accomplishes the same outcome. Other sudden movements or sounds, such as clapping your hands or clearing your throat, also work. Again, such behaviors are used to interrupt those accessing cues initiating trance-interfering conscious processes. They typically produce a mild state of uncertainty, which the therapist can immediately utilize for hypnotic developments.

Besides restricting the subject's motoric output, hypnotherapists can restrict their own movements to interrupt the subject's conscious patterns. For example, the therapist might sit very still, gaze meaningfully at the subject with unblinking eyes, breathe comfortably, and so on. As Chapter 3 noted, this externally oriented state facilitates trance in both therapist and client. If preceded by nonverbal mirroring, it will often elicit a similar response in the client; at the very least, it usually interrupts effortful patterns. It is thus particularly useful with, say, a person who "talks your ear off." Everybody has had experience with such individuals, and recognizes that sometimes they are pretty hard to interrupt. At the same time, most people reinforce this incessant talking by nodding, fidgeting about, trying to verbally respond, and so on; that is, they respond with the predictable patterns of a listener in a conversation. Simple experimentation will demonstrate that very few people can continue to talk if not reinforced by such minimal cues, especially the incessant talkers, whose "gabbing" is often a way of distracting from painful emotional processes. Thus, the hypnotist's motoric inhibition will frequently have the effect of quieting a person while also accessing therapeutically utilizable experiences.

For example, a client recently entered my office, sat down, and began a continuous stream of speculation about the possible causes of her considerable unhappiness. It being the third session with her, I realized the futility of attempting to straightforwardly depotentiate this not very useful monologue of hers, and thus simply shifted into an externally oriented trance characterized by motoric inhibition. As I continued to look meaningfully but silently at her, her tempo initially sped up in nervousness, then began to grow more arrhythmic (signaling increasing nervousness). On the several occasions when she asked me what I thought or what I was doing, I said simply and cryptically, "I'm waiting . . . you've been holding on for many years . . . a few more minutes won't hurt." It became increasingly difficult for her to continue; her self-consciousness seemed to grow rapidly; emotional turmoil began to develop, as evidenced by dilated pupils, restricted and irregular breathing, facial flush, damp eyes, and so forth. When she looked almost overwhelmed by this turmoil, although she was still struggling to maintain her verbal distractions, I said very gently, "Mary, you don't have to hold on any longer. Close your eyes now and feel it letting go. I'm here and will be here so you don't have to worry. So go ahead and close your eyes and let yourself experience what you've been holding onto for so very long noww!!" She closed her eyes and began to cry, whereupon I moved in and assisted her in handling the deep emotional experience she had accessed.

With another client, a woman I had seen for about a half dozen sessions, I remained totally silent as she walked in and sat down. Accustomed to having me direct the conversation in the initial part of a session, she began to nervously fidget about, looking away, squirming in her chair, restricting her breathing, and so forth. The first several times she asked me what I was up to I simply continued with my meaningful but soft gaze into her eyes; the next several times I said cryptically, "Is it time?", then subtly nodded my head. After about 15 minutes, the woman began to softly cry, whereupon I gently held her hands and directed her through a hypnotic integration process.

I have used this sort of technique in many other cases and generally find it to be a highly effective way to dissipate conscious "resistances" and to access therapeutically relevant experiences. Of course, one needs to have established a trusting relationship with clients before they will allow such personal and emotional experiences to develop. In the above case, previous sessions were spent establishing such a trust. Also, one needs to nonverbally convey not only meaningfulness, expectancy, and congruency, but also gentleness and caring support for the client. By using what Erickson referred to as an "iron hand in a velvet glove" approach, these methods are generally of outstanding therapeutic value.

My understanding of the therapeutic dynamics of this motoric restriction technique is that clients usually have well-developed ways of ensuring that neither they nor anybody else (e.g., the therapist) attend to certain key experiences.[2] When the hypnotherapist shifts into an externally oriented trance, clients typically sense that their well-honed distraction techniques are ineffectual and that the therapist can "see" through the "veil of dissociation." This arouses fear that the key experiences may be revealed; this thinking further activates the experiences, thereby prompting new distraction attempts. But as long as the therapist maintains rapport and intense absorption, the client cannot shift into other processes. This leads to increased uncertainty in the client, which the therapist, having established a context of trust and caring, can therapeutically utilize by offering gently hypnotic directives.

In summary, then, restriction of the subject's and/or hypnotist's motoric output can be effectively utilized as an interruption technique, both in terms of hypnotic inductions and hypnotherapy. To ensure success, the hypnotist needs to be able to communicate a supportive yet firm attitude with the individual, and generally needs to have some trust developed before extended utilizations can occur. The technique is usually most effective when combined with others.

## The Handshake Induction

Shaking someone's hand is one of the most common social patterns in our experience. Because the motor patterns involved are so well-practiced and thus automatized, interrupting this pattern before its completion will typically produce a momentary confusion quite utilizable for the induction of trance. It is therefore not surprising that Erickson used the handshake as the basis for one of his most innovative and effective induction methods. An interesting application of this technique occurred in South America when Erickson, who did not speak fluent Spanish, was lecturing and demonstrating hypnosis to medical groups. To bypass his language limitation, he demonstrated various "pantomime" inductions with selected subjects. Erickson (1964c) de-

---

[2]Of course, desperate attempts to *not* think of something generally increase the dominance of that something. For example, try hard not to think of "blue." An assumption here is that in a primary system like the unconscious it is impossible to "negate" something; thus, "not blue" is equivalent to "blue." Of course, an easy way out of this in the present context is to simply think of something else – e.g., white. This points to a key distinction between *attempted negation* and *rejection* of an idea; the former is impossible while the latter isn't. A person's attachment to an unacceptable experience makes it impossible to reject; attempted negations only increase its prominence.

scribed how he presented the handshake induction technique with one such subject in the following way:

> She was brought through a side door to confront me. Silently we looked at each other, and then, as I had done many times previously with seminarians in the United States in seeking out what I consider clinically to be "good responsive" subjects before the beginning of a seminar and hence before I was known to them, I walked toward her briskly and smilingly and extended my right hand and she extended hers. Slowly I shook hands with her, staring her fully in the eyes even as she was doing to me and slowly I ceased smiling. As I let loose of her hand, I did so in a certain irregular fashion, slowly withdrawing it, now increasing the pressure slightly with my thumb, then with the little finger, then with the middle finger, always in an uncertain irregular, hesitant manner and finally so gently withdrawing my hand that she would have no clearcut awareness of just when I had released her hand or what part of her hand I had last touched. At the same time, I slowly changed the focus of my eyes by altering their convergence, thereby giving her a minimal but appreciable cue that I seemed to be looking not at but through her eyes and off into the distance. Slowly, the pupils of her eyes dilated, and as they did so, I gently released her hand completely, leaving it in mid-air in a cataleptic position. A slight upward pressure on the heel of her hand raised slightly. Then catalepsy was demonstrated in the other arm also and she remained staring unblinkingly. . . . Slowly I closed my eyes and so did she. (In Rossi, 1980a, pp. 331–332)

Note how this description conforms to the general five-step procedure for confusion cited earlier (Table 7.1). After *identifying* a prominent pattern in the interaction – the handshake – Erickson *paced* it by extending his hand regularly and shaking the woman's hand. (Note also how he mirrored her nonverbal behavior, particularly her facial expression.) He then introduced *confusion* by *interrupting* the typical handshake pattern via changes in facial expression (from a friendly, sociable look to a deep, meaningful one), hand release pattern, and eye focus. He then *amplified the confusion* via the alternating and unpredictable pressures on her hand. Finally, Erickson *utilized the confusion* by developing catalepsy (by leaving the hand suspended once it was actually cataleptic) and nonverbally leading into trance (by defocusing and then closing his eyes).

Handshake interruption techniques can be used to develop trance in other ways as well. For example, Erickson (1964a/1980a, p. 287) described another lecture he gave, this one to a group of American physicians, where a medical doctor expressed interest in hypnosis but also showed hostile and aggressive behavior. During the pre-lecture social hour, the doctor – who was much bigger and stronger than Erickson – gave the latter a bone-crunching handshake, declaring that he would like to "see any damn fool try to hypnotize me." When Erickson later asked for volunteers to demonstrate hypnosis, the man strode up to the stage and loudly proclaimed his confidence that he could never be hypnotized. Erickson graciously offered his hand and then, as the belligerent fellow reached out to take it, suddenly bent down to tie his shoe. The man froze in amazement, his hand cataleptically suspended in air for the moment. Erickson immediately utilized by softly but meaningfully instructing the man to "just take a deep breath, sit down in that chair, close your eyes, and go deeply into a trance." After being briefly mesmerized, the startled man exclaimed, "Well I'll be damned! But how? Now do it again so I can know how you are doing it." Erickson proceeded to offer him a variety of induction techniques. When the man responded hypnotically to a hand levitation method, his trance was used to demonstrate various hypnotic phenomena to him and the rest of the group.

This case reveals an important point about confusion techniques, namely that the person rigidly entrenched in a particular pattern – belligerence, self-pity, superrational, placating, and so on – is most responsive to them. In other words, *the more identified a person is with a certain way of being, the more confused and uncertain he or she will be when that way of being is interrupted.* By calmly accepting the man's belligerence, Erickson was in a position to depotentiate it and thus use it as the basis for the trance induction. It is important to note that the physician did not immediately develop an extended trance; however, his "resistances" were dissipated to the point of making him responsive to further induction techniques. To reiterate, interruption techniques often disrupt trance-inhibiting patterns without developing a deep trance; the hypnotist's task in such cases is to promptly utilize the receptive state for trance development.

There are many other variations on the handshake induction method. It can be applied in a lecture/demonstration or a one-on-one clinical setting; the participants can be standing up or sitting down; it can be initiated as an "innocent" handshake or in a role-playing situation; it can be introduced in the beginning, the end, or even the middle of an interaction. Whatever the situation, the technique will work to the extent that the subject trusts the hypnotist and the situation. In the lecture situation this is accomplished by the prestige of the lecturer, his or her demeanor and remarks preceding the technique, nonverbal behavior expressed during the technique, and the perceived safety of the social setting. Because this perceived safety will not always be immediately present when a client is alone with the hypnotist, the technique generally should not be applied in the office setting for at least several sessions. Again, the point here is that interruption techniques can effect a "frozen" trancelike state for several seconds, whereupon subjects' interpretations of the situation will affect further responses (e.g., letting themselves go deeper into trance or coming out altogether).

The handshake induction technique may be applied along the lines of the 5-step process outlined in Table 7.1. This technique is somewhat different from the one described by Erickson (1964a; Erickson, Rossi, & Rossi, 1976; Erickson & Rossi, 1981). In the first step—*creating contact and expectancy*—the hypnotist essentially absorbs the subject's attention while maneuvering appropriate positions. I often like to do this while standing up and facing the (also standing) subject directly. This might be at the beginning or end of a session, or I might arrange it during the middle of a session by expressing an interest to show the client something—for example, how patterned behavior is, or how people can introduce themselves in various ways. The point here is that the subject should be attentionally absorbed and relatively unaware of the pending handshake interruption; also, the hypnotist should be relaxed and comfortable, thereby enabling the subject to feel the same. (If from past experience or reports the subject expects the handshake interruption, the hypnotist might elicit the beginning of a handshake—e.g., the subject lifting his or her hand in readiness—then shift attention by becoming "distracted" by something else. Several reiterations of this pattern interruption will typically build response potential so the subject feels increasingly compelled to shake hands to complete the frustrated pattern.) Once the subject is properly positioned and absorbed, the hypnotist might talk about some innocuous but interesting topic while periodically gazing briefly at the subject's hand, then looking at the subject and nodding subtly. The intent of such nonverbal behavior is to begin to focus unconscious attention on the hand; this can be enhanced through very subtle gesturing for the hand to begin to reach out.

In the second step—*initiating the pattern*—the hypnotist moves towards the subject with outstretched hand, indicating a desire to shake hands. As naturalistic experimentation will show, this invariably prompts the other person to automatically begin to extend his or her hand. During these several seconds, the hypnotist is still looking deeply into the subject's eyes and continuing conversation, so as to maintain attentional absorption.

The third step—*interrupting the pattern*—occurs when the hypnotist is about four feet away from the subject. At this point, the hypnotist—still walking forward with right hand outstretched—suddenly but gracefully accelerates to lift his or her *left* hand under the subject's outstretched hand. Continuing with one graceful motion, the hypnotist uses his or her thumb and index finger to lift the subject's hand to about shoulder level. (I have found that lifting it higher often creates muscle tensions requiring effort to maintain, thereby inviting conscious participation.) *This lifting should be done with minimal pressure and graceful gentleness, so the subject does not feel intruded upon or dominated.* The hypnotist merely guides the already lifting hand of the subject; this is done rather quickly, so that the element of surprise is present.

During this time the hypnotist's right hand (which has continued to lift, albeit at a slower rate than the left hand) rises to about the subject's eye level and points towards the subject's face (a good distraction and interruption technique); then quickly, in conjunction with the whole body, it swings around to point at the subject's now lifted right hand. The hypnotist, who has been looking at the subject in a surprised, intense, and absorbing fashion, now gazes with incredulity at the raised right hand of the subject. This typically will deeply disorient and surprise the subject to effect a rapid dissociation, evidenced by a lightness in the lifted right hand, a "frozen" look and posture, dilated pupils, restricted breathing, and so forth.

At this point, the hypnotist proceeds with the fourth step of *amplifying the confusion*. The subject is instructed in a soft but meaningful voice to "pay very close attention to all of the coloration changes beginning to occur in the fingers of your (lifted) hand." This statement, which sounds perfectly logical but is, to say the least, rather unusual, usually further disorients the subject while fixating attention on the hand. (In the occasional case where attentional absorption in the hand is not immediately procured, the hypnotist can look deeply into the subject's eyes to develop eye fixation and then direct it to the hand. An exception to this is when the subject is not surprised at all and in fact rather indignant, in which case other utilizations described below can be undertaken.) Because the disorientation will enhance both a willingness to follow simple directives and an ability to develop perceptual alterations, subjects will often begin to actually perceive coloration changes. These hypnotic developments can be facilitated by touching *very lightly* the fingertips of the lifted hand—which should produce tingling sensations – while concomitantly naming the touched digits. For example, the hypnotist might say:

> That's right . . . and just let yourself continue to *pay very close attention to all those coloration changes* . . . whether they are in the index finger (touching the index finger) or the middle finger (touching the middle finger) or the thumb (touching the thumb) or the ring finger (touching the ring finger) or the little finger (touching the little finger) or the thumb (touching the thumb) or the little finger (touching the thumb). . . .

After a minute or so, confusion can be amplified by speeding the rate of delivery while beginning to *misname* the fingers. This can lead into the fifth step of *utilizing the confusion* by interspersing trance suggestions. For example:

> . . . and the little finger (touching the middle finger) and the index (touching the thumb) and the thumb (touching the middle) or the index (touching the index) or the thumb again (touching the index) or the big one (touching the little finger) or the little (touching the index) or the middle (touching the ring finger) or the *dropping down into trance* as you go from the bigger, the smaller, the feeling of comfort, the changes in the middle, the little, the ring (now beginning to touch the digits in rapid succession), the *dropping down deeper now* . . . that's right . . . the eyes blinking, dropping, the trance developing . . . (etc.).

During this entire period (from the start of Step #3) the hypnotist's left hand remains underneath the subject's right hand. If the subject's hand feels totally cataleptic and light, which it often will, the hypnotist can stop supporting it and let his or her hand drop down about six inches. (Dropping the hand all the way down may distract or startle the subject's visual fixation.) If the hand feels somewhat light but still needs support, some very gentle rhythmic pressures of lifting up and down ever so slightly under the hand with a finger or two will usually develop the catalepsy fully, thereby enabling a gradual release of support. These lifting and letting go rhythms should be so gentle and light that the subject can barely distinguish when the touch begins and when it ends. (If the subject's hand feels quite heavy, the hypnotist should proceed with other utilizations described below.)

Of course, the specific verbal and nonverbal communications should be modified according to the subject's responses. To the extent this is done, a profound cataleptic trance is usually achievable. At this point the hypnotist can utilize further with any of a number of different possibilities. For example, hypnotic phenomena or hypnotherapeutic procedures can be introduced, especially dissociational processes such as hypnotic dreams. The subject might be eased down into a chair for such explorations, or kept standing up.

To reorient the subject, an interesting possibility is the *reorientation in time* technique developed by Erickson in which just as the subject opens his or her eyes to emerge from trance, the hypnotist completes the suspended handshake pattern and then acts congruently as if nothing had happened between the interruption and completion of the pattern. In that individuals typically are very responsive when shifting from trance to waking states, such a maneuver will often effect amnesia for the trance development and utilizations. (As Chapter 2 noted, amnesia helps to protect experiential learnings from immediate conscious compartmentalization and is a basic strategy used by the Ericksonian therapist in many cases. For specific discussion of naturalistic amnesia techniques, see Zeig, 1985c.)

To summarize, the handshake technique described above involves absorbing the subject's attention; initiating the handshake pattern; rapidly lifting the subject's outstretched right hand with your left hand, shifting all attention onto the supported right hand, then suggesting perceptual distortions of it; producing tingling by touching and naming the digits, then amplifying confusion by misnaming the digits; utilizing the confusion to develop trance, then utilizing the trance for hypnotherapeutic explorations; and reorienting the subject, possibly with the amnesia technique of reorientation in time. When carried out in a confident, smooth, and meaningful fashion, the technique is a tremendously effective confusion method.

Of course, even the most graceful utilizations will not always elicit hypnotic responses. Sometimes, for example, subjects may not be too surprised and consequently will not develop catalepsy. In such cases, the heaviness of the hand can be utilized just as promptly to induce trance. For example, the hypnotist might appreciate the heaviness of the hand as a nice indication of body relaxation, and therefore compliment the subject on demonstrating an ability to relax and so be ready to enter trance. It can then be suggested that the subject "fully relax and begin to develop a nice trance only *when and just when* the hand goes all the way back down to its resting position . . . and your unconscious can have all the rest." The hypnotist can then slowly lower the hand at a rate appropriate for trance development.

Another possibility in such instances is to use more distraction. For example, the hypnotist might suddenly look at the subject's (unraised) left hand and observe in a cryptic and surprised fashion that "your left hand is *not* lifting *yet* NOWW!"[3] As in the technique described earlier in the chapter, the hypnotist can lift the left hand at the same time, thus creating a surprise-inducing incongruency. Attention can then be rapidly shifted from one hand to the other. This extra confusion will often serve to depotentiate the conscious processes of previously unaffected subjects.

Thus, the utilization principle prevails in applying this technique, as in all others. Of course, a few subjects won't respond hypnotically to any versions of the technique. This is often due to a failure to establish rapport (since the person must feel safe to respond hypnotically); a failure to absorb attention experientially; or a lack of confidence or meaningful communication on the hypnotist's part. Whatever the case, the hypnotist should always feel free to abandon the technique if it clearly isn't working. To the extent that this is done confidently and gracefully, it poses no real problems. As previously noted, the hypnotist might quickly distract the subject, make a joke about apparently being "absentminded," speak seriously and earnestly, and so forth, depending on what seems appropriate to reestablish rapport with the subject.

## Polarity Plays

*Polarity plays* are maneuvers in which the operator assumes the "resistant" or trance-inhibiting part of the client and plays it better than the person. When performed congruently and dramatically, this typically serves to interrupt the person's entrenchment in that role, thereby allowing deeper experiential realities to unfold. For example, Erickson (1964a) described how a woman entered his office hesitatingly and expressed a deep interest in being hypnotized for therapeutic purposes. She reported that numerous previous attempts at hypnosis with three other doctors had all failed, and that Erickson had been recommended as someone who could handle her "resistances." From these and other remarks, Erickson concluded that while the woman was interested seriously in hypnosis and therapy, her many ambivalences would stimulate

---

[3]A variation on this technique is to point at one hand intently while describing the other hand. For example, you might look and point at the right hand while exclaiming, "The left hand is not lifting yet." Or focusing nonverbally on the left hand, you might exclaim, "Your right hand is not *left* up *right* yet NOWW!!!"

"no-win" relationship struggles. Because traditional inductions would fail under such circumstances, Erickson proceeded in the following way:

> . . . She was told rather brusquely, "Well, let's get this clear. Three doctors, all good men, just as good as I am, have worked hard and long on you. They found you to be too resistant, *as I will too. So let's have that understood at once.*" With markedly differing inflections and tempo, the following was said to her as a two-part statement, "I CAN'T HYPNOTIZE YOU, *just your arm.*"
>
> In a bewildered fashion she said, "Can't hypnotize me, just my arm – I don't understand what you mean."
>
> Again she was told with heavy emphasis with the words spoken slowly, "THAT'S EXACTLY WHAT I MEAN. I CAN'T HYPNO-TIZE YOU"; then with a soft gentle voice I added rapidly as if it were one word, *"justyourarm,see."*
>
> "As I said the word "See," I gently "lifted" her left arm upward, the touch of my fingers serving only to direct the upward move-ment, *not actually to lift it.* Gently I withdrew my fingers, leaving her hand cataleptically in midair. As she watched her arm in its upward course, I said softly and sighingly, "Just close your eyes, take a deep breath, go deeply asleep and as you do so, your left hand will slowly come to rest on your thigh and remain there continuously as you sleep deeply and comfortably until I tell you to awaken."
>
> Within five minutes after her entrance into the office, she was in a deep, and as it proved to be, somnambulistic trance. What happened? The woman was desperately seeking therapy, had come a long distance to seek it in response to repeated advice; she came with a rigid counter-set for any conventional traditional ritualistic or other techniques that she could watch, hear and understand. Believingly, agreeingly, she heard me say clearly and understand-ably, "I can't hypnotize you," to which was appended softly, quick-ly, and gently while she was still in a believing or accepting frame of mind, the inexplicable three words, *"just your arm."* (In Rossi, 1980a, p. 289)

The polarity play in this example involved taking the patient's belief of "I can't be hypnotized" and feeding it back dramatically and emphat-ically. In essence, Erickson "took over" that part of the patient, thus leaving her in an uncertain and receptive state, which Erickson prompt-ly utilized to develop trance.

This technique can be applied in a variety of ways. A client of mine, for instance, was mired deeply in a depression which he maintained by telling himself how incapable he was. Needless to say, his continual "induction" made him rather impervious to straightforward induction and therapy techniques. To unfetter him from this rigid outlook, I first arrested his attention by dramatically announcing that he was misleading me. After pausing for dramatic effect, I proceeded to tell him that he had severely underestimated his shortcomings. He couldn't do *anything* right, I proclaimed, taking 10 minutes or so to increasingly deride all his faults. I made sure to state these as exaggeratedly as possible. As expected, he eventually began to challenge my wild generalizations with claims that he could do *some* things fairly well. After letting him state several such abilities, I feigned disbelief, thus riling him into further disputatiousness. I utilized this by questioning his ability to "sit in a chair without moving, something so simple even a child could do it." When he began to do just this, I begrudgingly acknowledged it before offering a series of further challenges regarding his ability to, for instance, "pay attention to me and listen to what I had to say," to "breathe deeply, comfortably, and easy," to "relax without me having to tell you how to do so," and so on. By playing his polarity in this way, I was able to induce a trance within 20 minutes. The trance was utilized to develop in the client a state of comfort and security; this provided a foothold for further hypnotherapy that proved successful.

A somewhat different polarity play was used with another client, a middle-aged woman beset by many worries and anxieties. When I agreed to her request for hypnosis, she immediately began to ask question after question about the various possible trance experiences and what she should do in each situation. After a while it became clear that these inquiries were being used to maneuver away from the requested experience of trance. To utilize her pattern, I therefore announced that I would use a "special" technique with her: *she* would be the hypnotist and *I* the subject. Her objections were overridden and distracted as I quickly and good-naturedly changed seats with her. She looked at me from the "hypnotist's chair," confused and befuddled. I began to ask her questions similar to the ones she had put to me, but in a more exaggerated fashion. For example, I asked her after a while whether she could guarantee that my trance experience would be fantastic, whether she could accurately predict *exactly* what I would experience, whether she was willing to promise that it would solve all my problems, and so on. When she replied in the negative to such questions, I feigned astonishment and disappointment. I increasingly exaggerated this surprise, to the point where it became absurd and actually humorous. When we both began to laugh, I continued for a while longer before switching roles again and discussing how it was best to just allow one's self to experientially explore the many possible hypnotic realities, knowing that this could be done in a safe and secure fashion. My polarity play having interrupted and then depotentiated her trance-interfering gamut, she agreed to this suggestion, and a pleasurable and educational trance was developed.

To summarize, polarity plays involve enacting more dramatically and congruently a dominant behavioral pattern of the client, thereby interrupting the person's ability to continue with such behavior. It is an especially effective induction technique when the behavioral target is a trance-inhibiting pattern expressed by the subject. The assumption is that the person seeking trance yet expressing resistance to it has complementary structures "co-operating" simultaneously. Most hypnotists and therapists get stuck in enacting the complementary structure of the person who wants to experience trance or therapeutic change, thereby leaving the person mired in the opposite part. Playing the "resistant" part better than the client interrupts his or her ability to do so, thereby creating an uncertainty and consequent receptivity to suggestions; it also paces the "resistant' part in a way that enables the introduction of leading maneuvers. In the hypnotic context, this means that effective polarity plays constitute effective interruption techniques paving the way to meaningful hypnotic explorations.

### OVERLOAD TECHNIQUES

*Overview*

Besides interrupting patterns, confusion techniques can also be accomplished by *overloading* patterns. This method follows the five-step procedure outlined in Table 7.1: (1) behavioral patterns, especially trance-inhibiting ones, are identified; (2) the person is paced appropriately; (3) involvement in a dominant pattern is intensified and overloaded, thereby making it difficult to continue to process information at a normal rate; (4) the ensuing confusion is amplified to create more uncertainty and consequent response potential; and (5) the confusion is utilized to introduce a simple directive to which the person can respond in order to reduce the uncertainty. In accord with the utilization principle and as the complement to interruption techniques, overload techniques encourage clients to continue what they are doing, but even more so (to the point of information overload).

The effective use of overload requires a meaningful nonverbal delivery style. As Erickson (1964a) noted:

> A primary consideration in the use of a confusion technique is the consistent maintenance of a general casual but definitely interested attitude and speaking in a gravely earnest intent manner expressive of certain, utterly complete, expectation of their understanding of what is being said or done. . . . Also of great importance is a ready flow of language, rapid for the fast thinker, slower for the slow-minded but always being careful to give a little time for a response but never quite sufficient. Thus the subject is led almost to begin a response, is frustrated in this by then being presented with the next idea, and the whole process is repeated with a continued development of a state of inhibition, leading to confusion and a growing need to receive a clear-cut comprehensible communication to which he can make a ready and full response. (In Rossi, 1980a, p. 259)

An appreciation of overload as a viable therapeutic technique is enhanced by recognition of how commonly it occurs in everyday experience. For example, we all have experienced how confusing it can be to try to follow several speakers talking at the same time; to try to carry out several complex unrelated tasks simultaneously; or to comprehend a fast-paced lecture on a topic about which we know very little. In such situations our arousal usually increases along with psychological uncertainty, until finally we feel a need to do something about it. This is often easily accomplished: we might leave the situation, or simply stop paying attention, or otherwise disconnect from it. But sometimes disengagement from the source of confusion is not altogether possible. For example, we may be harassed by *internally generated* processes, such as incessant internal dialogue that questions and tries to analyze everything; or by *externally generated* stimuli, such as persistent loud voices. In such situations, our motivation to reduce the overloading stimuli increases with the confusion and uncertainty resulting from it.

Of course, there are times when we deliberately seek out overload in order to let go of mental sets: listening to loud music, singing together, running a marathon, and so forth. In such situations, we become immersed in and surrender to the intensity of the experiential stimuli, thereby allowing an effortless and more unified state of consciousness to emerge.

Thus, the value of overload depends greatly on the context and interests of the participants. The therapist therefore sets out to create appropriate contexts wherein confusion can be utilized therapeutically. A relationship is first established in which the client trusts the therapist and believes him or her to be an intelligent person whose communications are somehow relevant. Within this relationship, the therapist uses nonverbal communications indicating that what is being said is important and should be comprehended. With the client thus feeling compelled to attend to what is happening and to try to make sense of it, the therapist introduces confusion (e.g., by speeding the rate of delivery, interspersing nonsequiturs, shifting topics or orientations rapidly) to depotentiate psychological fixations, whereupon simple suggestions (e.g., to drop into trance) are delivered gently and straightforwardly.

As a cautionary note, it should be reiterated that the intent in using an overload technique is to disengage *willing but unable* subjects from fixed conscious processes that are severely limiting trance development as well as psychological functioning in general. In other words, the Ericksonian operator assumes that individuals are far more than the conscious processes with which they may be identified (confused), and uses overload techniques to enable deeper connection with experiential generativity. The therapist thus maintains a deep respect for the individual's integrity at all times, for to do otherwise would be not only unethical but also highly ineffective.

In a major sense, the effectiveness of an overload technique owes greatly to the subject's inability to let go of constant conscious processing. Thus, *what the person is doing is always that which can be used to induce trance*. The therapist operates like the fabled monkey catchers of India, who place a jar of rice in a clearing for a monkey. When the monkey arrives and places a hand in the jar in an attempt to grab some rice, they shout and run towards it. The monkey tries to escape, but cannot remove the rice-filled hand from the narrow-mouthed jar. It apparently never occurs to the monkey to simply release the rice, for previous experience has emphasized that once food is in hand, you should never let it go. Similarly, willing but unable subjects rarely realize that they simply need to let go of effortful conscious processes to exit from overload, and thus are engrossed and eventually entranced by such overload techniques. The therapist utilizes the ensuing trance states to assist clients in becoming unconstrained by rigidified frames, such that they can use them but not be used by them.

Like interruption techniques, overload can be carried out in any experiential modality(s) in a variety of ways. This section outlines six representative techniques: (1) temporal disorientation: the Erickson Confusion Technique; (2) spatial disorientation: internal referent shifts;

(3) spatial disorientation: the Mobius House; (4) spatial disorientation: external referent shifts; (5) conceptual disorientation; and (6) double inductions.

## Temporal Disorientation: The Erickson Confusion Technique

Originally developed by Erickson (see 1964a) as an age regression method, this is perhaps the most well-known of all his confusion techniques. It basically involves absorbing the subject's attention with some talk about some innocuous, commonplace activity (e.g., eating) and then gradually introducing various confusion maneuvers (e.g., rapid temporal referent shifts, nonsequiturs, and an increasingly rapid delivery style) to stimulate disorientation. The ensuing state of uncertainty is utilized to reorient to a different time/space coordinate – that is, the past or imagined future. The following is an abbreviated example with commentary, adapted from Erickson (1964a), in which regression is sought. (The italics indicate words or phrases given special tonal emphasis.)

### STEP # 1: Absorb Attention

| *Example:* | *Commentary* |
|---|---|
| " . . . And what a nice thing to know that as you're sitting there, you can recognize that there are a lot of experiences that you have enjoyed and have experienced on many occasions. . . . " | To begin, the subject must generally be in an attentive frame of mind. To establish this, many techniques can be used (e.g., those in Chapter 6). To introduce the verbal remarks, an innocuous pacing of the present can be used (as in the above example). |

### STEP # 2: Refer to a Common Event in the Present Tense

| *Example:* | *Commentary* |
|---|---|
| "For example, you probably ate lunch or breakfast today . . . most people do, although sometimes they skip a meal. . . . " | The hypnotist now mentions a commonplace activity (e.g., eating, sleeping, talking) which the subject has most likely engaged in and uses it to mention the present tense in a seemingly innocuous fashion. A slight nonsequitur ("although |

sometimes they skip a meal") is used to create mild uncertainty. All of this is delivered in a meaningful but decidedly casual fashion, so as to compel the subject to continue to listen and try to understand the significance of the utterances.

*STEP # 3: Use Common Event to Link Present With Past and Future*

| *Example* | *Commentary* |
|---|---|

" . . . And perhaps you had something today that you had before, perhaps some day *last* week, or the week before . . and you probably will have the same thing again sometime *next* week or the week *after* that . . . and perhaps that day *last* week, if there was one when you had *that* which you ate *today*, was a today *then* as *this* today is *now*. . . .

In other words, that which was *then* perhaps is like that which is *now* . . . perhaps it was a Monday like today, or a Tuesday, I don't know . . and maybe in the future it will be eaten again on a Monday or a Tuesday, but Wednesday should never be ruled out, even if it is the middle of the week . . . *and what does it really mean to be the middle of a week?* I don't really know, but I do know that at the beginning of the week, Sunday comes before Monday and Monday before Tuesday, and Tuesday after Sunday *except when five days before. . . .*"

The hypnotist now gradually assumes a more rapid delivery as the event is used to refer to days of the week, which in turn are used to refer to the different time tenses. The major purpose of these remarks – which can be modified (e.g., extended or shortened) according to the subject's responses – is to begin to overload and temporally disorient the subject. Note that all the statements are undeniably true, since any errors will give the overly rational subject an opportunity to stop listening intently.

At this point, subjects will usually either be struggling to follow, or will "give up" and just let themselves become absorbed in experiential processes. Either response can be utilized by speaking quicker and more asynchronously, so as to amplify any confusion. (Of course, the technique can be aborted or otherwise modified with the occasional subject who begins to argue or grow otherwise belligerent with the hypnotherapist. Such a response generally indicates insufficient preparation.)

*STEP # 4: Continually Equate Past, Present, and Future*

| *Example* | *Commentary* |
|---|---|
| " . . . And this is true *this* week, *was* true *last* week, and will be *next* week . . . but whether this week, last week, or next week really isn't that important . . . because Monday comes on the same day of the week this week as it did last week and will next week . . . and Sunday as well, *not to mention Tuesday* . . . and so the days of the week and the weeks of the month have many similarities shared between and among them. . . . " | Continuing to increase speech tempo while speaking mean- ingfully and intentfully, the hyp- notist now also shifts temporal referents by noting similarities of the past, present and future. Again, this can be lengthened if the subject seems to need more overloading. Note also the con- tinued use of nonsequiturs. |

*STEP # 5: Shift to Months of Year*

| *Example* | *Commentary* |
|---|---|
| " . . . And the months of the year follow a similar pattern as well . . . September before Octo- ber and after August, and August before September . . . this year, next year, and last year. . . . " | The referent shift from days to months adds variety and begins to generalize the constant rela- tions seen from changing van- tage points. That is, the content of the units changes, but the referential variability remains. (The difficulty in consciously comprehending this paradoxical relationship attests to its viabili- ty as an overload technique. Slow and deliberate contempla- tion will reveal that it all makes sense.) |

*STEP # 6: Gradually Shift Toward Past*

| *Example* | *Commentary* |
|---|---|
| " . . . And Labor day of this year, where were you *then now*? . . . And it really isn't Labor day yet, is it . . . and so you don't | The temporal referents are now all to the past, thus encouraging the subject to regress back to those times. Specific occasions |

have to labor at all . . . *you can let your unconscious take care of things and drop deeply into trance* . . . but where are you now? . . . No need to verbalize, just imagine and it is *that* which was *then now* . . . but summer of 1981 (or the present year) is behind us, and all that which occurred, most of which has been forgotten, do you remember? And *May* I continue by pointing out that any fool can begin *April* but a *March* through time leaves one wondering: Who really remembers *February* 19th? And the end of *January*, a new year already underway . . . and New Year's Day, and all of the activities of the night before . . . and the holidays of 1980 (or the year before the current one) and all of the things to do . . . but that was after Thanksgiving, was it — *is* it not *now*? . . . And this was true *then now* and also last year . . . and in [name two years previous to current one]. . . . "

(Christmas day, Feb. 19th, etc.) are used to enhance this revivification process. Phrases containing sudden tense shifts (e.g., "that was nice, isn't it?") are used to confuse the conscious mind while accessing and then placing in the present reality memories for the unconscious.

*STEP # 7: Access Specific Time*

| *Example* | *Commentary* |
|---|---|
| " . . . And continuing back, back, back . . . all the way back to the years of yesteryear *now* that are *now* becoming part of the undeniable present *now* . . . that which once was long ago is now *that which is now* . . . and you can enjoy how easy it is for your unconscious to recall a long-forgotten experience, a pleasant experience which you have not remembered for so long . . . because you can *drift all the way* | The subject is now generally directed to revivify a specific incident from the past. The subject is also asked to signal the revivification with a finger levitation. |

*back*, all the way back to that
time long ago as a child, long
ago where you really had an enjoyable, pleasant experience . . .
that's right . . . and take all the
time in the world . . . and when
you've let yourself completely
revivify that experience . . . your
unconscious can signal by letting the index finger of your
right hand slowly lift up. . . . "

Much of the effect of this technique depends on the hypnotist's delivery. To reiterate, subjects will often respond to their initial confusion
by wondering about the hypnotist's integrity, intelligence level, present
state, intent, and so forth. It is therefore important that the therapist
first develops a context in which he or she is perceived as a relatively
intelligent, well-intentioned, and effective communicator, then speaks
congruently, confidently, and rhythmically while delivering the technique. When these criteria are met, most subjects will either try to
follow closely what is being said – a near-impossible task almost inevitably leading to profound disorientation – or simply give up a need
to understand; both responses are ideal for trance development. However, the hypnotist must always remain tuned to the subject's ongoing
responses, so that the communications can be calibrated accordingly.
For example, tempo is quickened when subjects become mildly confused; rhythm grows more asynchronous when the temporal markers
(past, present, and future) are rapidly shifted; tempo is slowed and
intensity softened when simple hypnotic directives are given to utilize
the confusion. To masterfully adjust to these parameters, it is necessary
to practice – not only alone (e.g., taping into a recorder and then listening back; looking in a mirror while verbalizing the induction to get a
sense of facial expression; writing an entire induction out and critiquing
it), but with live subjects as well. Such practicing will pay off, for the
hypnotherapist will discover himself or herself able to work successfully
with many individuals previously branded unhypnotizable or resistant.

### Spatial Disorientation: Internal Referent Shifts

This technique is similar to Erickson's confusion technique, except
that the disorientation is accomplished via rapid shifts in *spatial referents – this/that/there/here, right/left/up/down/diagonally/the middle third,*

*east/west/south/north/straight down*, and so forth. One particularly effective way to do this is to intersperse the spatial referent shifts within an absorbing story. The following is an example of a general story I have found effective. For reasons made apparent by reading the story, I call it the *autohypnosis directional maneuver*. The story is usually best delivered after about 10-15 minutes of inductional communications have developed a light trance, or at least a receptive state, in the subject. (The italics indicate embedded suggestions, while capitalizations mark words or phrases delivered with special intensity.)

... And there are so many directions you can follow when you allow your unconscious to do it for you ... just as there are many different directions you can follow physically ... I'll give you an example. ... Some summers ago, I was traveling all alone on the highway in my car, just allowing myself to *pay close attention* to the sound of the engine, and knowing that slowly but surely I was heading into another state. And in that state there was a particular destination I was headed for, a particular person I wished to see, a particular experience I was looking forward to in that other state. However, while I knew the general set of directions regarding how to get to where I wanted to go, I could not for the life of me remember the proper order in which those turns occurred. I did know that from where I was *there then*, I thought to myself, "I don't want to be *here now*; I want to be *there now*, and all I can remember is that to get *there now*, or at least soon *now* from *here*, I take a combination of three *right* turns and *three left* turns ... but I don't know quite which is the *right* series of *rights* and *lefts* ... but I do want to get *there* and I am *here now*." And so I said, "All *right, pay very close attention*, because we've got to make it *right* or we'll be *left* behind." ... And *then* I said, "All *right*, let's begin ... I'll take a *right here* – I think that's *right*; it'd better be, or we'll be left in the wrong place – and *then* a *left* and *now* I'm *left* with two *lefts* and another couple of *rights*. ... So all *right*, I'll take another *left*, which means I'm now *left* with a *left* and a *right* and a *right*. ... And if *now* I take a *right* I'll be *left* with a *right* and a *left*, straight up and *straight down, all the way down* (spoken softly but intently) ... but if I take a *left* I'll be *left* with a *right* and then again a *right*. ... But I don't think *that's right*, so I'll take a *right now*, and *then* a *left* ... and now I'm *left* with a *right* ... and ... DEAD END! ... it's the *wrong* way. ... And so now I've got to go back to my starting point, so as not to get completely *left* behind. ... So I begin to back track back the same way as I just tracked forwards, except NOW EVERYTHING IS REVERSED: THAT WHICH JUST WAS LEFT IS NOW RIGHT AND THAT WHICH JUST WAS RIGHT IS NOW LEFT ... AND THE diagonals ARE REVERSED AS WELL . . . and so for every *right then* it is *right now* to take a *left* . . . and for every *left then* it is *right now* to take a *right now* and go all the way back to the beginning, ready to start again . . . and so I begin this time. . . .

The story can be elaborated and reiterated, each time with a different series of directional turns. When the subject looks completely confused, utilization suggestions can be offered. For example, to continue from above:

> . . . And after a while I became so tired, so confused, that I didn't know what to do, didn't care where to turn next . . . I couldn't tell a *right* from a *left*, nor a *left* from a *right*. . . . I couldn't figure out whether taking a *left* was *right* or whether taking a *right* was *right*. . . . So I pulled off to the side of the road, turned off the engine, and sat there with my eyes closed and said to myself, "*To hell with trying to figure it out. Stop all this activity and just relax and drop into trance!!*" (This is uttered in a slower, softer, but more intense and emphatic fashion.) . . . and I did . . . (The hypnotist now shifts to a more relaxed, almost relieved tone.) And I was able to *just allow that trance to fully develop* . . . there was the recognition that there really is no need in such situations to pay attention to any needs except the need to attend to one's own internal needs . . . and what a nice thing to know that you can simply *let your unconscious do the work for you*. . . .

Investigation will reveal that all these statements are valid and consistent with each other. Also, the effectiveness of the story will depend in large part on the delivery style. As with any Ericksonian technique, especially those involving confusion, the hypnotist needs to absorb and maintain the subject's attention, and must therefore speak meaningfully, impressively, and congruently. Because the intent is to create and then utilize informational overload, the hypnotist usually begins with a relatively quick tempo, increases and intensifies it when the subject begins to grow confused, then dramatically reduces to a slower and softer voice right at the point of utilization (i.e., the apex of the confusion). In terms of tonal patterns, it is extremely effective to mark out — as indicated by the italics above — both (1) the directional and ambiguous terms (e.g., right/left) and (2) embedded suggestions regarding paying attention and dropping into trance. When these and other nonverbal delivery techniques are judiciously applied, the story will usually work quite well as a confusion technique designed to depotentiate conscious interferences.

I should note that if you initially lack confidence in using this technique, you are not alone. Many therapists in my training workshops are fascinated by my demonstration of the technique and marvel at its effectiveness, but feel clumsy and often confused in initially trying it themselves. One helpful strategy is to not really listen closely to the story yourself as you tell it. Just let yourself develop a nice rhythm where you can continue to talk and shift tenses. To remain consistent and accurate in your statements, you might use the fingers of your right and left hands to keep tabs on the numbers of rights and lefts actually taken. For example, in telling the above story, which contained three rights and three lefts, you would start by holding out (unnoticeably to the subject) three fingers on each hand. Then, every time you describe actually making a turn – rather than noting simply that you *could* – you withdraw a finger on the same-referent (right or left) hand. In this way, all you really have to keep track of during the story is the number of rights and lefts you have left to take.

Of course, this strategy alone will not guarantee a smooth and effective delivery style. Like most of the overload techniques described in this section, a good deal of time should be devoted to practicing and refining your delivery style.

## Spatial Disorientation: The Mobius House

Overload via spatial disorientation can also be accomplished by absorbing clients in surreal or self-reflexive imagery. The unusual nature of such imagery will frequently depotentiate the rationally oriented conscious processes to enable trance development and hypnotherapeutic explorations. Of course, clients must be willing and able to become absorbed in the suggested imagery. For this reason, such imagery is often most effective as a deepening technique, that is, introduced after a light trance has already loosened the person up a bit.

There are many possible imaginal descriptions one can offer; for ideas, the work of Dali and Escher might be studied. One technique I have found particularly effective involves a "Mobius House" in the "Middle of Nowhere," where everything – directions, dimensions, colors, and so on – is experienced as leading to its (complementary) inverse. Thus, walking towards the Mobius house leaves one walking away from it; you stand on the ceiling once inside; white is black and black white; and so forth. The following exemplifies how communications might proceed after a light trance has been induced:

... That's right ... and so just continue to let yourself explore
your unconscious ... and what a nice thing to know that you can
be all alone, so very securely, with your unconscious and just a
voice ... my voice ... and you can hear my voice, and be here with
my voice, and it needn't bother you in any way, because what's
more important is simply letting yourself attend to the need to
attend to those unfolding, internal, hypnotic realities ... and you
can float all alone in the Middle of Nowhere ... and your unconscious does know where Nowhere is ... and you can be all alone,
very secure, floating, drifting, not attached to anything in particular ... simply being able to discover that secure drifting in the
Middle of Nowhere, unattached to a particular time or a particular
space, just very securely letting that comfortable, easy, and secure
place of the Middle of Nowhere unfold all around you ... (elaborate
for a while if needed).

... And you can experience a lot of different things in the Middle of Nowhere ... not attached to time, not attached to space, recognizing that time and space are variables that you can let your
unconscious use to create and generate experiences appropriate
for you as an individual ... and so what a nice thing to know that
in the middle of the Middle of Nowhere you can discover the
Mobius House ... and some people know that a mobius strip is
a two-dimensional strip in which the *inside* is *outside* and the *outside* is *inside* ... and so you can securely and pleasurably discover
that the Mobius House is a three-dimensional mobius configura-
tion in which *up* is *down*, *down* is *up*, *right* is *left* and vice-versa
... and *west* is *east* and *north south* ... *and even the diagonals are
reversed!!* ... And so as you walk towards the Mobius House you
find yourself walking away from it ... and maybe you *consciously
give up and forget trying*, I don't know, but in doing so you find
yourself *left right* in the middle of the Mobius House ... and standing on the ceiling looking up at the floor in the Mobius House, you
begin to notice a variety of different things. ... For example, that
in looking West you can see the sun coming up ... and as you look
east the sun is going down ... and walking outside you find yourself in the kitchen, again in the middle, the center, and you begin
to recognize that everything is its opposite and then some ... and
so you begin to think that *right* being *left* you go *left* for *right* but
discover that's not *right*, that's wrong! ... and you try to go *right*
for *right* but find you're *left* with going *left* again, and that's not
*right* ... and being turned round in these ways, you begin to recognize that it's not the physical dimensions, it's the mental attitude
... the Mobius House is in the Middle of Nowhere ... and its
inverse ways are in relation to mental expectations, not undeniable
realities ... in other words, you can allow both sides of that fence

to integrate within the common ground!! . . . and so thinking *right* is *left* makes it *left*, thinking north is south makes south south and north north . . . but *thinking* that thinking *right* is *left* makes *left left* actually makes *left right*. . . . (This can be continued if subject appears to need more overloading.)

. . . And so why not give up the thinking and simply enjoy yourself thoroughly, letting that reality unfold all round, letting yourself be ever more immersed in Nowhere, in discovering the pleasure of perceptual variability, of mental flexibility, of experiential variety, of *developing mental understandings of value to the entire Self*. . . .(etc.).

These communications can be continued in various ways. One involves having clients discover a library room in the Mobius House. In this library is a "Book of Time" (with the client's name on the cover) containing all past, present, and future events. The Book of Time can be used to direct clients back (or forward) in time to key experiences that can be therapeutically utilized.

Another possibility is to introduce a Mobius House room containing mirrors on opposite walls. The image on one wall is identified as reflecting some self-valued ("positive") representation of the person, while the opposite wall's image is described as showing an opposite, self-devaluing ("negative") aspect. The client is shuttled between the opposite images in increasingly rapid cycles, until eventually the two are integrated within a Self-valuing framework. As the imaginative hypnotherapist will quickly discover, there are many other possibilities in which the general framework of the Mobius House in the Middle of Nowhere can be used to facilitate therapeutic explorations.

*Spatial Disorientation: External Referent Shifts*

This general method, developed by Erickson in the 1930s, basically involves absorbing attention before directing it in an increasingly rapid fashion to various external stimuli. Like any confusion technique, it can be applied in a number of ways. An interesting example of the technique can be found in Erickson's (1964a) description of his interactions with a colleague, an Indian psychiatrist interested in gaining a better understanding of schizophrenic processes. As an experiment designed to experientially demonstrate perceptual disorientation, Erickson arranged two chairs in two respective corners of a 12-foot square space, then positioned himself and the psychiatrist in each of the remaining corners. He labeled the chairs A and B respectively, and himself and the psy-

chiatrist C and D respectively. He then summoned an excellent som-
nambulistic subject who had volunteered for the experiment. After
inducing the subject into a deep trance and instructing her to remain
in rapport with both him and the Indian psychiatrist (Dr. G), Erickson
asked her to sit in Chair A (nearest to Erickson) while facing Chair B
(near Dr. G). He then stated in an elaborate and somewhat cryptic
fashion that his intent was to teach Dr. G something about "geography"
and that the subject was to remain in her seat during the entire lesson.
Having thus focused Dr. G's attention onto the subject, Erickson began
a rather disorienting patter. The following is an excerpt:

> (speaking to subject) I want you to know that that chair (pointing
> to A) you are in is *here* to you (pointing to subject) and *that* chair
> (pointing to B) is *there* but as we *go around* . . . the *square*, I am
> *here* and you are *there* but you know you are *here* and you know
> I am *there* and we know *that* chair (B) and Dr. G are *there* but he
> knows he is *here* and you are *there* and *that* chair (B) is *there* and
> I am *there* and he and I know that you and *that* chair (A) is *there*
> and that I who am *here* am really *there* and if *that* chair (B) could
> think, it would know that you are *there* and that Dr. G and I both
> think we are *here* and that we know that you are *there* even though
> you think you are *here* and so the three of us know that you are
> *there* while you think you are *here* but I am *here* and you are
> *there*. . . . (In Rossi, 1980a, p. 268)

Erickson continued in this way, all the while speaking slowly, impressively, and rhythmically. After a while, Dr. G appeared to grow rather
disoriented, alternating confused glances to the spaces beneath him and
then at Erickson. At this point Erickson instructed the deeply hypnotized subject to take over his role in "explaining" in rapid fashion the
different orientations of "here" and "there." Briefly stated, Dr. G developed a rather profound alteration in consciousness, a development that
was utilized for various hypnotic explorations and later discussion.

Erickson (1964a) described how modified versions of this technique
were employed successfully with other individuals interested in hypnotic explorations. In my own work, I have found this spatial disorientation method rather effective, especially when various dissociations are
desired—for example, with a person desiring to separate from severe
physical pain (e.g., in surgery or chronic pain cases), or with individuals
who feel a need to consciously follow everything the hypnotist is saying
and doing. This latter category applies especially to mental health professionals interested in pursuing hypnotic inquiry with both themselves

and their patients. Such individuals often assume (erroneously) that the best way to develop skills as a hypnotist is to maintain continual conscious vigilance of all demonstrated techniques, a belief that frustrates their attempts to experience deep trances. I have found spatial disorientation to be an excellent method for developing a dual consciousness ("conscious observer" and "deep trance participant") that satisfies the needs to be "a part of yet apart from." The basic technique is to have one chair designated for "the conscious mind" and one for "the unconscious mind." The subject sits in the "conscious mind" chair prior to the induction and is shifted to the "unconscious mind" chair when trance development is appropriate. A brief induction (5–15 minutes) is usually used to experientially absorb the subject and build some response potential. A modified version of the "here/there" shifts is then used to locate the "conscious mind"—the part that needs to observe, analyze, recognize, and so on—in its designated chair, while the "unconscious" can experience deep trance in the other chair. In other words, subjects are instructed to imagine sitting in one chair, watching themselves go deeply into trance in the other chair.

For example, a trainee in an advanced hypnotherapy training program complained that although he could easily induce others into trance, numerous attempts to personally experience trance had all met with frustrating failure. After observing and discussing with him his futile efforts, it seemed that a major stumbling block was an incessant internal dialogue, which rationally analyzed from an operator's viewpoint all hypnotic communications presented to him. To address this, I accepted his request to serve as a demonstration subject and asked him to leave his seat and sit next to me in "the trance subject's chair." After opening with about 15 minutes of a conversational induction that stimulated a light trance at best (with eye closure), I began to use the above-described dissociational method. Upon hearing the referent shifts, the subject smiled in recognition. I graciously acknowledged his ability to be so attentive, then suddenly assumed an extremely serious demeanor and wondered aloud slowly and deliberately if he *really* recognized what I was saying. Having thrown him off balance with this cryptic remark, I urged him to "pay very close attention even though you might not understand all!!" I then shifted to an increasingly rapid and arrhythmic tempo and discussed spatial orientation and the value of dissociation. Each time I spoke about his conscious processes I directed my voice to his previous seat "over *there*"; all communications about his unconscious and trance development were vocally directed to the present (seating) position *"here now."* The following is an excerpt:

. . . And Kevin, I really am so glad that you've volunteered as a subject *today*. And however you participate, what a nice thing to know that you've left your chair *over there* and come *up here* to listen to *me here. Now* when you *were over there* you really *were* able to listen critically, knowledgeably, and enjoyably to all of the proceedings that have occurred over the past several days in *this here* room. And *now* I really don't think you should *stop listening consciously*; after all, when somebody has brought you a long way, you don't *forget* easily. And so keep in mind that as you *were over there* you can continue to be *that* way *over there*. And you have other interests as well, and you can attend to those, *develop those here*, all the while continuing to attend to those conscious interests *there*. Because what a nice thing to know that your unconscious can *operate independently from your conscious mind*. You regulate your breathing unconsciously, you sleep unconsciously, you carry out a lot of different things without conscious interference. And you dream at night unconsciously; and what does it *really* mean to *dream deeply and soundly*? I really don't know, but I do know that your unconscious can operate independently, intelligently, meaningfully. And your conscious mind does not have to go away at all; it can remain *there* as it did *then* and can now again be seated in *that* chair over *there*, and your unconscious can be *here* and *hear* me *here* . . . and your conscious mind *there* can listen and watch closely as well . . . your conscious *there*, your unconscious *here* . . . your concerns and rational intrigue over *there*, your trance ability *here now*, developing even more, that's right, even as your *conscious* can begin to recognize it . . . be a part of it yet apart from it . . . the comments, ever so fully, over *there*; the development of novel phenomenological reality *here* . . . and you can *hear* from *there* and *see* from *there* and yet *hear from here as well, if not better* . . . and what a nice thing to be a part of yet apart from *those normal operations over there* . . . and *there* you were up front with me and *here* you can be on my side . . . and I am talking in your left ear, because I am to your left as you face outwards . . . and yet if you were turned around facing *that* direction which just a moment ago was behind us and still is — but is it now not different and continuing to be so very different? . . . you can *feel it, Kevin* . . . *feel it happening* . . . that which was *there* is now again *there* and all the while you *drop deeper into trance HERE NOW* as you hear now that you've got two hands and so I'm wondering which will begin to lift up first? All the time in the world . . . watch it from *there* . . . feel it *here*. . . . *see from THERE* . . . *feel it HERE*. . . . *(etc.)*

These sorts of communications were extended for another 10 minutes or so, with an intense, rapid, and arresting delivery style maintained

throughout their presentation. The subject appeared increasingly cataleptic and deeply entranced, and various dissociation phenomena – hand
levitation, automatic talking, and "disconnected hands" – were all successfully developed. Before ending the trance, I instructed his "conscious mind over there" to "shift back with the rest of your body up
here." I then consolidated some of the learnings by elaborating how his
dissociational experiences were evidence of a general ability to "enjoy
autonomy" in a variety of valuable ways.

The subject was then reoriented from trance and questioned about
his experience. He reported initially thinking that the disorientation
technique, which he recognized as such, would not work, but that then
he became increasingly confused in trying to figure out whether I was
(as I had cryptically hinted during the induction) doing something else
besides the disorientation technique. He added that his confusion led
to profound perceptual alterations (e.g., the room began to swirl around,
his body seem to grow distorted). These developments surprised and
actually pleased him, as they were indications that trance was developing. He had then been disappointed briefly at the realization that his
conscious processes were "still hacking away," until suddenly the major
surprise of the experience occurred: he became aware that his "conscious
mind" was sitting in the front row seat watching him seated up on the
stage in a deep trance. This "blew his mind," as he put it, and he maintained this fascination as he watched "himself" on stage demonstrating
hand levitation. He had then, upon my suggestion, experienced himself
shifting back into his body on the stage chair and coming out of trance.
All in all, he remarked in an amazed fashion, it had been one of the most
intense experiences of his life. Not only did he finally develop a deep
trance, he gained deep insight into dissociational processes as used in
the hypnotic context.

A major reason for the technique's effectiveness is that it paced nicely
the subject's processes. A part of Kevin wanted to experience trance;
another part wanted to watch and comment extensively. The question
thus was, "How can both parts be utilized in an induction?" The spatial
disorientation method offered an ideal solution, enabling both parts to
participate in a noninterfering, complementary fashion.

Remember, however, that the appropriateness of a technique does
not guarantee its success. Although it may seem unduly repetitive, I
emphasize again the need for the hypnotist to (1) employ a nonverbal
delivery style that compels the subject to attend and respond in an
experiential fashion, and (2) continuously monitor and calibrate communications to the subject's ongoing responses. For example, more
confusing (pattern interrupting and informational overloading) com-

munications are added when conscious processes appear dominant; ongoing behavior is indirectly or generally paced in the induction; more direct and softer communications are used to offer trance suggestions at the peak of confusion. Observing these guidelines will enhance greatly the effectiveness of any technique, especially those involving confusion.

In experimenting with spatial disorientation, it is important to keep in mind that there are many modifications possible. For example, the therapist can have individuals physically moving from chair to chair, a Gestalt therapy technique especially effective with clients expressing conflicts about developing trance or any other therapeutic development. Thus, clients are instructed that every time they feel themselves wanting to experience trance, they should immediately sit in the designated "trance" chair; but every time they experience an objection or hesitation they should occupy the "objection" chair. (If there appears to be more than one type of objection, more chairs can be used.) In using this method, clients may have to be initially prompted to switch chairs when they switch parts, since their psychological shifts are often automatic and hence unconscious.

Depending on the person's responses, the technique can be used to develop trance in various ways. The spatial disorientation technique usually serves initially to separate the conflicting parts. The therapist might then engage the parts in serious discussion, working out a way to develop trance that satisfies the needs of all the parts. Another possibility – and one I find often to be quicker and more effective – is to gradually increase the rate at which the client shifts chairs. As long as the therapist remains sensitive and supportive, most individuals find it quite releasing to have their conflicts dramatized and carried to an absurd extreme; their laughter dissociates them from rigid identification with any one part, thereby paving the way for trance. If the client remains fixated in conscious processes (e.g., continuing to rationally analyze all hypnotic communications) the hypnotist might add to the proceedings some of the spatial disorientation communications described above. When delivered meaningfully, even the most difficult subjects desiring trance can find their wishes come to fruition.

*Conceptual Disorientation*

Besides temporal and spatial disorientation, the therapist can also use *conceptual disorientation* as an overload technique for inducing trance. Essentially, this technique involves employing a compelling, meaningful, and rapid nonverbal communicational style to deliver a loosely connected, free-associational stream of verbalizations. The intent is to first absorb a client in attending to and trying to comprehend the utterances, then switch topics so rapidly that the conscious mind overloads and depotentiates, whereupon embedded suggestions and other techniques are used to develop trance.

The specific statements are quite variable, being generated in a free-flowing fashion. To enable such a stream of utterances, the hypnotist shifts into an externally oriented trance (Chapter 3) to tune with the subject's ongoing processes, thereby ensuring that associations will be stimulated by the latter's behavior. Communications are offered in a meaningful and intense fashion, giving rise to the sense that what is being said is quite relevant. Having created this context, the hypnotist can select any topic or observation as the basis to begin. For example, if I were inducing a trance with someone while sitting here at my computer, I might say something like:

> . . . And I'm sitting here right now and you're there, and I'm using my fingers to type out the letters to you . . . and I've typed many times in the past, so I can *feel comfortable* in doing so . . . and there's a lot of different ways to type . . . you can type at a typewriter, you can type at a desk, you can typecast a particular person, whether you're in a play or not . . . and I often wonder what type of trance will one go in sitting there . . . what type of trance will it be? . . . and there's a type where you can go in and out . . . there's a type where you *go all the way down* . . . and what does it mean to *go all the way down*? . . . some people know what it is to get down or to be down or to feel down, but what does it really mean to *go into trance*? . . . you can go into a department store and shop around and not have to commit yourself to anything, and you can do the same in trance . . . and you can visit a lot of different places . . . and whether it's officially a vacation or not is not important . . . because you can relax anyway, anywhere, anytime NOWW!! . . . You can work and be comfortable, you can stay home and feel at home, you can go out and feel secure inside . . . and in the winter or the summer, it's nice to be comfortable and secure inside, not to mention any other times . . . and the times really are a changing . . . the New York Times has taken on a new old look . . . the Los Angeles Times has grown more conservative . . . and so many unexpected things can change after all . . . and change is nice to have, and bills even nicer, as long as they're one dollar, five dollar, 10 dollar, 20, 100 dollar bills . . . and in trance you can develop a wealth of different experiences and enrich your ability to take care of your needs in unique and appropriate fash-

ions . . . and the fashions change every year, but one thing does not: your ability to drop into trance and utilize the unconscious as your ally . . . and you don't have to be Luke Skywalker to need an ally and feel the Force . . . you can be here now and know that whenever, however, whatever happens, your unconscious can help you along. . . . (etc.)

This stream of consciousness is deliberately unedited to illustrate how the statements need not be brilliant; they simply need to follow associationally from the previous statement and be delivered in a meaningful and rhythmic way. As with any overload technique, subjects who have been properly absorbed will typically grow increasingly disoriented and then respond in one of two ways. The first, evidenced by the person who tries to understand everything rationally, is one of bewilderment and a growing desperateness to try to understand what is being said; the second is one of giving up trying to understand and simply enjoying the "trip" offered by the associations. With the first type of response, the hypnotist remains utterly serious while increasing the rate of delivery and rate of associational crossovers; with the second type, the hypnotist can be more gentle and more amusing, as the person is generally quite willing to completely let go and should be supported in doing so. Both types of responses can be utilized by interspersing trance suggestions, especially via rhetorical questions and embedded suggestions (Chapter 6). Of course, each subject will respond somewhat differently, thus making it imperative for the hypnotist to observe closely and adapt accordingly to the subject's ongoing processes.

In experimenting with this technique, one usually discovers that its mastery requires more "unlearning" than "learning." That is, the ability to free associate is something we all naturally have but learn to suppress at least partially; through "hypnotic" dictums such as "stick to the topic," "get to the point," "concentrate," and so forth, we train ourselves to constrain associations so as to adhere to a particular frame of reference. Although valuable and necessary for rational thinking, rigid adherence to such a constraint stifles various creative processes, including the present technique. Thus, a useful (and quite enjoyable) training exercise is to sit alone or with a friend for 10 minutes a day, select some stimulus randomly as a starting point, and let yourself free associate wildly. Once you find this easy to do, begin to weave in trance-relevant communications (e.g., regarding the person's ongoing behavior, their interests).

In practicing this technique, you will probably discover numerous ways to make associational crossovers. A few possibilities might be noted here.

*1. Different meanings.* One way is to shift to different meanings of a stated word or concept. For instance, the above example included "typing" to "typecast" to "types of trance"; "other times" to "changing times" to the newspaper "Times"; and "change" to "(dollar) bills" to "wealth of experience."

*2. Theme weaving.* A related, more elaborate strategy is to spin off and return to a theme in various ways. The following brief example weaves suggestions by playing off the themes or central ideas of *time* and *body parts*:

> (looking at watch on hand) . . . And what a nice thing to know that you've got time on your hands and you can use it in so many different ways . . . you can be able to look at your *watch carefully* and know whether *it is time*, John . . . and what does it mean to have all the time in the world . . . what does it mean for time to *come to a standstill*, for time to tick merrily, to have time on your hands . . . and, John, it *is* a handy thing to know that you don't have to give an arm and a leg to relax into a trance . . . because your unconscious has a holistic body of knowledge that it can use to stand on its own two feet, to reach out, to feel comfortable with. . . .

*3. Last word duplication.* A third strategy is to take the last word(s) in each statement and make them the first word(s) of the next statement. This repeated word is, however, placed in a different semantic context, thereby shifting the conceptual frame. For example:

> . . . And you really can have a good time in trance . . . and what does trance really mean? Everybody knows what it means to transfer (trance for), to translate (trance late), to have a translator (trance later), a transformation (trance formation), a transcendental, a trance now, a deep trance, a very deep trance NOWW. . . . And you can have a trance now *or* later, because sooner or later is something we all know about . . . and we all know so many different things, about so many different experiences . . . and different experiences are natural, they are undeniable . . . and you don't have to deny yourself something that is natural . . . and trees are natural, the Sierra Club knows that, even (former Interior Secretary) James Watt knows that . . . and Watt (what) does it mean to have enough energy to produce a light bulb . . . the emergence of a creative idea . . . and creativity emerges in so many different ways. . . .

*4. Cross-contextualizing general predicates.* A fourth strategy is to shift general predicates across various contexts, such that the experiential process is constant while the situation (persons, places, times) changes. For example:

> ... And in trance you can develop experiential comfort ... and what does it mean to develop experiential comfort? A child knows how to develop experiential comfort ... every child has had the experience of lying down for a nice cozy nap in the afternoon and really feeling good about it ... and every businessman knows the pleasure of coming home from a hard day's work and easing into a state of experiential comfort ... and the athlete needs to develop experiential comfort before and after the game ... and the student as well ... and so whether sitting at home, in bed, in the park on a nice sunny afternoon, wherever, you can *develop experiential comfort* in so many different ways and styles.

*5. Bridging.* Chapter 6 described the specific-to-general-to-specific bridging technique, wherein the hypnotist generalizes the present topic to cross over to another topic, then emphasizes some aspect of the new topic unrelated to the previous one.[4] For example:

> ... And trance is a learning experience ... and you have had so many different learning experiences before ... for example, sitting in a hard seat in a classroom as a youngster you learned a lot of different things ... and sitting in a hard seat can be uncomfortable ... and yet many people enjoy baseball games so much that sitting in a hard seat need not matter ... and you can forget about discomfort in many different ways ... for example, when you sleep at night, you really find how difficult it is to be consciously concerned about anything ... and you dream so deeply at night. ...

*6. Associational crossovers.* A final strategy is to make crossovers via associations from particular events, concepts, persons, and so forth. For example:

---

[4]The socially acceptable way to bridge is to emphasize those aspects of the new topic shared by (i.e., relevant to) the old topic. For example, if I say that your trance responses remind me of another subject, Bill, and then begin to talk about Bill, my comments about Bill are generally expected to pertain to your trance responses. If they do not—for example, say I talk about Bill's divorce from his wife, which has nothing to do with you, especially your present experience—you typically will become slightly uncertain and then exhibit responses appropriate to the context (e.g., anger, boredom, confusion). In the hypnotic context, the Ericksonian operator works to ensure that the appropriate response is further trance-utilizable uncertainty.

. . . And a trance state is an opportunity to explore a lot of different things . . . and what a nice thing to know that whatever state you're in in the United States, you can feel free to do so many things . . . and everybody has a right to vote . . . and you can afford comfort whether you voted (in 1976) for a Ford or a Carter . . . and while Ford and Chevy still are dominant in this country, I really like a nice German car . . . and over in Europe people wonder how (in 1980 and 1984) Reagan won so handily . . . but whether you're interested in old cowboy movies or not, you should recognize that Indians have a right to be red-faced and angry . . . and how representative were the actors then? . . . Do the images you have really represent history accurately?. . . . and how representative is your conscious mind of your unconscious needs, wishes, and desires? . . . why not take the opportunity to find out; it's the only democratic way. . . .

In concluding, it should be mentioned that while these associational strategies are presented here as the basis for conceptual disorientation, they certainly can be applied in other, less confusing ways. As discussed in the preceding chapter, they are also valuable in generalizing a point, gracefully shifting topics, connecting ideas, speaking metaphorically, speaking fluidly and continually, thinking creatively, and so forth. Because much of the effect depends on the accompanying nonverbal communications, the hypnotist can elicit different general responses by altering demeanor accordingly.

## Double Inductions

A double induction involves two hypnotists simultaneously doing inductions with a single subject.[5] I have found it to be one of the most effective confusion techniques available: not only does it interrupt the ingrained social rule of one person speaking at a time, it is virtually impossible for someone to consciously follow two persons speaking at the same time. Some subjects, particularly those mired in internal dialogue, will try desperately to keep up with the hypnotists; others will delight in just "giving up" the need to understand and will let themselves "go with the flow"; almost all will eventually become entranced by a

---

[5]This technique has been used by various people. Influenced by our work with Bandler and Grinder (1975) and by the writings of Castenada (1972), Paul Carter and I developed our own version. Approximately eight years later, we discovered that Kay Thompson and Robert Pearson had developed their own version of the technique many years earlier.

double induction. For these and other reasons – for instance, it can be used to simultaneously address different parts of a person – it is an outstanding hypnotic and therapeutic method.

The general procedure is as follows. The two hypnotists sit facing the subject. (I have usually found it best to sit on either side of the subject, so that he or she can only focus on one hypnotist at a time, thus enabling the other hypnotist to work more with unconscious processes.) To establish the proper context, rapport and trust must first be developed. Also, it is usually best to straightforwardly inform the person that a double induction will be offered for the purpose of assisting trance development. The exception to this is when an element of surprise is needed for a particularly recalcitrant subject; even then, however, a relationship in which the subject believes the hypnotists to be trustworthy and well-intentioned must be established by prior communications.

Subjects entrenched in trying to rationally analyze everything are instructed to try to follow along carefully, *even though they may not understand all*; subjects more able to set aside their conscious processes are instructed to feel free to alternate between attending to both, one, or neither of the voices during the induction. To gradually lead in to the double induction, the hypnotists can begin to speak sequentially, with one's comments complemented by the other's, thus encouraging the subject to shift attention back and forth. After several minutes, the hypnotists begin to talk simultaneously, both performing inductions that utilize the subject's ongoing processes.

A very important aspect of the hypnotists' processes is their nonverbal communications, especially in their relation to each other. At a most general level, these communications should complement each other. Of the many ways this can be done, the simplest is straightforward synchronization – that is, both hypnotists use the same rhythm, tempo, inflection patterns, pauses, and so on. This can be accomplished easily enough by coordinating with the subject's ongoing processes, and is a nice way to start out. The hypnotists are using different verbalizations, of course, and so the effect is like two guitarists playing the same melody but singing different lyrics. The matching of nonverbal styles tends to absorb unconscious processes, while the differences in verbalizations tends to overload the conscious mind.

Another type of nonverbal complementarity is a syncopated rhythm in which the hypnotists employ the same rhythms, though one follows a half beat behind the other. It's like two tapes of the same melody being played concurrently, with one tape a half second later than the other. A nice way to do this in relation to the subject's processes is for one hypnotist to time downward intonation inflections to the subject's exhalations, while the other hypnotist calibrates inflections to inhalations. This syncopated pattern is rather disruptive to any analytical processes still operative.

Nonverbal processes can also be combined with verbal processes to address different parts of the person. For example, one hypnotist might concentrate on depotentiating the conscious mind (e.g., by offering confusion techniques with a rapid-fire and arrhythmic nonverbal delivery), while the other hypnotist accesses unconscious processes (e.g., by using a soft, gentle, and soothing voice to offer straightforward suggestions such as "let yourself go . . . you don't have to listen to that . . . drop into trance . . . "). Or one hypnotist might distract the subject's conscious processes with irrelevant stories that *sound* quite relevant, while the other whispers trance suggestions in the other ear. Or one hypnotist might offer communications to support a part of the person wanting to stay out of trance for a while, while the other encourages development of deep trance. In all these cases, an interesting possibility is for the hypnotists to switch their respective functions in midstream; for instance, the one using confusion suddenly becomes very supportive, while the other assumes a confusion approach. This is rather disorienting and especially useful when the subject seems to be following along consciously without any difficulty.

This general strategy of simultaneously addressing different psychological processes has many values. Two or more "parts" of the person can be simultaneously paced and utilized; this is especially useful in ensuring that the subject (and the hypnotists) don't identify with one part to the exclusion of the other(s). It also enables psychological parts to be untangled and separated, something that can be extended therapeutically in various ways (like the Gestalt therapy "chair sorting" technique). For example, two therapists might stage an argument, each therapist identifying with a different "part" of the person — for example, "letting go into trance" vs. "holding on." This can be dramatically extended so that the client becomes engrossed in the argument, thereby projecting the conflict into another structure. (This is the essence of symbolic psychotherapy.) At some point, the therapist can begin to integrate the two positions or, better yet in some cases, ask the client how it might be worked out. Regardless of whether the client has a solution readily available, the drama will secure experiential absorption, thus creating receptivity to hypnotic explorations.

Several other general points should be mentioned about double inductions. The first regards the amount of overloading appropriate during a double induction. As with any confusion technique, disorienting communications are valuable to the extent that the subject's conscious processes are actively interfering with the development of trance. This will be evidenced by various minimal cues discussed in Chapter 4: furrowing of the brow, moving around, licking of the lips, talking, and so on. Such effortful participation can be utilized by taxing the conscious processes even more: assuming a more rapid tempo, giving the subject tasks, asking rhetorical questions, becoming more asynchronous in relation to each other, using other confusion techniques, and so forth. The confusion resulting from this increased overloading can be amplified and utilized with simple suggestions from one or both of the hypnotists to drop into trance.

Once trance has been established, further confusion is often counterproductive, as the conscious processes targeted by confusion have been depotentiated and the unfolding experiential processes of the unconscious now need support and guidance, not confusion. Further overloading is particularly inappropriate when elaborate instructions for a hypnotherapy process (e.g., hypnotic dreams) are given, as the disoriented subject will likely be unable to comprehend them. Similarly, it generally should not be used while the entranced subject is exploring some suggested hypnotic experience(s). It should also be reduced if the subject becomes angry or otherwise emotionally upset. In these various cases, overloading can be minimized by the hypnotists slowing down, speaking sequentially, being very gentle and clear, and utilizing the accessed experience via therapeutic procedures. Of course, a more overloading approach can be resumed if needed.

A second general point is that double inductions can be accomplished without two hypnotists. With persons besieged by internal dialogue, I sometimes turn on a tape recorded-induction and have them attend to it while I do an induction (usually "playing off" the taped induction). This both distracts and overloads their conscious processes. For self-hypnosis, this can be modified by having the subject listen to either a tape of a double induction or two tapes of different inductions. I have found listening to a double induction tape one of the most powerful self-hypnosis methods for most clients.

Another possibility, one demonstrated exquisitively by Erickson, is for a single hypnotist to use the principles and processes of the double induction. For example, I observed Erickson lean to his right and talk to a subject's conscious mind (e.g., "You may want to stay out of a trance for awhile . . . and your conscious mind can wonder") and then shift to his left and talk to the unconscious (e.g., "And your unconscious may wish to *develop a trance* and begin to wander into hypnotic realities"). He would alternate back and forth, using slightly different voices for the two parts, before settling on a left-leaning ("unconscious") orientation. This pacing and leading technique, which I have found remarkably effective in my own work, is a classic example of how auditory localization in space (Erickson, 1973) can be used to address different parts of the person.

Of course, there are other ways in which aspects of the double induction technique can be applied. Subjects might be asked to listen to some music during the induction; or switch chairs as they shift into different attitudes about trance or some therapeutic issue; or comment aloud for every suggestion offered by the hypnotist as to why it would not work. (This latter possibility is especially appropriate for the sophisticated subject who tries to follow the techniques closely; not only does it make the trance-inhibiting commentary of the subject part of the induction, but it also provides valuable information as to why a particular approach may not be appropriate, thus enabling the evolution of a more appropriate one.) In this regard, one of the most valuable aspects of the double induction technique is its highlighting of some important hypnotic communicational processes — for example, acknowledging, separating, and utilizing all relevant parts of a person; overloading conscious processes; the different effects of asynchronized and synchronized communicational rhythms; the value of distraction; and incorporating conscious processes — particularly objections — into the induction. By becoming skilled in double inductions, the therapist becomes much more effective at utilizing these processes in any hypnotic situation.

## CLINICAL DISCUSSION

Many therapists, while fascinated and impressed with confusion techniques, find themselves unwilling or unable to freely utilize them. Part of this is due to the normal and understandable *hesitation* about trying something seemingly rather unorthodox, and can be remedied by practicing alone or with colleagues, or by integrating confusion methods slowly into one's therapeutic style. Part is also due to a *lack of understanding* about exactly when and how to utilize confusion in the complex and delicate interaction of therapy, and a *lack of confidence* in experimenting with the somewhat sophisticated techniques (e.g., the fear that the technique won't work as planned); the discussion below addresses these points. But perhaps the most formidable barrier to effectively using confusion is a *misunderstanding* of its purpose – for instance, thinking its automatic effect is to humiliate individuals or make them feel stupid. This belief is understandable, given the negative cultural value attached to uncertainty states, but should be recognized as erroneous. To reiterate, *the Ericksonian operator uses confusion to support the person by creating the opportunity to disengage from the rigid limits of normal ways of being and experience the Self in other, more nurturing ways; confusion can liberate a person from a false and limiting identity.* In this sense, it is similar to a good joke, a Marx Brothers movie (the true masters of confusion techniques), a giggling spell or tickling session with a good friend, jogging, sex, and so forth; all are viable methods for depotentiating the normal frame of reference to enable new ways of being.

That inducing confusion *can* be tremendously supportive doesn't mean it always is. To reemphasize, the effect of a technique on a person's quality of experience depends on the integrity and intent of the user. Thus, the Ericksonian operator must develop, maintain, and communicate the belief that the client is an intelligent, capable, and unique individual deserving of the utmost respect, and that the intent of hypnotic communications – no matter how bizarre they may seem at times – is to support the person. To do otherwise is not only unethical but impractical, for at best clients will become angry and distrustful of the therapist; at worst they will be seduced and brainwashed. In any case, the satisfaction reaped from integrity will be accorded no one, especially the operator.

The integrity of the hypnotist is necessary but not sufficient for confusion to have beneficial effects. The remainder of the chapter briefly discusses some practical points regarding clinical applications.

*1. Confusion should usually be introduced gradually.* Partly because of the way they have been presented in the literature, many people assume that confusion techniques are suddenly sprung upon clients without prior notice. To say the least, this belief creates a bit of trepidation among therapists interested in applying them. It should be therefore be emphasized that confusion is usually best introduced only after certain understandings have been established. I rarely use an elaborate confusion technique (e.g., temporal disorientation, the handshake induction) before spending *at least* a session or two securing rapport with a client. I first establish that it is my dual intent to (1) fully respect and protect the person's needs and values while (2) stimulating his or her ability and desire to develop desired changes. After developing some trust, I make it clear through discussion and example (not necessarily in that order) that fulfilling these intentions will require my communicating in a variety of ways, one being confusion. I begin to intersperse slightly confusing communications: a meaningful nonsequitur, motoric restriction, a cryptic remark, or an astonished glance at their hand. This is usually done humorously, around a topic unrelated to the identified problem(s), with no attempt being made to develop a trance or extend past a nonthreatening and mild uncertainty state. Clients typically enjoy such unspectacular confusion techniques, and thus are receptive when I then discuss with them the potential value of uncertainty, especially in regard to how it creates a flexibility and receptiveness to internal resources. During this time I also address any concerns they might have. This generally paves the way for the success of more elaborate and dramatic confusion techniques.

I use confusion techniques with the vast majority of my clients (to varying degrees, of course); most are receptive to these techniques. In fact, many find confusion one of the most valuable approaches I use with them; they learn quickly that not only is it phenomenologically enjoyable and often humorous, but it also usually leads to positive experiential developments (i.e., therapeutic trance explorations). They thus feel secure in letting themselves follow the confusion-utilizing suggestions offered.

Of course, some subjects will not respond positively to confusion. This may be due to any number of reasons; for example, they may distrust the hypnotist; they may access some unpleasant childhood experience where they were confused; the hypnotist might not have absorbed their attention adequately or communicated compellingly enough; the amount of confusion may have been insufficient; the hypnotist may have attempted to utilize too quickly (i.e., before the subject had been adequately confused) or too late (e.g., the subject stopped listening because the confusion was getting too anxiety-provoking). The hypnotist can usually identify the reason by desisting from further confusion and talking directly with the client, or by using the five steps of confusion (Table 7.1) to review how confusion was applied (and perhaps misapplied) with the person in question. Appropriate measures can then be taken to rectify the situation.

*2. It is sometimes inappropriate to use confusion techniques.* It was mentioned above that confusion should be curtailed during certain points in an hypnotic interaction — for example, when a trusting relationship is not secure, when the subject feels unsafe or unprotected, once the subject is quite confused, and when instructions are being given. Just as importantly, there are some clients with whom confusion should not be used at all. This applies especially to those *already* deeply confused, such as the genuinely suicidal individual, the grieving person, the war veteran suffering from flashbacks. The hypnotist does not have to *produce* confusion in such people; it is already there. The hypnotist simply needs to utilize it. Providing gentle, direct, and simple pacing and leading is often all that's needed. For example, a suicidal woman entered my office. She had recently seen a psychiatrist who, in the first half hour with her, tried some crude attempts at confusion techniques. In her tremendously vulnerable and confused state, the woman felt incredibly violated. She panicked and ran out of the office crying hysterically, her suicidal urges augmented. Luckily, a friend – a student of mine – was able to settle her down. When she came to me upon referral from her friend, she was obviously still deeply upset and in a crisis period. After speaking with her briefly to establish rapport, I very gently acknowledged how terrible she felt, how she wanted to kill herself, how she had also come to me in apparent hopes of doing something else, how she could feel free to cry or not, how I wasn't going to hurt her, how she could continue to breathe, how it was safe here, and so forth. When she broke down crying, I took hold of her hands and continued in a similar fashion. After an hour or so, she felt much more stable and less suicidal. This relationship context expanded to allow further changes in therapy over the next several months.

The last thing people in such crisis periods need is for the therapist to confuse them. They have a desperate need to reduce the uncertainty, to find a basis of security and self-appreciation. The hypnotherapist should therefore skip the first four steps of a confusion technique and proceed immediately to the final step of utilizing the confusion. In this regard, it is useful to recognize that the confusion clients often exerience while exploring a therapeutic issue can be similarly utilized. The major ways in which therapists often deal with such uncertainty states include labeling it as resistance, demanding that the subject act rationally, ignoring or not recognizing it, trying to cheer the client up, and distraction. Another possibility – one I have found far more effective – is to recognize it as self-induced confusion and utilize with direct suggestions. For example, the therapist might say something like:

> That's right, John . . . you don't know what to do . . . you don't know what to say . . . but you can look at me . . . and as you do I'd like you to just let your eyes close and go inside for a moment . . . that's right . . . and as you do I'd like you to take a deep breath and

pay attention to what's happening, knowing that I am here with
you and will continue to be . . . but just breathe right now, John,
and tell me what you're beginning to become aware of. . . . (etc.)

Further directives could be issued according to the client's needs and
the therapist's stylistic preferences. Utilizing naturally-occurring confusion in such a manner not only is therapeutically effective, but it can
also yield some nice insights into how confusion works naturalistically
and thus enhance one's skill with confusion methods in general.

An exception to not using confusion with disturbed people is with
clients rigidly entrenched in their self-confusion, such as psychotics and
chronic depressives. Such individuals, while incredibly unhappy for the
most part, are usually not caught in a crisis period. On the contrary,
their misery and distorted views are often maintained in well-developed
and systematic ways that make them impervious to straightforward
interventions. Confusion is an ideal strategy in such cases, as it can
stimulate movement in the self-locked psychological processes. However, it should be applied sensitively, as underneath most severe chronic
symptoms is a great deal of pain and loneliness. Thus, the hypnotherapist should be willing and able to switch to an extremely supportive and
gentle approach once the confusion has dislodged the person from his
or her rigidity. Also, such individuals often have problems paying attention to anything outside of their own haunting internal processes. Thus,
the hypnotherapist usually needs to identify the exact nature of those
internal processes and design a confusion technique uniquely suited to
them. (Examples of this are included below; also, the special case of
psychotics is addressed in Chapter 8.)

Finally, confusion is sometimes inappropriate with subjects who are
perfectly willing and able to develop trance. It often is an unnecessary
sidetrack for such individuals, for they have little difficulty setting aside
the conscious processes that are the targets of confusion techniques.
They may even be held up and consequently frustrated by and resentful
of any attempts to confuse them. To avoid this possibility, a good rule
of thumb is to first attempt to induce trance without using confusion.
If it works, fine, don't use confusion. But if a person cannot experience
trance via a relatively permissive and straightforward induction, consider confusion and other approaches that depotentiate rational attentiveness (e.g., boredom, distraction, dissociation, and metaphor).

*3. The subject's processes should be the basis for selecting (or devel-
oping) confusion techniques.* Keeping in mind the general utilization
principle that *whatever a person is doing is exactly that which will allow*

*trance to develop* can help the therapist realize what type of confusion technique might work, and how and when it should be applied. For example, subjects caught up in social customs may be especially susceptible to the handshake induction; those who try to distract away from their problems will probably be strongly influenced by motoric restriction techniques; those insecure about their intelligence will be prone to meaningful nonsequiturs; and those with incessant internal dialogue will likely be powerfully affected by double induction or conceptual disorientation techniques. Of course, each subject's responses will be unique; thus, the hypnotist must be willing and able to utilize accordingly. This may mean abandoning a confusion approach in midstream, adding or shifting into a different confusion technique, simply modifying the present technique, and so on. The important point to grasp is that confusion is a naturalistic form of communication that is hypnotically effective only when the subject feels respected and protected as a person.

Also remember that the confusion techniques cited in this chapter are only some of the possibilities. They are most valuable in illustrating principles and providing reference structures which can guide the therapist in using confusion with a given client. Some examples may help underline this very important point.

One client, a man in his fifties, complained of depression. In short, he burdened himself with an incredible number of responsibilities: he was married and father of four children, worked 10 hours a day at his business (though financially well off), headed the PTA and a couple of citizen groups, contributed volunteer work on weekends, and so forth. He toiled joylessly at these commitments, never taking time for himself, insisting politely that his personal needs weren't that important. Casual conversation with him disclosed that he strongly identified himself as a man of honesty and integrity. Thus, after spending several sessions gaining rapport and familiarizing him with trance, I used a very simple but powerful confusion technique. I fully absorbed his attention before asking in a very slow and meaningful fashion if anybody had ever called him a liar. When he replied that nobody had ever done such a thing, I paused meaningfully before saying – again deliberately and intently – *"Well, let me be the first."* As I looked at him seriously and expectantly, he grew very confused, his mouth dropping open in an attempt to sputter a response. After several seconds he finally got out the words, "Well, I don't know . . . I don't know if I can take that." I utilized his profound confusion by replying, "Neither do I know if you can take that yet . . . but you can breathe, Fred, and you can and are looking at me . . . and so can you, why don't you close your eyes NOWWW!!! . . . and drop deeply into trance . . . that's right . . . all the way down NOWW!!!" He followed the suggestions and developed a nice trance. I suggested first that he have an integrating hypnotic dream, then guided him through some age regression experiences relevant to the therapeutic goals of feeling less depressed.

Another client, a 30-year-old woman, was interested in developing some assertiveness, among other things. After a half dozen hypnotherapy sessions with her, I suggested while she was in trance that her unconscious begin to create opportunities for her to realize her goals. Several days later, she went to pick up her car at a gas station, where she left it for a tune-up only after being repeatedly assured she could pick it up to drive to an extremely important meeting late that afternoon. When the car wasn't ready, forcing her to miss the appointment, she suppressed her anger as usual. She drove away meekly an hour and a half later, proceeding about a mile before the car broke down completely, strange sounds and steam escaping from under the hood. Perhaps taking cue from the steam letting off, she stormed back to the station and unleashed a scathing attack on the attendant, appropriately berating his arrogance and questioning his integrity. Her fury left him and all bystanders speechless and motionless, until she finally stalked off an hour later. As she was walking home, she suddenly realized what she had done (having apparently been in a dissociated trance during the outburst). She felt overwhelmed and frightened by her behavior, having always been meek and placating, and grew increasingly worried.

When she called me that evening, she was hysterically shouting that she was losing her mind. I spent a few minutes collecting a report of the transpired events and then, after calling her name and pausing to gain her complete attention, said simply, "Congratulations!" I could hear and feel that she was totally shocked by this statement. After all, she was losing her mind and here was somebody whom she trusted very much congratulating her about it! I repeated my congratulations in the same meaningful way, knowing this would amplify her confusion, and then instructed her to simply close her eyes, breathe deeply and easily, and drop into trance. After accessing some self-appreciation (anchored during previous trance work) to stabilize her state, I had her come down that evening and further work was done to utilize the crisis event.

In both the above cases, interruption of an important aspect of the person's psychological identity was the basis of the confusion technique. This utilization of client-presented (rather than therapist-developed) opportunities is usually both simpler and more effective, as it clearly

involves naturalistic communications and meaningful experiences. Similar strategies can be undertaken with overloading principles. For example, a woman suffering from psychosomatic pain had seen several
other hypnotherapists before being referred to me. She would request
trance with apparent eagerness, but responded to any traditional induction with complaints of growing pains throughout her body. My strategy was to first congratulate her on "the ability of her unconscious to
express itself in so many unique ways" while remarking that she was
obviously "aching to go into trance." Her uncertainty produced by my
effusive compliments was used to absorb her attention and meaningfully deliver the following series of comments:

> That's right, Mary, that pain really is payin' off (pain off) . . . and
> you want to experience a trance and you have tried repeatedly in
> the past and you have not succeeded at all . . . so obviously a dif-
> ferent approach is needed, one more appropriate for *your* style of
> operating, *your* rate of development, *your* way of responding . . .
> but what a nice thing to know that the unconscious can respond
> in so many different ways . . . some people's unconscious lift a
> finger . . . some people's unconscious lift an entire hand . . . some
> develop the ability to look and not see or listen and not hear or hear
> and not listen . . . and apparently your unconscious has selected
> your body as a way to express its feeling of aching to go into trance
> . . . and so let your unconscious get to work . . . and I wonder, and
> you can wonder too, which part of your body will begin to ache first
> . . . will it be a hand?. . . . the right or the left?. . . . will it be your
> head, and if so, will it, is it now not a regular headache or perhaps
> an ache in the back of the head . . . *but don't discriminate against
> the middle third, Mary* . . . the middle third is where both halves
> add up . . . but where is the pain, Mary? (She says it's in her foot.)
> . . . Your foot . . . just one? . . . why not make it two? . . . why dis-
> criminate in this day and age . . . a hot foot doubled is an exciting
> experience . . . and the other sensations . . . your ear . . . your right
> ear . . . your neck . . . your chest . . . and I wonder how many dif-
> ferent types of sensation you will develop . . . an ache in the stom-
> ach along with a tickling sensation in the head? . . . I don't know,
> but please tell me how your unconscious is nicely expressing itself
> . . . and I wonder how that will *hypnotically transform (trance-
> form)*. . . . (etc.)

I continued these communications for another 20 minutes or so, delivering them all in an absorbing and meaningful fashion. Each time Mary
reported some localized pain, I followed compliments with chastise-

ments for not spreading things around and letting *all* of her participate in the process. Over a half hour she remained thoroughly absorbed in my communications, being initially surprised and then, in succession, intrigued, bewildered, apparently titillated, worried, and emotionally overwhelmed. I adapted my nonverbal communications to fit each general response, pacing and then exaggeratedly encouraging it to where it could no longer be maintained. When she began to exhibit trance (e.g., eyelid flutters, motoric restriction, latency in verbal response) and increasing emotional involvement (e.g., tears in her eyes, irregular breathing), I very gently and softly asked her to close her eyes, take a deep breath, and begin to recognize that "it's finally time to let go." The therapeutic trance that ensued was so pleasant and motivating (i.e., it gave her a taste of what was possible) that from then on she was willing and able to develop trance without the disruptive aches and pains arising. Thus, the simple strategy of accepting and then overloading the "resistance" – psychosomatic pain used apparently to avoid potentially unpleasant personal experiences – enabled both trance development and consequent therapeutic work with the client.

These same basic principles were applied with an experimental psychologist seeking to learn autohypnosis to curb an insomnia problem. His previous experience with hypnosis included scoring "0" on several hypnotizability tests, and some futile induction attempts by a hypnotherapist friend. Despite this, his desire to sleep better and a strong recommendation from a mutual friend motivated him to approach me for possible assistance. In assessing the situation, it became clear that his personality characteristics (e.g., a need to be in charge, an intensely logical mind that wanted to know the "why" of everything, and an extreme attentiveness to detail) made him rather impervious to traditional induction attempts. I thus calculated confidently that confusion techniques would be ideal, but discovered to my chagrin that some of my most effective techniques (temporal and conceptual disorientation) were met with a rather puzzled disgust and rejection. My smugness still somewhat intact, I figured he simply needed *more* confusion, and was thus further surprised by an even more intense rejection on his part. Finally gaining the sense to ask him about what was happening, I identified several fascinating patterns in his mental processes. First, he would automatically reject from consideration anything sounding to him like "nonsense" (such as the confusion techniques presented). Second, he formulated virtually all communications into experimental hypotheses which he then tested in some way. For example, having heard that a behavioral criterion of trance was motoric inhibition, during an induction he would periodically test for trance by trying to lift his head voluntarily, which he invariably could do, and then conclude he wasn't in trance. Needless to say, these mental processes stymied naturalistic trance development.

I saw him again the following week, after thinking extensively about how to effectively utilize his processes. I began by talking about various research developments in psychology, noting how interesting it was that "facts" about a phenomenon certainly change rapidly in the experimental field. Following his anticipated agreement on this point, I noted that this was especially true in the area of hypnosis. I pointed out that his knowledge of hypnosis seemed to be from research done 10 years previously, when theories and methodologies were rather crude, and that a much more sophisticated and diverse view of hypnosis had since emerged. As he seemed to accept this claim, I continued by emphasizing how hypnosis could be examined in terms of "multifactor, probabilistic" models that posited that one could test trance scientifically only by examining many behavioral criteria simultaneously. I identified six likely correlates of trance: temperature changes in the feet; respiration changes (usually slowing but occasionally quickening, depending on other variables); swallowing inhibition; changes in eye blink rate; hand heaviness; and lightness in the head. I added that another recent finding was that it was best for the subject to be a "mutual partner" in developing the trance.

With this groundwork accomplished, I had him sit comfortably and establish a "baseline check of the respective values" of the identified variables. I urgently requested that he continually and systematically monitor all the variables for "possible changes" during the induction, looking especially for interactional effects. My induction consisted mainly of rapidly alternating attentional focus among these variables, wondering aloud whether they were changing or if they would change, whether they were interacting, whether something unpredictable (e.g., "activity of an unknown variable") was occurring or could or would occur, and so forth. All the while, strong encouragement was given for him to continue his checking process. After about a half hour of steady, rapid patter, he began to look a bit confused, his eyelids fluttering and his eyes dilating. I thus sped things up, beginning to intersperse embedded suggestions for trance and "letting go." Predictably, this amplified the confusion to where further suggestions elicited eye closure and a nice trance. Various trance phenomena were developed and suggestions for further trance experiences were given. Upon arousing, he reported being excited and impressed about having a "first hand" experience of trance.

Further work with him was much easier. An effective self-hypnosis method of overloading himself via a taped induction, along with his own self-monitoring procedure, was developed. Although he reported being unable to really "completely let go," he obtained significant relief from his insomnia.

Again, the strategy here, while seemingly complex, was really quite simple. The question of how the subject's trance-inhibiting processes could be accepted and utilized as the basis for trance development led eventually to the straightforward strategy of encouraging such processes to the point where they became destabilized. The resulting uncertainty and confusion were utilized to develop a trance that opened the door to further effective hypnotic work.

In conclusion, confusion is a powerful method for depotentiating conscious processes that inhibit more direct therapeutic explorations. The numerous techniques described in the chapter exemplify some of the many ways in which confusion can be applied. The cases in this section emphasize that the most effective methods are those generated from the client's unique patterns and processes. Keeping these points in mind, along with the importance of establishing and maintaining an appropriate relationship, the hypnotherapist will find few individuals, if any, who cannot benefit from hypnotic communications.

## SUMMARY

The chapter emphasized how confusion principles and techniques are an important part of Ericksonian communications, especially during the induction phase. The first section described how most confusion techniques follow the five general steps of identifying a pattern, pacing it, interrupting or overloading it, amplifying the resulting confusion, then utilizing the confusion to offer an alternative (e.g., trance). Because the response to confusion will vary according to the perceived communicational context — e.g., individuals may get angry if they think they're being used, afraid if they feel unsafe and unprotected, or go into trance if they feel secure and acknowledged — special importance was assigned to (1) spending time prior to the confusion technique securing rapport and trust with subjects (so they feel safe), and (2) speaking meaningfully during the confusion (so subjects feel compelled to follow along).

The second section focused on interruption techniques, which are generally short, brief, and usually surprising communications designed to disrupt trance-inhibiting psychological or behavioral patterns. The specific techniques outlined included (1) meaningfully delivered nonsequiturs; (2) syntactical violations; (3) motoric restriction (in the subject or hypnotist); (4) the handshake induction; and (5) polarity plays. It was mentioned that a single interruption technique will often not suffice to produce a deep trance, but it usually creates a state of uncertainty which further confusion techniques (or other hypnotic communications) can utilize to develop a therapeutic trance.

The third section discussed how confusion can also be created and utilized by *overloading* psychological or behavioral patterns. The intent in overloading is to unbind attachments to fixed ways of being, thereby paving the way for therapeutic explorations. This disorientation can involve temporal referents (the Erickson Confusion technique); external or internal spatial referents (e.g., here/there; right/left; this/that); surreal imagery (e.g., the Mobius House); conceptual disorientation (e.g., rapid topic shifts); or verbal overloading (e.g., the double induction). Because overload techniques are usually ways of talking about unavoidably basic ideas (e.g., time and space), special attention must be paid to employing a delivery style meaningful enough to develop and maintain attentional absorption.

The final section addressed the clinical use of confusion. The discussion detailed how confusion should usually be introduced gradually, when it may be inappropriate, and how it should be based on the client's idiosyncratic patterns. As with all communications, its value depends on the interpersonal context in which it is applied.

# CHAPTER 8

# Balancing Associational and Dissociational Strategies: Practical Issues Regarding Therapeutic Inductions

The last several chapters discussed how hypnotic inductions can be accomplished through *associational* strategies (which access experiential responses) or *dissociational* strategies (which depotentiate analytical processes) as the basis for trance development. To reiterate, the former type of strategy is most effective with subjects willing and able to enter trance, while the latter type is used to handle potential conscious interferences. Because most properly prepared therapy clients will be relatively willing to experience trance yet somewhat unable to completely set aside their normal control patterns, most effective inductions combine associational and dissociational strategies.

This chapter illustrates some of the ways in which this can be done. The first section provides an induction transcript with detailed commentary. The transcript illustrates how associational and dissociational techniques blend together and emphasizes some practical points regarding clinical inductions. The second section describes how Ericksonian techniques can be modified in special situations such as those involving children, psychotics, emergencies, or groups. The final section discusses how the hypnotherapist might proceed when a variety of induction strategies have all proved ineffective.

### INDUCTION WITH COMMENTARY

As Chapter 5 discussed, the first step in a naturalistic induction involves adequately preparing both therapist and client. During this time, the therapist secures the trust and comfort of the client while emphasizing the safe and beneficial nature of trance. The therapist also uses this time to take care of his or her own needs, such as beginning to develop an interpersonal trance while gathering information about what might facilitate or inhibit trance (associations, past experiences, etc.).

Upon developing mutual rapport and attentional absorption, the therapist gradually and subtly introduces hypnotic communications to elicit trance responses. More than anything else, this involves shifting nonverbal processes: speaking more slowly, with short pauses to encourage accessing (Chapter 6); pacing and leading communicational rhythms, such as calibrating vocal intonation patterns to breathing patterns; and orienting all attention to the subject. Verbalizations complement this absorbing demeanor to shift the subject to a more experiential and internal orientation. For example, questions become more personal, more meaningfully asked, and more related to possible trancelike experiences; abstract theorizing is discarded for more experiential inquiries; and comments about trance are delivered as embedded suggestions. Of course, the rate at which this shift occurs depends entirely on the subject's responses; generally speaking, the hypnotist introduces other induction techniques only when the subject begins to exhibit trance-indicating minimal cues (see Table 4.2). An effective ordering of such techniques might include (1) *questions* to further access trancelike responses, (2) *general statements* and *stories* to deepen involvement in the accessed experiences, (3) *confusion techniques* to depotentiate any conscious interference, and (4) *utilization procedures* to utilize the trance state for beneficial gains.

To illustrate how such an induction might unfold, presented below is a partial transcript of a demonstration induction I did in an advanced training workshop on Ericksonian hypnotherapy. The subject was a young man who had some personal experience with Erickson, both as a student and patient, shortly before Erickson's death. He stated that he really wanted to experience a deep trance, but had failed to do so on numerous previous attempts. After observing him over several days and chatting with him for about 20 minutes during a break, I accepted his request to participate as a demonstration subject. The transcript below is a record of part of the induction.

| *Transcript* | *Commentary* |
|---|---|
| (1) *Hypnotist:* And Bill, how do you feel today? | (1) After shifting into an externally-oriented state, the hypnotist begins to pace by simply |

*Subject:* Not bad.

*H:* All right. And I want to tell you that I am very happy that you've volunteered as a subject here today . . . and I want to thank you for that . . . because I think everybody can learn from personal and direct experience. . . . And I also want to assure you, Bill, that I'm going to speak generally here with you, because I really have no right in this situation to probe into your specific affairs . . . so I'm not going to ask you to talk or do anything except become as involved and absorbed in your experience as you would like to. . . . Is that all right with you?

*S:* Yes.

(2) *H:* And how do you feel about sitting up here?

*S:* A little nervous.

*H:* A little nervous . . . and do you think that the nervousness will increase or decrease before it leaves?

*S:* I don't know . . . I hope it will decrease.

*H:* Are you willing to find out?

*S:* Yes.

*H:* All right then. . . . Pay very close attention to the fact that you can begin to *breathe comfortably and deeply* and look here at me at the same time . . . that's right . . . and what do you begin to notice?

acknowledging the subject's willingness to participate, and then leads by presupposing the subject will have direct and personal experiences. He then paces the potentially trance-inhibiting fact that the subject is in front of a group of peers with a hypnotist he's never worked with before, and offers assurances that the subject's integrity and privacy will be fully respected. It is important to handle such issues because they are connected to two major trance-inhibiting fears: the fear of being controlled by the hypnotist and the fear of losing control and making a fool of oneself. Since the subject congruently communicates that he feels safe, no further communications are offered on the topic.

(2) Following the utilization maxim of using whatever the person is doing as the basis for developing trance, the hypnotist now tunes into the subject's immediate experience. The hypnotist's reply to the subject's report of nervousness presupposes its dissipation while introducing the idea that change can occur in many ways, some unexpected (e.g., nervousness increasing before decreasing). The subject's willingness to explore uncertainty is then elicited and utilized to develop an experiential (i.e., nonanalytical) and fixated (on hypnotist) attention.

At the same time, the subject's task of focusing and breathing will generally lead to

*S:* I'm feeling more relaxed.

*H:* That's right . . . you can *feel more relaxed* as you continue to sit here . . . and there really is no law against that, is there?

*S:* No.

*H:* And you really didn't have to effortfully do anything at all, did you?

*S:* No.

*H:* In other words, you have the ability to achieve comfort *and other things* by simply becoming more aware of what can unfold . . . and *trance* really is a lot like that.

(3) . . . But before you do *go all the way into trance*, Bill, I want you to hold out for a while . . . not too quickly . . . and let your eyes remain open until you're fully ready to *go all the way into trance* . . . because you really should wait until you're fully ready to go in. . . . But of course you can continue to let yourself *focus* on that which is important, exercising your ability to let yourself *become absorbed* in a selective fashion. . . . And you can really let yourself orient into a position that will be *very comfortable* for an extended period of time. . . .

reduced anxiety. When this occurs, it is framed as the subject's ability to effortlessly and pleasurably let experiences develop. In other words, this interchange utilizes the subject's responses to *experientially* demonstrate a naturalistic trance ability. Because it is the first demonstration, it is deliberately unspectacular. This enables a gradual shift into trance which is subtle and therefore difficult to resist.

(3) Still in a waking state, the subject began to close his eyes deliberately, a general sign that there is a conscious effort to develop trance. Forestalling eye closure until trance development enables the hypnotist to more effectively absorb and fixate the subject's attention while disenabling the waking-state subject's trance-inhibiting tendency to become mired in internal dialogue upon eye closure.

The subject is further encouraged to "hold out" a bit longer in a way which 1) continues attention absorption, 2) presupposes trance will occur, 3) paces the part of the subject that wants to stay out of trance for awhile, and 4) builds response potential in the parts of the person that are ready and willing to go into trance. The subject is next encouraged to find a comfortable seating position since, as noted earlier, any uncomfortable position will often disrupt the entranced subject, who will generally be motorically immobile and internally oriented.

(4) . . . And maybe you heard Erickson say before that a good trance subject has both feet flat on the floor . . . that's right . . . and both hands free, resting comfortably apart on your lap. . . . And maybe you didn't hear those exact words, because Erickson had so many different things to say about the experience of trance, did he not?

*S:* Yes.

*H:* And how did you feel, by the way, when you first met him?

*S:* Real nervous and excited.

*H:* Nervous and excited. More nervous and excited than you were here a moment ago?

*S:* I think so . . . I really did not know what to expect with him. . . .

*H:* And do you know what to expect here?

*S:* (laughs) Not really.

*H:* (after asking several other questions about the subject's experience with Erickson) And incidentally, how did you feel when Erickson demonstrated a trance induction?

*S:* Real warm and comfortable.

*H:* You were able to *develop the*

(4) The initial statement continues to suggest a trance-appropriate position. It also subtly tests readiness for trance: by placing both feet flat on the floor he would define himself as a good trance subject; by maintaining crossed legs or arms he would signal that he is not ready to define himself as such, and thus needs more preparation. (He uncrossed his arms and legs.)

The initial statement also references Erickson in order to begin to access the trance-related responses the subject has associated with Erickson. These experiential associations are further revivified through meaningfully asked questions (Chapter 6). The accessed experiences are generalized to the present situation by questions regarding nervousness and uncertainty. A similar strategy is used to access and generalize the sensory experiences of warmth and comfort.

*feeling of warmth and comfort*
. . . and it is nice to *feel warm
and comfortable*, is it not?

*S:* (nods head)

*H:* That's right, Bill . . . and you
really can feel warm and comfortable and *let that feeling extend* to a variety of things. . . .

(5) And how do you feel about
going *into a deep trance* in the
next 10 minutes?

*S:* I don't know if I
could. . . . I'm a little apprehensive about trying.

*H:* That's right. . . . It really is
important to hold on to apprehension for a while at times . . .
because apprehension tells you
to *slow down*, take it
easy . . . and how do you feel
about going into a light trance
in the next five minutes?

*S:* No sweat.

*H:* That's right, Bill . . . you really don't have to sweat about
dropping into trance. . . . You
can be warm and comfortable,
yet also cool in the *security* of
knowing that trance is a secure
place where you can really get
to know yourself at a *deeper
level* of experience . . . and
trance is an opportunity to *let
your unconscious do the work
for you* . . . it really is an effortless process . . . and so you really don't have to do anything at
all. . . . You don't have to move
. . . you don't have to talk . . .
you just *let your unconscious do
the work for you*. . . .

(5) The subject's willingness to
develop deep trance is accessed
through a simple question. Note
how the seemingly innocuous delineation of a 10-minute time
frame subtly suggests possible
differences, e.g., in trance receptivity, between the time during
and after the time frame. The
apprehension apparent in the
subject's verbal and nonverbal
responses is utilized to offer the
less stressful possibility of light
trance. This is an example of a
general Ericksonian pattern
noted in Chapter 7: create a responsive state of uncertainty
(e.g., anxiety) by leading too
quickly, then utilize by offering
the opportunity to respond to a
lesser directive. When the subject agrees to the lesser directive ("light trance"), the hypnotist utilizes his present and
previous statements ("no sweat"
and "warm and comfortable," respectively) to begin to develop
trance. This exemplifies again
how at even the most basic
levels the effective Ericksonian
operator generates communications from what the subject has
offered.

After pacing, the hypnotist
leads by emphasizing the need

to just let things happen. This process of letting go of conscious control, reiterated throughout the induction, is perhaps the most important – and sometimes most difficult – lesson to be learned by the person desiring trance.

The final statements suggest motoric immobility which, as noted in Chapter 7, constitutes an effective interruption technique for developing trance. Such instructions were given when the subject began to indicate trance responsiveness (e.g., motoric inhibition, eye fixation), thus serving to ratify, define, and develop the responses as trance-inducing.

(6) And many people wonder how they can do anything effortlessly and how they can do something without trying . . . and in that regard it's important to recognize this: *your unconscious can and does operate independently*, intelligently, and autonomously in many different ways all the time . . . you can sit in a chair, sit in an office, listen to stories and recognize that all of those associations, and that which was then, could and is becoming that which is now, in a selective and appropriate fashion . . . and during that time you can let your unconscious do what it already does so well, and then some. . . .

(6) The subject furrowed his brow, suggesting conscious internal dialogue in response to the preceding statements of letting things happen. This possibility is initially paced at a general level ("many people") and then led by emphasizing the naturalistic nature of unconscious autonomy in responding. Further associations to Erickson ("sitting in an office listening to stories") continue the process of indirectly accessing appropriate reference structures. The final several words are uttered cryptically, thus raising the possibility of unexpected unconscious activity.

(7) For example, you can *breathe easily and comfortably*, because

(7) Specific examples of the preceding general statements

your unconscious regulates your breathing most of the time . . . you breathe in and out, in and out, and you really don't need to try to breathe . . . you do it *effortlessly and easily.* . . . And the same is true for your pulse rate, your ability to fall asleep at night, your heart rate, your ability to enjoy spontaneously a good laugh, a happy time, and all of those other things . . . and so *your unconscious can operate independently*, autonomous from conscious mediation. . . .

(8) And you can extend that to a variety of other experiential processes in productive fashions. . . . For example, with the *blinking* of your eyes . . . and normally you really don't exercise conscious volition over your eye *blink*. You don't try to blink them, you just *let them blink* . . . that's right . . . and we really know that we can blink the eyes volitionally as easily . . . (pause). that's right . . . you can will them to *blink* and they will blink. . . . But did you know that your eyes can also *blink nonvolitionally*? . . . And you can discover that by trying not to blink the eyes . . . and it really isn't important whether you feel them *blink unconsciously* or keep them open . . . because you can go into a trance with your eyes open or you can *close your eyes and drop all the way into trance* when your unconscious is ready. . . . But whether you have them open . . . or *let them blink* . . . that's right . . . and

are now given. The statements about breathing in and out are timed respectively to the inhalations and exhalations of the subject. The examples are all undeniable instances of activities generally unmediated by rational effort. After presenting these "irrefutable facts," a general statement is again made to consolidate acceptance of the general point being made.

(8) The generalization is now applied to the specific behavior of eye blinking. The "eye blink induction" technique is remarkably effective. Initially, it usually effects rapid eye fixation and a self-consciousness in the subject, with full or partial body catalepsy often resulting. In the present example, the hypnotist uses the subject's nonvolitional blinking to experientially demonstrate unconscious activity. This involves initially pacing by simply talking about how natural it is for eyes to blink, pausing meaningfully and expectantly until the subject blinks and then ratifying that response ("that's right").

What makes the technique almost invariably effective is that any response can be utilized to develop trance. If the subject develops ideomotoric blinking, as did the present subject, the hypnotist can lead by gradually increasing speech tempo, giving embedded com-

then come up again . . . and
blink *again* . . . that's
right . . . and back up and
*down* . . . and up and
*down* . . . and you can *feel
it* . . . your unconscious really
can operate independently. . . .
and so at some point in time, as
you go back and forth, up and
*down*, you can let your eyes
*close and drop all the way down
into trance NOWWWW!!!*

mands for blinking, suggesting
that the subject consciously try
not to blink (thus enabling the
demonstration of the unconscious responding independent
of conscious volition), and continuing to calibrate statements
(e.g., "up and down" pacing) to
blink responses and then acknowledging and reinforcing
blink occurrences verbally or
nonverbally. The eye flutter
response which usually develops
can be met with an increased
speech tempo, thereby augment-
ing both the flutter response
and the growing uncertainty of
the subject. As in confusion
techniques, the hypnotist can
then utilize with simple suggestions to "let your eyes close and
drop all the way into trance
NOWWW!!!" This last word is
best delivered emphatically and
dramatically.

If the subject doesn't blink,
the hypnotist can recognize and
accept this as eye catalepsy,
which can, and usually will, lead
naturally to further trance-
inducing responses such as full
body catalepsy and tunnel vision. The hypnotist thus defines
the eye catalepsy as a legitimate
trance response. Again, the hypnotist simply accepts whatever
the subject offers as the basis
for the induction.

(9) And just drop deeply and
comfortably into trance . . . and
allow yourself to really begin to
*experience* all of that wonderful
and *secure state unfolding* . . .
and what a nice thing to know

(9) As in the utilization phase of
confusion techniques, the eye
closure resulting from the eye
blink technique is a transition
point where the subject is highly
responsive to trance-deepening

that you can be all alone in the Middle of Nowhere, all alone with just a voice . . . my voice . . . and you can *hear my voice,* be with my voice, because *your unconscious can hear and respond* in an appropriate fashion. . . . Because what's important is your own developing ability to experience yourself drifting into *secure* hypnotic realities all alone in the Middle of Nowhere . . . and your unconscious does know where Nowhere is . . . and what a pleasant thing to *let that experience fully develop.* . . .

directives. The hypnotist thus shifts immediately to a slower, softer voice and delivers direct suggestions to dissociate into the Middle of Nowhere (Chapter 7). After further encouraging the subject to just let things happen, the hypnotist notes that he can hear his voice without needing to actively listen to it. This is useful in freeing up the subject to become fully absorbed in hypnotic realities; it is analogous to being able to watch a movie without having to continuously listen and respond to an outside commentator. Most hypnotized subjects hear the hypnotist's voice only part of the time, usually during lighter portions of trance.

(10) And what a nice thing to know that you can experience a lot of things in trance . . . because *trance is a learning experience* . . . and you've had so many different learning experiences in the past. . . . For example, you've probably had the experience of sitting in a classroom as a child and listening to the sound of the teacher as he droned on and on . . . and listening to the teacher, when the seat was hard, the lecture boring, the day hot, you began to wonder: When is he going to get to the point? When is he going to get to the point? . . . And a minute seemed like an hour . . . and an hour like a day . . . and you looked at the clock, noting the first hand, the second hand, and the third hand . . . *and what does it mean*

(10) Further deepening suggestions are offered. Notice how topic shifts are gracefully accomplished by shifting to a general statement that can bridge any two topics. The framing of trance as a learning context is then used to lead into the common childhood experience of daydreaming through a boring class. This type of story, delivered slowly and monotonously, serves numerous purposes. First, it accesses boredom, which is a good depotentiation technique. Second, as an indirect regression technique it deepens trance by orienting away from the present time/space coordinates. Third, the remarks about the slowed sense of time associated with boredom access the trance-

*to have a third hand*? And the face on the clock: Why does the clock have a face? And looking at the face, and watching the time going by *so slowly* . . . and really beginning to *drift into another world* . . . really letting yourself *become increasingly absorbed* in that reality.

related experience of time distortion. Fourth, the rhetorical questions about a "third hand" and "face of the clock" are confusion techniques designed to distract and depotentiate any conscious interference. Finally, the statements about daydreaming in the classroom are essentially indirect suggestions to shift deeper into hypnotic daydreaming realities.

(11) And you really can become absorbed in those activities which are of interest to your unconscious . . . and you can let the unconscious *develop those hypnotic realities* in accord with your own internal needs . . . and so let it happen in a way, at a rate, and in a style which is *appropriate for you* as an individual . . . and you have all the time in the world to *let it happen*. . . .

(11) The accessed daydreaming experiences are now generalized through permissive and open-ended suggestions. The subject is encouraged to drift in and out of various hypnotic realities, not sticking with one focus for any significant period of time. Encouraging this loose-association style of exploration is especially useful with novice subjects and at the beginning of trance since it 1) lets the subject become acquainted with a broad range of trance possibilities and 2) enables the hypnotist to observe and catalogue the subject's patterns in trance (e.g., likes and dislikes). Also, the single-topic and sequential style of exploration is often highly associated to the trance-inhibiting rational mode of thought (e.g., maintaining effortful concentration on something).

(12) And what does it really mean to have *all* the time in the world? What does it *really* mean to have time on your hands? And what does it mean when someone says that "there once

(12) The subject began to exhibit minimal cues indicating trance arousal, e.g., postural adjustment, swallowing, and breathing shifts. To handle this increasing conscious activity, a

was a time" or "this is the time" or "there will come a time"? . . . And you really can orient to time in a variety of different ways . . . you know, for example, that *that* which once *was* is not the *past* but once *was* the present *only* after it was the *future*. . . . And you also know that although today tomorrow is tomorrow, tomorrow it will be today, and the day after that it will be yesterday . . . and yet from all reference points Saturday is Saturday . . . and though Saturday does come after Friday, it is before Sunday; yet Sunday will be here soon enough and Sunday is a day of rest, and you really can *rest in trance, Bill, and let the unconscious do all the rest.* . . .

(13) Because while in a waking state you have the past tense, the future tense, the present tense, in a trance state you *really don't need to tense at all* . . . you can *relax fully and comfortably*, and know that you can orient to a variety of different realities and experience them unfolding in a way which is appropriate and comfortable for you as an individual. . . .

(14) And normally you orient toward time and orient toward space in a constant fashion. . . . For example, you say that over *there* is over *there* and *here* is *here* and that if you're *here* you can't be *there also* . . . but in a trance your unconscious really can operate as a part of, yet

temporal disorientation confusion technique (Chapter 7) was used. Note how rhetorical questions are used to first occupy and distract the conscious mind. As temporal reference shifts are introduced, the hypnotist shifts into a faster speech tempo and more syncopated rhythm. The voice slows suddenly and dramatically when the embedded suggestions to rest in trance are delivered. To reiterate, the purpose of disorientation techniques is to unbind the subject from any rigid attachment to a particular viewpoint – temporal, spatial, or conceptual – thereby freeing up the ability to explore hypnotic realities.

(13) The temporal disorientation remarks are now used to lead into the potentially confusion-reducing suggestions regarding "no tense," a play on words suggesting both a lack of tension and the timelessness often associated with trance. Other open-ended and permissive suggestions address the development of a general trance orientation.

(14) The subject's nonverbal cues indicated continued activity by his conscious mind. Thus, another disorientation technique – the visual overload method outlined in Chapter 7 – was delivered. The task of mentally overloading the subject was addressed through multiple path-

*apart from*, those normal constraints. . . . You can *hear me here* and know that if I were *there* you could also *hear* just as well . . . and if you were *there* you could *hear me here* just as well . . . and I could go *there* yet *still* be from vantage point *here* even though it would be a change from my previous reference . . . because wherever I go, it will always be *here* for me. . . . And you can *hear me there* and here also, and normally to go there you would have to use effort, use muscular activity, use tension, but in a trance you don't need to use tension at all . . . you can *let the unconscious do it completely* . . . you can *feel it* . . . you can *feel it* . . . you can *feel it* . . . the conscious *doubts* over *there*, the *unconscious* activity *here* . . . the internal processing of the *conscious mind* over *there*, the ease, comfort, and unexpected and integrating surprises of the *unconscious here* . . . the *effort there*, the continuing development of *trance here* . . . the *wondering there*, the *wandering here*. . . . You can *feel it* . . . you *can* feel it . . . *you* can feel it. . . .

ways, including 1) the rapid shifting of spatial orientations, 2) dramatic localization shifts in the hypnotist's voice as he mentioned "here" and "there," 3) a rapid and syncopated delivery style, and 4) the ambiguous use of "here" and "hear."

When minimal cues indicated the subject was growing increasingly confused, the hypnotist suggested spatial dissociation of the conscious ("over there") and unconscious ("over here"). In shifting from confusion to dissociation strategies, the quick and syncopated delivery style was replaced by a more intense and focused one. The techniques seemed to work: the subject became still and "frozen" looking, indicating dissociation; his breathing, after being rapid and irregular during the overload, was slower and more regular; his closed eyelids displayed rapid movement, indicating visualizations; and his cheeks flattened out, indicating trance. He later reported that this was a perfect technique for him, as it handled a major problem of wanting to both listen and record the techniques being used while also going deeply into trance. The dissociation enabled him to seat his studious and rational part 10 feet away, while the rest of him could enjoy thoroughly a nice deep trance.

(15) And as you do, let the *unconscious operate autonomously* . . . let those experiences develop . . . and I don't know and

(15) With the subject now fairly immersed in trance, the hypnotist speaks in a softer and slower manner, encouraging the

you don't know exactly how *that will happen* . . . perhaps your unconscious will begin to *revivify a long forgotten pleasant memory*, a memory that will be very *comforting*, very *enjoyable*. . . . Perhaps several memories will become revivified, sequentially or simultaneously . . . and whether from the period of a young toddler or a growing child learning his ABCs or a developing adolescent or a young adult really isn't that important. . . . What's important is that your *unconscious* can begin to explore areas of your *experience* in a way which really is *secure* and educational. . . .

subject to let himself explore hypnotic realities. Different possibilities regarding pleasant age regressions are mentioned, with *some* regression experience presupposed by the permissive suggestions. These suggestions also emphasize the subject's unconscious as the source of power, not the hypnotist or the subject's conscious mind. This theme is pursued repeatedly in Ericksonian communications as it emphasizes the responsibility and hence the capabilities and potentialities of the unconscious. Again, the hypnotist's major task is to guide and supervise the subject in discovering valuable resources. The Ericksonian operator is directive and assertive only when the subject's conscious processes actively interfere with trance or when a client is overwhelmed by some experiential trauma and needs assistance. Generally, the Ericksonian hypnotherapist refrains from imposing strategies and solutions on the client.

(16) And perhaps it will involve a dream because your unconscious does dream many times every night, and thus knows how to *use dreams to explore and integrate meaningful experiences* . . . and I really don't know how your unconscious will choose to *explore those hypnotic experiences*. . . . All I know is that your unconscious is very intelligent and so why not take a few moments of clock time, all the time in the world for your

(16) The subject, still in a dissociated trance, didn't exhibit any of the minimal cues typically prominent when a childhood experience is accessed, such as increased facial coloration, emotional expressions of a subtle sort, actually looking younger; thus, dreaming was mentioned. Regression perhaps could have been developed with more time or with other accessing techniques; but since the intent was simply to give the individ-

unconscious to let those explorations happen . . . *let them unfold* . . . two minutes of clock time, all the time in the world, and my voice can be silent, because you can let those explorations *develop and integrate* in a very natural fashion . . . all the way, beginning NOWWW!!!

ual an opportunity to experience deep trance, the option of dreaming was instead offered. As with any hypnotic phenomenon, dreams are introduced as a naturalistic phenomenon for which the subject already has a number of pleasant reference structures, thereby implying that they can be easily developed, safely experienced, and beneficially used.

The several-minute time period is then mentioned, along with general time distortion suggestions. Then, as was also noted, the hypnotist remains silent but closely observant of the subject during the two minutes, thereby enabling full absorption in the dream.

(17) (After two minutes of clock time) That's right . . . and just let yourself drop back down into the Middle of Nowhere, very comfortably and very easily . . . and just *let yourself drift*, let yourself take the opportunity to *fully appreciate yourself* . . . not for what you've done, not for what you will do, but for who you are . . . that incredibly unique essence of Self that is you . . . that essence that lets you experience that *you really are OK* just the way you are. . . . You have the ability to support yourself, to *love yourself*, to take care of yourself, in many different ways. . . .

(17) After the dream period, the subject is guided back to the Middle of Nowhere and given the opportunity to simply appreciate himself. Note how this dissociation is used to emphasize the ability to experience a Deep Self independent of specific behaviors or other content. This experiential state of self-appreciation has incredible potential for facilitating personal growth processes.

(18) . . . and you really can recognize that your unconscious is the best friend you have. . . . It

(18) A series of further general suggestions is offered. The unconscious is emphasized as a

will never leave you . . . it is always available to support you if you simply *acknowledge and appreciate* and allow it to be with you . . . and you can *utilize your unconscious resources* in many different ways. . . . For example, you can continue all of these explorations in your dreams, letting your unconscious begin to fully *integrate all of these learnings* and others. . . . I really don't know whether it will be the second dream or the fourth dream or the third or a combination thereof or some other combination. . . . All I know is that your unconscious *can* use your dreams to put into proper perspective, appropriate focus, those aspects of your life that are important to you. . . . You really can *trust your unconscious* in a variety of situations . . . whether in a communicational situation, working on a problem, sleeping at night, talking with friends, whether in a trance or asleep or in a waking state, you really can let the unconscious offer you the resources, the vase storehouse of experiential knowledge that it has available . . . because *your unconscious is your ally*, an ally that will always be with you. . . .

powerful ally, an idea I intersperse in virtually every trance induction. The ability of the unconscious to generate meaningful experiences is then generalized in an open-ended fashion. General posthypnotic suggestions are offered regarding a continuing integration of the trance explorations and other experiences during the subject's nocturnal dreams, with the question of *which* dream it will be presupposing that at least one will occur. Finally, the ability of the unconscious to support the Self in many ways is cross-situationally generalized.

(19) And so just take a few minutes to *appreciate yourself*, to let yourself know that you really are a capable individual who can respond to yourself and others with integrity, love, and honesty. . . . And know that you can shift back into this state any

(19) The self-appreciation suggestions are continued. Also, trance is anchored to the hypnotist ("when you hear this voice") and subject ("when you're alone and . . . "). Such anchors will often develop without explicit verbalizations; for ex-

time in the future when you would like to . . . when you hear this voice . . . or when you're all alone and would like to experience a trance, you can remember this experience, and in doing so, let it become revivified. . . .

(20) And you can let that feeling of well-being and self-appreciation *spread* and generalize to other aspects of your being. . . . Therefore, in a moment I'm going to count from 10 to 1 . . . and when I reach the number 1 you'll be all the way out of trance, coming back to the room comfortably refreshed and relaxed, and bringing back only those experiences and memories which are appropriate for you to consciously know at this time, leaving behind all that is appropriate to leave to your unconscious for the time being. . . .

(21) And so now I'm going to begin to count . . . 10 . . . 9 . . . 8 . . . 7 . . . 6 . . . 7 . . . 8 . . . 9 . . . 10 . . . 11 . . . 12 . . . 13 . . . 14 . . . 15 . . . 16 . . . 18 . . . 19 . . . 20 . . . that's right, all the way down *NOWWW!!!* . . . and just let yourself *drift* for a few moments, knowing that *your unconscious really can operate independently* from your normal constraints and controls . . . 19 . . . 18 . . . 17 . . . 16 . . . 15 . . . 14 . . . 13 . . . 12 . . . 11 . . . 10 . . . 9 . . . 8 . . . 7 . . . 6 . . . 5 . . . 4 . . . 3 . . . 2 . . . 1 . . . (subject opens eyes)

ample, most subjects I work with respond to the unique voice tone and facial expressions I use when I'm interested in having them develop a trance.

(20) It is now suggested that the present feeling of self-appreciation can be experienced in other contexts as well. This provides a nice transition back to the waking state. Before arousing the subject with counting, a method that allows for a gradual reorientation, general and permissive suggestions for full or partial amnesia are given.

(21) The hypnotist now uses the counting reversal technique whereby the counting is suddenly reversed. Since counting down has been defined as coming out of trance, counting up is implicitly defined as going into trance. The subject responded in a typical fashion: he started arousing as the numbers went down, looked rather startled and confused when the reversal began, and then, as the hypnotist shifted into a deeper voice tone and more trancelike demeanor, took a deep breath and exhibited signs of dropping deeply into trance. At the count of 20, the trance is deepened

through brief verbalizations, especially the word NOW! which, having been used at deep trance transitions twice previously, was anchored to deepening. The subject's hypnotic response was emphasized as an experiential demonstration of the autonomy of the unconscious. The numbers were then reversed and the subject taken out of trance.

The counting reversal process is essentially a confusion technique especially useful in experientially "convincing" subjects that they were in an altered state and that the unconscious really can operate autonomously from conscious volition or expectation. This depotentiates trance-inhibiting doubts many subjects, particularly novices, have about whether they were "really" in trance, thereby shifting the focus from "Was I in a trance?" to "What can I experience and develop in trance?"

(22) *Hypnotist:* Hello!
*Subject:* Hi. (shifts position and rubs eyes)

(22) As the subject opened his eyes, the hypnotist shifted to a quicker and more upbeat demeanor. Such a shift helps to uniquely associate the hypnotist's communicational patterns used during trance to the subject's trance experience, thereby making subsequent trance inductions much easier. Also, the word "hello" is a salutation signaling the *beginning* of something (waking state) and hence the end of something else (trance). This, combined with the fact that a significant alteration

in a speaker's delivery style will generally orient a listener to the speaker, typically has the effect of rapidly bringing the subject out of trance, thereby encouraging amnesia.

The present subject shifted his body posture and returned the salutation, thus indicating he was reorienting from trance. Occasionally subjects will not arouse immediately from trance, as evidenced by general motoric immobility and continued eye closure. This generally indicates that the person needs a little more time for integration or further explorations. In such instances, straightforward instructions can thus be given to take "a few more minutes of clock time, all the time in the world, to complete those explorations, knowing that you can return back later at an appropriate time and in an appropriate fashion, to continue those integrations."

Further interventions are needed if the client is manifesting muscular tension and arrythmic breathing. In such circumstances, the therapist needs to establish contact with the person (e.g., by calling the person's name, gently taking hold of his or her hand, giving breathing instructions, and repetitively mentioning the therapist's presence). The need for such interventions is not entirely common, but should be recognized as a possibility when dealing with severely dissociated clients. In such cases, further utilizations should emphasize shorter trances and stronger interpersonal connections with the therapist.

The subject expressed a pleasant surprise at his trance experience. His experience and the various techniques employed during the induction were the topic of group discussion for the next hour.

The above transcript illustrates how an Ericksonian induction might proceed. It highlights important points about induction processes, especially the following:

1. the utilization of the subject's reality (past experiences, present responses) as the basis for the induction;
2. the use of questions to absorb and direct attention;
3. the use of experiential demonstrations to introduce and develop key ideas;
4. the use of real sense memories to access trance;
5. the rhythmic shifting from the *specific* demonstration or story (to provide an experiential reference structure) to the *general* (to frame and/or generalize a response) and then back to a *specific* (to add another reference structure or lead to a new response);
6. the progressive and gradual development of each new response from the preceding one(s);
7. the use of conjunctions to link everything together;
8. the use of presuppositions that focus attention on *how* something will be done rather than *whether* it will be done;
9. the frequent interspersing of ideas regarding trance as a secure learning context where the unconscious can operate autonomously and intelligently;
10. the framing of trance phenomena as naturalistic processes;
11. the occasional silence to let the subject explore on his or her own;
12. the periodic shift in delivery style (e.g., quick for confusion, to slow and gentle for relaxation, to intense and focused for dissociation);
13. the use of confusion techniques to depotentiate conscious involvement; and
14. the general and permissive directive style employed by the hypnotist.

Of course, each induction will be different. With many subjects, for example, the amount of confusion employed in the above induction would be unnecessary or inappropriate, while with other subjects even more confusion might be effective.

Another point of great variability is the temporal duration of the trance. Many novice subjects, for instance, are not willing or able to remain in trance very long. In training such individuals, I therefore often use a version of the *refractionation technique* described in Chapter 5, whereby a cycle of alternating 5–10 minute periods of trance and discussion is repeated several times, with each trance slightly deeper than the preceding one.

Another time-related issue is how long an induction should be. To reiterate, rapid inductions will work with some individuals, although the therapeutic value of such trances is often limited. As discussed in Chapter 1, the "short-induction" trances developed in the authoritarian and standardized situations are described by many subjects, in comparison to trances developed via conversational Ericksonian approaches, as more unidimensional, lighter in depth, and often passive (i.e., completely directed by the hypnotist) or dominated by conscious efforting (e.g., "trying to imagine" what the hypnotist suggests). In contrast, descriptions of "Ericksonian" trances frequently emphasize feelings of being acknowledged and safely encouraged to explore an inner self, pleasant surprises (e.g., remembering a long-forgotten childhood experience), and enhanced feelings of self-esteem, competency, and self-acceptance.

In short, direct inductions tend to create a trance phenomenologically experienced as a limited and singular state directed by someone else (the hypnotist), while longer, conversational inductions frequently spawn a trance experienced as a general context for self-appreciation and transformation.

This is not to say that brief inductions are never used in the Ericksonian approach. As discussed in Chapter 5, I sometimes spend a half dozen or more sessions training an individual in trance experiences before examining specific therapeutic issues. Such a training period thoroughly familiarizes and trains the client in various trance processes, while permitting the hypnotist to establish the requisite rapport and specific anchors needed to rapidly reinduce a potential-laden trance. Thereafter, inductions can be shorter, thereby providing sufficient time for thorough utilization of trance for therapeutic gains.

While on the general topic of practical clinical issues, several miscellaneous points should be included. First, remember that a *time lag*, lasting from a minute to several sessions, between suggestion and response will often occur, especially with more complex responses such as dissociation or hallucinations. It is therefore wise to offer open-ended suggestions (e.g., "Take all the time in the world to let that develop fully"), cover all possibilities (e.g., "I don't know whether it will be the left or right hand that presses down or lifts up"), perhaps restate the suggestions in several ways, and then shift to another topic. This shift distracts any potentially interfering conscious processes while also providing more time to make necessary adjustments. As such, it is not uncommon for a response to occur only after the hypnotist has stopped talking about it directly.

Second, keep in mind the floating phenomenon (Chapter 2), whereby the depth of trance fluctuates. This is a major reason why the Ericksonian operator shies away from the various versions of the "deeper, deeper, deeper" incantations that dominate traditional inductions. Simply stated, subjects – especially novices – generally don't follow such a progression; they might go into trance a bit, come out, go back in a little more, and so forth. The hypnotist wishing to remain in rapport must adapt communications to such fluctuations, since deepening instructions given when subjects are lightening their trance make it impossible for them to stay with you. Accordingly, the Ericksonian operator closely observes and responds to trance-related minimal cues constantly being expressed by subjects. When the subject's trance appears to lighten, the hypnotist might respond with simple pacing (e.g., "That's right . . . and it really is important to come up for a while, take a rest, and wonder a bit before you wander back down into trance"), confusion, or any other technique which appropriately handles the heightened conscious processes of the subject. Relatedly, the subject deeply immersed in trance doesn't need confusion or comments about arousing from trance.

A final area of comment concerns the gradual external-to-internal orientation shift effected in the subject by most induction strategies. An example of a common progression appears on the following page. In such a progression, communications that externally orient the subject will initially constitute effective pacing, but generally become counterproductive as internal absorption is achieved. For example, many entranced subjects will experience an unexpected touch as a jarring interruption of their internal experience as well as a grave violation of an implicit trust. Physical contact should therefore be used sparingly (e.g., during some hand levitation techniques), and then only after the hypnotist has informed the subject of what is to be done. Relatedly, the

PACE AND LEAD VARIOUS EXTERNAL STIMULI
(whatever the subject is aware of)

↓

LEAD TO FIXATION ON EXTERNAL STIMULUS
(e.g., the hypnotist)

↓

INCLUDE COMMENTS ON SUBJECT'S
PERCEPTUAL EXPERIENCE
(e.g., visual alterations, kinesthetic feelings, or modalities which connect
internal and external realities)

↓

ORIENT INCREASINGLY TO SUBJECT'S INTERNAL WORLD
(e.g., images, memories)

subject's verbalizations and movements should be kept to a minimum, since they generally will encourage an external orientation.

Of course, the subject may reorient externally at some point during a trance, such as when disturbed by the loud noise of a ringing phone or a backfiring car, or when physically uncomfortable, or when emotionally insecure. This can be utilized in various ways, depending on the degree of reorientation. If the subject appears to completely reorient, perhaps even opening his or her eyes, the hypnotist might postpone further hypnotic communications, assume and communicate the attitude that arousal from trance was absolutely appropriate, then use discussion with the subject to decide whether or not trance should be reinstated. In the more common case where the degree of reorientation is partial or ambiguous, *general* or *indirect* pacing of the external stimuli is more appropriate. For example, the subject slightly adjusting his or her head might be instructed to:

. . . really let the unconscious make all the adjustments necessary for you to experience trance . . . because you really can *head* into an altered state of comfort and security. . . .

Similarly, a ringing phone might be paced as follows:

> . . . and what does it mean to let your unconscious call to mind an important message? . . . What does it mean to receive unexpected communications and respond with even further unconscious absorption . . . because your unconscious really can attend to those things which let you become ever more involved in those unfolding hypnotic realities. . . .

This type of pacing incorporates the potential interruptions into the trance experience in a manner that will not distract subjects so absorbed in trance that they did not notice the stimuli in question.

### SPECIAL CASE APPLICATIONS

Trance inductions, even adaptive Ericksonian inductions, have a general structure and set of content associated to them. Generally, they are used with the intent of shifting a person presupposed to be in a rational working state into a trance state. To do this, words like "the unconscious," "trance," "deeper," and so forth are typically interspersed among directives to let things happen. Such communications are inappropriate and ineffective with certain types of people and in certain situations. Sometimes this is because the person(s) in question is, in effect, already in a trancelike state and therefore unresponsive to communications which presuppose a rational waking state. At other times, the content of an induction just will not fit the situation. Whatever the case, Ericksonian principles of utilization can still be effectively applied, albeit in a modified form. This section briefly overviews some of these special case applications.

*Children*

Youngsters are generally not dominated by the rational mentations that inundate many an adult's experience; in fact, most children drift in and out of fantasy worlds rather freely. As such, developing trance in a child is often best done without formal inductions. Instead, it is easier to entrance children by naturalistically absorbing their attention and then utilizing their realities – for example, through competitive challenges, fantasy, or imaginative characters. As Erickson (1958) noted:

> Children have a driving need to learn and to discover. . . . The limited experiential background of the child, the hunger for new experiences and the openness to new learnings render the child a

good hypnotic subject. He is willing to receive ideas, he enjoys responding to them, and there is only the need of presenting those ideas in a manner comprehensible to him. . . . There is a need . . . to work primarily *with* and not *on* the child. The adult can better comprehend passive participation. . . . There should not be a talking down to the child, but rather a utilization of language, concepts, ideas, and word pictures meaningful to the child in terms of his own learnings. . . . The child must be respected as a thinking, feeling creature, possessed of a capacity to formulate ideas and understandings and able to integrate them into his own total of experiential comprehension; but he must do this in accord with the actual functioning processes he himself possesses. No adult can do this for him, and any approach to the child must be made with awareness of this fact. (Rossi, 1980d, pp. 174–176)

The variety of possibilities can be indicated by examples of working with children from three different age levels. The first occurred when my associate Paul Carter and I spent an evening at a friend's house while on a workshop tour through the Midwest. Our friend was the proud father of a darling two-year-old girl we'll call Ginny. The toddler was so enchanting in her cheery awakening of her parents during the wee hours of every morning that they felt powerless to lodge complaints against it. Unfortunately, the entranced but sleep-robbed father was growing increasingly baggy-eyed and unproductive in his work, and wondered aloud as to how long this could go on.

To see what we could do, Paul and I spent some time after dinner with Ginny and her father in the child's room. As "Dad" and I rested our weary bones in the corner, Paul absorbed Ginny's attention by inquiring about the many different dolls and stuffed animals scattered about the room. After the child tired of this, Paul reabsorbed her attention by looking into her eyes while gently stroking her belly. Concurrently, he soothingly spoke in the following paraphrased fashion:

And Ginny, you look so big since I last saw you . . . you're growing so much now . . . you're no longer a baby, are you? . . . you're a toddler now . . . and you're doing so many new things . . . your ability to walk is beginning to grow, you ability to talk is beginning to grow . . . your toes are growing . . . look at how big they've gotten . . . and your feet are growing too . . . and your legs are growing, aren't they? . . . yes, they are, and so nicely, too . . . and your arms are growing . . . your head is growing . . . your belly is growing . . . your mouth is growing . . . and you don't eat baby food any more, do you? . . . of course not, you eat grownup people's food

... that's because you're no longer a baby ... you're growing up, growing up in so many ways ... and you're going to continue to grow, Ginny ... you're going to grow taller and taller, just like mommy ... and you can be more and more of a grownup ... you're beginning to eat like a grownup ... you're beginning to talk like a grownup ... and you can begin to sleep more and more like a grownup, Ginny ... sleeping soundly through the night, knowing that your little body is growing bigger ... and you like to eat ... and you can enjoy sleep too, Ginny, sleep until Daddy and Mommy get up ... sleep just like a grownup. ... (continued for several more minutes)

As Paul elaborated on this "growth" theme, a thoroughly absorbed and cataleptic Ginny "grew" sleepier and sleepier. When she closed her eyes, we tiptoed out of the room and let her "dream on."

Ginny awoke at eight the next morning, four hours later than customary. Several months later, her considerably freshened father gratefully informed us that later waking times were becoming increasingly common.

A second example is an excerpt from the case reported by Erickson (1962) of a rebellious and hyperactive eight-year-old boy who was dragged into Erickson's office by his exasperated mother. Young Joe defiantly declared that he could "stomp" anybody, Erickson included, then proceeded to demonstrate his point by angrily crashing his foot down on the floor. Erickson calmly and condescendingly agreed that while the stomp was a remarkably strong one for an eight-year-old, it probably couldn't be repeated for very long. The disputatious boy irately claimed he could stomp a thousand times if he so desired. When Erickson doubted aloud that "a little boy" was capable of even half that many, the outraged boy vowed to prove him wrong.

Erickson dismissed the mother, whereupon Joe stomped his left foot on the floor. Erickson feigned astonishment while admitting he had underestimated the boy's strength, then expressed doubts about such ferocity continuing for long. Predictably, this was met with a series of further contemptuous stomps. After 30 or so repetitions, the increasingly fatigued boy began to realize his gross overestimation of his stomping ability, whereupon Erickson patronizingly suggested he pat the floor a thousand times with his foot since he certainly couldn't stand still without wanting to sit down. The desperate youngster accepted this indirect suggestion by adamantly voicing his intention to stand still. His resolute assumption of a stiff upright position was promptly utilized to fixate his attention on the desk clock, especially the "slowness of the minute hand and the even greater slowness of the hour hand despite the seeming rapidity of the ticking of the clock" (in Rossi, 1980b, p. 513). After delivering these hypnotic communications, Erickson turned to his desk and engaged in various tasks while peripherally keeping his attention on the boy.

Joe found it increasingly difficult to maintain his cataleptic position. After half an hour his hand sought support from a nearby chair, but was quickly withdrawn when Erickson seemed to "glance reflectively" about the room. After another hour, during which Erickson left the room briefly several times to enable Joe to rest, the boy was told to follow Erickson's instructions exactly when his mother returned. The mother, upon being summoned, looked wonderingly at her silent and rigidly upright son. Erickson signaled her to be silent and then commanded Joe to demonstrate the mightiness of his stomp. The startled boy obliged, whereupon he was directed to exhibit his ability to be stiff, straight, and still. Erickson then informed mother and son that the interview was a secret between Erickson and Joe, and that "it was enough" that only the two of them knew what had transpired. This turned out to be the case. Joe's misbehaving diminished to manageable and expectable proportions.

This case description, while only part of the therapy done with the boy, nicely exemplifies how utilization principles can be applied with youngsters. Erickson appreciated the boy's rebelliousness as an expression of the childhood need to define boundaries of power, strength, and reality. He therefore set out to utilize the boy's reality to produce a "reality confrontation" enabling "the identification of a secure reality." In doing so, Erickson employed many induction principles and strategies:

1. completely *accepting* the dominant responses to absorb attention
2. *leading* behavior through challenges and "polarity plays" (i.e., eliciting a response by strongly advocating its opposite)
3. *depotentiating* dominant response patterns through *overload* (the repeated stompings)
4. *utilizing overload* to fixate attention and develop catalepsy (standing and gazing at the clock)
5. *building response potential* by inhibiting a desirable response (sitting down)
6. *utilizing response potential* by enabling the response in a face-saving manner (by walking out of the room)
7. therapeutically *reframing* (gaining therapeutic control by demanding its occurrence and then associating it with the therapeutically developed response of silent and cataleptic fixation)
8. therapeutically *consolidating* the changes (by assuring the boy

that "it was enough" and that the humbling experience would be kept a secret).

This sequence of maneuvers produced enduring change in a graceful and supportive fashion.

A third example of working with children is the case of a 16-year-old boy who, under threat from his parents, reluctantly saw me about his reliance on drugs. He bore several things in common with many other American teenagers: (1) the increasingly sophisticated yet remarkably unrigid mind which makes for an excellent trance subject and (2) the rebellious and suspicious attitude toward "the establishment" which fosters a resistance to directives by authority figures. To utilize the former while bypassing the latter, I used slang talk to compare his favorite "drug highs" to ones I experienced during my adolescent experiments with altered states of consciousness. Upon securing rapport through this mutual sharing, I casually mentioned my discovery of how these "wild mind trips" could be used to generate all the "drug highs" plus some "even more far out ones." His interest clearly perked, I continued by happily describing learning to use these "mind trips" to shut out my mother's voice when so desired and to generate "psychedelic spin-outs" where I didn't "crash heavily" afterwards.

After offhandedly mumbling how I taught some friends to do the same, I deliberately changed the topic so, rather than my laying a trip on him, *he* would ask *me* how he might learn to do the same. When he did exactly that, I hemmed and hawed before agreeing to do so on the condition that he wouldn't practice more than several times a day. As I then began to demonstrate self-hypnosis, he shifted rather rapidly from observing to participating in the experience of trance, which I utilized by introducing "trippy" hypnotic phenomena such as perceptual distortions, time distortion, and dissociation. After emphasizing that "there's a lot more where that came from," I reoriented him from trance.

Over the next several months I turned him on to other "hypnotic highs" while gradually addressing how these hypnotic abilities could be applied directly to specific intra- and interpersonal challenges. A six-month follow-up revealed that the boy was not using drugs and was making satisfactory adjustments at home and in school.

To summarize, these three cases exemplify how Ericksonian strategies might be applied with younger people, often without formal inductions. Of course, there are many other possibilities, such as dramatically delivered metaphorical stories or fairy tales, hypnotic dreams, and similar imaginal techniques (e.g., hallucinating a television program). The young person's vivid imagination might also be utilized through external props such as "Rocky," the adorable racoon puppet employed by a colleague, Deborah Ross, when she works with hospitalized children. For example, I once observed Ross first buoy the spirits of a depressed child refusing food and then stimulate his appetite by having Rocky "steal" morsels from his food plate. The basic strategy in all of these techniques is one of recognizing, respecting, and utilizing the various aspects of the young person's rapidly changing reality. The therapist truly willing to do this will find most youngsters remarkably eager to develop therapeutic changes.

## Psychotics

Psychotics are generally mired in deeply self-devaluing trances. For the most part, their experience is dominated by classic hypnotic phenomena: hallucinations, perceptual distortions, age regressions, dissociation, time distortion, and so forth. Unfortunately, their experience is far less pleasant than the typical hypnotic trance. To be sure, most diagnosed psychotics live a distorted existence at the mercy of twisted unconscious processes, trying desperately to resist a mobius-like mind which dominates ever more oppressively with each struggle to dissociate from it. Such individuals, being generally unwilling to trust and unable to concentrate, are rather unresponsive to traditional inductions, which essentially demand that the psychotic come out of his or her tortuous trance to enter one suggested by the hypnotist. For these and other reasons, it is generally inappropriate to use hypnotic inductions with psychotics.

However, Ericksonian principles of hypnotic communication can certainly be applied therapeutically. The basic strategy is one of (1) recognizing that the person is in a dissociated trance state, (2) gaining rapport while gathering information about the unique nature of that trance state, (3) completely accepting and pacing the psychotic's reality, and then (4) gradually leading to other ways of being. In other words, the hypnotherapist comments inwardly: "OK, forget the induction – there's no need for it because this person's already in trance. What kind of trance is it? What's it like for the person? How can I accept and utilize it?"

A classic example of this type of strategy is Erickson's (1965) description of working with a mental-hospital patient who spewed out incessant streams of word salad. The understandable statements occasionally uttered by the patient were restricted to "Good morning," "Good night," and "My name is George." Repeated therapeutic attempts to elicit other responses had failed miserably. Upon joining the staff during the sixth year of George's hospitalization, Erickson studied his behavioral patterns intently. After recording and trying in vain to make sense out of the word salad, Erickson perfected a similar, yet unidentical style of speaking word salad. In enacting a therapeutic strategy, he initially sat silently next to George on a bench. After days of this pacing maneuver, Erickson led by identifying himself aloud while looking away from George. When he repeated this the following day, this time looking at George, the patient launched angrily into his word salad. Erickson listened politely while periodically countering with an equal amount of his own word salad. When a confused George eventually lapsed into silence, Erickson walked away.

This pattern of interchange continued for some time, finally escalating to a 12-hour session in which George served up a four-hour salad to which Erickson replied in kind, then another two hours which the wearying but determined Erickson returned. The next day, George interrupted some Erickson word salad with the demand that the psychiatrist "talk sense." Erickson complied by asking for George's last name, which was promptly supplied. George was thanked and then presented with a few more rational statements followed by a bit of word salad. George replied in a similar manner.

Over the next year, Erickson utilized this style of interchange to obtain a complete history and conduct a successful therapy with George. The word salad utterances were gradually reduced to infrequent unintelligible mumbles. George was discharged from the hospital and found a job which, as Erickson learned three years later, he maintained and enjoyed.

This case brilliantly illustrates how trance utilization principles can be used with psychotics. The patient's dissociation from the rest of the community certainly would have rendered ineffective any formal inductions initially attempted. Erickson therefore proceeded by accepting, entering, then utilizing the patient's already-established "dissociated trance" state. It is important to recognize how gradually this was done — the meticulous preparations, the extended pacing, the minuscule leads at first, and so on. To establish lasting therapeutic changes with people as confused and dissociated as George, extensive ground work is usually necessary. This includes spending time with the client to develop rapport and gather information, as well as spending time with oneself thinking of the many possible ways in which the client's unique situation might be handled.

This is not to say that the therapist must always begin mildly. Sometimes an effective opening gambit involves outrageous behavior. For example, Paul Carter and I worked with a psychotic who terrorized all the psychiatrists on his ward with gross hallucinations regarding dead babies, hot dogs coming out of his ears, and other truly bizarre images. We carefully observed at a distance for an extended period, noting when and how his hallucinatory episodes developed. When we began to interview him, he looked wildly about and then asked us if we saw the hallucinations. We matter-of-factly agreed with him, then looked crazily into space before asking *him* if he saw *our* hallucinations. Of course, this was all done elaborately and dramatically. Briefly stated, he was understandably stunned by our response; after all, *he* was supposed to be crazy, not us. He tried to counter with more hallucinations, which we again accepted and then led by introducing more of our own.

After a while, we disappointedly confessed that we had asked to see him because we were interested in becoming better hallucinators and had been told he was an expert on such matters. But, as we pointed out, there had obviously been a mistake; after all, we had 10 good hallucinations down while he had only three mediocre ones. Besides, we continued, the guy on the next ward had half a dozen, and of a much better variety.

Needless to say, this produced a state of profound confusion in the patient, which we promptly utilized by offering to teach him to be a better hallucinator. He agreed to this, and so over the next several months we showed him how to generate other hallucinations, how to hallucinate in a relaxed fashion, and how to have comforting hallucinations. We gradually led from very frightening and uncontrollable hallucinative processes to more relaxed and valuable sorts of hallucinations and then to dropping hallucinations altogether. Once he gained choice about his hallucinatory ability, he benefited from additional therapy with a psychiatric resident on the ward.

In summary, psychotics are generally bound up into an unpleasant "hypnotic reality" which renders them impervious to conventional forms of communication. Effective hypnotherapeutic strategies must therefore accommodate and utilize these unique realities. Trance inductions are often inappropriate, especially initially, but unorthodox trance utilization procedures that are sensitively applied can stimulate meaningful changes. It should be realized, however, that such changes will at best be temporary unless an intense relationship is developed and maintained. Thus, the principles are applied with an appreciation of the significant time and effort invariably needed to accomplish successful therapy with such individuals.

*Emergency Situations*

Chapter 7 emphasized how the sudden occurrence of an unexpected and impactful event will interrupt conscious processing and make the person highly responsive to suggestions which reduce the ensuing state of uncertainty. This is particularly true in naturalistic situations involving significant physical or psychological pain, such as those involving accidents or psychic traumas. Because the function of a formal induction has already been handled in such situations, trance utilization strategies can be introduced immediately.

A simple and amusing example of this transpired when I was visiting a friend at her house. As I was following her into the kitchen, my bare-footed hostess rammed her toe into a protruding cabinet. I immediately expressed exactly what I anticipated she would do in a moment — let loose with a loud, shrill cry of pain. Startled and shocked by the scream, she froze and looked at me in a bewildered fashion, whereupon I rapidly and dramatically said something like: "That's right . . . the pain is *here* . . . and you are *there* . . . and you can breathe . . . so breathe deeply and sit down all the way comfortably in *that* chair here now . . . deeply, Carol, and close your eyes and let your unconscious wrap you in unquestioned wonderment at your growing comfort." She sat down and closed her eyes, but opened them when after about 30 seconds she burst into laughter at the recognition of what had just happened. She proceeded to chide me goodnaturedly for "tricking" her.

As can be noted, the strategy was one of utilizing the moment of receptivity between physical insult and psychological reaction to dissociate (project) the anticipated scream (and, by implication, the pain) onto myself. The consequent confusion was utilized to consolidate the dissociation by placing the pain *"here"* and her *"there"* and then led to the uncertainty-reducing response of sitting down into a comfortable trance.

In other situations, more straightforward pacing and leading might be used. For example, Erickson (1958) described an incident in which his son Robert, then three years old, fell down the back stairs. Erickson did not try immediately to move the screaming boy, who lay sprawled in agony on pavement spattered with blood from his profusely bleeding mouth. Instead, he waited for the boy to take the fresh breath he needed to scream anew and then acknowledged in a simple and sympathetic fashion the "awful" and "terrible" pain Robert was experiencing. By demonstrating this understanding of the situation, Erickson secured rapport and attention, which he then consolidated by commenting that it would keep right on hurting. He paced further by voicing aloud the boy's desire to have the pain ease, then led by raising the *possibility* (*not* the certainty) of the pain diminishing within several minutes. He next distracted Robert by closely examining with his wife the "awful lot" of blood on the pavement before announcing that it was "good, red, strong blood" and suggesting that the blood could be better examined against the white background of the bathroom sink. By this time, absorption and interest in the quality of his blood had replaced Robert's pain and crying. This was utilized to demonstrate repeatedly to the boy that his blood was so strong and red that it could make "pink" the water being poured over his face. Questions of whether the mouth was bleeding and swelling properly were then raised and, after close examination, answered affirmatively.

The potentially negative response to the next step of stitching was paced before Erickson "regretfully" informed Robert that he probably couldn't have as many stitches as he could count or as many as several older siblings. This focusing of Robert's attention on counting the number of stitches served indirectly to secure freedom from pain. Robert was disappointed when he received "only" seven stitches, but cheered some when the surgeon pointed out that the stitches were of better quality than those given his siblings and that they probably would leave a W-shaped scar similar to the letter of his Daddy's college.

This example magnificently illustrates how emergency situations can be promptly utilized. The pain and likely concerns of the unlucky victim are first paced directly, simply, and sympathetically. Upon securing attention and rapport, the therapist can gradually mention a possible reduction in pain *but does not overemphasize this*. Attention is then redirected to another aspect of the situation, thereby enabling diminution of pain. Further utilizations sustain the distraction while simultaneously reframing the situation in positive terms.

This general approach can of course be modified according to situational and personality needs. For example, as a black belt in martial arts I was refereeing a karate match between a black belt and a brown belt in my club. The black belt unleashed a savage blow which accidentally crashed into the onrushing brown belt, collapsing him into a crumpled heap on the floor. I rushed to the side of the felled fighter, a young black man, as he lay writhing in pain from what turned out to be a broken arm. Employing a soft, sympathetic, yet absorbing tone, I said something like the following:

| *Communications* | *Commentary* |
|---|---|
| (1) Damn, Ray, you really got popped. I bet that sucker hurts like hell, hurts like a son of a | (1) The pain is first acknowledged appropriately, thereby facilitating rapport and securing |

bitch. So you better breathe deeply, Ray, breathe real deeply and look at me, 'cause you gotta use your mind now to do something . . . you gotta keep breathing too, just like in stretching, you gotta keep breathing and let the pain do its thing . . . because you know how pain turns into heat when you're stretching . . . but it takes a while . . . so just breathe and let that heat take you where it will. . . .

attention. This is used to elicit deep breathing to spread the pain while reducing any anxiety. The brief, general statement about the mind's ability to "do something," followed promptly by a topic shift, inconspicuously plants a seed for hypnotic work at an unconscious level. Leading communications then introduce the reference structure of stretching, familiar to most practiced martial artists, where one learns to transform (i.e., reframe) the initial pain of stretching into a pleasurable (or at least tolerable) experience such as "heat surging through the body." This paces the present pain and then leads with implicit suggestions for pain control.

(2) . . . And look here at me, man, and look at my belt . . . it's black, isn't it . . . and I'm proud of that . . . and John's (his opponent's) belt is black too, so you got nothing to feel bad about, nothing to be ashamed of, 'cause you got to have respect for blackness. . . . But you don't have to black out, Ray, look here at my belt and know that it will be time for you in the not too distant future . . . because you train real hard, work real hard, *take care of yourself mentally as well as physically* . . . you know how to think, and you know that sometimes the mental thing is much more important. . . .

(2) It is often good to distract conscious attention immediately after presenting a hypnotic suggestion, thereby enabling the unconscious to freely develop an appropriate response. Shifting attention to my black belt, a major goal of Ray's, elicits respect and attention while also accessing future-oriented imagery; both responses will distract from pain. Mentioning his opponent's black belt further distracts while depotentiating any embarrassment possibly being experienced about being "beat up." The pride and self-sufficiency Ray has associated to a black belt is then used to subtly overlap to the self-supporting abilities he has connected to his personal identity. Further compliments about his

training efforts and mental capabilities access more pride (and hence less pain) while implicitly framing the positive context of achieving a black belt.

(3) . . . And it probably still hurts some, so why not *close your eyes, Ray,* that's right, close them easily and comfortably, all the way down, and let your mind begin to do its thing . . . let yourself think about what it's going to be like when you get your black belt . . . how are you going to feel? . . . how are you gonna look? . . . let yourself imagine it . . . all the sweat, the pain, the dedication will be in the past now when you reach that goal.

(3) Still periodically grimacing in pain, Ray calmed somewhat as he grew increasingly absorbed in my communications. I utilized his receptive state by presenting direct suggestions for eye closure and subsequent general instructions for dissociated (from the present) imaginal activity. Again, the pain is placed within a context ("training for a black belt") which implicitly makes it easier to accept and thus to deal with. Generally, this sort of total shift into a future-oriented fantasy is not that difficult to accomplish rapidly in emergency situations, as the subject will usually be extremely motivated to dissociate.

Several more minutes of similar statements emphasized how Ray could maintain this trancelike reality "in an appropriate manner" as he was escorted to and treated at the hospital. He later reported how "far out" it was to "fade in and out of these trippy spaces" as a means to handle the pain.

The general strategy used with Ray is structurally equivalent to the one described above that Erickson used with his son. The operator first procures attentional fixation and receptivity by directly pacing the experience and then utilizes aspects of the subject's personal identity – in Ray's case his reference structures and motivations regarding martial arts – to dissociate and ultimately reframe the pain. The differences in detail (e.g., specific phrases or suggestions) between the two cases cited illustrate how this general strategy – which, incidentally, is the general strategy of a formal induction – is specifically applied according to the unique realities of the particular subject. Thus, the operator closely observes and utilizes each unfolding response, not knowing exactly which path will best lead to the desired state.

*Group Inductions*

I am sometimes asked whether the emphasis of the Ericksonian approach on flexibly adapting to the uniqueness of each person precludes its application in group situations. The answer is a resounding "no." In fact, I use group hypnosis as a major tool in training hypnotherapists, especially in advanced workshops. Group hypnosis also has value in group therapy situations.

Group inductions follow the same principles as individual inductions, albeit in a modified fashion. I usually spend at least 15 minutes talking about the nature of hypnosis and clearing up misconceptions, while framing trance as a general context for secure exploration of the Self. I emphasize that I will speak only generally during the induction and will not ask anybody to talk, move about, explore painful experiences, or do anything else potentially embarrassing. I mention the many different rates and styles of trance development (e.g., the floating phenomenon), and stress that each person should allow him/herself to discover his/her own rate and style, simply experiencing whatever is happening without needing to try to immediately have wild and dramatic experiences. Sometimes, especially if the group seems a bit reserved, I will provide a demonstration, either through self-hypnosis or by working with a willing and able subject.

I typically keep the first induction with a group brief and simple — for example, five minutes of relaxation and internal absorption instructions, five minutes of general statements and stories to elicit internal search processes, five minutes to revivify a pleasant memory, and five minutes of self-appreciation suggestions. Postinduction reports are solicited to emphasize the diversity of possible responses and to clear up any remaining misconceptions. Deeper and longer trances might then be developed at a rate appropriate to the group. The first two to six of these inductions might be used as a training period in which general and permissive suggestions are used to (1) introduce the major hypnotic phenomena and (2) have subjects develop "self-appreciation" or "security" anchors (Chapter 6), to both themselves and the hypnotist. Further inductions then focus on specific change processes.

An obvious advantage of a group induction is that both time and money can be saved. Also, the many different experiences reported by group participants expands a person's viewpoint about how trances can be developed and beneficially utilized. More generally, such reports demonstrate dramatically that people think and respond in many different ways, all of which can be valid. In my opinion, the *experiential* realization of this point is critical to the progress of both the hypno-therapy trainee and the psychotherapy client.

A potential disadvantage of group inductions is that the depth and quality of trance is, for some people, less than that experienced in an individual setting. Much of this owes to individual differences preclud-ing continual utilization of each individual's responses in the group situation. This problem can be at least partially circumvented in several ways. First, the hypnotist should speak more generally than usual, mak-ing sure to cover all possibilities while presupposing trance responses. For example, age regression suggestions might include the following sort of comments:

> And what a nice thing to know that you've had a variety of dif-ferent experiences in your childhood . . . as a baby, a toddler, a young boy or girl, all the way up to your adolescence . . . and trance is so very secure, you really can let your unconscious share with you pleasant, long-forgotten memories . . . and so I'm wondering and you can wonder, because neither of us really know just which long-forgotten memory will become revivified. Maybe it will be an experience at home, or maybe in a playground, or perhaps in school . . . I don't know and you don't know but your unconscious can surprise you pleasantly . . . perhaps one experience, perhaps two or more at first, perhaps none just yet. . . . Maybe you will see it first or feel it first or hear it or perhaps even smell it first, before all the rest of experience comes. . . . You can let your unconscious proceed at a rate and pace appropriate for you as an individual.

Second, the hypnotist inducing a group can scan the progress of subjects and give general suggestions for enjoyable hypnotic experi-ences to entranced subjects before zeroing in on the minority of par-ticipants having difficulty in developing trance. Embedded suggestions, generalities, and rapid dissociation techniques, all delivered within the flow of the group induction, are especially effective with these latter individuals. Third, special individual sessions might be scheduled for the handful of subjects hypnotically unresponsive to group inductions. This special training is needed most with psychotherapy clients who need specific assurances and guidance in letting go into trance.

In concluding, it should be noted that the response variability across different groups matches that observed across different individuals. Each group will have its own "personality," its own concerns, its own rate and style. A major task of the hypnotist is to remain sensitive and responsive to a given group's progress.

## Summary

To summarize, this section overviewed some special applications of Ericksonian induction principles and induction strategies. A major point has been that an induction should not be construed as a set of verbal incantations that repetitively emphasize "trance," "deeper and deeper," "relax," and other words classically associated with hypnotic experiences. While such incantations may be helpful in developing trance in most situations, especially when both hypnotist and subject feel comfortable with them, they can unduly limit the flexibility and consequent effectiveness of the hypnotherapeutic inquiry. The Ericksonian approach considers hypnotic inductions as interactional sequences that absorb and direct a person's attention into a therapeutically utilizable altered state of consciousness. In this general framework, the critical factor in inducing trance is *not* the subject's responsiveness to hypnotic directives, but rather the hypnotist's willingness and ability to accept and utilize the subject's reality. This sometimes necessitates unorthodox strategies and communications; it invariably requires ongoing flexibility.

If all this sounds terribly complicated to fathom — much less apply — it should be emphasized that things become immeasurably easier when one realizes that these naturalistic views of trance are really ways to conceptualize therapeutic change in general. In other words, most effective therapies involve some "induction" whereby the client is shifted from a rigid and limiting frame of mind to a more open and willing state ("trance") wherein experiential changes can be developed. It is therefore not essential that therapists interested in integrating Ericksonian approaches into their practices think in terms of formal hypnosis. It is far more useful for practitioners to first recognize how they already naturalistically induce and utilize trance states in clients. They can then assess their own personal comfort with "trance" terminology and respond accordingly. Some clinicians discover a preference for formal hypnotic approaches; others find other frameworks more appropriate. Regardless, the realization of how the Ericksonian framework complements other therapeutic approaches will significantly enhance one's abilities as a clinician.

## DEALING WITH UNSUCCESSFUL INDUCTION ATTEMPTS

What does the therapist do if a number of inductions have apparently failed to induce trance in a person desiring one? Chapter 1 noted how most traditional hypnotists would brand the subject as "insusceptible" or "resistant," while Ericksonian practitioners assume that the subject's experience has not been adequately utilized. To fairly claim this latter position, one must demonstrate that willing but previously insusceptible subjects can experience trance. To succeed at this task, both the hypnotist's and subject's processes in the hypnotic interaction should first be clearly assessed. This section explores questions valuable in this regard. The questions, many of them overlapping in scope, deal with topics discussed earlier. They can be answered through a combination of direct and indirect questioning of the subject, observation, intuition, and reflection on previous interactions.

The first question addresses the possibility that trance occurred without the subject's recognition:

*1. Has the subject experienced trance without knowing it?* While subjects claiming they did not experience trance are usually correct, this is not always the case. Sometimes, for instance, dramatic preconceptions about trance bar subjects from recognizing a light trance as such. These subjects, usually novices steeped in popular misconceptions about hypnosis, often incorrectly interpret the absence of certain expected experiences (e.g., "blacking out," not hearing the hypnotist, having wild religious-like experiences) as the absence of trance. The hypnotist might try to first clear up these misconceptions through discussion, emphasizing especially that (1) trance is an experiential continuum of involvement rather than an "all or none" phenomenon, (2) most initial trances, often light in depth, resemble ordinary waking consciousness in some ways but differ in others (e.g., greater effortlessness and enhanced perception, see Chapter 2), and (3) the best way to let trance develop is to set aside preconceptions and expectations and just accept whatever develops. This discussion might be followed with an induction containing "convincer techniques" (e.g., tunnel vision, ideomotor signals, dissociation, time distortion) that experientially demonstrate to the subject that he or she is in an altered state.

In addition to light trances not being recognized because of misconceptions, deep trances may not be recognized because of amnesia. This often creates unnecessary anxiety in the subject that needs to be handled. For example, a hypnotherapy trainee, spontaneously amnesic for several deep trances, grew increasingly worried about these hour-long "gaps" in her experience. Another woman, a hypnotherapy client given hypnotic amnesias to protect unconscious change processes from conscious interference, began to question the therapeutic progress. Both persons were instructed to remain in an open-eyed waking state while I used ideomotor finger responses (see Erickson & Rossi, 1981) to (1) have the unconscious communicate whether meaningful trance experiences had transpired and (2) elicit a subjectively compelling hypnotic response that could be consciously observed and remembered. This simple procedure allayed the concerns, thereby permitting the resumption of trance learnings.

The next five questions deal with the subject's *willingness* to develop trance:

*2. Does the subject misunderstand the nature of hypnosis?* This may be the case even with the subject properly informed by the hypnotist. For example, a client saw "hypnosis" demonstrated twice by stage hypnotists. The fact that in both cases the subjects were made to look foolish discouraged him greatly from participating in that role. Accordingly, he interpreted my straightforward attempts to distinguish clinical hypnosis from stage acts as efforts to "trick" him. With such individuals, it is often best to shelve further discussion in favor of experiential demonstration via self-hypnosis or My-friend-John techniques. Such techniques constitute indirect inductions; they also provide reference structures to replace the trance-inhibiting misconceptions about hypnosis.

*3. Does the subject anticipate unpleasant consequences?* Some subjects do not question the potential value of trance or their own trance ability, but do doubt their psychological stability. For example, one distraught client thought he would "fall apart" and "go over the deep end" if he relaxed even just a bit; another subject's previous trance experiences were dominated by frightening traumatic memories. Understandably, both persons were hesitant to enter trance. To transform such unwillingness, the therapist usually needs to proceed slowly and sensitively. Several sessions may be needed to simply develop rapport. Then, techniques might be used to identify what knowledge, assurances, or experiences the client would need to allow trance development. After developing and anchoring the identified resources for later use (Chapter 6), the therapist might offer opportunities to realize trance as a safe context through any of a variety of different methods: refractionation, withholding information from the hypnotist, having a cue for trance arousal, and so forth.

*4. Does the subject trust me?* Trances, especially therapeutic ones, involve opening up to new ways of being. Not surprisingly, many subjects will be reluctant to do this until they trust the hypnotist. Lack of trust may owe to a paucity of previous hypnotist-subject interactions, often remedied by a little time spent together. Or it may stem from previous experiences such as with a client of mine sexually seduced by her previous therapist, or another client whose miserable childhood had "taught" him to distrust everyone. With such individuals, the therapist must first demonstrate his or her integrity as a person and as a clinician. In doing so, the therapist should find out what the client needs in order to experience trust in the relationship, and should identify and pace those behavioral patterns most likely to incur the client's distrust. For example, say the therapist determines (through questioning, observing, listening to spontaneous reports, etc.) that the client immediately distrusts anybody bubbling with cheerful optimism. This could be respected by simply refraining from expressing such an attitude; or by commenting directly that the client has been burned before and therefore shouldn't believe anything said until trying it out at his or her own rate and style; or by periodically running "polarity plays" (Chapter 7) in which the therapist is more pessimistic than the client. The sensitive utilization of such strategies can transform unwillingness into cooperation.

Another possible source of distrust is the hypnotist's expressions, which may inadvertently violate the preferences, values, or needs of the client. Sometimes this results from inadequate knowledge, as when a client of mine temporarily stopped trusting me when I failed to recognize her remarkably unpleasant childhood and told stories about the pleasant childhood experiences "everyone" has had. Other times distrust arises from oversight, as when a hypnotist stressed eye closure to a highly trained subject who previously had clearly stated her preference to experience trance with her eyes open. The negative impact of distrust on the subject's willingness to enter trance behooves the hypnotist to (1) take sufficient time to complete the trance preparation phase discussed in Chapter 5 (e.g., gathering information, developing rapport), (2) maintain close observation of nonverbal behavior for signs of distrust (e.g., diminished rapport), (3) periodically explore issues of trust directly or indirectly (e.g., through questions, stories, or frank discussions), and (4) convey sincere and direct apologies when the subject's values or preferences have been violated.

*5. Is the subject experiencing anything unpleasant at the onset of trance?* Occasionally a subject will start to develop trance and then suddenly "pop out" with a reluctance to continue. This most often occurs with rapidly developing trances, which may produce sudden perceptual or emotional alterations frightening to the person. For example, one subject who easily developed eye fixation was unsettled by the ensuing visual distortions involving tunnel vision and double images; another subject was terrified upon discovering she couldn't move her body as she entered trance; a third person was seized with the panicking thought that her mind could be totally overtaken. Such experiences can be easily observed by the attentive therapist (in terms of disrupted rhythms, muscular contractions, and so forth), and the subject will usually be willing to talk about what transpired. Thus, it is generally not too difficult for the therapist to develop an understanding of the trance-interrupting fears and respond accordingly. Possibilities include *assurances* that the experiences in question are safe, common, and naturalistic; *specific suggestions* to adjust behavior – for example, telling the "visually distorting" subject described above to breathe deeply and blink her eyes if again petrified by tunnel vision; *slowing the rate of induction* so the subject doesn't "rush in" and become "uncentered"; *shifting demeanor* to a less overpowering style; and *accessing and anchoring resources* to ensure feelings of safety.

6. *Are there any unconscious objections?* Now and again a person will have an objection to developing trance that is not apparent to his or her conscious mind or to the therapist. This possibility should be explored, especially when other explanations have failed to account for or remedy a seeming unwillingness to experience trance. This can be done in a relatively straightforward way, for example, by using ideo-motor signals to check for the presence of unconscious objections or by using generalities or metaphors as "fishing in the dark" techniques (Chapters 4 and 6).

The next quartet of questions addresses the possible *inability* of the subject to develop trance:

7. *Does the subject need more time?* Some subjects need a fair amount of time to learn the skill of developing trance. This is why Chapter 5 emphasized the value of a pressure-free training period involving up to six sessions of extended inductions. Therapists who fail to respect each person's need to develop trance at his or her own rate will discover a good many "resistant" and "insusceptible" subjects on their hands. This is not to say that other factors are not also involved; to be sure, the hypnotist should always consider at least briefly the other questions

listed in this section. However, unless the situation clearly indicates otherwise, serious concern about trance inability is generally not warranted until adequate time has been provided.

*8. Does the subject understand his or her role?* A person may be willing but unable to develop trance because of misunderstanding about how to respond as a subject. One novice subject waited eagerly and suspensefully for the hypnotist to "cause" some dramatic shift in his consciousness; another person effortfully tried to immediately accommodate each suggestion given; a third subject, trained in traditional hypnosis, thought trance occurred when the subject was "outfoxed" by the hypnotist in a subtle "battle of wits." In each case, the trance desired by the subject was blocked by efforts to help it along. Because such efforts are usually well-intentioned, they can generally be handled by suggesting the substitution of a more appropriate response strategy.

*9. Are the subject's conscious processes interfering?* This is almost invariably the case with subjects having difficulty experiencing trance. Methods of identifying and utilizing such interference have already been discussed extensively, especially in the preceding chapter. General strategies include having subjects keep their eyes open, boredom, "polarity plays," My-friend-John techniques, metaphor, dissociation, confusion, and distraction.

*10. Is the subject already in a "dissociated trance"?* The preceding section described how some people are already in naturalistic, dissociated trance states that make them relatively impervious to formal inductions. It also discussed strategies for proceeding in such cases.

Another set of questions deal with the hypnotist's processes.

*11. What general strategies have I used?* A good first step in analyzing previous induction failures is to list all the techniques and strategies thus far used with the subject. Alongside each listed item, the hypnotherapist might briefly note the subject's general response(s) to it. This will often yield insights into why things have not worked as well as expected. For example, I noted that I had used a tremendous amount of confusion with one client. She would typically respond to such techniques by starting to talk about something else, which I interpreted as increased conscious interference that needed to be depotentiated by "better" and more confusion techniques. In contemplating this, it struck me that this "more of the same" strategy was perhaps the problem, not the solution. Sure enough, shifting to a less dominating and confusing approach enabled increased rapport and the consequent development of trance.

*12. What general strategies have I not used?* On the same sheet listing attempted strategies, unattempted strategies might also be jotted down. As with the previous question, considering the items on such a list often provides ideas about how to proceed more effectively with a subject. For example, the observed absence of metaphors with a rationally oriented subject led to successful inductions filled with stories (Chapter 6); with another person, an insecure woman seeking specific guidance, recognizing the paucity of direct suggestions thus far offered to her prompted a more effective induction involving an interspersal of straightforward communications to develop trance.

*13. How would I know if the subject were in a trance?* This question is asked to identify possible misconceptions about necessary conditions for trance. Such misconceptions may bar the hypnotherapist from recognizing and ratifying a trance. This usually leads to communications implying that the subject is not yet in trance. The subject may respond to this remarkable lack of pacing by remaining in trance but losing rapport with the therapist or by developing doubts which hinder further trance experiences.

For example, a psychiatrist I supervised assumed erroneously that (1) the hypnotized subject follows any suggestion given by the hypnotist and (2) hand dissociation is always manifested in the form of hand levitation. He was thus rather perplexed when a subject apparently in deep trance responded to hand dissociation suggestions by becoming extremely heavy-handed. The psychiatrist's conclusion that trance was absent made things difficult for both him and the subject. When it was demonstrated to him that extreme heaviness is a valid dissociational response, he was able to ratify and utilize the subject's responses in later sessions.

The point here is that while there are general characteristics and indicators of trance (Chapters 2 and 4), none is *essential* for a trance to occur. Thus, rather than relying on rigid rules for assessing the presence of trance (e.g., deep relaxation, suggestibility), the hypnotist should be sensitive to the many different ways in which trance can be developed, experienced, and manifested.

*14. What are the subject's behavioral patterns?* A failure to induce trance almost invariably reflects a failure to utilize the person's behavior and experience. Thus, the stymied hypnotist might write down the recalcitrant subject's behavioral patterns, however trivial or unrelated to trance they may seem. That is, list whatever you can observe the subject doing repetitively, such as looking around, hand movements, saying "You know what I mean" every third or fourth statement, or shaking his or her head. Creative contemplation of how to utilize these patterns as the basis for induction will yield a wealth of potential induction strategies suitable for that person, as exemplified by the many examples appearing in this book.

*15. What have I discouraged the subject from doing?* When hypnotists fall into the common rut of thinking that an induction must proceed in a certain way (e.g., progressive relaxation), they will discourage certain behavioral and mental processes – for example, moving around, questioning things continually, attending to external stimuli, tensing up, keeping eyes open, and so forth. Since utilizing the subject's dominant patterns is generally the best induction strategy, it can be extremely valuable to identify any such patterns being discouraged.

For example, I supervised a case in which the hypnotherapist grew increasingly frustrated with the client's periodic laughter during hypnotherapeutic processes. He interpreted such behavior as indicating self-consciousness or exhibitionism, declaring that trance could not be developed until the laughter stopped. When it did not, he gave up and asked me if I could handle this apparently recalcitrant individual. I sat down with the client, an actress of a most extroverted nature. My observations indicated she was clearly enjoying herself and seemed quite internally absorbed during her spells of laughter. I thus commented cheerfully that it really was important to keep a sense of humor in all situations, especially hypnotic ones, and that her unconscious could laugh her all the way into trance if it so desired. At the same time, I took hold of her hands and held them gently to ensure she was experientially "grounded." Briefly stated, these simple utilizations paved the way for a successful induction. Once she developed trance, suggestions for mirthful laughter were interspersed among directives to develop various other emotional states as well.

A similar case involved a client overwhelmed with itches all over his body at the slightest development of trance. He just *had* to itch here, then there, and finally everywhere. I initially tried to handle this perceived "problem" through dissociation, distraction, and confusion, all to no avail. Finally it dawned on me: I was being blinded by an unconscious assumption that trance requires body immobility; the itching could and should be accepted as the basis for the induction. Thus, in the next session I first ascertained that itching of such magnitude occurred only during hypnotic communications. I thus proceeded to explain that creative unconscious processes and trance development could be manifested in many ways, including itching. This set the stage for a successful induction in which the itching was accepted, encouraged, directed (to various parts of the body), alternately increased and decreased, then transformed into different sensations (e.g., an itch of curiosity, a prickling of anticipation, a tickle of pleasure).

*16. What are the subject's valued associations?* This question was discussed in Chapters 4 and 5. To reiterate, a person's assets (e.g., skills, pleasant memories, achievements, etc.), however trivial and irrelevant they may seem, can be utilized to absorb attention, access confidence, generate effective stories, enhance motivation, provide compelling explanations and acceptable instructions, and frame trance in appropriate fashions. Thus, identifying a person's strengths can provide insight into past induction failures as well as ideas for effective future inductions.

*17. What are the subject's devalued associations?* Chapters 4 and 5 also noted how the subject's weaknesses (e.g., problems, deficiencies, fears, lack of skills) can be used for trance development in the same general way that strengths can.

*18. Is there a part of the subject that I'm unwilling or unable to accept?* Chapter 3 discussed how the unacceptable experiences of the therapist will preclude cooperation with similar experiences in the client. It thus behooves therapists to identify aspects of the client they devalue. As Chapter 5 noted, this can be accomplished by noting clinical or other pejorative labels used to describe some ways of being expressed by the client.

### SUMMARY

This chapter explored practical aspects of therapeutic trance inductions. The first section provided a transcript with commentary to illustrate how a complete induction might proceed. The transcript was used as a basis for further points about clinical hypnosis, including the time needed to generate effective therapeutic trance states. The second section overviewed how Ericksonian induction principles can be applied in nonformal, naturalistic fashions with children, psychotics, emergency situations, and groups. Especially emphasized was the utilization of existing, albeit self-devaluing, trance states that many clients are already experiencing. The final section offered questions that the hypnotherapist can ask to generate effective induction strategies with clients experiencing difficulties in developing trance.

# *Epilogue*

We have touched upon a variety of ideas over the past eight chapters. The following are the most important:

1. Cooperation is the basic principle of transformational change.
2. The Ericksonian therapist cooperates by joining the way a client is constructing his or her reality, then moves experientially to expand the range of possibilities within that reality.
3. Hypnosis is a model for constructing experiential realities.
4. Hypnosis is an experientially absorbing interactional sequence that culminates in an altered state of consciousness wherein unconscious expressions develop without conscious (analytical) mediation. In other words, hypnosis is a relationship that produces trance and trance phenomena.
5. Trance can be the basis of both problems and solutions, depending on the context in which it occurs.
6. Trance is an experiential process in which paradoxical logic applies, such that a person can experience seemingly contradictory states simultaneously.
7. Trance is developed within the therapeutic relationship via the therapist's use of processes that (a) experientially absorb attention, (b) pace and then deframe fixed conceptual orientations, and (c) elicit and amplify experiential (trance) processes. This induction process is naturalistic, such that most techniques unfold from the client's ongoing "techniques" (i.e., self-expression patterns).
8. The Ericksonian therapist is equally an observer and a participant. Thus, trances that develop within the therapeutic context are often interpersonal in nature, wherein therapist and client are each "a part of and apart from" the other.
9. The unconscious is respected as generative and creative. The therapist thus works to trust and utilize his or her own unconscious as a means to invite and enable the client to do the same in regard to the needs and goals of the client.

To illustrate how these ideas may be applied in the therapeutic context, a number of techniques have been presented in the preceding pages. About these techniques, one thing for certain can be said: They will become obsolete sooner or later. That is, their value is in facilitating developmental growth in therapist and client alike. As new levels of understanding and functioning are reached, new challenges requiring new techniques arise. At that point, T. S. Elliot's (1963) words ring true:

> Last season's fruit is eaten
> And the fulfilled beat shall kick the empty pail.
> For last year's words belong to last year's language
> And next year's words await another voice. (p. 218)

Thus, it is my hope that you, the reader, appreciate the ideas and principles, while remaining flexible with the techniques. Much learning is required to master the technical craft of hypnotherapy, yet even more work is needed to appreciate that the techniques are merely "hints and guesses," suggesting possibilities of deeper aliveness. In the immortal words of Bruce Lee, don't fixate on the finger pointing at the moon, or you will miss the moon.

Milton Erickson pointed me towards the moon in a variety of different ways. It is thus fitting that I bring closure to this volume by relating an encounter I had with him during a training session. Orienting to the topic of diagnostic acumen, Erickson handed me a folder containing a letter from a patient, along with the directive to find that information revealing that the patient wasn't telling the truth. After I had failed miserably in my appointed task, Erickson pointed out that the patient announced she was taking "the last train from St. Louis" to see him. Erickson seized upon my puzzled state to emphatically and hypnotically declare, *"There is no last train from St. Louis.* You will never know a last train from anywhere. There's always the possibility of another train."

The last 10 years have seen me return to that puzzled state on numerous occasions in hopes of consciously appreciating the value of that seemingly ridiculous statement, which somehow resonated deep within me. Lately, it's dawning on me: There is no last train.

Good luck.

# References

Asante, M. K. The African-American mode of transcendence. *Journal of Transpersonal Psychology*, 1984, *16*, 167–177.

Bain, A. *The emotions and the will*. New York: Appleton, 1859.

Bandler, R., & Grinder, J. *Patterns of the hypnotic techniques of Milton H. Erickson, M. D.: Volume I*. Cupertino, CA: Meta Publications, 1975.

Bandler, R., & Grinder, J. *Frogs into princes*. Moab, UT: Real People Press, 1979.

Bandler, R., & Grinder, J. *Reframing: Neuro-Linguistic Programming and the transformation of meaning*. Moab, UT: Real People Press, 1982.

Bandler, R., Grinder, J., & Satir, V. *Changing with families: Volume I*. Palo Alto: Science & Behavior Books, 1976.

Bandura, A. *Social learning theory*. Englewood Cliffs, NJ: Prentice-Hall, 1977.

Barber, T. X. *Hypnosis: A scientific approach*. New York: Van Nostrand-Reinhold, 1969.

Barber, T. X. Suggested ("hypnotic") behavior: The trance paradigm versus an alternative paradigm. In E. Fromm & R. E. Shor (Eds.), *Hypnosis: Research developments and perspectives*. Chicago: Aldine-Atherton, 1972.

Barber, T. X., & Calverly, D. S. "Hypnotic" behavior as a function of task motivation. *Journal of Psychology*, 1962, *54*, 363–389.

Bartlett, E. E. My first experience with Milton Erickson. *American Journal of Clinical Hypnosis*, 1977, *20*, 6–7.

Bateson, G. *Naven: A survey of the problems suggested by a composite picture of the culture of a New Guinea tribe drawn from three points of view* (2nd Ed.). Stanford: Stanford University Press, 1958.

Bateson, G. *Steps to an ecology of mind*. New York: Ballantine, 1972.

Bateson, G. *Mind and nature: A necessary unity*. New York: E. P. Dutton, 1979.

Bateson, G., Jackson, D. D., Haley, J., & Weakland, J. H. Toward a theory of schizophrenia. *Behavioral Science*, 1956, *1*, 251–264.

Bernheim, H. *Suggestive therapeutics: A treatise on the nature and uses of hypnotism*. New York: Putnam, 1895.

Blum, G. S. *A model of the mind*. New York: Wiley & Sons, 1961.

Bogen, J. E. The other side of the brain: An appositional mind. *Bulletin of the Los Angeles Neurological Societies*, 1969, *34*, 135–162. Reprinted in R. E. Ornstein (Ed.), *The nature of human consciousness: A book of readings*, San Francisco: W. H. Freeman, 1973.

Bower, G. H., & Gilligan, S. G. Remembering information related to one's self. *Journal of Research in Personality*, 1979, *13*, 420–432.

Bower, G. H., Gilligan, S. G., & Monteiro, K. P. Selectivity of learning caused by affective states. *Journal of Experimental Psychology: General*, 1981, *110*, 451–473.

Brown, G. S. *Laws of form*. New York: E. P. Dutton, 1979.

Castenada, C. *Tales of power*. New York: Simon & Schuster, 1972.

Cheek, D. B., & LeCron, L. M. *Clinical hypnotherapy*. New York: Grune & Stratton, 1968.

Chomsky, N. *Syntactic structures*. The Hague: Mouton, 1957.

Chomsky, N. *Aspects of the theory of syntax*. Cambridge, MA: MIT Press, 1965.

Cooper, L. F., & Erickson, M. H. *Time distortion in hypnosis* (2nd Ed.). Baltimore: Williams & Wilkins, 1959.

Cooper, L. M. Hypnotic amnesia. In E. Fromm & R. E. Shor (Eds.), *Hypnosis: Research developments and perspectives.* Chicago: Aldine-Atherton, 1972.

Davis, P. J., & Hersh, R. *The mathematical experience.* Boston: Houghton-Mifflin, 1981.

Day, M. E. An eye movement phenomenon related to attention, thought, and anxiety. *Perceptual and Motor Skills,* 1964, *19,* 443–446.

Day, M. E. An eye movement indicator of type and level of anxiety: Some clinical observations. *Journal of Clinical Psychology,* 1967, *66,* 438–441.

Deikman, A. Experimental meditation. *Journal of Nervous and Mental Disorders,* 1963, *135,* 329–373.

Deikman, A. Deautomatization and the mystic experience. *Psychiatry,* 1966, *29,* 324–388.

de Shazer, S. *Patterns of brief family therapy: An ecosystemic approach.* New York: Guilford Press, 1982.

Diamond, M. J. The modification of hypnotizability: A review. *Psychological Bulletin,* 1974, *81,* 180–198.

Dilts, R. B., Grinder, J., Bandler, R., Delozier, J., & Cameron-Bandler, L. *Neuro-Linguistic Programming I.* Cupertino, CA: Meta Publications, 1979.

Dorcus, R. M. Fallacies in predictions of susceptibility to hypnosis based on personality characteristics. *American Journal of Clinical Hypnosis,* 1963, *5,* 163–170.

Doyle, A. C. *The complete Sherlock Holmes.* New York: Doubleday, 1905.

Drewes, H. W. *An experimental study of the relationship between electroencephalographic imagery variables and perceptual-cognitive processes.* Unpublished doctoral dissertation, Cornell University, 1958.

Ekman, P. Communication through nonverbal behavior: A source of information about an interpersonal relationship. In S. S. Tomkins & C. E. Izard (Eds.), *Affect, cognition, and personality.* New York: Springer Press, 1965.

Ekman, P. Universal and cultural differences in facial expressions of emotions. In J. Cole (Ed.), *Nebraska symposium on motivation, Volume 19.* Lincoln: University of Nebraska Press, 1972.

Ekman, P. Biological and cultural contributions to body and facial movement in the expression of emotions. In A. Rorty (Ed.), *Explaining emotions.* Berkeley: University of California Press, 1980.

Eliot, T. S. Four Quartets. In T. S. Eliot, *Collected Poems: 1909–1962.* London: Faber & Faber, 1963.

Ellenberger, H. *The discovery of the unconscious: The history and evolution of dynamic psychiatry.* New York: Basic Books, 1970.

Epstein, M. O. On the neglect of evenly suspended attention. *Journal of Transpersonal Psychology,* 1984, *16,* 193–205.

Erickson, M. H. Hypnotic psychotherapy. *The Medical Clinics of North America.* 1948, 571–584. New York: W. B. Saunders Co. Reprinted in Rossi, 1980d.

Erickson, M. H. Deep hypnosis and its induction. In L. M. LeCron (Ed.), *Experimental hypnosis.* New York: Macmillan, 1952. Reprinted in Rossi, 1980a.

Erickson, M. H. Hypnotherapy of two psychosomatic dental problems. *Journal of the American Society of Psychosomatic Dentistry and Medicine,* 1955, *1,* 6–10. Reprinted in Rossi, 1980d.

Erickson, M. H. Pediatric hypnotherapy. *American Journal of Clinical Hypnosis,* 1958, *1,* 25–29. Reprinted in Rossi, 1980d.

Erickson, M. H. Further clinical techniques of hypnosis: Utilization techniques. *American Journal of Clinical Hypnosis,* 1959, *2,* 3–21. Reprinted in Rossi, 1980a.

Erickson, M. H. Identification of a secure reality. *Family Process,* 1962a, *1,* 294–303. Reprinted in Rossi, 1980d.

Erickson, M. H. Basic psychological problems in hypnotic research. In G. Estabrooks (Ed.), *Hypnosis: Current problems.* New York: Harper & Row, 1962b. Reprinted in Rossi, 1980b.

Erickson, M. H. The confusion technique in hypnosis. *American Journal of Clinical Hypnosis,* 1964a, *6,* 183–207. Reprinted in Rossi, 1980a.

Erickson, M. H. The "Surprise" and "My friend John" techniques of hypnosis: Minimal cues and natural field experimentation. *American Journal of Clinical Hypnosis*, 1964b, *6*, 293–307. Reprinted in Rossi, 1980a.

Erickson, M. H. Pantomime techniques in hypnosis and the implications. *American Journal of Clinical Hypnosis*, 1964c, *7*, 64–70. Reprinted in Rossi, 1980a.

Erickson, M. H. An hypnotic technique for resistant patients: The patient, the technique, and its rationale and field experiments. *American Journal of Clinical Hypnosis*, 1964d, *7*, 8–32. Reprinted in Rossi, 1980a.

Erickson, M. H. The use of symptoms as an integral part of therapy. *American Journal of Clinical Hypnosis*, 1965, *8*, 57–65. Reprinted in Rossi, 1980d.

Erickson, M. H. The interspersal technique for symptom correction and pain control. *American Journal of Clinical Hypnosis*, 1966a, *8*, 198–209. Reprinted in Rossi, 1980d.

Erickson, M. H. The experience of interviewing in the presence of others. In L. A. Gottschalk and A. H. Auerback (Eds.), *Methods of research in psychotherapy*. New York: Appleton-Century-Crofts, 1966b. Reprinted in Rossi, 1980b.

Erickson, M. H. Laboratory and clinical hypnosis: The same or different phenomena? *American Journal of Clinical Hypnosis*, 1967, *9*, 166–170. Reprinted in Rossi, 1980b.

Erickson, M. H. A field investigation by hypnosis of sound loci importance in human behavior. *American Journal of Clinical Hypnosis*, 1973, *16*, 147–164. Reprinted in Rossi, 1980b.

Erickson, M. H., & Kubie, L. S. The translation of the cryptic automatic writing of one hypnotic subject by another in a trancelike dissociated state. *The Psychoanalytic Quarterly*, 1940, *9*, 51–63. Reprinted in Rossi, 1980c.

Erickson, M. H., & Rosen, H. The hypnotic and hypnotherapeutic investigation and determination of symptom-function. *Journal of Clinical and Experimental Hypnosis*, 1954, *2*, 201–219. Reprinted in Rossi, 1980d.

Erickson, M. H., & Rossi, E. L. Varieties of double bind. *American Journal of Clinical Hypnosis*, 1975, *17*, 143–157. Reprinted in Rossi, 1980a.

Erickson, M. H., & Rossi, E. L. Autohypnotic experiences of Milton H. Erickson, M. D. *American Journal of Clinical Hypnosis*, 1977, *20*, 36–54. Reprinted in Rossi, 1980a.

Erickson, M. H., & Rossi, E. L. *Hypnotherapy: An exploratory casebook*. New York: Irvington, 1979.

Erickson, M. H., & Rossi, E. L. *Experiencing hypnosis: Therapeutic approaches to altered states*. New York: Irvington, 1981.

Erickson, M. H., Rossi, E. L., & Rossi, S. I. *Hypnotic realities*. New York: Irvington, 1976.

Féré, C. *Sensation et mouvement*. Paris: Alcan, 1887.

Freud, S. (1909). Analysis of a phobia in a five-year old boy. *Standard Edition, 10*, 3–152. London: Hogarth Press, 1955.

Freud, S. (1912). Recommendations to physicians practicing psychoanalysis. *Standard Edition, 18*, 235–254. London: Hogarth Press, 1955.

Freud, S. (1923). Two encyclopedia articles. *Standard Edition, 23*, 209–253. London: Hogarth Press, 1955.

Fromm, E. Activity and passivity of the ego in hypnosis. *International Journal of Clinical and Experimental Hypnosis*, 1972, *20*, 238–251.

Fromm, E., Oberlander, M. I., & Gruenwald, D. Perceptual and cognitive processes in different states of consciousness: The waking state and hypnosis. *Journal of Projective Techniques and Personality Assessment*, 1970, *34*, 375–387.

Ghiselin, B. (Ed.) *The creative process*. New York: Mentor, 1955.

Gill, M. M., & Brenman, M. *Hypnosis and related states: Psychoanalytic studies in regression*. New York: International University Press, 1959.

Gilligan, S. G. Ericksonian approaches to clinical hypnosis. In J. K. Zeig (Ed.), *Ericksonian approaches to hypnosis and psychotherapy*. New York: Brunner/Mazel, 1982a.

Gilligan, S. G. *Effects of emotional intensity on learning*. Unpublished doctoral dissertation, Stanford University, 1982b.

Gilligan, S. G. Generative autonomy: Principles for an Ericksonian hypnotherapy. In J.

K. Zeig (Ed.), *Ericksonian psychotherapy, Volume I: Structures.* New York: Brunner/Mazel, 1985.

Gilligan, S. G. The trance dance: Ericksonian hypnotherapy with couples. Manuscript in preparation, 1986.

Gilligan, S. G., & Bower, G. H. Cognitive consequences of emotional arousal. In C. E. Izard, J. Kagan, & R. Zajonc (Eds.), *Emotion, cognitions, and behavior.* New York: Cambridge Press, 1984.

Glass, A. L., Holyoak, K. J., & Santa, J. L. *Cognition.* Reading, MA: Addison-Wesley, 1979.

Grinder, J., & Bandler, R. *The structure of magic: Volume II.* Palo Alto, CA: Science & Behavior Books, 1975.

Grinder, J., Delozier, J., & Bandler, R. *Patterns of the hypnotic techniques of Milton H. Erickson, M.D., Volume II.* Cupertino, CA: Meta Publications, 1977.

Gordon, D. *Therapeutic metaphor: Helping others through the looking glass.* Cupertino, CA: Meta Publications, 1978.

Gordon, D., & Meyers-Anderson, M. *Phoenix: Therapeutic patterns of Milton H. Erickson.* Cupertino, CA: Meta Publications, 1981.

Haley, J. *Strategies of psychotherapy.* New York: Grune & Stratton, 1963.

Haley, J. *The power tactics of Jesus Christ and other essays.* New York: Grossman, 1969.

Haley, J. *Uncommon therapy: The psychiatric techniques of Milton H. Erickson, M.D.* (paperback edition). New York: W. W. Norton, 1973.

Haley, J. *Problem-solving therapy: New strategies for effective family therapy.* San Francisco: Jossey-Bass, 1976.

Hall, E. T. *The silent language.* Garden City, New York: Doubleday & Co., 1959.

Hall, E. T. *The hidden dimension.* Garden City, New York: Doubleday & Co., 1966.

Hall, E. T. *The dance of life: The other dimension of time.* Garden City, New York: Anchor Press/Doubleday, 1983.

Hartland, J. *Medical and dental hypnosis and its clinical applications* (2nd Ed.). London: Baillière Tindall, 1971.

Hartmann, H. *Ego psychology and the problem of adaption.* New York: International Universities Press, 1958.

Higgins, E. T., Herman, C. P., & Zanna, M. P. *Social cognition: The Ontario Symposium, Volume I.* Hillsdale, NJ: Erlbaum, 1981.

Hilgard, E. R. *Hypnotic susceptibility.* New York: Harcourt, Brace, Jovanovich, 1965.

Hilgard, E. R. *Divided consciousness: Multiple controls in human thought and action.* New York: Wiley & Sons, 1977.

Hilgard, E. R., & Bower, G. H. *Theories of learning* (4th Ed.). Englewood Cliffs, NJ: Prentice-Hall, 1975.

Hull, C. L. *Hypnosis and suggestibility.* New York: Appleton-Century, 1933.

James, W. *Principles of psychology* (2 volumes). New York: Holt, 1890.

Janet, P. *The major symptoms of hysteria.* New York: Macmillan, 1907.

Janet, P. The subconscious. In R. G. Badger (Ed.), *Subconscious phenomena.* Boston: Gorham Press, 1910.

Katz, R. *Boiling energy: Community healing among the Kalahri Kung.* Cambridge, MA: Harvard University Press, 1982.

Koestler, A. *The act of creation: A study of the conscious and unconscious in science and art.* New York: Macmillan, 1964.

Knapp, M. L. *Nonverbal communication in human interactions.* New York: Holt, Rinehart, & Winston, 1972.

Kramer, E. Hypnotic susceptibility and previous relationship with the hypnotist. *American Journal of Clinical Hypnosis*, 1969, *11*, 175–177.

Kris, E. *Psychoanalytic explorations in art.* New York: International Universities Press, 1952.

Kroger, W. S. *Clinical and experimental hypnosis.* Philadelphia: Lippincott, 1963.

Kubie, L. S. *Neurotic distortions of the creative process.* Lawrence, KS: University of Kansas Press, 1958.

Kubie, L. S., & Margolin, S. The process of hypnotism and the nature of the hypnotic state. *American Journal of Psychiatry*, 1944, *100*, 611–622.

Lakoff, G., & Johnson, M. *Metaphors we live by*. Chicago: University of Chicago Press, 1980.

Lankton, S. R. *Practical magic: A translation of basic Neuro-Linguistic Programming into clinical psychotherapy*. Cupertino, CA: Meta Publications, 1980.

Lankton, S. R., & Lankton, C. H. *The answer within: A clinical framework for Ericksonian hypnotherapy*. New York: Brunner/Mazel, 1983.

Lankton, S. R., & Lankton, C. H. *Enchantment and intervention in the family: Training in Ericksonian approaches*. New York: Brunner/Mazel, 1986.

Lay, W. Mental imagery. *Psychological Review Monograph Supply*, 1897, *92*, 1–59.

Leonard, G. *The silent pulse*. New York: E. P. Dutton, 1978.

Mandler, G. *Mind and emotion*. New York: Wiley & Sons, 1975.

Marshall, G. *The affective consequences of "inadequately explained" physiological arousal*. Unpublished doctoral dissertation, Stanford University, 1976.

Maslach, C. Negative emotional biasing of unexplained arousal. In C. E. Izard (Ed.), *Emotions and emotion-cognition interactions in psychopathology*. New York: Plenum Press, 1977.

Masters, R., & Houston, J. *Mind games*. New York: Dell Publishing, 1972.

Orne, M. T. The nature of hypnosis: Artifact and essence. *Journal of Abnormal and Social Psychology*, 1959, *58*, 277–299.

Orne, M. T. On the mechanisms of posthypnotic amnesia. *International Journal of Clinical and Experimental Hypnosis*, 1966, *14*, 121–134.

Pearce, J. C. *The bond of power*. New York: E. P. Dutton, 1981.

Perry, C., Gelfand, R., & Marcovitch, P. The relevance of hypnotic susceptibility in the clinical context. *Journal of Abnormal Psychology*, 1979, *88*, 592–602.

Perry, C., & Laurence, J. R. Hypnotic depth and hypnotic susceptibility: A replicated finding. *International Journal of Clinical and Experimental Hypnosis*, 1980, *28*, 272–280.

Perry, C., & Walsh, B. Inconsistencies and anomalies of response as a defining characteristic of hypnosis. *Journal of Abnormal Psychology*, 1978, *87*, 547–577.

Pribram, K. H. *Languages of the brain: Experimental paradoxes and principles in neuropsychology*. Englewood Cliffs, NJ: Prentice-Hall, 1971.

Prince, M. *Psychotherapy and multiple personality: Selected essays*. Cambridge, MA: Harvard University Press, 1975.

Richardson, A. *Mental imagery*. London: Routledge & Kegan Paul, 1969.

Richeport, M. Erickson's contributions to anthropology. In J. K. Zeig (Ed.), *Ericksonian approaches to hypnosis and psychotherapy*. New York: Brunner/Mazel, 1982.

Ritterman, M. *Using hypnosis in family therapy*. San Francisco: Jossey-Bass, 1983.

Rogers, C. R. *A way of being*. Boston: Houghton-Mifflin, 1980.

Rogers, C. R. Reaction to Gunnison's article of the similarities between Erickson and Rogers. *Journal of Counseling and Development*, 1985, *63*, 565–566.

Rosen, G. History of medical hypnosis. In J. M. Schneck (Ed.), *Hypnosis in modern medicine* (2nd ed.). Springfield, IL: Thomas, 1959.

Rosenhan, D. On the social psychology of hypnosis research. In J. E. Gordon (Ed.), *Handbook of clinical and experimental hypnosis*. New York: Macmillan, 1967.

Rossi, E. L. (Ed.) *The collected papers of Milton H. Erickson, Volume I: The nature of hypnosis and suggestions*. New York: Irvington, 1980a.

Rossi, E. L. (Ed.) *The collected papers of Milton H. Erickson, Volume II: Hypnotic alteration of sensory, perceptual, and psychophysiological processes*. New York: Irvington, 1980b.

Rossi, E. L. (Ed.) *The collected papers of Milton H. Erickson, Volume III: Hypnotic investigation of psychodynamic processes*. New York: Irvington, 1980c.

Rossi, E. L. (Ed.) *The collected papers of Milton H. Erickson, Volume IV: Innovative Hypnotherapy*. New York: Irvington, 1980d.

Rossi, E. L., & Jichaku, P. Therapeutic and transpersonal double-binds: Continuing the legacy of Gregory Bateson and Milton H. Erickson. Paper presented at the Annual Scientific Meeting of the American Society of Clinical Hypnosis. October, 1984, San Francisco.

Rossi, E. L, Ryan, M. O., & Sharp, F. A. (Eds.) *Healing in hypnosis: The seminars, workshops, and lectures of Milton H. Erickson.* New York: Irvington, 1983.

Sachs, L. B. Construing hypnosis as modifiable behavior. In A. Jacobs & L. Sachs (Eds.), *Psychology of private events.* New York: Academic Press, 1971.

Sarbin, T. R. Contributions to role-taking theory: I. Hypnotic behavior. *Psychological Review,* 1950, *57,* 255-270.

Sarbin, T. R. Physiological effects of hypnotic stimulations. In R. M. Dorcus (Ed.), *Hypnosis and its therapeutic applications.* New York: McGraw Hill, 1956.

Sarbin, T. R., & Coe, W. C. *Hypnosis: A social psychological analysis of influence communication.* New York: Holt, Rinehart, & Winston, 1972.

Schacter, S., & Singer, J. E. Cognitive, social, and physiological determinants of emotional states. *Psychological Review,* 1962, *69,* 379-399.

Sheehan, P. W., & Perry, C. W. *Methodologies of hypnosis: A critical appraisal of contemporary paradigms of hypnosis.* Hillsdale, NJ: Erlbaum Press, 1976.

Shor, R. E. Hypnosis and the concept of the generalized reality orientation. *American Journal of Psychotherapy,* 1959, *13,* 582-602.

Shor, R. E. Three dimensions of hypnotic depth. *International Journal of Clinical and Experimental Hypnosis,* 1962, *10,* 23-28.

Shor, R. E., Orne, M. T., & O'Connell, D. N. Psychological correlates of plateau hypnotizability in a special volunteer sample. *Journal of Personality and Social Psychology,* 1966, *3,* 80-95.

Sjoberg, B. M., & Hollister, L. E. The effects of psychotomimetic drugs on primary suggestibility. *Psychopharmacologica,* 1965, *8,* 251-262.

Sokolov, E. N. *Perception and the conditioned reflex.* New York: Macmillan, 1963.

Spiegel, H., & Spiegel, D. *Trance and treatment: Clinical uses of hypnosis.* New York: Basic Books, 1978.

Tart, C. The influence of the experimental situation in hypnosis and dream research: A case report. *American Journal of Clinical Hypnosis,* 1964, *7,* 163-170.

Tart, C. (Ed.) *Altered states of consciousness.* Garden City, NY: Doubleday, 1969.

Tinterow, M. M. *Foundations of hypnosis from Mesmer to Freud.* Springfield, IL: Thomas, 1970.

Varela, F. *Principles of biological autonomy.* New York: Elsevier North Holland, 1979.

Walter, W. G. *The living brain.* London: Duckworth, 1953.

Watzlawick, P., Beavin, J. H., & Jackson, D. D. *Pragmatics of human communication: A study of interactional patterns, pathologies, and paradoxes.* New York: Norton, 1967.

Watzlawick, P., Weakland, J., & Fisch, R. *Change: The principles of problem formation and problem resolution.* New York: Norton, 1974.

Weitzenhoffer, A. M. *Hypnotism: An objective study in suggestibility.* New York: J. Wiley & Sons, 1953.

Weitzenhoffer, A. M. *General techniques of hypnotism.* New York: Grune & Stratton, 1957.

Weitzenhoffer, A. M. Hypnotic susceptibility revisited. *American Journal of Clinical Hypnosis,* 1980, *22,* 130-146.

White, R. W. A preface to the theory of hypnotism. *Journal of Abnormal Social Psychology,* 1941, *36,* 477-505.

Wolberg, L. R. *Medical hypnosis.* New York: Grune & Stratton, 1948.

Young, A. M. Consciousness and cosmology. In C. Muse & A. M. Young (Eds.), *Consciousness and reality: The human pivotal point.* New York: Avon Books, 1972.

Zeig, J. K. (Ed.) *Ericksonian approaches to hypnosis and psychotherapy.* New York: Brunner/Mazel, 1982.

Zeig, J. K. (Ed.) *Ericksonian psychotherapy, Volume I: Structures.* New York: Brunner/Mazel, 1985a.

Zeig, J. K. (Ed.) *Ericksonian psychotherapy, Volume II: Clinical applications.* New York: Brunner/Mazel, 1985b.

Zeig, J. K. The clinical use of amnesia. In J. K. Zeig (Ed.), *Ericksonian psychotherapy, Volume I: Structures.* New York: Brunner/Mazel, 1985c.

Zeitlin, H. Cult induction: Hypnotic communication patterns in contemporary cults. In J. K. Zeig (Ed.), *Ericksonian psychotherapy, Volume I: Structures.* New York: Brunner/Mazel, 1985.

Zimbardo, P. G., Rapaport, C., & Baron, J. Pain control by hypnotic induction of motivational states. In P. G. Zimbardo (Ed.), *The cognitive control of motivation.* Glenview, IL: Scott, Foreman, & Co., 1969.

Zukav, G. *The dancing Wu-Li Masters.* New York: Bantam Books, 1979.

# Index